The Raccolta of Indulgenced Prayers and Good Works by Ambrose St. John

of the
Oratory of Saint Philip Neri, Birmingham

Copyright © 2018 Edition
With the Original 1910 Prayers, Explanations and Devotions
in Latin and English

Hope and Life Press

NIHIL OBSTAT: HENRICUS S. BOWDEN, Censor Deputatus.
IMPRIMATUR: EDMUNDUS SURMONT, Vicarius Generalis.
Westmonasterii, die 10 Maii, 1909.

APPROBATION 8
PREFACE TO THE EDITION IN MEMORIAM AMBROSE ST JOHN 9
ON INDULGENCES 10
DECISIONS OF THE SACRED CONGREGATION OF INDULGENCES - STATE OF GRACE 11
LIST OF ABBREVIATIONS 14
INSTRUCTIONS 14
I. THE HOLY TRINITY 15
1. The Angelic Trisagion 15
2. Gloria Patri seven times, said by three Persons 15
3. Mass and Prayers in Thanksgiving for Our Lady's Privileges 15
4. Gloria Patri thrice 16
5. Prayers of Thanksgiving for Our Lady's Assumption 16
6. Three Offerings of Thanksgiving To obtain a Good Death 17
7. Triduo, or Novena (made at any time in public or private in honour of the Holy Trinity) 17
8. The Sign of the Cross 17
9. Thanksgiving on New-Year's Eve 17
10. Prayer 17
11. Acts of Adoration and Thanksgiving to the Blessed Trinity 18
12. Prayer to the Holy Trinity 18
13. Renewal of Baptismal Vows 18
II. ALMIGHTY GOD 18
14. Acts of Faith, Hope and Charity 18
15. Chaplet of Acts of the Love of God 19
16. Prayer 20
17. Prayer of St Francis Xavier for the Conversion of Infidels 20
18. Prayer for Peace 21
19. Offerings for the Beginning of the Day and for Mass 21
20. An Offering 22
21. A Morning Offering 22
22. An Act of Faith 22
23. Prayer of St Bonaventure 22
24. Prayer 23
25. Prayer of St Ignatius 23
26. Prayer 23
27. Prayer 23
28. Prayer for the Supreme Pontiff 23
29. Ejaculation of Resignation to the Will of God 24
30. Ejaculation 24
31. Invocation 24
32. Ejaculation 24
33. Ejaculation 24
34. Ejaculation 24
III. THE HOLY GHOST; 24
35. The Hymn and Sequence 24
36. Novena of the Holy Ghost 25
37. Novena for Pentecost 26
38. Gloria Patri seven times 26
39. Prayer for the Church 26
40. Prayer for the Propagation of the Faith 26
41. Veni Sancte Spiritus, reple, etc 26
42. Chaplet of the Holy Spirit 26

43. Prayer to the Holy Spirit. ... 27
IV. JESUS CHRIST ... 27
44. Rosary of Our Lord. ... 27
45. Invocation of the Holy Name. ... 29
46. Hymns and Psalms in Honour of the Holy Name. ... 29
47. Prayer for a Holy Death. ... 32
48. Prayer. ... 32
49. Prayer. ... 32
50. Prayer. ... 32
51. Prayer of St Thomas Aquinas. ... 33
52. Prayer of St Thomas Aquinas. ... 33
53. Petitions of St Augustine. ... 33
54. Prayer for the Conversion of Scandinavia. ... 34
55. Devotion to the Holy Name. ... 34
56. Litany of the Holy Name of Jesus. ... 35
57. Prayer for Grace to do the Will of God. ... 36
58. Prayer for the Preservation of Faith. ... 36
59. Prayer for the Love of God. ... 37
60. Prayer in Honour of the Holy Family. ... 37
61. Ejaculation. ... 37
62. Ejaculation of St Jerome Emilian. ... 37
63. Ejaculation. ... 37
64. Ejaculation. ... 38
65. Ejaculation. ... 38
66. Ejaculation. ... 38
67. Ejaculation. ... 38
68. Prayer to Jesus our Redeemer. ... 38
69. Invocation. ... 38
70. Prayer for the Conversion of Sinners. ... 38
71. Prayer to our Lord. ... 38
72. Prayer to Jesus, Lover of Children. ... 38
V. THE CHILD JESUS. ... 39
73. Christmas Day. To all who say or assist in Church at the Divine Office. ... 39
74. Novena for Christmas. ... 39
75. Mysteries of the Holy Childhood. ... 39
76. Novena for the Twenty-fifth Day of every Month. ... 40
77. Prayer before the Crib. ... 41
78. Prayer. ... 41
79. The Month of January. ... 41
VI. THE BLESSED SACRAMENT. ... 42
80. Novena for Corpus Christi. ... 42
81. Feast and Octave of Corpus Christi. ... 42
82. Triduo on Friday, Saturday and Sunday, during the Octave of Corpus Christi. ... 42
83. Corpus Christi. ... 42
84. Act of Adoration during the Elevation. ... 42
85. Frequent Communion. ... 43
86. Visit during the Forty Hours Exposition. ... 43
87. Visit during Exposition between Septuagesima Sunday and Ash Wednesday. ... 43
88. Prayers before the Blessed Sacrament. ... 43
89. Acts of Adoration and Reparation. ... 44
90. Act of Reparation and Ejaculations. ... 45
91. One Hour's Prayer on Holy Thursday, Corpus Christi, and other Thursdays. ... 45
92. Visit to the Holy Sepulchre on Holy Thursday and Good Friday. ... 45
93. Prayer. ... 45
94. The Hymn Pange Lingua, with Versicle and Prayer. ... 45
95. Invocations. ... 46
96. Prayer of St Alphonsus Liguori, to be said at a Visit to the most Holy Sacrament. ... 47
97. Prayer. ... 47
98. Visit to the Blessed Sacrament, with Pater, Ave, and Gloria five times, and Pater, Ave, and Gloria once for the intention of the Pope. ... 47
99. Prayer for a Visit. ... 47
100. Following the Blessed Sacrament. ... 48
101. Following the Blessed Sacrament to the Sick. ... 48
102. Prayer to be said during the Elevation in the Mass. ... 48
103. Ejaculation. ... 48
104. Act of Spiritual Communion of Saint Alphonsus Liguori. ... 48
105. Act of Homage to Christ, our God and our King. ... 48
106. Hymn of St Thomas Aquinas. ... 49
107. Prayer. ... 50
108. Ejaculation. ... 50
109. Ejaculation after Mass. ... 50
110. First Communicants and their Friends. ... 50
111. Prayer for the Increase of Daily Communion. ... 50

112. Prayer to our Lady of the Blessed Sacrament.	50
113. Prayer to our Lord in the Blessed Sacrament.	50
114. Prayers during a Procession of the Blessed Sacrament.	51
115. Prayer to be said at the Beginning of Mass.	51
116. Ejaculation.	51
VII. JESUS CRUCIFIED	51
117. The Stations of the Cross.	51
118. Chaplet of the Stations of the Gross.	54
119. The "Scala Santa" in Rome.	54
120. Pious Exercise on Fridays.	54
121. Devotions in Honour of the Five Wounds.	54
122. Devotion of the Seven Words.	56
123. The Three Hours on Good Friday and any other Friday.	59
124. Devotion for Lent.	59
125. The Prayer, Deus, qui pro Redemptione, etc.	59
126. Chaplet of the Five Wounds.	59
127. Prayer, En Ego.	60
128. Prayers of St Pius V, with the Apostles Creed five times.	60
129. Invocation of St Thomas Aquinas to the Cross.	60
130. Prayers of St Clare of Assisi.	60
131. Hymn, Vexilla Regis.	61
132. Prayer to Our Lord scourged at the Pillar.	62
133. Ejaculation.	62
134. Invocation.	62
135. Prayer to Our Lord on the Cross.	63
136. Prayer to Jesus Dead.	63
137. Prayer for a Happy Death.	63
VIII. THE PRECIOUS BLOOD	63
138. Chaplet of the Precious Blood.	63
139. Prayer.	65
140. Devout Aspirations.	66
141. Seven Offerings, in reparation for all the outrages received by Our Lord in the Precious Blood.	66
142. Act of Oblation in thanksgiving for blessings received.	67
143. Month consecrated to the Precious Blood.	67
144. Prayer to Jesus of Nazareth.	67
145. Ejaculation.	68
146. Offering.	68
IX. THE SACRED HEART	68
147. Visit to a Representation of the Sacred Heart, exposed for public veneration.	68
148. Act of Oblation to be made before a Representation of the Sacred Heart.	68
149. Acts of Devotion.	68
150. Chaplet.	69
151. Visit to any Church or Public Oratory where the Feast of the Sacred Heart is being kept.	70
152. Novena of the Sacred Heart.	70
153. Prayer for those in their agony.	71
154. Month of June.	71
155. Acts of Homage to the Eucharistic Heart of Jesus.	71
156. Daily Act of Oblation.	73
157. Act of Consecration of B. Margaret Mary.	73
158. Devotions for Fridays.	73
159. Ejaculation.	73
160. Ejaculation.	73
161. Ejaculation.	73
162. Ejaculation.	73
163. Ejaculation.	73
164. Ejaculation.	74
165. Litany of the Sacred Heart.	74
166. Prayer to the Sacred Hearts of Jesus and Mary for the Conversion of Jews and Turks.	75
167. Prayer.	75
168. Ejaculation.	76
169. Little Office of the Sacred Heart.	76
170. Prayer to the Eucharistic Heart.	76
171. Prayer to the Sacred Heart.	76
172. Consecration of the Family to the Sacred Heart.	76
173. Prayer to the Sacred Heart.	77
174. Ejaculation.	77
175. Ejaculation.	77
176. Ejaculation.	77
177. Ejaculation.	77
178. Ejaculation.	77
179. Ejaculation.	77
180. Ejaculation of B. Margaret Mary.	77
X. MARY	77

A. GENERAL ... 77
181. The Rosary of St Bridget. ... 77
182. The Angelus and Regina Cœli. ... 78
183. Invocation of the Name of Mary. ... 79
184. The Salve Regina and Sub Tuum Præsidium. ... 79
185. Prayers of St Alphonsus Liguori for everyday of the Week, with Ave Maria thrice. ... 80
186. Month of May. ... 82
187. Psalms in Honour of the Name of Mary. ... 82
188. Twenty-five Days Preparation for the Nativity, after the example of St Catharine of Bologna. ... 84
189. The Litany of Loreto. ... 85
190. Prayer of St Alphonsus. ... 87
191. Three Offerings. ... 87
192. Prayer, with Ave Maria, thrice, etc. ... 87
193. Prayer, O Excellentissima. ... 87
194. Prayer. ... 87
195. The Crown of Twelve Stars. ... 88
196. The Memorare. ... 88
197. Prayer, Ave Augustissima. ... 89
198. The Tota Pulchra, etc. ... 89
199. Five Novenas for the Principal Feasts of Our Lady. ... 89
200. Eleven Novenas in Honour of Our Lady. ... 99
201. One Ave and Prayer, O Domina Mea! for Victory in Temptations, especially those against Chastity. ... 99
202. Prayer, O Beata Virgo. ... 100
203. Prayer of St Alphonsus to be said before a representation of Our Lady. ... 100
204. Prayer for a Good Death. ... 100
205. Psalms and Prayers of St Bonaventure for every day in the week. ... 100
206. Chaplet of the Twelve Privileges of Our Lady. ... 100
207. Prayer for the Conversion of Heretics and Schismatics. ... 101
208. Prayer for the Conversion of Greek Schismatic's. ... 102
209. Act of Reparation. ... 102
210. Prayer. ... 102
211. Prayer. ... 102
212. Office of the Blessed Virgin. ... 103
213. Hymn, Ave Maris Stella. ... 103
214. Reparation for Blasphemy against Our Lady. ... 103
215. The Magnificat. ... 103
216. Prayer of St Aloysius Gonzaga. ... 104
217. Prayer for England. ... 104
218. Prayer for Reunion. ... 104
219. Aspiration. ... 104
220. Ejaculation. ... 105
221. Three Invocations with Ave thrice. ... 105
222. Ejaculation of St Philip Neri. ... 105
223. Chaplet of the Seven Joys of Our Lady. ... 105
224. Ejaculation. ... 105
225. Ejaculation. ... 105
226. Ejaculation. ... 105
227. Ejaculation. ... 106
228. Prayer to Our Lady. ... 106
229. Prayer to Our Lady. ... 106
B. MARY SORROWING ... 107
230. The Rosary of the Seven Dolours. ... 107
231. One Hour's Prayer. ... 108
232. Devotions in honour of the Sorrowful Heart of Mary. ... 108
233. Devotions for Holy Week and Fridays. ... 109
234. Ave Maria, etc., seven times. ... 109
235. Devotions during the Carnival. ... 109
236. Stations of Our Lady's Dolours. ... 109
237. The Month of September. ... 109
238. Hymn, Stabat Mater. ... 109
239. Prayer. ... 111
240. Prayer. ... 111
C. MARY IMMACULATE ... 111
241. Chaplet of the Immaculate Conception. ... 111
242. Seven Sundays in Honour of the Immaculate Conception. ... 111
243. The Little Office of the Immaculate Conception. ... 111
244. Antiphon, Versicle and Prayer. ... 111
245. Ejaculation. ... 112
246. Ejaculation. ... 112
247. Ejaculation. ... 112
248. Ejaculation. ... 112
249. Invocation. ... 112
250. Invocation. ... 112

E. OUR LADY OF THE ROSARY ... 115
260. The Rosary blessed by Canons Regular of St Augustine of the Order of the Holy Cross. ... 115
261. The Rosary of St Dominic. ... 115
262. The Month of October. ... 117
263. Prayer. ... 117
264. The Fifteen Saturdays. ... 117
265. Our Lady of the Rosary of Pompeii. ... 117
266. Prayer to Our Lady of the Rosary. ... 117
F. VARIOUS TITLES OF OUR LADY ... 117
267. Prayer to Our Lady of Pity. ... 117
268. Prayers to Our Lady of Perpetual Succour. ... 118
269. Prayer to Our Lady of Good Counsel. ... 118
270. Prayer to Our Lady of Mount Carmel. ... 119
271. Prayer to Our Lady, Mother of Divine Providence. ... 119
272. Prayer to Our Lady of the Cœnaculum. ... 119
273. Prayer to Our Lady Help of Christians. ... 119
274. Prayer to Our Lady Help of Christians. ... 119
275. Prayer to Our Lady of Africa for the Conversion of the Mussulmans and other Infidels. ... 120
276. Invocation to be said Morning and Evening. ... 120
277. Prayer to Mary our Helper. ... 120
278. Prayer to Our Lady, Queen of Prophets. ... 121
279. Prayer to Our Lady, Mother of Confidence. ... 121
280. Prayer to Our Lady of Lourdes. ... 121
281. Ejaculation. ... 122
282. Prayer to Our Lady "Reparatrice." ... 122
283. Prayer to Our Lady of Lourdes for a Sick Person. ... 122
284. Our Lady of Ransom. ... 123
285. Seven Saturdays of Our Lady of Ransom. ... 123
286. Ejaculation to Our Lady "del Pilar" of Saragossa. ... 123
XI. THE HOLY ANGELS ... 123
ST MICHAEL ARCHANGEL ... 123
289. Hymn, Antiphon, etc. ... 123
290. Novena of St Michael. ... 124
291. Angelical Crown. ... 124
292. Prayer to St Michael. ... 125
293. Antiphon. ... 126
ST GABRIEL AND ST RAPHAEL ... 126
294. Novena. ... 126
295. Prayer. ... 126
THE GUARDIAN ANGEL ... 126
296. Invocation. ... 126
297. Novena of the Guardian Angel. ... 126
XII. ST JOSEPH ... 127
298. Responsory, Antiphon, etc. ... 127
299. Psalms in honour of the Name of St Joseph. ... 127
300. Seven Sorrows and Seven Joys. ... 130
301. Novena of St Joseph. ... 131
302. Month of March. ... 131
303. Prayer. ... 131
304. Prayer. ... 131
305. Prayer to St Joseph, Patron of the Universal Church. ... 131
306. Prayer. ... 132
307. Prayers for those in their Agony. ... 132
308. Prayer. ... 132
309. Prayer of St Bernadine of Siena. ... 132
310. Invocation. ... 132
311. Invocation. ... 133
312. Ejaculation. ... 133
313. Prayer for the Observance of Sundays and Feast Days. ... 133
314. Prayer to St Joseph. ... 133
315. Prayer to St Joseph. ... 133
XIII. VARIOUS SAINTS ... 133
ST JOACHIM ... 133
316. Prayer. ... 133
317. Prayer. ... 134
318. Prayer. ... 134
ST ANNE ... 134
319. Prayer. ... 134
SS. PETER AND PAUL ... 134
320. Prayer. ... 134
321. Responsory of St Peter. ... 135
322. Responsory of St Paul. ... 136
323. Veneration of St Peter's Statue. ... 137

ST JOHN, APOSTLE & EVANGELIST	138
325. Prayer.	138
ST EMIGDIUS, BISHOP & MARTYR	138
326. Prayer.	138
327. Invocation.	138
ST CHALCEDONIUS, MARTYR	138
328. Prayer.	138
ST GREGORY VII	138
329. Prayer.	138
ST PIUS V	139
330. Hymn.	139
ST NICHOLAS OF BARI	140
331. Prayer.	140
ST ALPHONSUS LIGUORI	140
332. Prayer.	140
ST LOUIS OF TOULOUSE	140
333. Prayer.	140
ST DOMINIC	141
334. Prayers.	141
ST FRANCIS OF ASSISI	141
335. The Five Sundays.	141
336. Hymn.	141
337. Feast of St Francis.	142
THE SEVEN HOLY FOUNDERS OF THE SERVANTS OF MARY	142
338. Prayer.	142
339. Seven Prayers.	142
ST JOHN OF MATHA	143
340. Prayer.	143
ST FRANCIS OF PAOLA	143
341. The Thirteen Fridays in honour of Christ and his Twelve Apostles.	143
ST IGNATIUS LOYOLA	143
342. The Ten Sundays.	143
343. Prayer.	144
ST PHILIP NERI	144
344. Prayers for every Day of the Week.	144
345. Prayer.	145
ST JOSEPH CALASANCTIUS	146
346. Prayer.	146
ST CAMILLUS OF LELLIS	146
347. The Seven Sundays.	146
348. Prayer.	146
ST VINCENT OF PAUL	146
349. Novena.	146
350. Prayer.	146
ST PAUL OF THE CROSS	147
351. Prayer.	147
352. Novena.	147
ST PETER FOURIER	147
353. Prayer.	147
ST THOMAS AQUINAS	147
354. Prayer to St Thomas, Patron of Schools.	147
355. Little Office of St Thomas Aquinas.	148
356. The Six Sundays.	148
357. Invocation, before Lecture or Study.	148
ST ANTHONY OF PADUA	148
358. Responsory.	148
359. Pater, Ave, and Gloria, thirteen times, in honour of the Saint.	148
360. St Anthonys Bread. Prayer.	149
361. St Anthony's Bread. Thanksgiving.	149
362. The Thirteen Tuesdays, or Sundays.	149
363. Prayer to St Anthony.	149
ST VINCENT FERRER	149
364. Prayer.	149
ST JOHN OF THE GROSS	149
365. Prayer.	149
ST ANDREW AVELLINO	150
366. Prayers.	150
ST MICHAEL DE SANTI	150
367. Prayer.	150
ST ANTHONY, ABBOT	150
368. Prayer.	150
ST ALOYSIUS GONZAGA	151
369. Feast Day.	151

370. The Six Sundays.	151
371. Prayer.	151
372. Act of Consecration.	151
ST STANISLAUS KOSTKA	151
373. Feast Day. Ten Sundays, etc.	151
374. Prayers.	152
ST JOHN BERCHMANS	152
375. The Five Sundays.	152
ST BENEDICT JOSEPH LABRE	152
376. Prayer.	152
ST LUCY, VIRGIN AND MARTYR	152
377. Prayers.	152
378. Prayer to St Lucy.	153
ST AGNES, V.M.	154
379. Prayer.	154
380. Prayers.	154
ST BARBARA, VIRGIN	154
ST JULIANA FALGONIERI	154
382. Prayer.	154
ST THERESA, VIRGIN.	155
383. Prayer of St Alphonsus.	155
ST MARY SALOME	155
384. Prayer.	155
ST ELIZABETH OF HUNGARY	155
385. Prayer.	155
ST MARGARET OF CORTONA	156
386. Prayer.	156
387. Prayer to St Blaise.	156
ST STEPHEN	156
388. Antiphon and Prayer.	156
ST JOHN THE BAPTIST	156
389. Prayers.	156
ST FRANCIS XAVIER	157
390. Novena in honour of the Saint.	157
ST PAUL OF THE CROSS	157
391. Prayer.	157
ST RITA	157
392. Prayer.	157
ST JOHN DE LA SALLE	157
393. Prayer.	157
SS. BRIDGETT AND CATHARINE OF SWEDEN	158
394. Prayers.	158
ST CATHARINE OF ALEXANDRIA	158
395. Prayers for the Promotion of Studies.	158
396. BLESSED FRANGUS, Carmelite Confessor.	159
XIV. BLESSED CROSSES, CRUCIFIXES, ROSARIES, MEDALS, etc., FROM THE HOLY LAND	159
397.	159
XV. THE DYING AND THE APOSTOLIC BLESSING	160
398. Praying for the Dying.	160
399. Offering of Masses for the Dying.	160
400. The Apostolic Blessing.	160
401. Plenary Indulgence in Articulo Mortis.	160
XVI. THE FAITHFUL DEPARTED	160
402. The Office of the Dead.	160
403. The Heroic Act.	160
404. The De Profundis.	161
405. Holy Week.	161
406. Pater and Ave five times, etc.	161
407. All Souls Day.	161
408. Prayers.	162
409. Prayers for Nine or Seven Days.	162
410. League of Perpetual Suffrage.	162
411. Month of November.	163
412. Devotion to the Five Wounds.	163
413. Prayers.	164
414. Prayer for the Dead.	164
415. VV. & RR. for the Dead.	164
XVII. MISCELLANEOUS	164
416. Visits to the Churches of the Stations.	164
417. Visit to the Seven Churches and the Seven Privileged Altars.	167
418. The Portiuncula.	167
419. The Gradual or Penitential Psalms.	167
420. Christian Doctrine.	167

- 421. Mental Prayer. 167
- 422. Explanation of the Gospel. 168
- 423. Prayer after saying Office. 168
- 424. Prayers to be said after the Sacrosanctæ. 168
- 425. Prayer for the Conversion of the Dutch. 168
- 426. The Divine Praises. 168
- 427. Ejaculations for a Happy Death. 168
- 428. Beati Mortui, etc. 169
- 429. Prayer for those in their Agony. 169
- 430. Visiting the Sick in Hospitals. 169
- 431. Almsgiving. 169
- 432. Prayer for Deaf-Mutes. 169
- 433. Propagation of the Faith. 169
- 434. Against an Unprovided Death. 169
- 435. Ejaculation. 170
- 436. In Honour of the Blessed Trinity, etc. 170
- 437. Spiritual Canticles. 171
- 438. Prayer, with Ejaculation. 171
- 439. Prayers for a Happy Death. 171
- 440. Invocations and Petitions. 172
- 441. Prayers in Times of Calamity. 172
- 442. Prayers for the Conversion of Japan. 173
- 445. Prayer of St Benedict Joseph Labre for Times of Necessity. 174
- 446. Prayers for Purity. 175
- 447. Temperance Pledge. 175
- 453. Christian Acts. 177
- 454. Assisting at a First Mass. 177
- 455. Prayer of St Thomas Aquinas for grace to lead a holy life. 177
- 456. Prayer in Times of Calamity. 178
- 457. Prayer for the Christian Family. 178
- 458. Prayers to the Holy Family. 179
- 459. Prayer for Benefactors. 179
- 463. Prayer for the Sanctification of Priests. 180
- 464. Two Prayers for the Increase and Preservation of the Clergy. 180
- 465. For Clerics and Students putting on a Cotta. 181
- FOR SPECIAL CLASSES 181
- I. FOR PRIESTS 181
- 466. Intention before Mass. 181
- 467. Prayer after Mass. 181
- 468. Prayer to St Joseph, before Mass. 181
- 469. Prayer to our Lady before Mass. 182
- 470. Preparation and Thanksgiving. 182
- 471. Prayer before Hearing Confessions. 182
- 472. Prayers before and after Confession. 183
- 473. First Mass. 183
- II. FOR PRIESTS AND OTHERS IN SACRED ORDERS 183
- 474. Prayer to our Lord. 183
- 475. Ejaculation. 183
- 476. Prayer for the Preservation of Chastity. 183
- III. FOR YOUNG STUDENTS 183
- 477. Consecration of Studies to Mary Immaculate. 183
- 478. Prayer in Choosing a State of Life. 184
- 479. Prayer for one aspiring to the Priesthood. 184
- 480. Prayer to Our Lady. 184
- 481. Prayer for Children in Purgatory. 184
- APPENDIX 185
- 482. Prayer for the Conversion of Freemasons. 185
- 483. Pious Reading of the Gospel. 185
- 484. Prayer to the Sacred Heart for Pope Pius X. 185
- 485. Prayer to the Queen of Angels by the Ven. Louis Edward Gestac. 185
- 486. Ejaculation to the Sacred Heart. 186
- 487. The Twelve Saturdays immediately preceding the Immaculate Conception. 186
- 488. Prayer to St Paul. 186
- 489. Litany of St Joseph. 186
- 490. Medals of the Child JESUS. 187
- 491. Kissing the Ring of a Cardinal or Bishop. 187

APPROBATION

MOST BLESSED FATHER, In order to promote thereby the piety of the faithful in England, Ambrose St John, Priest of the Oratory of St Philip Neri, in the Diocese of Birmingham, humbly prays for permission

to print in English a translation of the book entitled *Raccolta di Orazioni, &c., alle quali sono ammesse le SS. Indulgenze,* having first obtained the approbation of His Eminence the Cardinal Archbishop of Westminster; and also that the faithful who make use of this translation may gain all the indulgences annexed to the original. After an audience of the Holy Father, granted February 3, 1856, our most Holy Lord Pius IX, by Divine Providence Pope, on an application made by me, the undersigned Secretary of the Sacred Congregation for the Propagation of the Faith, has of his goodness answered by Rescript in favour of the grace, according to the terms of the petition, provided the translation be made from the last Roman edition, and it being understood that the Decree printed at the end of this edition remains in full force. Given at Rome from the House of the same Sacred Congregation, on the day and year aforesaid. Gratis, without any payment on any plea whatever.
AL. BARNABO, Secretary.
In the place of the seal.
WE approve of the Translation by virtue of the above
Rescript of His Holiness.
N. CARDINAL ARCHBISHOP.
Westminster, October 23, 1857.

PREFACE TO THE EDITION IN MEMORIAM AMBROSE ST JOHN

AMBROSE St John was the younger of the two sons of Henry St John, and grandson of St Andrew St John, D. D., Dean of Worcester, of the ancient family of St John of Staunton St John, Oxfordshire. He was born June 29, 1815, went to Westminster School, and afterwards graduated with Honours at Oxford. From Christ Church he entered the Anglican Ministry, and, after accepting a curacy under the Rev. Henry William Wilberforce, then incumbent of Bransgore, Hants, joined Dr Newman at Littlemore, where he remained till 1844.

He was received into the Church September 29, 1845, at Prior Park, near Bath, and accompanied Dr Newman to Rome, where the two converts were ordained Subdeacon together in the private chapel of Cardinal Franzoni May 26, 1847. Three days later they received the Diaconate at St John Lateran's, and the Priesthood the following day, Trinity Sunday. After a short novitiate they returned to England as Oratorians, and in the foundation of the Oratory in England by Father Newman Ambrose St John figures as his right hand at Maryvale, at Alcester Street, and finally at Edgbaston.

Bright and cheerful in aspect and manner, and many sided in his accomplishments, Father St John devoted himself most assiduously to the service of GOD and his neighbour in the Oratory. He was a typical son of St Philip, indefatigable alike in the confessional and in the pulpit, and a true father, whether to the Italian organ-grinders or to the poor factory girls of Birmingham. Later on, at Dr Newman's request, he sacrificed himself to the exacting work of the Oratory School, founded in 1859, of which as Headmaster from 1862, under the guidance of his Superior, he may be said to have laid the permanent foundations. His memory is held in grateful recollection by many old Oratory boys.

The translation of the Raccolta by Father St John was one of the first books of popular devotion issued by the Fathers of the Birmingham Oratory, and it supplied them with the congregational prayers, still in use in their church, for the Stations of the Cross, for the month of May, the Triduo and Novenas in preparation for the Feasts of our Lady, and similar devotions. The fifth edition of the book, brought out after Father St John's death, was printed in Birmingham by the direction and under the supervision of Cardinal Newman himself. Concurrently with the issue of the English Raccolta Father St John translated and published a work on Indulgences by the Abbate Dominico Sarra, Recorder of the Sacred Congregation of Indulgences and Holy Relics, a handy popular treatise on the doctrine and use of Indulgences published by authority at Rome.

This Edition has been conformed to the latest Roman Raccolta, approved July 23, 1898, and the Supplement, approved July 31, 1902; and contains also the Indulgences and decisions since recorded in the *Acta Sanctæ Sedis* up to the present time. The immediate occasion of Father St John's death was an act of neighbourly kindness, which led him to assist one very hot day as Deacon at the Festa of St Paul of the Cross, to which he had been invited by the Passionist Fathers at Harborne, his health being at the time very uncertain. He had recently translated from the German Dr. Fessler's *True and False Infallibility*, a work approved by the Holy See, which Dr Newman thought of great importance in the controversy which had arisen out of Mr Gladstone's *Vaticanism*; the work had been done against time, and the effort, made in the midst of multifarious duties, had proved a great strain. The High Mass at Harborne was celebrated in a large conservatory, then in use as a temporary church, and the sun, beating down through the glass, brought on a kind of sunstroke and brain fever, to which he succumbed. Dr Newman in replying to a letter of condolence says: " I do not like not to acknowledge your kind sympathy in my sorrow, but I am so pulled down that I cannot write without bringing on a flood of tears not I trust from want of resignation, but from love of him I have lost, so I say only a few words. You who have undergone bitter losses will make allowance for me."

Their friendship is recorded in the concluding sentences of the Apologia, in which that work is offered as a memorial of affection and gratitude to the Fathers of the Oratory : "And to you especially, dear Ambrose St John, whom GOD gave me when He took everyone else away; who are the link between my old life and my new; who have now for twenty one years been so devoted to me, so patient, so zealous, so tender; who have watched me so narrowly, who have never thought of yourself if I was in question."

Father St John was buried in the private cemetery of the Oratorian Fathers at Rednal, and Cardinal Newman left strict injunctions that he himself should be laid in his friend's grave. A single head-stone bears their brief epitaphs. In the present issue of the Raccolta, brought up to date, the editor would claim for them and for himself, from all who use this book, a remembrance in their prayers.
R.G.B.
The Oratory, Birmingham,
November 2, 1908.

ON INDULGENCES

PUNISHMENT, like a shadow, follows all sin, whether mortal or venial, and it is not usually remitted to the full when forgiveness is obtained.
Eternal punishment, incurred by mortal sin, is always remitted with the guilt, but some temporal punishment generally remains due to the justice of GOD. This temporal punishment is inflicted by GOD either in this life or in Purgatory; but a man may anticipate the divine justice by works of penance, or by means of Indulgences.

The guilt, then, of sin is one thing, the punishment another. The guilt is remitted when a man truly repents, either with or without the Sacrament of Penance; but though the punishment, or a portion of it, may be remitted with the guilt, some usually remains, as a debt of satisfaction, to be paid in this world or the next. This truth is clearly indicated in the sacramental penances which always accompany Absolution. These penances have, in course of time, under pressure of external circumstances, lost much of the severity which characterized them in earlier ages, but they still testify to the principle that after forgiveness satisfaction remains due. The comparative lightness of modern sacramental penances ought to suggest that they alone are not sufficient to satisfy the justice of GOD, and that they should be supplemented either by other penances, self-inflicted or patiently accepted at the hand of GOD, or by some equivalent. And in the case of sins forgiven either indirectly in the Sacrament, or by means of contrition alone, the satisfaction remaining due is left altogether to the individual's patience under chastisement from GOD, or to his personal activity in applying himself either to works of penance, or to some equivalent. That equivalent is to be found in Indulgences.

What, then, is an Indulgence? An Indulgence is the remission by the Church, on specified conditions, of the whole or a part of the debt of satisfaction remaining due for sin. The Church has power to absolve from guilt; she has also power to remit the punishment. The one she exercises in the Sacrament of Penance; the other she exercises when she grants an Indulgence. And it is clear from what has been said that an Indulgence is supplemental to Absolution, and presupposes the forgiveness of the guilt of sin.

Theologically considered, an Indulgence is not a mere exercise of spiritual power and authority on the part of the Church ; it is truly a payment of the debt, made out of her Treasury of satisfactory merit; for in this are stored up the superabundant merits of JESUS CHRIST, and the accumulated merits of our Lady and all the Saints. With this inexhaustible fund at her command, she has the means of satisfying the debts due from her children to the justice of GOD.

In form, an Indulgence emanates from the Pope; leaving out of account the limited power exercised by Bishops in favour of their flocks and by Cardinals, Nuncios and others; and it is registered in a Decree or Rescript of the Congregation of Indulgences, or some similar document. It attaches to a specified prayer or good work an additional satisfactory value, such value being expressed in the terms of an ancient canonical penance, viz., so many days, Quarantines (which lasted forty days), or years, to which the Indulgence is there by declared to be equivalent. The earliest Indulgences were, in fact, remissions of these very penances.

Indulgences are either Plenary or Partial, according as a remission of all, or of part, of the debt of punishment due is granted. In either case the actual benefit obtained depends upon the dispositions of the penitent, and the care and accuracy he employs in fulfilling the conditions laid down. For the sake of clearness and facility of reference, the general and special conditions required for obtaining Indulgences are set out in tabular form below.

It only remains to add that, though the Church has no direct jurisdiction over the souls in Purgatory, she authorizes and encourages, as a work of supreme charity, the application of Indulgences, by way of suffrage, to the needs of those afflicted souls; and we may confidently assure ourselves that these suffrages are most acceptable to the Divine Majesty, and that what the Church would thus, as it were, indirectly loose in Purgatory is speedily loosed also in Heaven, amid the rejoicing of all the heavenly court, to the great glory of GOD, and to the incalculable benefit, as well of the suffering souls as of their earthly benefactors.

General Conditions required for all Indulgences.
1. STATE OF GRACE. (See Decisions i, 2,)
2. INTENTION. (See Decisions 3, 4,)
3. ACCURACY and DEVOTION in fulfilling the specified conditions. (See N.B. ibid.)
Special Conditions usually required for Plenary, and sometimes for Partial, Indulgences.
i. CONFESSION.
ii. COMMUNION.
iii. VISIT to a church or public chapel. (See p, xiii.)
iv. PRAYER according to the intention of the Pope. (See p. xiii.)

N.B. Too much stress cannot be laid on the importance of carefully noting and exactly fulfilling all that may be required for gaining a particular Indulgence. If there is any deviation, even though unintentional, from the strict letter of the specified conditions, no Indulgence can be gained.

To gain the full benefit of a Plenary Indulgence, it is necessary to have a true hatred of every, even venial, sin committed, and to be wholly free from all voluntary attachment to what is sinful.

NOTE. In the case of gaining Indulgences for the dead, the necessity of a state of grace is questioned by some theologians, unless it is specified or implied in the Grant; and therefore, in this particular case, the necessity cannot be insisted upon as absolutely certain; nevertheless, in practice, a state of grace should always be considered of the first importance, the opinion above quoted being" only probable.
The following decisions of the Congregations of Indulgences should be carefully noted:

DECISIONS OF THE SACRED CONGREGATION OF INDULGENCES - STATE OF GRACE
1. A state of grace ought to precede everything, but in case it should not, it must at least be attained before the last of the acts prescribed for the Indulgence is completed. (Raccolta, p. vii.)
2. Although for Partial Indulgences Confession is not usually required as a condition, the usual formula being, "with at least a contrite heart," in case of conscious mortal sin it should precede the other acts; but in case of difficulty in getting to confession an act of true contrition with a firm purpose of confessing

suffices. (December 17, 1870.) Under ordinary circumstances, the formula above quoted implies nothing more than a state of grace.

INTENTION

3. A general intention of gaining all Indulgences is sufficient. It should be renewed from time to time, say every morning. (Raccolta, p. viii.)

4. By a further general intention all, or by a particular intention any, Indulgences may be applied to the Holy Souls in Purgatory, either to the Holy Souls in general, or to individual souls (Ib.) N.B. Indulgences to be applicable to the holy souls require a positive declaration to that effect in the grant. (Cf, Instruction 8, p. i.)

CONFESSION

5. Confession, whenrequiredas a condition, is binding even on those who are not conscious of mortal sin. (May 19,1759.)

6. The Confession, or Confession and Communion, required as conditions may be made on the day previous to that appointed for an Indulgence, provided other acts remain to be done on the day itself. (January 12, 1878.)

6a. In cases of special feasts enriched with Indulgences, and of those days when as in the case of the Portiuncula many indulgences can be gained in succession; on account of the concourse of penitents, the Confession can now be made, in the first case, i.e. when a single Indulgence is in question, two days, and in the second case three days before the feast. (March n, 1908.)

7. Habitual weekly Confession, for those in a state of grace, suffices for all Indulgences during the week, except Jubilees. (March 12, 1855.)

8. By weekly Confession is meant Confession every seven days. (November 23, 1878, February 25, 1886.)
N.B. Daily Communicants are no longer required to make this weekly Confession. See Frequent Communion," No. 85, p. 70.

9. In cases of devotion extending over a period of days, the Confession and Communion may be made any time within eight days after the end of such a period. (December 8, 1 897.)

10. If the Bishop of the Diocese applies for it, a concession is made in favour of places where, through want of Confessors, people have a difficulty in getting to Confession before an indulgenced feast. In such cases, Confession made eight days before suffices, and covers all Indulgences during the period. (June 12, i822; September 28, 1838; December 15, 1841.)

11. Under similar circumstances, and if the Bishop applies for the concession, the habitual Confession made once a fortnight, i.e. every thirteen days, suffices for all the Indulgences during the period. (November 23, 1878; February 25, 1886.)

12. Confession and Communion made on Easter Day satisfy for the Paschal precept and for the Indulgence attached to the Papal blessing given by the Bishop. (March 19, 1841.)

13. For a Jubilee, ordinary or extraordinary, a special Confession and Communion must be made. (May 10, 1844.)

COMMUNION

14. One Communion satisfies for all the Indulgences of the day. (May 29, 1841.)

15. The Paschal Communion satisfies for the Paschal precept and the Indulgence of the day. (May 10, 1844.)

16. Unless specially required, the Communion for an Indulgence attached to a particular church need not be made in that church. (May 19, 1759.)

17. In cases of chronic infirmity, or physical impediment, the Confessor can commute the Communion for some other good work. And this has been made applicable to Communities. (September 18, 1862; January 16, 1886.)

VISIT TO A CHURCH OR PUBLIC CHAPEL

18. Separate visits must be made for two or more Indulgences. (February 29, 1864.)

19. If the Communion be made in a church or chapel prescribed, or available for the visit, special prayer said at the time of Communion satisfies for one visit. (Raccolta, p. xviii.)

20. The chapels of monasteries, seminaries, and convents, to which the faithful have not public access, are not available for the visit. (August 22, 1842.)

21. Confessors can commute the visit in the case of chronic invalids, or those who cannot go out. And this has been made applicable to Communities. (September 1 8, 1 862; June 16, 1 886.)

22. The visit may be made before or after the other acts, i.e., any time from midnight to midnight, unless otherwise specified, e.g., from first Vespers on the vigil to sunset on the feast. (May 19, 1759; January 12, 1878.)

PRAYER ACCORDING TO THE POPE'S INTENTION

23. The Pope's intention always includes the following objects:

i. The progress of the Faith and triumph of the Church.

ii. Peace and union among Christian Princes and Rulers.

iii. The conversion of sinners.

iv. The uprooting of heresy.

These intentions may be fittingly recalled and prayed for after Communion, or at the visit; but a general intention of praying according to the mind of the Pope is sufficient; and any prayers may be used which are not already of obligation, e.g., the Little Hours of a priests Office. (July 12, 1847; May 29, 1841.)

THE DEAF AND DUMB

24. Vocal prayer is commuted for devout elevation of mind and heart. (February 16, 1852.)

25. At public Devotions, presence and a devout attitude of mind and heart suffice. (Ibid.)

26. Confessors can commute private prayers for other external works. (Ibid.)

27. Vocal prayers may be said by signs or mentally, or they may be read over without articulation. (July 16, 1902).

GENERAL

28. Indulgenced prayers may be said in any language, provided that the version in the vernacular is a faithful rendering of the original; and this may be guaranteed, either by the Cardinal Prefect of the Congregation of Indulgences, or by one of the Ordinaries of the country where the language in question is spoken. (December 20, 1884.)

29. Unless specially required, indulgenced prayers need not be said kneeling. (September 18, 1862.)

30. Unless other wise declared, e.g., "from first Vespers on the vigil to sunset on the feast," the day is calculated from midnight to midnight. (January 12, 1878.)

31. Devotions which admit of being said alternately, such as the Angelus or Rosary, may be said by several persons together. (February 29, 1820.)

32. A prayer or good work, enriched with diverse indulgences, must be repeated, if several Indulgences are to be gained, unless such repetition is impracticable, e.g. Communion, or unusual, e.g. Confession. (February 29, 1820; January 12, 1878.)

33. A Plenary Indulgence, granted for visiting a church on certain days, or doing some other pious work, can be gained only once a day, save that of the Portiuncula (March 7, 1678), and similar concessions granted T.Q.

34. An indulgence attached to a visit to a church or chapel, even though described as quotidiana plenaria, can be gained once only in the year, unless it is clearly stated in the indult that it can be gained every day. (February 16, 1852.)

35. By feasts of our LORD, when spoken of in connexion with Plenary Indulgences, must be understood the Nativity, Circumcision, Epiphany, Easter, Ascension, and Corpus CHRISTI. And by feasts of our Lady must be understood the Immaculate Conception, Nativity, Annunciation, Purification, and Assumption. (September 18, 1862.)

36. If Partial indulgences are granted to "other" feasts of our LORD and our Lady, this must be understood of feasts which are common to the Universal Church.

37. In all cases by feasts of the Apostles are meant those feasts which commemorate their entrance into eternal life. (September 18, 1862.)

ROSARIES, MEDALS, ETC.

38. Blessed objects can only be used by the person for whom they were originally blessed, or if blessed for distribution, can be passed on by that person to others; but they can go no further. They cannot be given away, or lent with the intention of transferring the indulgences attached to them. If they be so dealt with, the indulgences are lost, and the objects return to their original unblessed condition. They cannot be sold or exchanged. And if a person undertakes to get such objects blessed for others, he must be careful, if he wishes to receive payment for them, either to obtain the money before getting them blessed, or at least a

precise commission to buy them, sufficient to determine the ownership of the goods. (February 6, 1657; January 10, 1839; July 16, 1887; July 10, 1896.)

LEAFLETS, ETC.

39. Anyone obtaining a grant of an Indulgence, of universal extension, must, under pain of nullity, present the original to the Secretary of the Sacred Congregation of Indulgences.

40. Thus all leaflets, circulars, little books or papers, purporting to contain prayers indulgenced for all the faithful, not to be found in the Raccolta (as distinguished from similar documents belonging to Confraternities, Pious Societies, etc., which are purposely omitted), are certainly spurious and worthless, unless they have annexed to them the approbation of the said Congregation. (January 22, 1858; January 8, 1861; January 19, 1756; April 14, 1856.)

N. B. It follows from what has been said above, that only Indulgences granted to all the Faithful in general are to be found in the Raccolta, and that the Indulgences belonging to Confraternities, Pious Societies and the like, which are not therefore of universal extension, must be sought for elsewhere, in the Rules and Regulations of such Societies.

LIST OF ABBREVIATIONS

Bl., Bull.
Bps., Congregation of Bishops and Regulars.
Br., Brief.
Res., Rescript.
Mem., Secretariate of Memorials.
Enc., Encyclical.
Con., Constitution. Aff., of Special Ecclesiastical Affairs.
Mot. pr., Motu proprio.
Pr. ma., Propria manu.
Bfs., of Briefs.
Indul., Congregation of Indulgences
Sta., of State.
Pen., Penitentiary.
Ind. , of the Index. Off. , Holy Office.
Rit., of Rites.
A.S.S., Acta Sanctæ Sedis.
Prop., of Propaganda.
T.Q., Toties quoties, i.e., any number of times.

INSTRUCTIONS

1. THE conditions, general and special, for gaining Indulgences, with the decisions of the Congregation of Indulgences which follow, should be carefully studied and often referred to.

2. Unless otherwise stated, e.g., "once a day," a partial Indulgence may be gained any number of times in succession. This is indicated by the letters T.Q.

3. To gain a "Plenary, once (or twice, etc.) a month," the prayer or at must be repeated daily or a month; and the Communion may be made, unless otherwise declared, on any day of the month, or within eight days after.

4. The Roman numerals, I, II, III, IV, placed after an Indulgence, indicate the special conditions, viz., I, CONFESSION; II, COMMUNION; III, VISIT to a church or public chapel; IV, PRAYER according to the Pope's intention (see pp. xi-xiii).

5. The references at the foot of the page correspond with the indulgences; and the dates are those of rescripts of the Congregation of Indulgences, unless otherwise noted (see p. xv).

6. The Our FATHERS, Hail Mary's, and Glories prescribed for an Indulgence are indicated throughout by the Latin Pater noster, Ave Maria, and Gloria Patri, or in short, Pater, Ave, and Gloria. They can of course be said in English, and this applies to similar references in Latin to familiar prayers, antiphons, etc. N.B. All the indulgences which follow, except those granted "in articulo mortis, " i.e., for the point of death, and except those marked with an asterisk, are applicable to the holy souls in Purgatory (S.C. Indul., Dec. 8. 1897).

I. THE HOLY TRINITY.

1. The Angelic Trisagion.

i. 100 Days, once a day. ii. 100 Days, three times a day, on Sundays and during" the Octave of Trinity Sunday. iii. Plenary, once a month. I, II, IV. (See Instructions above.) 1 Clement XIV, June 6, 1769; June 26. 1770.

SANCTUS, Sanctus, Sanctus, DOMINUS DEUS exercituum: Plena est terra gloria tua: Gloria PATRI, Gloria FILIO, Gloria SPIRITUI SANCTO.

HOLY, Holy, Holy, Lord God of Hosts, earth is full of thy Glory, Glory be to the FATHER, Glory be to the SON, Glory be to the HOLY GHOST.

2. Gloria Patri seven times, said by three Persons.

i. 100 Days, once a day. ii. Seven Years and Seven Quarantines, on Sundays. iii. Plenary, twice a month, on any two Sundays. I, II, IV. (See Instructions) 2 Pius VI, May 15, 1784.

In order to gain these Indulgences there must be a pious union of three persons, who shall agree to recite, either together or separately, thrice a day, morning, afternoon and evening, Gloria Patri seven times, and Ave Maria once, in honour of the Holy Trinity. Should any one of the three die, or cease to belong to the union, a substitute must be found.

3. Mass and Prayers in Thanksgiving for Our Lady's Privileges.

i. 300 Days, once a day. ii. Plenary, twice a month. I, II, IV. (See Instructions) 3 Pius VII, Rit. April 15, June 13, July 13, 1815; Mem. Jan. 10, 1817.

In this Devotion, originally restricted to the Church of Our Lady of Loreto in the Forum of Trajan, Rome, one Votive Mass of the Most Holy Trinity can be celebrated each day, and this in one church alone in any city or village; this church must be designated by the Ordinary. The Mass may be said on days when the office is of an ordinary double festival. On days when the rite is a major double, or double of the second class, the Mass of the day must be said with a Commemoration of the Most Holy Trinity; this permission, however, does not extend to Sundays of the first class or doubles of the first class. This Mass may be applied according" to the intention of benefactors, or for any other pious object, or in suffrage for the dead, even on days when the Rubric requires Missa pro defunctis.

Prayers to be said by priest and people after the Mass.

MOST Holy Trinity, FATHER, SON, and HOLY GHOST, Three Persons and one GOD, we adore Thee, and with all the love of our whole hearts we give Thee thanks for the high gifts and privileges granted to Mary most holy in her glorious and Immaculate Conception. Gloria PATRI thrice, and Ave Maria once.

MOST Holy Trinity, FATHER, SON, and HOLY GHOST, we adore Thee, and with all the love of our whole hearts we give Thee thanks for the high gifts and privileges granted to Mary most holy in her glorious Nativity. Gloria PATRI thrice, and Ave Maria once.

MOST Holy Trinity, FATHER, SON, and HOLY GHOST, we adore Thee, and with all the love of our whole hearts we give Thee thanks for the high gifts and privileges granted to Mary most holy in her glorious Presentation in the Temple. Gloria PATRI thrice, and Ave Maria once.

MOST Holy Trinity, FATHER, SON, and HOLY GHOST, we adore Thee, and with all the love of our whole hearts we give Thee thanks for the high gifts and privileges granted to Mary most holy in her glorious Annunciation. Gloria PATRI thrice, and Ave Maria once.

MOST Holy Trinity, FATHER, SON, and HOLY GHOST, we adore Thee, and with all the love of our whole hearts we give Thee thanks for the high gifts and privileges granted to Mary most holy in her glorious Visitation. Gloria PATRI thrice, and Ave Maria once.

MOST Holy Trinity, FATHER, SON, and HOLY GHOST, we adore Thee, and with all the love of our whole hearts we give Thee thanks for the high gifts and privileges granted to Mary most holy in her glorious Purification. Gloria PATRI thrice, and Ave Maria once.

MOST Holy Trinity, FATHER, SON, and HOLY GHOST, we adore Thee, and with all the love of our whole hearts we give Thee thanks for the high gifts and privileges granted to Mary most holy in her most glorious Assumption. Gloria PATRI thrice, and Ave Maria once.

LASTLY, we give Thee most hearty thanks, for that Thou hast exalted and glorified the most holy and most sweet name of Mary throughout the whole world.

Prayer to the most Holy Virgin.

MARY, dear Mother! Mother most amiable! tender Mother! Mother full of love and sweetness for thy clients and children! we pray thee, by this our loving act of thanksgiving to the Most Holy Trinity, obtain for all of us grace ever to employ the powers of our souls, and our bodily senses, to the honour and glory of GOD, one in Three Persons, directing all our actions to Him, and loving Him with pure hearts, even as thou didst love Him here on earth; that thus we may be able to attain to the enjoyment of Him in the bliss of heaven with thee for ever and ever.

Bless us in the name of the FATHER, and of the SON, and of the HOLY GHOST.

All say the Salve Regina (see p. 184).

V/. Let us bless the FATHER, SON, and HOLY GHOST.

R/. Let us praise and exalt Him above all forever.

Let us pray.

ALMIGHTY and eternal GOD, who hast given to us thy servants grace by the confession of the true faith to acknowledge the glory of the eternal Trinity, and in the power of thy Majesty to worship the Unity; grant, we beseech Thee, that by the firmness of this our faith we may ever be defended from all adversities. Through CHRIST our LORD. **R/.** Amen.

4. Gloria Patri thrice.

i. 100 Days, thrice a day, for saying morning, noon, and evening-, Gloria Patri thrice, in thanksgiving to the Most Holy Trinity for the graces and privileges granted to most holy Mary, especially in her glorious Assumption into heaven.

ii. Plenary, once a month. I, II, IV. (See Instructions) 4 Pius VII, July 11, 1815.

5. Prayers of Thanksgiving for Our Lady's Assumption.

i. 300 Days, once a day. ii. Plenary, once a month. I, II, IV. (See Instructions, p. i.) 5 Pius VII, Mem. July 19, 1822

Adore the eternal FATHER with a PATER, Ave, and Gloria; then say,

I ADORE Thee, Eternal FATHER, my LORD and my GOD, in union with all the heavenly host, rendering Thee infinite thanks for every grace and favour Thou hast granted to Mary, most holy Virgin, thy well-beloved daughter, and, above all, for that height of power to which Thou didst exalt her by her Assumption into heaven.

Adore the Eternal SON with a PATER, Ave, and Gloria; then say

I ADORE Thee too, Eternal SON, my GOD, my LORD, and my REDEEMER, in union with all the heavenly host, rendering Thee infinite thanks for every grace and favour Thou hast granted to Mary, Virgin most blessed, thy well-beloved Mother, and, above all, for the gift of highest wisdom with which Thou didst glorify her on her Assumption into heaven.

Adore the HOLY GHOST with a PATER, Ave, and Gloria; then say,

I ADORE Thee also, O HOLY GHOST, the PARACLETE, my GOD and my LORD, and in union with all the heavenly host I render Thee infinite thanks for every grace and favour Thou hast granted to the most blessed Virgin, thy most loving Spouse, and, above all, for that most perfect and divine charity with which Thou didst inflame her most holy and most pure heart in the act of her most glorious Assumption into heaven. In the name of thy most chaste Spouse, I humbly beg of Thee to grant me the grace of remission of all my most grievous sins which I have committed from the first moment when I was able to sin until this day, for all of which I grieve exceedingly, firmly purposing rather to die than ever again offend thy Divine Majesty; and relying on the high merits and most powerful protection of this thy most loving Spouse, I beg of Thee to grant me the most precious gift of thy grace and Divine love, by vouchsafing me those lights and special helps whereby thy eternal providence has determined to will my salvation, and to bring me to Thyself.

Then say three times,

HOLY Mary, all ye holy men and women, saints of GOD, intercede for us to our LORD, that we may merit his help and be saved. Amen.

To the Most Blessed Virgin.

I ACKNOWLEDGE thee and I venerate thee, most holy Virgin, Queen of Heaven, Lady and Mistress of the Universe, as Daughter of the Eternal FATHER, Mother of his well-beloved SON, and most loving Spouse of the HOLY SPIRIT. Kneeling at the feet of thy great Majesty, with all humility I pray thee, through that divine charity with which thou wast so bounteously enriched on thy Assumption into heaven, to vouchsafe me favour and pity, placing me under thy most safe and faithful protection, and receiving me into the number of thy happy and highly-favoured servants. Deign, Mother and Lady most tender, to accept my miserable heart, memory, will, powers, and senses, internal and external; govern them all in conformity to the good pleasure of thy Divine Son, as I intend by my every thought and deed to give thee glory and honour. And, by that wisdom with which thy well-beloved Son glorified thee, I pray and beseech thee to obtain for me light that I may clearly know myself and my own nothingness, and in particular my sins, that so I may hate and loathe them ; and that I may discern the snares of the infernal enemy, and all his modes of attack, whether open or hidden. Above all, most tender Mother, I beg of thee the grace of N. **Say three times,**

Virgin of all virgins,
To thy shelter take us,
Gentlest of the gentle,
Chaste and gentle make us.

Let us pray.
PARDON, O LORD, we beseech Thee, the sins of thy servants; that we, who of our own actions know not how to please Thee, may be saved by the intercession of the Mother of thy SON, our LORD. Through the same CHRIST our LORD. Amen. May the almighty and merciful LORD, FATHER, SON, and HOLY GHOST, bless and preserve us. Amen.

6. Three Offerings of Thanksgiving To obtain a Good Death.

i. 100 Days. T.Q. ii. Plenary, once a month, at the end of the month. I, II, IV. (See Instructions) 6. Leo XII, Pr. Ma., October 21, 1823; Pius IX, June 18, 1876.

WE offer to the Most Holy Trinity the merits of JESUS CHRIST, in thanksgiving for the Most Precious Blood which He shed in the garden for us; and through those merits we beseech his Divine Majesty for pardon of our sins. PATER, Ave, Gloria.

WE offer to the Most Holy Trinity the merits of JESUS CHRIST, in thanksgiving for his most precious death endured on the Cross for us ; and through those merits we beseech his Divine Majesty for the remission of the pains due to our sins. PATER, Ave, Gloria.

WE offer to the Most Holy Trinity the merits of JESUS CHRIST, in thanksgiving for his unspeakable charity, in descending from heaven to earth to take human flesh, and to suffer and die for us upon the Cross ; and by those merits we beseech his Divine Majesty to bring our souls to the glory of heaven after our death. PATER, Ave, Gloria.

7. Triduo or Novena (made at any time in public or private in honour of the Holy Trinity).

i. Seven Years and Seven Quarantines every day of the Triduo or Novena. ii. Plenary, to those who shall keep such Novena or Triduo completely, I, II, III & IV. (See Instructions.) 7 Pius IX, August 8, 1847.

8. The Sign of the Gross.

i. 50 Days. T.Q. ii. 100 Days, if made with Holy Water. T.Q. (See Instructions) 8 Pius IX, Br. July 28, 1863. Br. March 23. 1865.

N. B. The words must in either case be said. IN the name of the FATHER, and of the SON, and of the HOLY GHOST.

9. Thanksgiving on New-Year's Eve.

Seven Years, IV. (See Instructions.) 9 Pius IX, Br. December 5, 1876.

This Devotion consists of two half-hours, viz., the last of the old year and the first of the new, spent in thanksgiving to the Holy Trinity for benefits received, and in praying according 1 to the intention of the Pope.

10. Prayer.

200 Days, once a day. (See Instructions) 10 Leo XIII, March 15, 1890. N.B. All existing indulgences for the same are abrogated.

OMNIPOTENTIA PATRIS, adjuva fragilitatem meam, et e profundo miseriæ eripe me.

OMNIPOTENCE of the FATHER, help my frailty, and rescue me from the depths of misery.

Sapientia FILII, dirige cogitationes, verba et actiones meas omnes.

Wisdom of the SON, direct all my thoughts, words, and actions.

Amor SPIRITUS SANCTI, esto cunctarum animæ meæ operationum principium, quo jugiter sint

Love of the HOLY SPIRIT, be the source of all the operations of my soul, so that they may be entirely

| divino beneplacito conformes. | conformed to the divine will. |

11. Acts of Adoration and Thanksgiving to the Blessed Trinity.
300 Days, once a day. (See Instructions.) 11 Pius X, March 22, 1905.
MOST Holy Trinity, FATHER, SON, and HOLY GHOST, behold us prostrate in thy divine presence. We humble ourselves profoundly and beg of Thee pardon for our sins.
We adore Thee, Omnipotent FATHER, and with the outpouring of our hearts we thank Thee for having given us thy divine SON JESUS to be our REDEEMER, and for having left Him with us to the consummation of the world in the most august sacrament of the Holy Eucharist, in which mystery of faith and love He reveals to us the wonders of his Sacred Heart. Gloria PATRI.

O DIVINE Word, most adorable JESUS, we adore Thee in thy Sacrament, and with the outpouring of our hearts we thank Thee for having taken human flesh and for having- made Thyself, for our redemption, Priest and Victim in the sacrifice of the Cross, a sacrifice which, by an excess of the love of thy adorable Heart, Thou dost renew every moment on our altars throughout the world. O supreme Priest, O divine Victim, grant that we may honour the sacrifice of the most holy Eucharist with the united homage of most holy Mary and of all thy Church, in triumph, in suffering, and in warfare. We offer ourselves wholly to Thee, and since thou dost deign to have victims associated with Thee, accept our offering, and, uniting it with thine, bless us. Gloria PATRI.

O DIVINE SPIRIT and PARACLETE, we adore Thee, and with the outpouring of our hearts, we thank Thee for having, with so much love for us, wrought the ineffable blessing of the Incarnation of the divine Word, a benefit which is continually being extended and increased in the most holy Eucharist. By this adorable mystery of the love of the Sacred Heart of JESUS, grant to us and to all sinners thy grace; pour out upon us and upon all redeemed souls thy holy gifts, but in a special manner bestow them upon the holy Church, the Spouse of JESUS CHRIST and our Mother, upon its visible head the supreme Pontiff, upon all the Cardinals, the Bishops and pastors of souls, on all priests, and on all the other ministers of the Sanctuary. Amen. Gloria PATRI.

12. Prayer to the Holy Trinity.
300 Days.* T.Q. (See Instructions) 12 Pius X, April 18, 1906.
I ADORE Thee, O my GOD, one GOD in three Persons; I annihilate myself before thy Majesty. Thou alone art being, life, truth, beauty, and goodness. I glorify Thee, I praise Thee, I thank Thee, and I love Thee, all incapable and unworthy as I am, in union with thy dear SON JESUS CHRIST, our SAVIOUR and our FATHER, in the mercifulness of his heart and through his infinite merits. I wish to serve Thee, to please Thee, to obey Thee, and to love Thee always, in union with Mary immaculate, Mother of GOD and our Mother, loving also and serving my neighbour for thy sake. Therefore, give me thy HOLY SPIRIT to enlighten, correct, and guide me in the way of thy commandments, and in all perfection, until we come to the happiness of heaven, where we shall glorify Thee for ever. Amen.

13. Renewal of Baptismal Vows.
Plenary, I, II, & IV.. (See Instructions.) 13. Pius X, June 1, 1906.
This must be done solemnly and publicly, with ceremonial sanctioned by the Bishop, on Trinity Sunday.

II. ALMIGHTY GOD

14. Acts of Faith, Hope and Charity.
i. Seven Years and Seven Quarantines. T.Q. ii. Plenary, once a month. I, II, IV. iii. Plenary, in articulo mortis, (at the point of death), if frequently used during life. (See Instructions.) 14 Benedict XIII, January 15, 1728; Benedict XIV, January 28, 1756.
N.B. Any form of words may be used, provided that in each case it expresses the special motive peculiar to the virtue.

Act of Faith.

I MOST firmly believe, because GOD, who is the infallible Truth, hath so revealed to the Holy Catholic Church, and through the Church reveals to us, that there is one only GOD in three divine Persons, equal and distinct, FATHER, SON, and HOLY GHOST; that the SON became Man by taking to himself flesh and a human soul through the operation of the HOLY GHOST in the womb of the most pure Virgin Mary; that He died for us upon the Cross, rose again, ascended into heaven, and from thence shall come again at the end of the world to judge the living and the dead, to give Paradise for ever to the good and hell to the wicked; moreover, from the same motive I believe all that the same holy Church believes and teaches.

Act of Hope.
OMY GOD, because Thou art almighty, infinitely good and merciful, I hope that, by the merits of the Passion and Death of JESUS CHRIST our SAVIOUR, Thou wilt grant me eternal life, which Thou, most faithful, hast promised to all those who shall do the works of a good Christian, as I purpose to do by thy holy help.

Act of Charity.
O MY GOD, because Thou art the highest and most perfect good, I love Thee with my whole heart, and above all things; and rather than offend Thee, I am ready to lose all things; and moreover for thy love I love, and will love my neighbour as myself.

15. Chaplet of Acts of the Love of God.
1. 300 Days, once a day. ii. Plenary, once a year, to those who say them at least ten times a month, I, II, IV. (See Instructions.) 15 Pius VII, August 11, 1818.
O My GOD, and Sovereign Good, would that I had always loved Thee!
2. My GOD, I detest that time when I loved Thee not.
3. How could I ever live so long without thy holy love?
4. And Thou, too, my GOD, how couldst Thou bear with me?
5. My GOD, I give Thee thanks for thy great patience.
6. But now I desire to love Thee for ever.
7. I am content rather to die than love Thee not.
8. Take from me my life, O my GOD, if I am not to love Thee.
9. The grace I beg of Thee is to love Thee ever.
10. With thy love I shall be blessed. Gloria PATRI.

MY GOD, I would see Thee loved by all.
2. Happy should I be, could I but shed my blood that all might love Thee.
3. He who loves Thee not is blind indeed.
4. My GOD, give him thy light.
5. Miserable indeed are they who love not Thee, the Sovereign Good.
6. My GOD, let me never be one of those wretched ones who love Thee not.
7. My GOD, be Thou my joy, and all my good.
8. I would be wholly thine for ever.
9. Who shall separate me from thy holy love?
10. Come, all ye creatures, love ye my GOD. Gloria PATRI.

MY GOD, I would I had a thousand hearts wherewith to love Thee.
2. I would that I had all hearts of all men wherewith to love Thee.
3. I would there were more worlds, that all might love Thee.
4. How blessed would he be who could love Thee with the hearts of all possible creatures!
5. Thou meritest, my GOD, to be so loved.
6. My heart is too poor, too cold, to love Thee.
7. Alas for the dead coldness of men in not loving their Sovereign Good!
8. Alas for the miserable blindness of the world which knows not Thee, who art true love.
9. O blessed inhabitants of heaven, who know and love him!
10. O blessed necessity of loving GOD! Gloria PATRI.

MY GOD, when will the time come that I shall burn with love for Thee?
2. Oh, then what happiness were mine!
3. But, since I know not how to love Thee, I will at least rejoice that there are so many others who love Thee with their whole hearts.
4. In particular I rejoice that Thou art loved by all angels and all saints in heaven.
5. With the hearts of all these I unite the love of my poor heart.
6. In a special manner I intend to love Thee with the love with which those Saints who loved Thee best have loved Thee.
7. Wherefore I intend to love Thee with the love wherewith St Mary Magdalene, St Catherine and St Teresa loved Thee.
8. With the love wherewith St Augustine, St Dominic, St Francis Xavier, St Philip Neri and St Louis Gonzaga loved Thee.
9. With the love wherewith thy Holy Apostles, especially St Peter, St Paul, and the beloved Disciple, loved Thee.
10. With that same love wherewith St Joseph the great Patriarch loved Thee. Gloria PATRI.

MOREOVER, I intend to love Thee with that love wherewith Mary most holy, loved Thee when on earth.
2. In particular with that love wherewith she loved Thee when she conceived thy Divine SON in her virgin womb, when she brought Him forth, when she suckled Him, and when she saw Him die.
3. Yet more, I intend to love Thee with that love wherewith she loves Thee and will love Thee forever in heaven.
4. But to love Thee worthily, O my GOD of infinite goodness, not even this love suffices.
5. Wherefore I would love Thee as thy SON, the Divine Word made Man, did love Thee.
6. As He loved Thee when He was born.
7. As He loved Thee when He died upon the Cross.
8. As He loves Thee ever in those sacred tabernacles where He lies hid.
9. And with that love with which He loves Thee and will love Thee in heaven for all eternity.
10. Lastly, I would fain love Thee with that love with which Thou lovest thyself; but since that is impossible, grant me, O my GOD, of thy tender pity, that I may love Thee as far as I know how and am able, and as Thou art pleased that I should love Thee. Amen and Amen. Gloria PATRI.

Let us pray.
O GOD, who hast prepared invisible good things for them that love Thee, pour into our hearts such a desire of thy love, that we, loving Thee in all things and above all things, may attain thy heavenly promises, which exceed all that we can desire. Through CHRIST our LORD. Amen.

16. Prayer.
i. 40 Days. T.Q. ii. 100 Years and 100 Quarantines or saying it every Saturday for a month. (See Instructions.) 16 Leo XII. Pr. Ma. July 9. 1828.
LOOSEN, O LORD, we pray Thee, in thy pity, the bonds of our sins, and by the intercession of the blessed Mary ever Virgin, Mother of GOD, St Joseph, the blessed Apostles Peter and Paul, and all saints, keep us thy servants and our abodes in all holiness; cleanse us, our relations, kinsfolk, and acquaintances from all vices ; adorn us with all virtues ; grant us peace and health; repel our enemies visible and invisible; curb our carnal desires; give us healthful seasons; bestow thy charity upon our friends and our enemies; guard thy holy City; preserve our Sovereign Pontiff N.; defend all prelates, princes, and Christian people from all adversity. Let thy blessing be ever upon us, and grant to all the faithful departed eternal rest. Through CHRIST our LORD. Amen.

17. Prayer of St Francis Xavier for the Conversion of Infidels.
300 Days, once a day. (See Instructions) 17 Pius IX, Pr. Ma. May 24, 1847

ÆTERNE rerum omnium effector DEUS, memento abs te animas infidelium procreatas, casque ad imaginem et similitudinem tuam conditas. Ecce, DOMINE, in opprobrium tuum his ipsis infernus impletur. Memento JESUM FILIUM tuum pro

ETERNAL GOD, the Maker of all things, remember that the souls of unbelievers have been created by Thee, and that they have been made after thy own image and likeness. Behold, O LORD, to thy dishonour, with these very souls hell is filled.

illorum salute atrocissimam subiisse ne cem. Noli, quæso, DOMINE, ultra permittere, ut FILIUS tuus ab infidelibus contemnatur; sed precibus sanctorum virorum et Ecclesiæ sanctissimi FILII tui Sponsæ placatus, recordare misericordiæ tuæ, et oblitus idolatrias et infidelitatiseorum, effice ut ipsi quoque agnoscant aliquando quem misisti DOMINUM JESUM CHRISTUM, qui est salus, vita, et resurrectio nostra; per quem salvati et liberati sumus: cui sit gloria per infinita sæcula sæculorum. Amen.

Remember, O GOD, that for their salvation thy SON JESUS CHRIST underwent a most cruel death. O LORD, suffer not that thy SON be despised by unbelievers; but, appeased by the prayers of holy men and of the Church, the Spouse of thy most holy SON, remember thy own pity, and, forgetting their idolatry and their unbelief, bring to pass that they may at length acknowledge thy SON JESUS CHRIST, who is our salvation, life, and resurrection, through whom we are saved and set free; to whom be glory from age to age without end. Amen.

18. Prayer for Peace
i. 100 Days, T.Q. (See Instructions) ii. Plenary once a month. I, II, III, IV. 18 Pius IX. May 18, 1848

DA pacem, DOMINE, in diebus nostris: quia non est alius qui pugnet pro nobis nisi tu, DEUS noster.
V/ Fiat pax in virtute tua
R/ Et abundantia in turribus tuis.
Oremus.
DEUS, a quo sancta desideria, recta consilia, et justa sunt opera: da servis tuis illam, quam mundus dare non potest, pacem: ut et corda nostra mandatis tuis dedita, et hostium sublata formidine, tempora sint tua protectione tranquilla. Per CHRISTUM DOMINUM nostrum. Amen.

Give peace, O LORD, in our days; for there is none other that fighteth for us, but only Thou, our GOD.
V/ Let there be peace in thy strength, O LORD.
R/ And plenty in thy strong places.
Let us pray.
O GOD, from whom proceed all holy desires, all right counsels and just works; grant unto us thy servants that peace which the world cannot give, that our hearts may be devoted to thy service, and that, being delivered from the fear of our enemies, we may pass our time in peace under thy protection. Through CHRIST our LORD. Amen.

19. Offerings for the Beginning of the Day and for Mass.
i. Three Years, once a day for each prayer. ii. Plenary, to those who say both the prayers every day or a month. I, II, III, IV. (See Instructions.) 19Pius IX, Br. April 11, 1860; May 5, 1890.

At the Beginning of the Day.
O LORD GOD Almighty, behold me prostrate before Thee in order to appease Thee, and to honour thy Divine Majesty, in the name of all creatures. But how can I do this who am myself but a poor sinner? Nay, but I both can and will, knowing that Thou dost make it thy boast to be called FATHER of mercies, and for love of us hast given thy only-begotten SON, who sacrificed Himself upon the Cross, and for our sake doth continually renew that sacrifice of Himself upon our altars. And therefore do I sinner, but penitent; poor, but rich in JESUS CHRIST present myself before Thee, and, with the love of angels and of all thy saints, and with the tender affection of the Immaculate Heart of Mary, I offer to Thee in the name of all creatures the Masses which are now being celebrated, together with all those which have been celebrated, and which shall be celebrated to the end of the world. Moreover, I intend to renew the offering- of them every moment of this day and of all my life, that I may thereby render to thy infinite Majesty an honour and a glory worthy of Thee, thus to appease thy indignation, to satisfy thy justice for our many sins, to render Thee thanks in proportion to thy benefits, and to implore thy mercies for myself and for all sinners, for all the faithful, living and dead, for thy whole Church, and principally for its visible Head, the Sovereign Pontiff, and lastly for all poor schismatic's, heretics, and infidels, that they also may be converted and save their souls.

During, or (in the case of priests] before Mass.
ETERNAL FATHER, I offer to Thee the sacrifice which thy beloved SON JESUS made of Himself upon the Cross, and which He now renews upon this altar; I offer it to Thee in the name of all creatures, together with the Masses which have been celebrated, and which shall be celebrated in the whole world, in order to adore Thee, and to give Thee the honour which Thou dost deserve, to render to Thee due thanks for thy innumerable benefits, to appease thy anger, which our many sins have provoked, and to

give Thee due satisfaction for them; to entreat Thee also for myself, for the Church, for the whole world, and for the blessed souls in purgatory. Amen.

20. An Offering.
100 Days, once a day. (See Instructions.) 20 Pius IX, Pr. Ma. April 30, 1860.
ETERNAL FATHER, we offer Thee the Blood, Passion, and Death of JESUS CHRIST, and the sorrows of the most holy Mary and St Joseph, in payment for our sins, in suffrage for the holy souls in purgatory, for the wants of our holy Mother the Church, and for the conversion of sinners. Amen.

21. A Morning Offering.
i. 100 Days, once a day. ii. Plenary, once a month, during" the month. I, II, III, IV. (See Instructions.) 21 Pius IX, Br. September 6, 1867.
ETERNAL GOD, behold me prostrate before the immensity of thy majesty. I humbly adore Thee, and offer Thee all my thoughts, words, and works of this day. I intend to do everything for love of Thee, for thy glory, and for the fulfilment of thy divine will; in order to serve, praise, and bless Thee, to be enlightened in the mysteries of our holy faith, to secure my salvation, and to hope in thy mercy; to satisfy the divine justice for my many grievous sins, to assist the holy souls in purgatory, and to obtain the grace of a true conversion for all sinners. I desire, in fine, to do everything in union with that most pure intention which JESUS and Mary had during life, and which the saints now have in heaven, and the just on earth. Would that I could write down this intention with my own blood and repeat it as often as there be moments in eternity! O my GOD, accept my goodwill; grant me thy holy blessing and efficacious grace never to commit a mortal sin throughout the course of my life, but particularly on this day, on which I desire and purpose to gain all the indulgences which it is possible for me to gain, and to be present in spirit at all the Masses which will be celebrated today in the whole world, that I may apply them to the holy souls in purgatory, and free them from all pain. Amen.

22. An Act of Faith.
100 Days, once a day. (See Instructions.) 22 Pius IX, Aff. January 10, 1871.
O MY GOD! I believe in Thee; I believe all that Thou hast revealed, and that the holy Catholic Church proposes for my belief. I believe, first, that the most blessed Virgin is truly the Mother of God; I believe firmly, and with all certainty, that she is at the same time mother and virgin, and that she is free from even the least actual sin. I also believe most firmly, and with all certainty, that by a singular grace and privilege of Almighty GOD, in view of the merits of JESUS CHRIST, the Saviour of the human race, Mary was, in the first instant of her conception, preserved free from all stain of original sin. I believe most firmly and with all certainty that when the Roman Pontiff speaks ex cathedra that is, when, fulfilling the office of chief pastor and teacher of all Christians, he, in virtue of his supreme and apostolic authority, defines a doctrine concerning faith or morals to be held by the universal Church by the divine assistance, promised him in the person of St Peter, possesses that infallibility with which the divine REDEEMER wished his Church to be endowed when defining matters of faith or morals; and, therefore, that such definitions of the Roman Pontiff are, of themselves, and not from the consent of the Church, irreformable. I believe all this, because thy holy Church, which is the pillar and ground of truth, which has never erred and can never err, proposes it to be believed.

23. Prayer of St Bonaventure.
100 Days, once a day. (See Instructions.) 23 Pius IX, Res. aut. April 11, 1874.

DOMINE sancte, PATER omnipotens, æterne DEUS, propter tuam largitatem et FILII tui, qui pro me sustinuit passionem et mortem, et matris ejus excellentissimam sanctitatem, atque beati Francisci, et omnium sanctorum merita, concede mihi peccatori, et omni tuo benencio indigno, ut te solum diligam, tuo amore semper sitiam, beneficium passionis continuo in corde habeam, meam miseriam recognoscam, et ab omnibus conculcari et contemni cupiam: nihil me contristet nisi culpa. Amen.

O HOLY LORD, almighty FATHER, eternal GOD! through thy liberality and that of thy SON, who for me endured suffering and death, through the surpassing holiness of His Mother, and through the merits of blessed Francis, and or all the saints, grant me, a sinner, undeserving of all thy benefits, that I may love Thee alone, and always thirst for thy love; that I may constantly feel in my heart the benefit of thy Passion; that I may acknowledge my misery, and desire to be trampled upon and despised by all men; that nothing but sin may sadden my heart. Amen.

24. Prayer.
100 Days, once a day. (See Instructions) 24. Pius IX. June 15, 1862; Leo XIII, July 19, 1879.

O LORD Almighty, who permittest evil to draw good therefrom, hear our humble prayers, and grant that we remain faithful to Thee unto death. Grant us also, through the intercession of most holy Mary, the strength ever to conform ourselves to thy most holy Will.

25. Prayer of St Ignatius.
300 Days, once a day. (See Instructions) 25 Leo XIII, May 26, 1883.

SUSCIPE DOMINE universam meam libertatem. Accipe memoriam, intellectum atque voluntatem omnem. Quidquid habeo vel possideo mihi largitus es: id tibi totum restituo, ac tuæ prorsus voluntati trado gubernandum. Amorem tui so him cum gratia tuadones, et dives sum satis, nec aliud quidquam ultra posco.

TAKE, O LORD, all my liberty. Receive my memory, understanding, and entire will. Thou hast bestowed on me whatever I have or possess: I give all back to Thee, and deliver it to Thee to be entirely subject to thy will. Only grant me thy love and thy grace, and I am rich enough and ask for nothing more.

26. Prayer.
200 Days, once a day. (See Instructions.) 26 Leo XIII, January 19, 1889.

THOU seest, O LORD, how on all sides the winds are let loose upon us, and the sea is growing rough with the violent commotion of the waves. Do Thou, we beseech Thee, who alone art able, command the winds and the waves. Restore to mankind that true peace which the world cannot give, the peace which comes of good order. Let men impelled by thy grace return to a right and orderly course of life, practising again, as they ought, love towards GOD, justice and charity in dealing with their neighbour, temperance and self control in their own lives. May thy kingdom come and may those who now vainly and laboriously seek for truth and salvation, far removed from Thee, understand that they must live as thy servants in subjection to Thee. Thy laws show forth thy justice and paternal gentleness, and to enable us to keep them, Thou dost freely supply by thy grace the ready means. The life of man on earth is a warfare, but *"Thou dost thyself behold the strife, Thou dost help man to conquer, raise him when he falls, and crown him when he is victorious."* St. Aug. in Ps. 32.

27. Prayer.
100 Days, once a day. (See Instructions.) 27 Leo XIII, December 14, 1889.

O LORD, who in the mystery of the glorious Transfiguration of thy Divine SON, didst deign to make resplendent the truth of the holy Catholic Faith, and to confirm miraculously, by thy very word, spoken from a cloud, our perfect adoption as thy sons; we humbly beg of Thee to grant that we may in truth become coheirs of this same King of Glory, and share in thy everlasting happiness. Amen.

28. Prayer for the Supreme Pontiff.
200 Days, once a day. (See Instructions.) 28 Leo XIII, May 8. 1896.

O LORD, in union with millions of believers, and prostrate here at thy feet, we pray Thee to save, defend, and long preserve the Vicar of CHRIST, the Father of the glorious society of souls, our own Father. Today and every day he prays for us, fervently offering to Thee the sacred victim of love and peace. Turn then, O LORD, thy loving eyes upon us, who forgetful as it were of ourselves pray now above all things for him. Unite our prayers with his, and receive them into the bosom of thy infinite mercy, as a most sweet perfume of that living and efficacious charity, in which the children of the Church are united to their FATHER. All that he asks of Thee to-day we too ask for with him. Whether he sorrows or rejoices, or when he hopes or offers the victim of love for his people, we would be united with him. We desire that the utterance of our souls should be one with his.

Mercifully grant, O LORD, that no one of us be far from his mind and heart during- the hour of his prayer, and when he offers to Thee the sacrifice of thy blessed SON. And in the moment that he, our most revered Pontiff, holding in his hands the very body of JESUS CHRIST, shall say to the people over the Chalice of benediction the words: The peace of the Lord be ever with you, do Thou, O LORD, cause thy most sweet peace to descend with a new and manifest power into our hearts, and upon all the nations of mankind. Amen.

29. Ejaculation of Resignation to the Will of God.

i. 100 Days, once a day. ii. Plenary, once a year, to all who say it daily. I, II, IV. iii. Plenary, in articulo mortis (at the point of death), to those who, during- life, shall have frequently recited this Ejaculation, provided that, worthily disposed, they accept death with resignation from the hands of GOD. (See Instructions.) 29 Pius VII, May 19, 1818.

FIAT, laudetur, atque in æternum superexaltetur justissima, altissima, et amabilissima voluntas DEI in omnibus.

MAY the most just, most high, and most adorable will of GOD be in all things done, praised, and magnified forever.

30. Ejaculation.

50 Days. T.Q. (See Instructions.) 30 Leo XIII, May 4, 1888.

DEUS meus et omnia!

My GOD, and my all!

31. Invocation.

100 Days, once a day. (See Instructions.) 31 Leo XIII, March 15, 1890.
MY GOD, grant that I may love Thee, and as the sole reward of my love, grant that I may ever love Thee more and more.

32. Ejaculation.

i. 300 Days, once a day. ii. Plenary, once a month, during the month. I, II,III, IV. (See Instructions.) 32 Leo XIII, Br. March 13, 1902.
MY GOD, my only good, Thou art all mine; grant that I may be all thine.

33. Ejaculation.

50 Days. T.Q. (If said devoutly on hearing a blasphemy.) (See Instructions.) 33 Pius X, November 28, 1903.
DEUS sit benedictus.   Blessed be GOD.

34. Ejaculation.

300 Days. T.Q.(See Instructions.) 34 Pius X, January 21, 1905 ; May 30, 1908.
MY GOD, unite all minds in the truth and all hearts in charity.

III. THE HOLY GHOST;

35. The Hymn and Sequence.

i. 100 Days for each. IV. T.Q. ii. 300 Days, on Whit Sunday, and its octave for either. IV. iii. Plenary, once a month for one, or other. I, II, IV. (See Instructions.) 35 Pius VI. Br. May 26, 1796.

Hymn.	
VENI, Creator SPIRITUS,	COME, O Creator SPIRIT blest!
Mentes tuorum visita,	And in oursouls take up thy rest;
Imple superna gratia	Come, with thy grace
Quæ tu creasti pectora.	and heavenly aid,
	To fill the hearts which
	Thou hast made.
Qui diceris PARACLITUS,	Great PARACLETE ! to Thee we cry :
Altissimi Donum DEI,	O highest gift of GOD most high !
Fons vivus, Ignis, Charitas	O fount of life ! O fire of love !
Et spiritalis Unctio.	And sweet Anointing from above!
Tu, septiformis munere,	Thou in thy sevenfold gifts art known!
Digitus Paternæ dexteræ,	Thee, Finger of GOD's hand we own
Tu rite promissum PATRIS,	The promise of the FATHER Thou !
Sermone ditans guttura.	Who dost the tongue with pow'r endow.
Accende lumen sensibus,	Kindle our senses from above,
Infunde amorem cordibus,	

Infirma nostri corporis	And make our hearts o'erflow with love ;
Virtute firmans perpeti.	With patience firm, and virtue high,
	The weakness of our flesh supply.
Hostem repellas longius,	Far from us drive the foe we dread,
Pacemque dones protinus;	And grant us thy true peace instead ;
Ductore sic te prævio	So shall we not, with Thee for guide,
Vitemus omne noxium.	Turn from the path of life aside.
Per te sciamus da PATREM,	O, may thy grace on us bestow
Noscamus atque FILIUM,	The FATHER and the SON to know,
Teque utriusque SPIRITUM	And Thee, through endless times confess'd,
Credamus omni tempore.	Of Both th'eternal SPIRIT blest.
DEO PATRI sit gloria	All glory, while the ages run,
Ejusque soli FILIO,	Be to the FATHER and the SON,
Cum SPIRITU Paraclito	The same, O HOLY GHOST, to Thee,
Nunc et per omne sæculum. Amen.	Now and through all eternity. Amen.
Temp. Pasch.	Paschal Time.
DEO PATRI sit gloria,	All glory while the ages run
Et FILIO, qui a mortuis	Be to the FATHER and the SON,
Surrexit, ac Paraclito,	Who rose from death ;
In sæculorum sæcula. Amen.	the same to Thee, O HOLY GHOST, eternally. Amen.
Sequence.	
VENI, SANCTE SPIRITUS,	
Et emitte cœlitus	HOLY SPIRIT! LORD of light!
Lucis tuæ radium.	From thy clear celestial height,
Veni, PATER pauperum	Thy pure beaming radiance give :
Veni, dator munerum;	Come, Thou FATHER of the poor!
Veni, lumen cordium.	Come, with treasures which endure !
Consolator optime,	Come, Thou Light of all that live !
Dulcis hospes animæ,	Thou, of all consolers best,
Dulce refrigerium.	Visiting the troubled breast,
In labore requies,	Dost refreshing peace bestow;
In æstu temperies,	Thou in toil art comfort sweet ;
In fletu solatium.	Pleasant coolness in the heat;
O lux beatissima,	Solace in the midst of woe.
Reple cordis intima	Light immortal! Light Divine!
Tuorum fidelium.	Visit Thou these hearts of thine,
Sine tuo numine	And our inmost being fill:
Nihil est in homine,	If Thou take thy grace away,
Nihil est innoxium.	Nothing pure in man will stay;
Lava quod est sordidum,	All his good is turn'd to ill.
Riga quod est aridum,	Heal our wounds our strength renew;
Sana quod est saucium.	On our dryness pour thy dew;
Flecte quod est rigidum,	Wash the stains of guilt away :
Fove quod est frigidum,	Bend the stubborn heart and will
Rege quod est devium.	Melt the frozen, warm the chill;
Da tuis fidelibus	Guide the steps that go astray.
In te confidentibus	Thou, on those who evermore
Sacrum septenarium.	Thee confess and Thee adore,
Da virtutis meritum,	In thy sevenfold gifts, descend :
Da salutis exitum,	Give them comfort when they die;
Da perenne gaudium. Amen.	Give them life with Thee on high ;
	Give them joys which never end. Amen.

36. Novena of the Holy Ghost.
i. 300 Days, each day. ii. Plenary, once during the Novena or eight succeeding days, I, II, IV. (See Instructions.) 36 Pius IX, Res. January 5, 1849; November 26, 1876.

This Novena may be made at any time, with any form of prayers approved by competent ecclesiastical authority.

37. Novena for Pentecost.
i. Seven Years and Seven Quarantines, each day. ii. Plenary, once during the Novena, Feast or Octave, I, II, IV. (See Instructions.) 37 Leo XIII, Br. May 5. 1895; Enc. May 9, 1897.
This Novena may be made publicly or privately, and the same Indulgences are granted for special prayers said every day during the Octave. Any prayers to the HOLY GHOST may be used.

38. Gloria Patri seven times.
To obtain the Seven Gifts, for the Propagation of the Faith, and for the intention of the Pope. Seven Days. IV. T.Q. (See Instructions.) 38 Pius IX, Prop. March 12, 1857.

39. Prayer for the Church.
300 Days, once a day. (See Instructions.) 39 Leo XIII, August 26, 1889.

O CREATOR SANCTE SPIRITUS, adesto propitius Ecclesiæ Catholicæ, eamque contra inimicorum incursus tua superna virtute robora et confirma; tua caritate, et gratia spiritum famulorum tuorum, quos unxisti, renova, ut in te clarificent PATREM FILIUM que ejus unigenitum JESUM CHRISTUM DOMINUM nostrum. Amen.

O HOLY SPIRIT, CREATOR, be propitious to the Catholic Church; and by thy heavenly power make it strong and secure against the attacks of its enemies; and renew in charity and grace the spirit of thy servants, whom Thou hast anointed, that they may glorify Thee and the FATHER and his only begotten SON, JESUS CHRIST, our LORD. Amen.

40. Prayer for the Propagation of the Faith.
100 Days, once a day. (See Instructions.) 40 Leo XIII, July 31, 1897.

SPIRITUS SANCTE, Spiritus veritatis, veni in corda nostra; da populis claritatem lucis tuæ, ut in fidei imitate tibi complaceant.

O HOLY SPIRIT, Spirit of Truth, come into our hearts; shed the brightness of thy light on all nations, that they may be one in Faith and pleasing to Thee.

41. Veni Sancte Spiritus, reple, etc.
300 Days. T.Q. (See Instructions.) 41 Pius X, May 8, 1907.

VENI SANCTE SPIRITUS, reple tuorum corda fidelium, et tui amoris in eis ignem accende.

COME, O HOLY GHOST, fill the hearts of thy faithful, and kindle in them the fire of thy love.

42. Ghaplet of the Holy Spirit.
i. Seven Years and Seven Quarantines, once a day. ii. Plenary, on the Feast, or during- the Octave, of Pentecost, for all who make a practice of this Devotion. I, II, III, IV. (See Instructions.) 42 Leo XIII, Br. March 24, 1902.

Short Act of Contrition.
I GRIEVE, O my GOD, for having sinned against Thee, because Thou art so good; and with the assistance of thy grace I will never sin again.
Come, O Creator SPIRIT blest, etc. (See 35.)
V/: Send forth thy SPIRIT, and they shall be created.
R/: And Thou shalt renew the face of the earth.
Let us pray.
O GOD, who didst instruct the hearts of the faithful by the light of the HOLY SPIRIT, grant us in the same SPIRIT to be truly wise and ever to rejoice in His consolation, through JESUS CHRIST our LORD. Amen.

FIRST MYSTERY. JESUS was conceived of the Virgin Mary by the power of the HOLY GHOST.
Meditation. The HOLY SPIRIT shall descend upon thee, and the power of the most high shall overshadow thee, and therefore the Holy one that shall be born of thee shall be called the SON of GOD" (St Luke i, 35).

Application. Pray earnestly for the help of the divine SPIRIT and, through the intercession of Mary, for grace to imitate the virtues of JESUS CHRIST, who is the example of all virtue, and so to be conformed to the image of the SON of GOD. PATER and Ave once, Gloria seven times.

SECOND MYSTERY. The SPIRIT of GOD rests upon JESUS.
Meditation. "Jesus being baptized came forth immediately from the water, and behold the Heavens were opened, and He saw the SPIRIT of GOD descend like a dove, and coming, stand over Him" (St Matt, iii, 16).
Application. Hold in the highest esteem the priceless gift of sanctifying grace, which the HOLY SPIRIT infused into your heart in Baptism. Keep the promises to the observance of which you have bound yourself. By continual exercise, increase Faith, Hope and Charity. Live always as becomes children of GOD, and members of his true Church, in order that after this life has run its course, you may be worthy to receive your heavenly inheritance. PATER and Ave once, Gloria seven times.

THIRD MYSTERY. JESUS was conducted by the SPIRIT into the desert.
Meditation. "But JESUS, full of the HOLY SPIRIT, retired from the Jordan, and was conducted by the SPIRIT into the desert for forty days; and was tempted by the Devil" (St Luke iv, i, 2).
Application. Be always grateful for the seven gifts given to you by the HOLY SPIRIT in Confirmation; for the spirit of wisdom and understanding, of counsel and fortitude, of knowledge and piety, and of the fear of the LORD. Faithfully adhere to your divine Guide, acting manfully in all the dangers of this life and in temptation, as becomes a perfect Christian and a brave athlete of JESUS CHRIST. PATER and Ave once, Gloria seven times.

FOURTH MYSTERY. The HOLY SPIRIT in the Church.
Meditation. "And suddenly there was a sound from Heaven as of a mighty wind coming where they were assembled; and they were all filled with the HOLY SPIRIT, and began to discourse of the wonderful works of GOD" (Acts ii, 2, 4,11).
Application. Thank GOD for making you a child of his Church which the divine SPIRIT, sent into the world on the day of Pentecost, ever vivifies and rules. Hear and obey the Supreme Pontiff, who by the assistance of the HOLY SPIRIT is the infallible teacher, and the Church, which is the pillar and foundation of truth. Hold fast her doctrines, maintain her cause, defend her rights. PATER and Ave once, Gloria seven times.

FIFTH MYSTERY. The HOLY SPIRIT in the soul of the just man.
Meditation. "Do you not know that your members are the temple of the HOLY SPIRIT, who is in you" (i Cor. vi, 19). "Do not extinguish the SPIRIT" (i Thess. v, 19). "And grieve not the HOLY SPIRIT of GOD, whereby you are sealed unto the day of redemption " (Ephes. iv, 30).
Application. Be ever mindful of the HOLY SPIRIT who is in you, and watch with all possible care over purity of soul and body. Faithfully obey his divine inspirations, so as to gather therefrom the fruits of the SPIRIT: Charity, joy, peace, benignity, goodness, longanimity, mildness, faith, modesty, continency, chastity. PATER and Ave once, Gloria seven times.
End with the Creed, as a profession of faith, and PATER and Ave once according to the intention of the Pope.

43. Prayer to the Holy Spirit.
300 Days, once a day. (See Instructions.) 43 Pius X, June 5, 1908.
OHOLY SPIRIT, divine spirit of light and love, I consecrate to Thee my understanding, heart and will, my whole being for time and for eternity. May my understanding be always submissive to thy heavenly inspirations, and to the teaching of the Catholic Church, of which Thou art the infallible Guide; may my heart be ever inflamed with love of GOD and of my neighbour; may my will be ever conformed to the divine will, and may my whole life be a faithful imitation of the life and virtues of our LORD and SAVIOUR JESUS CHRIST, to whom with the FATHER and Thee be honour and glory for ever. Amen.

IV. JESUS CHRIST
44. Rosary of Our Lord.
This Rosary is composed of the Pater, said thirty-three times in remembrance of the thirty-three years He lived on earth, and of the Ave five times in honour of his five most holy wounds; the first three of which are said, one at the beginning of each of the three divisions comprising the Pater said ten times; of the two remaining one Ave is said before saying Pater noster thrice in conclusion, and the other after saying them. This Rosary finishes with the Credo in honour of the holy Apostles.

In order to gain the following Indulgences it is necessary that
1. The Rosary be blessed by the Reverend Fathers of the Camaldolese Order, either hermits or monks, or else by those who have apostolical authority to bless them.
2. Every one saying this Rosary should, according to his capacity, meditate on the mysteries of the life of our LORD JESUS CHRIST.
i. 200 Years, every time, when said after confession, or at least with firm resolution to confess.
ii. 150 Years, to anyone who carries about him one of these Rosaries, and says it every Monday, Wednesday, and Friday, and also on all feasts of obligation. I, II.
iii. Plenary, once a year, to anyone who has made a practice of saying it at least four times a week, I,II.
iv. Plenary, once a month. I, II, IV.
44 Clement X, Br. July 20, 1674 ; Leo XII, August 11, 1824.
v. Plenary, at the point of death, to anyone who shall then invoke in his heart, if he cannot do so with his lips, the most holy Name of JESUS; provided he has said this Rosary once during his illness with the intention of gaining this Indulgence; in the event of his recovery, he gains 200 Years.
vi. 20 Days, to anyone who shall carry about him one of these Rosaries and invoke the adorable Name of JESUS after he has made an examination of conscience with contrition for his sins, and said thrice the Pater and thrice the Ave for the good estate of the Church.
vii. 20 Years, I, IV
viii. 10 Years, to anyone who, having about him this Rosary, shall say thrice the Pater and thrice the Ave, as often as he does any spiritual or temporal good work in honour of our LORD JESUS CHRIST, the Blessed Virgin Mary, or some saint, or for the good of his neighbour.
ix. 200 Years, on the days of the Stations in Rome, to those who carry about them one of these Rosaries. If in Rome, they must visit the church of the Station, or if out of Rome, some other church. But in either case, if the visit cannot be made, the recitation of this Rosary, together with the Penitential Psalms, the Litanies and prayers, may be substituted.
x. Plenary on Fridays in March. I, II. (See Instructions.)

Begin with an act of contrition.
FIRST DECADE.
THE Archangel Gabriel makes known to Mary the Incarnation of the Divine Word in her pure womb. Ave Maria.
1. The SON of GOD made man is born of Mary the Virgin in a stable. PATER noster.
2. The Angels rejoice and sing Gloria in excelsis Deo. PATER noster.
3. The shepherds hear the Angels tidings, and come and adore Him. PATER noster.
4. He is circumcised the eighth day, and called by the most holy Name of JESUS. PATER noster.
5. Is adored by the Magi with offerings of gold, frankincense, and myrrh. PATER noster.
6. Is presented in the Temple, and foretold to be the SAVIOUR of the world. PATER noster.
7. Flees from the persecution of Herod, and is carried into Egypt. PATER noster.
8. Herod finds him not, and murders the Innocents. PATER noster.
9. He is carried back by Joseph and his Mother into Nazareth, his home. PATER noster.
10. Disputes in the Temple with the doctors, being twelve years old. PATER noster.
(Add Eternal rest, etc. , if said for the departed.)

SECOND DECADE.
JESUS is most obedient to the Blessed Virgin his Mother, and to St Joseph. Ave Maria.
1. When thirty years old, He is baptized by John in the Jordan. PATER noster.
2. Fasts forty days in the desert, and overcomes the tempter. PATER noster.
3. Practises and preaches his own holy law, whereby is life eternal. PATER noster.
4. Calls his disciples, who forthwith leave all and follow Him. PATER noster.
5. Works his first miracle of changing water into wine. PATER noster.
6. Heals the sick, makes the lame to walk, gives hearing to the deaf, sight to the blind, life to the dead. PATER noster.
7. Converts sinful men and women, and pardons their sins. PATER noster.
8. When the Jews persecute Him even unto death, He chastises them not, but sweetly chides them. PATER noster.
9. Is transfigured on Mount Thabor, in the presence of Peter, James and John. PATER noster.

10. Enters triumphant into Jerusalem sitting on an ass's colt, and drives the profaners from the Temple. PATER noster.
(Eternal rest, etc. , as above.)

THIRD DECADE.
JESUS takes leave of his most holy Mother before He goes to die for our salvation. Ave Maria.
1. Celebrates the last Paschal Supper, washes the Apostles feet. PATER noster.
2. Institutes the most holy Sacrament of the Eucharist. PATER noster.
3. Prays in the garden, sweats blood, and is comforted by an angel. PATER noster.
4. Is betrayed by Judas with a kiss, is taken and bound by the officers of justice as a great malefactor. PATER noster.
5. Is falsely accused, is buffeted and spit upon, and shamefully used before four tribunals. PATER noster.
6. Looks tenderly on Peter after he had thrice denied Him, and converts him; whilst Judas despairs, hangs himself, and is lost. PATER noster.
7. Is cruelly scourged at the pillar, and receives innumerable blows. PATER noster.
8. Is crowned with thorns, shown to the people, who cry, Crucify Him ! Crucify Him ! PATER noster.
9. Is condemned to die, carries the heavy cross with grievous pain upon his shoulders to Mount Calvary. PATER noster.
10. Is crucified between two thieves, dies after three hours most painful agony, is wounded in the side with a lance, and is buried. PATER noster.
(Eternal rest, etc., as above.)
JESUS rises the third day, and visits first of all Mary his most holy Mother. Ave Maria.
1. Appears to the three Marys, and bids them tell the disciples they have seen Him risen from the dead. PATER noster.
2. Appears to the disciples, shows them his most holy Wounds, makes Thomas touch them. PATER noster.
3. The fortieth day after his resurrection, blesses most holy Mary his Mother and all his disciples ; then ascends into heaven. PATER noster.
Let us pray to the most holy Virgin to obtain for us also the blessing of her divine Son JESUS CHRIST, now and at the hour of our death. Ave Maria.
(Eternal rest, etc., as above.)
Then say the Credo in honour of the holy Apostles.

45. Invocation of the Holy Name.
i. 50 Days, every time anyone says to another: (See Instructions,) (45 Clement XIII, September 5, 1759.)
Laudetur JESUS CHRISTUS. Praised be JESUS CHRIST.
or answers: Amen, or,
In sæcula. For evermore.
ii. 25 Days, every time anyone invokes the most holy Name of JESUS.
iii. Plenary, at the point of death, to anyone who has had the devout practice of saluting- and answering as above, or of invoking- often the said most holy Name, provided that he then invokes this holy Name at least in his heart, if he is unable to do so with his lips.
The same Indulgences to preachers and others who exhort the faithful to salute each other in this way, and to invoke frequently the most holy Names of JESUS and Mary.

46. Hymns and Psalms in Honour of the Holy Name.
To those who recite certain psalms whose initial letters compose the most holy Name of JESUS, together with certain hymns and prayers:
i. Seven Years and Seven Quarantines. T.Q. ii. Plenary, once a month. I, II, IV. iii. Plenary, on the Feast of the most holy Name of JESUS (the Second Sunday after Epiphany) to all who say them frequently in the course of the year. I, II, IV. iv. Plenary, on the Feast of the Circumcision of our LORD JESUS CHRIST, January I, and the Feast of JESUS the Nazarene, October 23, for those who say them for a month together. I, II, IV.
(See Instructions.) 46 Pius VII, June 13, 1815 ; Nov. 13, 1821.

HYMN.

JESU, dulcis memoria,
Dans vera cordi gaudia:
Sed super mel, et omnia,
Ejus dulcis praesentia.
Nil canitur suavius,
Nil auditur jucundius,
Nil cogitatur dulcius,
Quam JESUS, DEI Filius.
JESU, spes pœnitentibus,
Quam pius es petentibus!
Quam bonus te quærentibus !
Sed quid invenientibus !
Nec lingua valet dicere,
Nec littera exprimere:
Expertus potest credere,
Quid sit JESUM diligere.
Sis, JESU, nostrum gaudium,
Qui es futurum præmium!
Sit nostra in te gloria,
Per cuncta semper sæcula. Amen.

J. Ant. In Nomine JESU.
Psalm, xcix.
JUBILATE DEO omnis terra : * servite DOMINO in lætitia.
Introite in conspectu ejus, * in exultatione.
Scitote, quoniam DOMINUS ipse est DEUS : * ipse fecit nos, et non ipsi nos.
Populus ejus, et oves pascuæ ejus: * introite portas ejus in confessione, atria ejus in hymnis; confitemini illi.
Laudate nomen ejus, quoniam suavis est DOMINUS, in aeternum misericordia ejus: * et usque in generationem et generationem veritas ejus.
Gloria PATRI, et FILIO, etc.

Ant. In Nomine JESU omne genuflectatur cœlestium, terrestrium, et infernorum.
E. Ant. Ego autem.
Psalm, xix.
EXAUDIAT te DOMINUS in die tribulationis: * protegat te nomen DEI Jacob.
Mittat tibi auxilium de sancto: * et de Sion tueatur te.
Memor sit omnis sacrificii tui: * et holocaustum tuum pingue fiat.
Tribuat tibi secundum cor tuum: * et omne consilium tuum confirmet.
Lætabimur in salutari tuo: * et in nomine DEI nostri magnificabimur.
Impleat DOMINUS omnes petitiones tuas: * nunc cognovi, quoniam salvum fecit DOMINUS christum suum.
Exaudiet ilium de cœlo sancto suo: * in potentatibus salus dexteræ ejus.
Hi in curribus, et hi in equis: * nos autem in nomine DOMINI DEI nostri invocabimus.
Ipsi obligati sunt, et ceciderunt: * nos autem surreximus, et erecti sumus.
DOMINE, salvum fac regem: * et exaudi nos in die, qua invocaverimus te.
Gloria PATRI, etc.

Ant. Ego autem in DOMINO gaudebo, et exultabo in DEO JESU meo.
S. Ant. Sanctum et terribile.
Psalm, xi.
SALVUM me fac, DOMINE, quoniam defecit sanctus, * quoniam diminutæ sunt veritates a filiis hominum.
Vana locuti sunt unusquisque ad proximum suum: * labia dolosa, in corde, et corde locuti sunt.
Disperdat DOMINUS universa labia dolosa, * et linguam magniloquam.
Qui dixerunt: linguam nostram magnificabimus, labia nostra a nobis sunt: * quis noster DOMINUS est?
Propter miseriam inopum, et gemitum pauperum, * nunc exurgam, dicit DOMINUS.

Ponam in salutari: * fiducialiter agam in eo.
Eloquia DOMINI eloquia casta, * argentum igne examinatum, probatum terrae, purgatum septuplum.
Tu, DOMINE, servabis nos, et custodies nos * a generatione hac in æternum.
In circuitu impii ambulant: * secundum altitudinem tuam multiplicasti filios hominum.
Gloria PATRI, etc.

Ant. Sanctum, et terribile Nomen ejus: initium sapientiae timor DOMINI.
U. **Ant.** Vocabis Nomen ejus JESUM.
Psalm, xii.
USQUEQUO, DOMINE, oblivisceris me in finem ? * usquequo avertis faciem tuam a me ?
Quamdiu ponam consilia in anima mea, * dolorem in corde meo per diem?
Usquequo exaltabitur inimicus meus super me? * respice, et exaudi me, DOMINE DEUS meus.
Illumina oculos meos, ne unquam obdormiam in morte; * nequando dicat inimicus meus: prevalui adversus eum. Qui tribulant me, exultabunt, si motus fuero: * ego autem in misericordia tua speravi.
Exultabit cor meum in salutari tuo: cantabo DOMINO, qui bona tribuit mihi, * et psallam nomini DOMINI altissimi.
Gloria PATRI, etc.

Ant. Vocabis Nomen ejus JESUM: ipse enim salvum faciet populum suum a peccatis eorum.
S. **Ant.** Sitivit anima mea.
Psalm, cxxviii.
SÆPE expugnaverunt me a juventute mea: * dicat nunc Israel.
Sæpe expugnaverunt me a juventute mea: * etenim non potuerunt mihi.
Supra dorsum meum fabricaverunt peccatores: * prolongaverunt iniquitatem suam.
DOMINUS Justus concidit cervices peccatorum: * confundantur, et convertantur retrorsum omnes, qui oderunt Sion. Fiant sicut fœnum tectorum, * quod priusquam evellatur, exaruit.
De quo non implevit manum suam, qui metit, * et sinum suum, qui manipulos colligit.
Et non dixerunt, qui praeteribant: Benedictio DOMINI super vos: * benediximus vobis in nomine DOMINI.
Gloria PATRI, etc.

Ant. Sitivit anima mea ad Nomen sanctumtuum, DOMINE.
HYMN
JESU, Rex admirabilis
Et triumphator nobilis,
Dulcedo ineffabilis,
Totus desiderabilis.
Quando cor nostrum visitas,
Tunc lucet ei veritas;
Mundi vilescit vanitas,
Et intus fervet charitas.
JESU, dulcedo cordium,
Fons vivus, lumen mentium,
Excedens omne gaudium
Et omne desiderium.
JESUM omnes agnoscite,
Amorem ejus poscite;
JESUM ardenter quærite,
Quærendo inardescite.
Te nostra, JESU, vox sonet,
Nostri te mores exprimant:
Te corda nostra diligant
Et nunc, et in perpetuum. Amen.
V/. Sit nomen DOMINI benedictum.
R/. Ex hoc nunc, et usque in sæculum.
Oremus.

DEUS, qui Unigenitum FILIUM tuum constituisti humani generis Salvatorem, et JESUM vocari jussisti: concede propitius; ut cujus sanctum Nomen veneramur in terris, ejus quoque aspectu perfruamur in cœlis. Per eumdem CHRISTUM DOMINUM nostrum. Amen.

47. Prayer for a Holy Death.
300 Days. T.Q. (See Instructions.) 47 Pius IX, June 10, 1856.

DIVINE JESU, FILI DEI incarnate, qui pro nostra salute in stabulo nasci, vitam in paupertate, ærumnis et miseria degere, et in crucis doloribus mori dignatus es, divino tuo PATRI dic, quæso, in momento mortis meæ : Pater ignosce ei; die matri tuæ dilectæ: Ecce filius tuus ; die animæ meæ : Hodie eris mecum in Paradiso. DEUS meus, DEUS meus, ne derelinquas me in ilia hora.

Sitio: utique, DEUS meus, anima mea sitit ad te, qui es fons aquarum viventium. Vita mea præterit velut umbra ; adhuc modicum et consummata erunt omnia. Quapropter, O SALVATOR mi adorabilis, ex hoc momento in omnem æternitatem, in manus tuas commendo spiritum meum. DOMINE JESU, accipe animam meam. Amen

DIVINE JESUS, incarnate SON of GOD, who for our salvation didst vouchsafe to be born in a stable, to pass thy life in poverty, trials, and misery, and to die amid the sufferings of the Cross, I entreatThee in the hour of my death, say to thy divine FATHER:"Father, forgive him "say to thy beloved Mother : "behold thy son "; say to my soul : "this day thou shalt be with me in Paradise." My GOD, my GOD, forsake me not in that hour. "I thirst": truly, my GOD, my soul thirsts after Thee, who art the fountain of living waters. My life passes like a shadow; yet a little while and all will be consummated. Wherefore, O my adorable SAVIOUR, from this moment, for all eternity, " into thy hands I commend my spirit. " LORD JESUS, receive my soul. Amen.

48. Prayer.
300 Days, once a day. (See Instructions.) 48 Pius IX, Pr. Ma. October 14, 1859.

O JESU, vivens in Maria, veni et vive in famulis tuis, in SPIRITU sanctitatis tuæ, in plenitudine virtutis tuæ, in veritate virtutum tuarum, in perfectione viarum tuarum, in communione Mysteriorum tuorum, dominare omni adversæ potestati in SPIRITU tuo ad gloriam PATRIS. Amen.

O JESUS, who dost live in Mary, come and live in thy servants, in the spirit of thine own holiness, in the fullness of thy power, in the reality of thy virtues, in the perfection of thy ways, in the communion of thy Mysteries; have Thou dominion over every adverse power, in thine own SPIRIT, to the glory of thy FATHER. Amen.

49. Prayer.
100 Days, once a day. (See Instructions.) 49 Pius IX, October 6, 1870,

O CLEMENTISSIME JESU, salus, vita, resurrectio nostra tu solus es. Te ergo quæsumus ne derelinquas nos in augustiis et perturbationibus nostris, sed per agoniam cordis tui sanctissimi et per dolores matris tuæ immaculatæ tuis famulis subveni, quos pretioso sanguine redemisti.

O MOST compassionate JESUS! Thou alone art our salvation, our life, and our resurrection. We implore Thee, therefore, do not forsake us in our needs and afflictions, but by the agony of thy most Sacred Heart, & by the sorrows of thy immaculate Mother, succour thy servants whom Thou hast redeemed by thy most Precious Blood.

50. Prayer.
100 Days, once a day. (See Instructions, p. i.) 50 Pius IX, November 26, 1876.

O GOOD JESU! O most tender JESU! O most sweet JESU! O JESU, Son of Mary the Virgin, full of mercy and kindness! O sweet JESU, according to thy great mercy, have pity on me! O most merciful JESU, I entreat Thee by that Precious Blood of thine, which Thou didst will to pour forth for sinners, to wash away all my iniquities, and to look upon me, poor and unworthy as I am, asking humbly pardon of Thee, and invoking this holy Name of JESUS. O Name of JESUS, sweet Name! Name of JESUS, Name of joy! Name of JESUS, Name of strength! Nay, what meaneth the Name of JESUS but SAVIOUR? Wherefore, O JESUS, by thine own holy Name, be to me JESUS, and save me. Suffer me not to be lost me, whom Thou didst create out of nothing. O good JESU, let not my iniquity destroy what thy almighty goodness made. O sweet JESU, recognize what is thine own, and wipe away from me what is not of Thee! O most kind JESU, have pity on me while it is the time of pity, and condemn me not when it is the time of judgment. The dead shall not praise Thee, LORD JESU, nor all those who go down into hell. O most loving JESU! O

JESU, most longed for by thine own ! O most gentle JESU ! JESU, JESU, JESU, let me enter into the number of thine elect. O JESU, salvation of those who believe in Thee; JESU, consolation of those who fly to Thee. JESU, Son of Mary the Virgin, pour into me grace, wisdom, charity, chastity, and humility, that I may be able perfectly to love Thee, to praise Thee, to enjoy Thee, to serve Thee, and make my boast in Thee, together with all those who invoke thy Name, which is JESUS. Amen.

51. Prayer of St Thomas Aquinas.
(To be said before study or class.) 300 Days. T.Q. (See Instructions.) 51 Leo XIII, June 21, 1879.

CONCEDE mihi, misericors DEUS, quæ tibi placita sunt ardenter concupiscere, prudenter investigare, veraciter agnoscere et perfecte adimplere ad laudem et gloriam nominis tui. Amen.

O MERCIFUL GOD, grant that I may eagerly desire, carefully search out, truthfully acknowledge, and ever perfectly fulfil all things which are pleasing to Thee, to the praise and glory of thy Name. Amen.

52. Prayer of St Thomas Aquinas.
(Before writing , preaching", etc.) 200 Days, once a day. (See Instructions.) 52 Leo XIII, February 21, 1880.

CREATOR ineffabilis, qui de thesauris sapientiæ tuæ tres angelorum hierarchias designasti et eas super cælum empyreum miro ordine collocasti, atque universi partes elegantissime disposuisti. Tu inquam, qui verus fons luminis et sapientiæ diceris ac supereminens principium, infundere digneris super intellects mei tenebras tuæ radium claritatis, duplices, in quibus natus sum, a me removens tenebras, peccatum scilicet et ignorantiam. Tu, qui linguas infantium facis disertas, linguam meam erudias, atque in labiis meis gratiam tuæ benedictionis infunde. Da mihi intelligendi acumen, retinendi capacitatem, addiscendi modum et facultatem, interpretandi subtilitatem, loquendi gratiam copiosam; ingressum instruas,progressum dirigas, egressum compleas, tu, qui es verus DEUS et homo. Qui vivis et regnas in sæcula sæculorum. Amen.

INEFFABLE CREATOR, who, of the treasures of thy wisdom hast formed the nine choirs of Angels, and set them on high above the heavens in a wonderful order, and hast exquisitely fashioned and knit together all parts of the universe; do Thou, who art the true fountain and one principle of light and wisdom, deign to shed the brightness of thy light upon the darkness of my understanding, and thus to disperse the twofold darkness of sin and ignorance wherein I was born. O Thou, who makest eloquent the tongues of babes, instruct my tongue, and pour forth on my lips the grace of thy blessing. Grant me acuteness in understanding what I read, power to retain it, subtlety to discern its true meaning, and clearness and ease in expressing it. Do Thou order my beginnings, direct and further my progress, complete and bless my ending-; Thou who art true GOD and true Man, who livest and reignest world without end. Amen.

53. Petitions of St Augustine.
50 Days, once a day. (See Instructions.) 53 Leo XIII, Br. September 25, 1883.

DOMINE JESU, noverm me, noverim te. Nec aliquid cupiam nisi te. Oderim me et amem te. Omnia agam propter te. Humiliem me,exaltemte. Nihil cogitem nisi te. Mortificem me et vivam in te. Quæcunque eveniant accipiam a te. Persequar me, sequar te. Semperque optem sequi te. Fugiam me, confugiam ad te. Ut merear defendi a te. Timeam mihi, timeam te, Et sim inter electos a te. Diffidam mihi, fidam in te. Obedire velim propter te. Ad nihil afficiar nisi ad te. Et pauper sim propter te. Aspice me, ut diligam te. Voca me ut videam te. Et in æternum fruar te. Amen.

LORD JESUS, may I know myself and know Thee. And desire nothing save only Thee. May I hate myself and love Thee. May I do everything for the sake of Thee. May I humble myself and exalt Thee. May I think of nothing except Thee. May I die to myself and live in Thee. May I receive whatever happens as from Thee. May I banish self and follow Thee. And ever desire to follow Thee. May I fly from myself and fly to Thee, That I may deserve to be defended by Thee. May I fear for myself and fear Thee, And be among those who are chosen by Thee. May I distrust myself and trust in Thee. May I be willing to obey on account of Thee. May I cling to nothing but to Thee. May I be poor for the sake of Thee. Look upon me that I may love Thee. Call me that I may see Thee, And ever and ever enjoy Thee. Amen.

54. Prayer for the Conversion of Scandinavia.
300 Days, once a day. (See Instructions.) 54 Leo XIII, April 18, 1885.

O GOOD JESUS, prostrate at thy feet, we humbly implore Thee, by thy most sacred wounds and by the Precious Blood which Thou didst shed for the salvation of the whole world, that Thou wouldst deign to cast a look of pity on the peoples of Scandinavia, seduced from the Faith for so many centuries, and plunged in the darkness of heresy, separated from thy Church, deprived of the participation of the adorable Sacrament of thy Body and Blood, and of the other sacraments instituted by Thee, as the refuge of souls in life and in death. Remember, O REDEEMER of the world, that for these souls too Thou didst suffer bitter death, with the loss of all thy blood. Bring back, O good Shepherd, these wandering sheep of thine to the one fold and to the healthy pastures of thy Church, so that they may form with us one flock, tended by Thee, and by thy Vicar on earth, the supreme Pontiff, whom, in the person of the Apostle St Peter, Thou didst commission to feed thy sheep and thy lambs. Graciously hear, O good JESUS, the prayers which we offer Thee with the most lively trust in the love of thy Sacred Heart, and to thy most holy Name be praise, glory, and honour, world without end. Amen.

55. Devotion to the Holy Name.
i. 300 Days. T.Q. ii. Plenary, on the Sunday after the Epiphany, if said daily, to all who visit a church where the Feast of the Holy Name is being celebrated. I, II, IV. iii. Plenary, to all who assist at the annual requiem for those who were devout to the holy Name. I, II, IV. (See Instructions.) 55 Pius X, November 26, 1906.

Gloria PATRI and May the holy Name of JESUS be infinitely blessed, five times.

56. Litany of the Holy Name of Jesus.

300 Days, once a day. (See Instructions.) 56 Leo XIII, January 16, 1886

KYRIE eleison.	LORD, have mercy on us.
CHRISTE eleison.	CHRIST, have mercy on us.
KYRIE eleison.	LORD, have mercy on us.
JESU, audi nos.	JESUS, hear us.
JESU, exaudi nos.	JESUS, graciously hear us

PATER de cœlis DEUS,		GOD the FATHER of heaven,	
FILI REDEMPTOR mundi DEUS,		GOD the SON, REDEEMER of the world,	
SPIRITUS SANCTE DEUS		GOD the HOLY GHOST,	
Sancta Trinitas, unus DEUS,		Holy Trinity, one GOD,	
JESU, FILI DEI vivi,		JESU, SON of the living God,	
JESU, splendor PATRIS,		JESUS, splendour of the FATHER,	
JESU, candor lucis æternæ,		JESUS, brightness of eternal light,	
JESU, Rex gloriæ,		JESUS, King of glory,	
JESU, sol justitiæ,		JESUS, sun of justice,	
JESU, Fili Mariæ Virginis,		JESUS, Son of the Virgin Mary,	
JESU amabilis,		JESUS, most amiable,	
JESU admirabilis,		JESUS, most admirable,	
JESU, DEUS fortis,		JESUS, the mighty GOD,	
JESU, PATER futuri sæculi,		JESUS, the Father of the world to come,	
JESU, magni consilii Angele,		JESUS, the Angel of great counsel,	
JESU potentissime,		JESUS, most powerful,	
JESU patientissime,		JESUS, most patient,	
JESU obedientissime,		JESUS, most obedient,	
JESU, mitis et humilis corde,	miserere nobis.	JESUS, meek and humble of heart,	have mercy on us.
JESU, amator castitatis,		JESUS, lover of chastity,	
JESU, amator noster,		JESUS, lover of us,	
JESU, DEUS pacis,		JESUS, the GOD of peace,	
JESU, auctor vitæ,		JESUS, the Author of life,	
JESU, exemplar virtutum,		JESUS, the example of virtues,	
JESU, zelator animarum,		JESUS, the zealous lover of souls,	
JESU, DEUS noster,		JESUS, our GOD,	
JESU, refugium nostrum,		JESUS, our refuge,	
JESU, pater pauperum,		JESUS, the father of the poor,	
JESU, thesaure fidelium,		JESUS, the treasure of the faithful,	
JESU, bone pastor,		JESUS, the good shepherd,	
JESU, lux vera,		JESUS, the true light,	
JESU, sapientia æterna,		JESUS, the eternal wisdom,	
JESU, bonitas infinita,		JESUS, infinite goodness,	
JESU, via et vita nostra,		JESUS, our way and our life,	
JESU, gaudium Angelorum		JESUS, the joy of Angels,	
JESU, Rex Patriarcharum,		JESUS, the King of Patriarchs,	
JESU, Magister Apostolorum,		JESUS, the Master of the Apostles,	
JESU, Doctor Evangelistarum,		JESUS, the Teacher of the Evangelists,	
JESU, fortitude Martyrum,		JESUS, the strength of Martyrs,	
JESU, lumen Confessorum,		JESUS, the light of Confessors,	
JESU, puritas Virginum,		JESUS, the purity of Virgins,	
JESU, corona Sanctorum omnium,		JESUS, the crown of all Saints,	
Propitius esto, parce nobis, JESU.		Be merciful unto us, spare us, O LORD JESUS.	
Propitius esto, exaudi nos, JESU.		Be merciful unto us, hear us, O LORD JESUS.

Ab omni malo,	From all evil,	
Ab omni peccato,	From all sin,	
Ab ira tua,	From thy wrath,	
Ab insidiis diaboli,	From the snares of the devil,	
A spiritu fornicationis,	From the spirit of fornication,	
A morte perpetua,	From everlasting death,	
A neglectu inspirationum tuarum,	From the neglect of thy inspirations,	
Per mysterium sanctæ Incarnationis tuæ,	Through the mystery of thy holy Incarnation,	
Per Nativitatem tuam,	Through thy Nativity,	
Per Infantiam tuam,	Through thy infancy,	
Per divinissimam vitam tuam,	Through thy most divine life,	
Per labores tuos,	Through thy labours,	
Per agoniam et passionem tuam,	Through thy Agony and Passion,	
Per crucem et derelictionem tuam,	Through thy Cross and dereliction,	
Per languores tuos,	Through thy sufferings,	
Per mortem et sepulturam tuam,	Through thy Death and burial,	
Per Resurrectionem tuam,	Through thy Resurrection,	
Per Ascensionem tuam,	Through thy Ascension,	
Per sanctissimam institutionem Eucharistiæ tuæ	By the most holy institution of thy Eucharist.	
Per gaudia tua,	Through thy joys,	
Per gloriam tuam,	Through thy glory,	

(libera nos, JESU. / JESUS, deliver us.)

AGNUS DEI, qui tollis peccata mundi, parce nobis, JESU.
LAMB of GOD, who takest away the sins of the world, JESUS, spare us.

AGNUS DEI, qui tollis peccata mundi, exaudi nos, JESU.
LAMB of GOD, who takest away the sins of the world, JESUS, graciously hear us.

AGNUS DEI, qui tollis peccata mundi, miserere nobis, JESU.
LAMB of GOD, who takest away the sins of the world, have mercy on us.

JESU, audi nos.
JESUS, hear us.

JESU, exaudi nos.
JESUS, graciously hear us.

Oremus.
Let us pray.

DOMINE JESU CHRISTE, qui dixisti: Petite, et accipietis ; quærite et invenietis ; pulsate, et aperietur vobis: quæsumus, da nobis petentibus divinissimi tui amoris affectum, ut te toto corde, ore et opere diligamus, et a tua nunquam laude cessemus.

LORD JESUS CHRIST, who hast said: Ask, and ye shall receive; seek, and ye shall find; knock, and it shall be opened unto you; grant, we beseech Thee, to our most humble supplications, the gift of thy most divine love, that we may ever love Thee with our whole hearts, words, and works, and never cease praising Thee.

Sancti Nominis tui, DOMINE, timorem pariter et amorem fac nos habere perpetuum, quia nunquam tua gubernatione destituis quos in soliditate tuæ dilectionis instituis. Qui vivis et regnas.

O LORD, give us a perpetual fear as well as love of thy holy Name, for Thou never ceasest to govern those whom thou foundest upon the the solidity of thy love, Who livest, etc.

57. Prayer for Grace to do the Will of God.

200 Days, once a day. (See Instructions.) 57 From the Imitation of Christ, iii, 15; v, 3. Leo XIII, February 27, 1886.

GRANT me, most kind JESUS, thy grace, that it may abide with me, labour with me, and persevere with me to the end. Grant me ever to desire and to will that which is the more acceptable to Thee and pleases Thee more dearly.

May thy will be mine, and my will ever follow thine, and be in closest accord with it. May it be my one care to will and to be unwilling with Thee, and may I be unable to will or not will anything but what Thou willest or willest not.

58. Prayer for the Preservation of Faith.

300 Days, once a day. (See Instructions.) 58 Leo XIII, April 11, 1888.

O My REDEEMER, will that terrible moment ever come, when but few Christians will be found animated with a spirit of faith? that moment when, provoked to indignation, Thou wilt remove from us thy protection? The vices, the evil habits of our children, have perhaps irrevocably moved thy justice this very day to vengeance! O Thou who art the author and finisher of our faith, we conjure Thee, in the bitterness of our hearts, humbled and contrite, not to permit the beautiful light of faith to be extinguished in us. Be mindful of thy mercies of old, cast a compassionate regard upon that vine which Thou hast planted with thy right hand, which was bedewed with the sweat of the Apostles, watered with the precious blood of thousands upon thousands of martyrs and the tears of so many generous penitents, and made fruitful by the prayers of so many confessors and innocent virgins. O divine Mediator, have regard for those zealous souls who incessantly raise their hearts to Thee and pray for the maintenance of that most precious treasure, the true Faith. Suspend, O must just GOD, the decree of our reprobation, turn away thine eyes from our sins, and fix them on the adorable blood, shed upon the Cross as the price of salvation, and daily pleading for it, on our behalf, upon our altars. Oh, preserve us in the true Catholic Roman Faith. Infirmities afflict us, annoyances wear us away, misfortunes oppress us: but preserve to us thy holy faith; for, endowed with this precious gift, we shall willingly bear every sorrow, and nothing can affect our happiness. On the other hand, without this supreme treasure of the faith, our misfortunes will be unspeakable and immense. O good JESUS, author of our faith, keep it pure; keep us safe within the bark of Peter, faithful and obedient to his successor, thy Vicar here on earth, that so the unity of holy Church may be preserved, holiness fostered, the Holy See kept free and protected, and the universal Church extended, to the advantage of souls. O JESUS, author of our faith, humble and convert the enemies of thy Church; bestow on all Kings and Christian Princes, and on all the faithful, peace and true unity; strengthen and maintain all in thy holy service, to the end that we may live by Thee and die in Thee. Ah! my JESUS, author of our faith, in Thee I would live, and in Thee would I die. Amen.

59. Prayer for the Love of God.
50 Days, twice a day. (See Instructions.) 59 Leo XIII, February 6, 1893.
O My JESUS, Thou well knowest that I love Thee; but I do not love Thee enough: Oh ! make me to love Thee more. O Love which burnest always and is never extinguished, my GOD, Thou who art Charity itself, kindle in my heart that divine fire which consumes the Saints and transforms them into Thee. Amen.

60. Prayer in Honour of the Holy Family.
200 Days, once a day. (See Instructions.) 60 Leo XIII, March 25, 1897.

FAC nos, DOMINE JESU, Sanctæ Familiæ tuæ exempla jugiter imitari, ut in hora mortis nostræ, occurrente gloriosa Virgine Matre tua cum beato Joseph, per te in æterna tabernacula recipi mere amur.

GRANT us, O LORD JESUS, faithfully to imitate the examples of thy Holy Family, so that in the hour of our death, in the company of thy glorious Virgin Mother and St Joseph, we may deserve to be received by Thee into eternal tabernacles.

61. Ejaculation.
100 Days. T.Q. (See Instructions.) 61 Pius IX, September 24, 1846.
My JESUS, mercy!

62. Ejaculation of St Jerome Emilian.
i. 50 Days. T.Q. ii. Plenary, on the feast of the Saint, July 20, from first Vespers, or during the octave, if said at least once a day for a year, I, II, III, IV. (See Instructions.) 62 Pius IX, August 11, 1851. November 29, 1853.
DULCISSIME JESU, non sis mihi Judex sed SALVATOR.
SWEETEST JESUS, be to me not a judge but a SAVIOUR.

63. Ejaculation.
50 Days. T.Q. For saying or inducing- others to say the following. (See Instructions.) 63 Pius IX, Pr. Ma. May 7, 1854
JESU, DEUS meus, super omnia amo te.   JESUS, my GOD, I love Thee above all things.

64. Ejaculation.
100 Days, once a day. (See Instructions.) 64 Leo XIII, February 27, 1886.
JESU, fili David, miserere mei (Luc. xviii, 38).   JESUS, Son of David, have mercy on me.

65. Ejaculation.
100 Days. T.Q. (See Instructions.) 65 Pius X, March 20, 1908.
O LORD, preserve to us the Faith.

66. Ejaculation.
50 Days, once a day. (See Instructions.) 66 Leo XIII. February 21, 1891.
SALVATOR mundi, miserere nobis.   SAVIOUR of the world, have mercy on us.

67. Ejaculation.
100 Days, once a day. (See Instructions.) 67 Leo XIII, September 13, 1893.
DULCISSIME JESU, da mihi fidei, spei et caritatis augmentum, cor contritum et humiliatum.
MOST sweet JESUS, increase my faith, hope, and charity, and give me a humble and contrite heart.

68. Prayer to Jesus our Redeemer.
i. 300 Days, once a day. ii. Plenary, once a month. I, II, HI, IV. (See Instructions.) 68 Leo XIII, May 13, 1903.
O JESUS, SON of the living GOD, my SAVIOUR and REDEEMER, behold us prostrate at thy feet. We beg pardon and make this act of reparation for all the blasphemies uttered against thy holy Name, for all the outrages committed against Thee in the most holy Sacrament of the altar, for all irreverence shown to thy most blessed and immaculate Mother, and for all the calumnies spoken against thy spouse, our holy Mother, the Catholic Church. O JESUS, who didst say: whatever you shall ask the FATHER in my Name, that I will do, we pray and beseech Thee for our brethren who are living in danger of sin, that Thou wouldst preserve them from the seductions of apostasy. Save them who stand over the abyss; give them light and knowledge of the truth, power and strength in the conflict against evil, and perseverance in faith and active charity. And therefore, most merciful JESUS, do we pray to the FATHER in thy Name, with whom Thou livest and reignest, in the unity of the HOLY SPIRIT, world without end. Amen.

69. Invocation.
300 Days. T.Q. (See Instructions.) 69 Pius X, October 10, 1904.
JESUS and Mary, invoked with the heart, if not with the lips.

70. Prayer for the Conversion of Sinners.
300 Days. T.Q. (See Instructions.) 70 Pius X November 22, 1905.
OLORD JESUS, most merciful SAVIOUR of the world, we beg and beseech Thee, through thy most Sacred Heart, that all wandering sheep may now return to Thee, the Shepherd and Bishop of their souls. Who livest and reignest with GOD the FATHER and the HOLY SPIRIT, GOD for ever and ever. Amen.

71. Prayer to our Lord.
300 Days, once a day. (See Instructions.) 71 Pius X, March 15, 1907.
O UNCREATED Word, exemplar and creator of all things, redeemer of men, who didst bestow on blessed Albert a powerful mind to contemplate all beings in their dependence one on another, from GOD and his infinite perfections to the constellations of Heaven, and the most minute of terrestrial creatures with all their wonderful qualities; grant that I too may understand, according to the humble proportion of my intellectual gifts, the bond which binds together the human sciences in their diversity, and the mutual assistance they can render one another in their common service of the one truth. Then shall I value them all, as well as those who cultivate the various branches of them, and I shall summon up in desire the blessed hour when all the learned shall agree to place their persevering labours, their acquired knowledge, and their many discoveries at the service of the Faith. I beg this favour of Thee, O LORD, for thy glory, for the honour of thy holy Church, and for the salvation of souls purchased by thy Precious Blood. Amen.

72. Prayer to Jesus, Lover of Children.
300 Days, once a day. (See Instructions.) 72 Pius X, March 15, 1906.

O JESUS, friend of children, who from thy most tender years didst grow visibly in wisdom and in grace before GOD and men; who at the age of twelve wast seated in the Temple, in the midst of the doctors, listening to them attentively, humbly asking them questions, and exciting their admiration by the prudence and wisdom of thy discourse; who didst receive so willingly the children, blessing them and saying to thy disciples: Let them come to Me, for of such is the Kingdom of Heaven, inspire me as Thou didst inspire Blessed Peter Canisius, model and guide of the perfect Catechist, with a profound respect and a holy affection for childhood, a taste and a marked devotion for instructing them in Christian doctrine, a special aptitude in making them understand its mysteries and love its beauties. I ask this of Thee, through the intercession of the blessed Virgin Mary. Amen.

V. THE CHILD JESUS

73. Christmas Day. To all who say or assist in Church at the Divine Office.
i. 100 Years, for **1**, Matins; **2**, Mass; **3**, 1st Vespers; **4**, Second Vespers. I, II. ii. 40 Years, for each of the Hours, Prime, Terce, Sext, None, and for Compline, I, II. (See Instructions.) 73 Sixtus V. Br. October 22, 1586.

74. Novena for Christmas.
i. 300 Days, each day. ii. Plenary, on Christmas Day, or during the Novena or Octave. I, II, IV. (See Instructions.) 74 Pius VII, Mem., August 12, 1815; Pius VIII, July 9, 1830.

This Novena may be made once more, at any time during the year. Any form of prayers may be used.

75. Mysteries of the Holy Childhood.
i. Plenary, on the twenty-fifth of every month, for assisting at these devotions in public. I, II, IV. ii. 300 Days, once a day on any other day. (See Instructions.) 75 Pius VII, November 23,1819.

V/. Incline unto my aid, O GOD.
R/. O LORD, make haste to help me.
V/. Glory be to the FATHER, etc.
PATER noster.

I. JESU, sweetest Child, who didst come down from the bosom of the FATHER for our Salvation, who wast conceived by the HOLY GHOST, who didst not abhor the Virgin s womb, and, the Word made flesh, didst take upon Thee the form of a servant; have mercy upon us.
R/. Have mercy on us, Infant JESUS, have mercy on us. Ave Maria.

II. JESU, sweetest Child, who, through thy Virgin Mother, didst visit Saint Elisabeth, and fill thy forerunner the holy Baptist with the HOLY GHOST, sanctifying him whilst yet in his mother's womb; have mercy upon us.
R/. Have mercy, etc. Ave Maria.

III. JESU, sweetest Child, who, shut up for nine months in thy Mother's womb, wast looked for with eager expectation by Mary and by Joseph, and wast offered to GOD the FATHER for the salvation of the world; have mercy upon us.
R/. Have mercy, etc. Ave Maria.

IV. JESU, sweetest Child, born in Bethlehem of Mary ever Virgin, swathed in rags, laid in the manger, announced by angels, visited by shepherds; have mercy upon us. **R/.** Have mercy, etc. Ave Maria.

O JESU, born of Virgin bright,
Immortal glory be to Thee;
Praise to the FATHER Infinite,
And HOLY GHOST eternally.

V/. CHRIST is at hand.
R/. Come let us worship.
PATER noster.

V. JESU, sweetest Child, wounded in thy circumcision the eighth day, called by the glorious Name of JESUS, and at once by thy Name and thy Blood foreshown as the SAVIOUR of the world; have mercy upon us. R/. Have mercy, etc. Ave Maria.

VI. JESU, sweetest Child, made known to the three Magi by a star, adored in the arms of thy Mother, presented with the mystic gifts of gold, frankincense, and myrrh; have mercy upon us. R/. Have mercy, etc. Ave Maria.

VII. JESU, sweetest Child, who wast presented in the Temple by thy Virgin Mother, who wast embraced by Simeon, and revealed to Israel by Anna the prophetess; have mercy upon us. R/. Have mercy, etc. Ave Maria.

VIII. JESU, sweetest Child, whom wicked Herod sought to slay, whom Joseph carried with Mary into Egypt, who wast taken from a cruel death and wast glorified by the blood of innocents; have mercy upon us. R/. Have mercy, etc. Ave Maria.

O JESU, etc., as above, V/. and R/. as above. **PATER noster.**

IX. JESU, sweetest Child, who didst dwell in Egypt with most holy Mary and the Patriarch holy Joseph until the death of Herod; have mercy upon us. R/. Have mercy, etc. Ave Maria.

X. JESU, sweetest Child, who didst return with Mary and Joseph out of Egypt into the land of Israel, who didst suffer many toils by the way, and didst enter into the city of Nazareth; have mercy upon us. R/. Have mercy, etc. Ave Maria.

XI. JESU, sweetest Child, who in the holy house at Nazareth didst remain subject to Mary and Joseph, didst dwell there most holily, wast wearied by poverty and labours, and didst advance in wisdom, age, and grace; have mercy upon us. R/. Have mercy, etc. Ave Maria.

XII. JESU, sweetest Child, at twelve years old brought to Jerusalem, sought for by Mary and Joseph with sorrow, and found with joy after three days amongst the doctors; have mercy upon us. R/. Have mercy, etc. Ave Maria.
O JESU, etc., as above.
For Christmas Day and its Octave.
V/. The Word was made flesh. Alleluia,
R/. And dwelt among us. Alleluia.
The Alleluia is omitted during the rest of the year.

For the Epiphany and its Octave.
V/. CHRIST hath manifested Himself to us. Alleluia.
R/. Come, let us adore. Alleluia.
Let us pray.
ALMIGHTY and everlasting GOD, LORD of heaven and earth, who dost reveal thyself to little ones; grant, we beseech Thee, that we,. duly honouring the holy mysteries of thy SON, the Infant JESUS, and daily imitating Him in our lives, may come to the kingdom of Heaven promised by Thee to little children. Through the same JESUS CHRIST, etc. R/. Amen.

76. Novena for the Twenty-fifth Day of every Month.

One Year, for each day of this Novena, made either in public or private, on nine days previous to the 25th day of any and each month. (See Instructions.) 76 Pius IX, September 23, 1846.
First Offering.
ETERNAL FATHER, I offer to thy honour and glory, and for my own salvation, and for the salvation of all the world, the mystery of the Birth of our Divine SAVIOUR. Gloria PATRI.
Second Offering.

ETERNAL FATHER, I offer to thy honour and glory, and for my eternal salvation, the sufferings of the most holy Virgin and of St Joseph in that long and weary journey from Nazareth to Bethlehem; I offer Thee their pain in finding no place wherein to shelter themselves, when the SAVIOUR of the world was to be born. Gloria PATRI.

Third Offering.
ETERNAL FATHER, I offer to thy honour and glory, and for my eternal salvation, the stable where JESUS was born, the hard straw which served Him for a bed, the cold He suffered, the swaddling clothes which bound Him, the tears He shed, and his tender infant cries. Gloria PATRI.

Fourth Offering.
ETERNAL FATHER, I offer to thy honour and glory, and for my eternal salvation, the pain which the divine Child JESUS felt in his tender infant body when He submitted it to the keen knife of circumcision; I offer Thee that Precious Blood which then first He shed for the salvation of the whole race of man. Gloria PATRI.

Fifth Offering.
ETERNAL FATHER, I offer to thy honour and glory, and for my eternal salvation, the humility, mortification, patience, charity and all the virtues of the Child JESUS; I thank Thee, and I love Thee, and I bless Thee without end, for this ineffable mystery of the Incarnation of the divine Word. Gloria PATRI.

V/. The Word was made flesh.
R/. And dwelt amongst us.

Let us pray.
O GOD, whose only-begotten SON was made manifest to us in the substance of our flesh; grant, we beseech Thee, that our souls may be inwardly renewed through Him, whom our eyes have seen externally like unto ourselves. Who liveth and reigneth with Thee for ever and ever. Amen.

77. Prayer before the Crib.
i. 200 Days, once a day, if said in the Basilica of St. Mary Major. ii. 100 Days, once a day, if said anywhere else. (See Instructions.) 77 Pius IX, Br. October 1, 1861.

I ADORE Thee, O Word Incarnate, true SON of GOD from all eternity, and true Son of Mary ever Virgin in the fullness of time. When I adore thy divine Person, and the Humanity united to thy Divinity, I venerate the poor manger which welcomed Thee when an Infant, and which was truly the throne of thy love. I prostrate myself before it with the simplicity of the shepherds, with the faith of Joseph, with the love of Mary. I bow down in veneration of this precious memorial of our salvation with the same spirit of mortification, poverty and humility with which Thou, though the LORD of heaven and earth, didst choose for thyself a manger wherein to lay thy tender infant limbs. And Thou, O LORD, who in thine Infancy didst design to lay thyself in this manger, vouchsafe also to pour into my heart a drop of that joy to which the sight of thy lovely Childhood, and the miracles which accompanied thy Birth, gave rise. By that holy Birth, I now implore Thee to grant to all the world peace and goodwill, and in the name of the whole human race I render thanks and honour to GOD the FATHER, and to GOD the HOLY SPIRIT, who with Thee live and reign one GOD world without end. Amen.

78. Prayer.
100 Days, once a day. (See Instructions.) 78 Leo XIII, January 18, 1894.

MOST dear LORD JESUS CHRIST, who, being made an infant for us, wast willing to be born in a cave, to free us from the darkness of sin, to draw us to thyself, and to inflame us with thy holy love ; we adore Thee as our CREATOR and REDEEMER, we accept and choose Thee for our King and LORD, and for tribute we offer Thee all the affections of our poor hearts. Dear JESUS, our LORD and GOD, deign to accept this offering, and that it may be worthy of thine acceptance, pardon us our faults, enlighten us, and inflame us with that holy fire which Thou earnest to bring into the world and enkindle in men's hearts. May our souls thus become a perpetual sacrifice in thy honour. Grant that we may ever seek thy greater glory here on earth, so that we may one day come to rejoice in thy infinite loveliness in Heaven. Amen.

79. The Month of January.
i. 300 Days, each day, if the Devotions are public, in a church or public chapel, ii. 100 Days, each day, if private. iii. Plenary, on the last day of the month, for daily attendance at public devotions. I, II, IV. (See Instructions.) 79 Leo XIII, Br, December 21, 1901.

Some devotion must be practised daily in honour of the holy Name of Jesus.

VI. THE BLESSED SACRAMENT.

80. Novena for Corpus Christi.

i. Seven Years and Seven Quarantines, each day. ii. Plenary, on the Feast or during- the Novena or Octave. I, II, IV. (See Instructions.) 80 Pius X, May 8, 1907.

The Novena may be made privately, with any pious practice or publicly with devotions prescribed by the Bishop.

81. Feast and Octave of Corpus Christi.

i. 200 Days, on the vigil of the Feast of Corpus CHRISTI, to all who, having confessed, shall fast, or do some other good work enjoined them by their confessor. I. ii. 400 Days, on the feast, to all who, having confessed, shall devoutly assist at or be present at First or Second Vespers, Matins, or Mass. 160 Days for each of the Little Hours Prime, Terce, Sext, None, and for Compline, I. iii. 200 Days, during the octave, for each Vespers, Matins, and Mass. 80 Days, for each of the Little Hours, and for Compline. iv. 200 Days, for accompanying the procession of the Blessed Sacrament on the feast or during the octave, to every priest who has said Mass, and to every layman who has gone to Communion praying according to the intention of the Pope.

(See Instructions.) 81 Urban IV, Con. August 11. 1264; Martin V, Con. May 26, 1429; Eugenius IV, Con. May 26, 1433.

82. Triduo on Friday, Saturday and Sunday, during the Octave of Corpus Christi.

i. Seven Years and Seven Quarantines, each day. ii. Plenary, during the Triduo. I,II, IV. iii. Plenary, on the Sunday. I, II, III, IV. (See Instructions.) 82 Pius X, April 10, 1907.

There must be each day a sermon, on the Holy Eucharist and Benediction. And on the Sunday a sermon, at the parochial Mass, on the Gospel and the Holy Eucharist. The devotions in the afternoon as above, with special sermon on frequent communion, and the Te Deum before the Tantum ergo. The Bishop may transfer the Triduo to another time.

N.B. This devotion is primarily for Cathedral Churches, but Bishops may order them, and specially the Sunday devotions, in other churches.

The Prayer, Dulcissime JESU, must be said after the sermon during exposition on each day.

O DULCISSIME JESU, qui in hunc mundum venisti, ut omnes animas vita ditares gratiæ tuæ, ad quam in illis servandam simulque fovendam in augustissimo Eucharistiæ Sacramento salutare pharmacum earum infirmitatibus sanandis, et cibum divinum debilitati sustinendæ temetipsum quotidie præbes, te supplices deprecamur, ut super eas sanctum tuum spiritum benignus effundas; quo repletæ, lethali labe si quae sint inquinatæ ad te revertentes, vitam gratiæ deperditam recuperent; quæ vero, te misericorditer largiente, jam tibi adhærent, quotidie, prout cui dabitur, ad tuam cœlestem dapem devote accedant, qua roboratæ, venialium culparum a se quotidie admissarum antidotum sibi comparare, vitamque gratiæ tuæ alere valeant, sicque magis magisque emundatæ, sempiternam in cœlis beatitudinem consequantur. Amen.

O SWEETEST JESUS, who came into this world to enrich the souls of all with thy grace, and who, in order to preserve and increase it in them, didst in the most august Sacrament of the Eucharist, give thyself to be a salutary remedy for our infirmities and divine food to sustain our weakness; we humbly beg of Thee mercifully to pour out upon all men thy HOLY SPIRIT, which may enable them, if stained with any mortal guilt, to recover the life of grace lost by sin, and return to Thee ; while those who through thy great mercy are still united with Thee may daily, so far as each may be able, approach thy heavenly table, where they may find strength, and an antidote for their daily faults, may nourish the life of grace within them, and, being more and more purified, may attain to everlasting happiness in Heaven. Amen.

83. Corpus Christi.

Plenary, for every visit, after the fashion of the indulgence of the Portiuncula, made on Corpus CHRISTI, from first Vespers to sunset next day, to a church of the Congregation of the Blessed Sacrament, I, II, III, IV. (See Instructions.) 83 Pius X, Br. July 30, 1906.

84. Act of Adoration during the Elevation.
Two Years, if made in church. One Year, if made in any other place. (See Instructions.) 84 Gregory XIII, Con. April 10. 1580.
Kneeling in prayer, when the bell rings at a conventual or parochial Mass.

85. Frequent Communion.
i. Five Years, every time on feast-days, I, II, IV. ii. Ten Years, every time they communicate, to those who have the good habit of communicating at least once a month, on all the Feasts of our LORD, of the Blessed Virgin, of the Holy Apostles, and on the birthday of St John Baptist, iii. Plenary, once a year, to all such persons, on the day when the principal feast of the city or country where they may happen to be is celebrated, I, II, IV. (See Instructions.) 85 Gregory XIII, April 10, 1580.
N.B. Those who are daily communicants, even though they miss once or twice a week, are not bound to confess weekly in order to gain all indulgences, except Jubilees (Pius X, February 14, 1906).

86. Visit during the Forty Hours Exposition.
i. Plenary, once during the Exposition. I, II, IV. ii. Ten Years and Ten Quarantines, for each other visit, iii. Indulgence of the Privileged Altar, to all the altars of a church during the time of Exposition there. (See Instructions.) 86 Pius IX, November 26, 1876 ; Leo XIII, December 8, 1897 : Pius VII. Card. Vic. May 10, 1807.

87. Visit during Exposition between Septuagesima Sunday and Ash Wednesday.
Plenary, to all who visit the Blessed Sacrament when exposed for three days in any church in any one or all of the weeks from Septuagesima up to Ash Wednesday ; the same to those who shall visit it when exposed on the Thursday after Sexagesima Sunday, the day commonly called in Rome "Giovedi grasso." I, II, IV. (See Instructions.) 87 Benedict XIV, Br. June 14, 1749; Clement XIII, July 23, 1765.

88. Prayers before the Blessed Sacrament.
i. Plenary, on the first Thursday of every month. I, II, IV. ii. Seven Years and Seven Quarantines, on any other Thursday. I, II, IV. iii. 100 Days, on any other day. (See Instructions.) 88 Pius VI, Mem. October 17, 1796.
V/. We adore Thee, CHRIST, and we bless Thee,
R/. Because by thy holy Cross Thou has redeemed the world.

I ADORE Thee, Eternal FATHER, and I give Thee thanks for the infinite love with which Thou didst deign to send thy only-begotten SON to redeem me, and to become the food of my soul. I offer Thee all the acts of adoration and thanksgiving that are offered to Thee by the angels and saints in heaven and by the just on earth. I praise, love, and thank Thee with all the praise, love, and thanksgiving that are offered to Thee by thine own SON in the Blessed Sacrament ; and I beg Thee to grant that He maybe known, loved, honoured, praised, and worthily received by all, in this most divine Sacrament. PATER, Ave, Gloria.

I ADORE Thee, Eternal SON, and I thank Thee for the infinite love which caused Thee to become man for me, to be born in a stable, to live in poverty, to suffer hunger, thirst, heat, cold, fatigue, hardships, contempt, persecutions, the scourging, the crowning with thorns, and a cruel death upon the hard wood of the Cross. I thank Thee, with the Church militant and triumphant, for the infinite love with which Thou didst institute the most blessed Sacrament to be the food of my soul. I adoreThee in all the consecrated hosts throughout the whole world, and I return thanks for those who know Thee not, and who do not thank Thee. Would that I were able to give my life to make Thee known, loved, and honoured by all, in this sacrament of love, and to prevent the irreverences and sacrileges that are committed against Thee ! I love Thee, divine JESUS, and I desire to receive Thee with all the purity, love, and affection of thy blessed Mother, and with the love and affection of thy own most pure Heart. Grant, O most amiable spouse of my soul, in coming to me in this most holy Sacrament, that I may receive all the graces and blessings which Thou dost come to bestow on us, and let me rather die than receive Thee unworthily. PATER, Ave, Gloria.

I ADORE Thee, Eternal SPIRIT, and I give Thee thanks for the infinite love with which Thou didst work the ineffable mystery of the Incarnation, and for the infinite love with which Thou didst form the sacred body of our LORD JESUS CHRIST out of the most pure blood of the Blessed Virgin Mary, to become in this Sacrament the food of my soul. I beg Thee to enlighten my mind, and to purify my heart and the hearts of all men, that they all may know this great benefit of thy love and receive worthily this most blessed Sacrament. PATER, Ave, Gloria.
Tantum ergo, with Versicle and Prayer (See 94).

89. Acts of Adoration and Reparation.

300 Days. T.Q. (See Instructions.) 89 Pius VII, Rit. August 26, 1814.

I

I ADORE Thee, my JESUS, in the Blessed Sacrament; I acknowledge Thee, true GOD and true Man. By this my act of adoration I intend to make Thee reparation for the coldness of so many of thy people, who pass before thy churches, nay, before thy very tabernacle, where hour after hour Thou dost deign to dwell in loving impatience to communicate thyself to thy faithful, yet do not even bow the knee before Thee, but like the Israelites in the wilderness, seem by their indifference to loathe this heavenly manna. I offer Thee thine own most precious Blood which Thou didst shed from the wound in thy Left Foot, in reparation for this hateful coldness, and entering therein, I cry, and will never cease to cry: ----
Blessed and praised every moment
Be the most holy and divine Sacrament!
PATER, Ave, Gloria.

II

I PROFOUNDLY adore Thee, my JESUS; I acknowledge Thee present in the most holy Sacrament. By this acl; of adoration I would fain make amends for the forgetfulness of so many Christian people, who, when they see Thee go to the poor sick, to be their strength in their great journey to eternity, leave Thee unescorted, and hardly give Thee even one outward sign of homage. I offer Thee, in reparation for this coldness, that most precious Blood which Thou didst shed from the wound in thy Right Foot, and entering therein, I cry, and will never cease to cry:----
Blessed and praised every moment
Be the most holy and divine Sacrament!
PATER, Ave, Gloria.

III

I PROFOUNDLY adore Thee, my JESUS, true Bread of life eternal; and by this my act of adoration I would fain make Thee compensation for all the wounds with which thy Sacred Heart bleeds daily to see the profanation of those churches wherein Thou dost vouchsafe to abide, beneath the sacramental species, to receive the love and adoration of thy people. I offer Thee, in reparation for all these irreverences, that most precious Blood which Thou didst shed from the wound in thy Left Hand, and, entering therein, I will ever cry: ----
Blessed and praised every moment
Be the most holy and divine Sacrament!
PATER, Ave, Gloria.

IV

I PROFOUNDLY adore Thee, my JESUS, Living Bread come down from heaven; and by this act of adoration I would fain make amends for all the acts of irreverence which thy people day by day commit whilst they assist at holy Mass, in which bloodless Sacrifice Thou dost renew the very Sacrifice which once Thou didst consummate on Calvary for our salvation. I offer Thee, in reparation for all this ingratitude, that most precious Blood which Thou didst shed from the wound in thy Right Hand; and, entering- therein, I unite my voice with the voices of the holy angels who adore around thy throne: ----
Blessed and praised every moment
Be the most holy and divine Sacrament !
PATER, Ave, Gloria.

I PROFOUNDLY adore Thee, my JESUS, true Victim of expiation for our sins; and I offer Thee this act of adoration in compensation for the sacrilegious outrages Thou dost receive from so many of thy ungrateful people, who dare to draw nigh to Thee and receive Thee in Communion with mortal sin upon their souls. In reparation for these hateful sacrileges, I offer Thee those last drops of thy most precious Blood which Thou didst shed from the wound in thy Side; and, entering therein, I approach Thee with acts of adoration, love, and thanksgiving, and, with all holy souls who are devout to Thee in this most holy Sacrament, I cry:---
Blessed and praised every moment
Be the most holy and divine Sacrament!
PATER, Ave, Gloria.
Tantum ergo with Versicle and Prayer (See 94).

90. Act of Reparation and Ejaculations.
200 Days. T.Q. (See Instructions.) 90 Pius VII, January 21, 1815.
JESUS, my GOD, my SAVIOUR, true GOD and true Man, in that lowly homage with which the faith itself inspires me, with my whole heart I adore and love Thee in the most august Sacrament of the Altar, in reparation for all the acts of irreverence, profanation and sacrilege, which I myself may ever have been so unhappy as to have committed, as well as for all such like acts that ever have been done by others, or that may be done in ages yet to come. I adore Thee, my GOD, not indeed as Thou deservest, nor as much as I am bound to adore, but as far as I am able; and I would that I could adore Thee with all the perfection of which a reasonable creature is capable. Meantime I purpose now and ever to adore Thee, not only for those Catholics who adore and love Thee not, but also for the conversion of all bad Christians, and of all Heretics, Schismatics, Mohammedans, Jews and idolaters. JESUS, my GOD, mayest Thou be ever known, adored, loved and praised every moment, in the most holy and divine Sacrament. Amen.

I ADORE Thee every moment, O living Bread of Heaven, great Sacrament! JESUS, treasure of Mary's heart, I pray Thee send thy blessing on my soul. Holiest JESU! loving SAVIOUR! 1 give Thee my heart.

91. One Hour s Prayer on Holy Thursday, Corpus Christi, and other Thursdays.
i. Plenary, to all who on Holy Thursday, either in public or private, shall for one hour practise some devotion in remembrance of the institution of the most holy Eucharist; to be gained after Confession and Communion on that day, or some day in the following 1 week. I, II. ii. Plenary, on the same conditions, on the Feast of CORPUS CHRISTI. i, II. iii. 300 Days, on any other Thursday.
91 Pius VII, Mem. February 14, 1815 ; April 6, 1816 ; Pius IX, June 18, 1876. (See Instructions.)

92. Visit to the Holy Sepulchre on Holy Thursday and Good Friday.
i. Ten Years and Ten Quarantines for each visit, IV. ii. Plenary, on Holy Thursday or Easter Sunday, I, II, IV. (See Instructions.) 92 Pius VII, March 7. 1815.

93. Prayer.
100 Days, once a day. (See Instructions.) 93 Pius VII, Mem. February 9, 1818.
BEHOLD, my most loving JESUS, to what an excess thy boundless love has carried Thee. Of thine own Flesh and Precious Blood Thou hast made ready for me a divine banquet in order to give me all thyself. What was it that impelled Thee to this transport of love? It was thy Heart, thy loving Heart. O adorable Heart of my JESUS ! burning furnace of Divine Love! within thy most sacred wound receive Thou my soul ; that in that school of charity I may learn to requite the love of that GOD who has given me such wondrous proofs of his love. Amen.

94. The Hymn Pange Lingua, with Versicle and Prayer.
i. 300 Days, once a day. ii. 100 Days, to those who say the Tantum ergo only, with the Versicle and Prayer. iii. Plenary, every year, on Holy Thursday, Corpus CHRISTI, or one day in its octave, and any one other day in the year, for saying either Pange lingua, or Tantum ergo with **V/.** and Prayer at least ten times a month, I, II, III, IV. (See Instructions.) 94 Pius VII, August 24, 1818.

PANGE lingua gloriosi	SING, my tongue, the
Corporis Mysterium,	SAVIOUR'S glory,
Sanguinisque pretiosi,	Of his Flesh the mystery sing;
Quern in mundi pretium,	Of the Blood, all price exceeding,
Fructus ventris generosi,	Shed by our immortal King,
Rex effudit gentium.	Destin'd, for the worlds redemption,
Nobis datus, nobis natus	From a noble womb to spring.
Ex intacta Virgine,	Of a pure and spotless Virgin
Et in mundo conversatus	Born for us on earth below,
Sparse verbi semine,	He, as Man with man conversing,
Sui moras incolatus	Stay'd, the seeds of truth to sow;
Miro clausit ordine.	Then He clos'd in solemn order
In supremæ nocte cœnæ	Wondrously his life of woe.
Recumbens cum fratribus,	On the night of that Last Supper,
Observata lege plene	Seated with his chosen band,
Cibis in legalibus,	He, the paschal victim eating,
Cibum turbæ duodenæ	First fulfils the Law's command;
Se dat suis manibus.	Then as food to all his brethren
Verbum caro, panem verum,	Gives himself with his own hand.
Verbo carnem efficit:	Word made Flesh, the bread of nature
Fitque Sanguis CHRISTI merum,	By his word to Flesh He turns;
Et si sensus deficit:	Wine into his Blood He changes
Ad firmandum cor sincerum	What though sense no change discerns?
Sola fides sufficit.	Only be the heart in earnest,
	Faith her lesson quickly learns.
TANTUM ergo Sacramentum	DOWN in adoration falling,
Veneremur cernui:	Lo! the sacred Host we hail;
Et antiquum documentum	Lo! o'er ancient forms departing,
Novo cedat ritui:	Newer rites of grace prevail;
Præstet fides supplementum	Faith for all defects supplying,
Sensuum defectui.	Where the feeble senses fail.
Genitori, Genitoque	To the everlasting FATHER,
Laus et jubilatio,	And the SON who reigns on high,
Salus, honor, virtus quoque	With the HOLY GHOST proceeding
Sit et benedictio:	Forth from each eternally,
Procedenti ab utroque	Be salvation, honour, blessing,
Compar sit laudatio.	Might, and endless majesty.
Amen.	V/. Thou gavest them Bread from heaven,
V/. Panem de ccelo præstitisti eis.	R/. And therein was sweetness of every kind.
R/. Omne delectamentum in se habentem.	
Oremus	Let us pray.

DEUS, qui nobis sub Sacramento mirabili Passionis tuæ memoriam reliquisti: tribue, quaesu- mus, ita nos Corporis et Sanguinis tui sacra mysteria venerari, ut redemptionis tuæ fructum in nobis jugiter sentiamus. Qui vivis et regnas in sæcula saeculorum. Amen.

O GOD, who under this wonderful Sacrament hast left unto us the memorial of thy Passion; grant us, we beseech Thee, so to venerate the sacred mysteries of thy Body and thy Blood that we may constantly experience within ourselves the fruit of thy redemption. Who livest and reignest, forever and ever. Amen.

95. Invocations.

i. 300 Days. T.Q. ii. Seven Years, if said after Communion, iii. Plenary, once a month. I, II, III, IV. (See Instructions.) 95 Pius IX, January 9, 1854.

ANIMA CHRISTI, sanctifica me. Corpus CHRISTI, salva me. Sanguis CHRISTI, inebria me. Aqua lateris CHRISTI, lava me. Passio CHRISTI, conforta me. O bone JESU, exaudi me. Intra tua vulnera absconde me. Ne permittas me separari a te. Ab hoste maligno defende me.. In hora mortis meæ

SOUL of CHRIST, be my sanctification. Body of CHRIST, be my salvation. Blood of CHRIST, fill all my veins. Water of CHRIST'S side, wash out my stains. Passion of CHRIST, my comfort be. O good JESU, listen to me. In thy wounds I fain would hide, Ne'er to be parted from thy side. Guard me

voca me, Et jube me venire ad te, Ut cum sanctis tuis laudem te. In saecula sæculorum. Amen.

should the foe assail me. Call me when my life shall fail me. Bid me come to Thee above. With thy Saints to sing thy love World without end. Amen.

96. Prayer of St Alphonsus Liguori, to be said at a Visit to the most Holy Sacrament.
i. 300 Days. T.Q. ii. Plenary, once a month. I, II, IV. (See Instructions.) 96 Pius IX, Pr. Ma. September 7, 1854

O MY LORD JESUS CHRIST, who for the love which Thou dost bear men dost remain night and day in this Sacrament, all full of tenderness and love, expecting, inviting, and receiving all those who come to visit Thee; I believe Thee present in the Sacrament of the Altar; I adore Thee in the depths of my own nothingness; and I thank Thee for all the graces which Thou hast granted me, especially for having vouchsafed to bestow thyself upon me in this Sacrament, for having given me thy own most holy Mother Mary for my advocate, and for having invited me to visit Thee in this church. I pay my homage this day to thy adorable Heart, and I do so for the following three intentions: first, in thanksgiving for this great gift itself; secondly, as a reparation for all the injuries which Thou hast received from all thy enemies in this Sacrament; thirdly, by this visit I intend to adore Thee in all those places where Thou, sacramentally present, art least reverenced and most abandoned. My JESUS, I love Thee with my whole heart. I repent of having so many times heretofore displeased thy infinite goodness. By thy grace I resolve never to offend Thee more for the time to come; and at this present moment, poor sinner as I am, I consecrate myself wholly to Thee. I renounce for myself, and I give to Thee, my will, my affections, my desires, everything that I call my own. From this day forth do Thou with me, and with everything- that belongs to me, whatever pleases Thee. I ask Thee only, and I wish only, for thy holy love, for final perseverance, and the perfect fulfilment of thy will. I commend to Thee the souls in purgatory, especially those who were most devoted to the most holy Sacrament, and to Mary most holy. Moreover, I commend to Thee all poor sinners. For this intention, O my dear SAVIOUR JESUS, I unite all my affections with the affections of thy most loving Heart; and thus united, I offer them to thy Eternal FATHER, and I entreat Him, in thy Name and for thy love, to accept and answer them.

97. Prayer.
100 Days, once a day. (See Instructions.) 97 Pius IX, Pr. Ma. January 1 1866.

DEAR JESUS, present in the Sacrament of the Altar, be for ever thanked and praised. Love, worthy of all celestial and terrestrial love! who, out of infinite love for me, ungrateful sinner, didst assume our human nature, didst shed thy most precious Blood in the cruel scourging, and didst expire on a shameful cross for our eternal welfare! Now, illumined with lively faith, with the outpouring of my whole soul and the fervour of my heart, I humbly beseech Thee, through the infinite merits of thy painful sufferings, give me strength and courage to destroy every evil passion which sways my heart, to bless Thee in my greatest afflictions, to glorify Thee by the exact fulfilment of all my duties, supremely to hate all sin, and thus to become a saint.

98. Visit to the Blessed Sacrament, with Pater, Ave, and Gloria five times, and Pater, Ave, and Gloria once for the intention of the Pope.
300 Days. T. Q. (See Instructions) 98 Pius IX, Br. September 15, 1876.

99. Prayer for a Visit.
100 Days, once a day. (See Instructions.) 99 Pius IX, February 4, 1877.

LOOK down, Holy FATHER and LORD, from thy sanctuary, and from heaven, thy dwelling-place on high, and behold this sacred Victim which our great High Priest, thy holy Child, our LORD JESUS, offers up to Thee for the sins of his brethren; and be appeased for the multitude of our transgressions. Behold, the voice of the Blood of JESUS, ourBrother, cries to Thee from the Cross. Give ear, O LORD! Be appeased, O LORD! Hearken, and do not tarry, for thine own sake, O my GOD, for thy Name is invoked upon this city and upon thy people; and deal with us according to thy mercy. Amen.

V/. That Thou vouchsafe to defend, pacify, keep, preserve, and bless this city,

R/. We beseech Thee to hear us.

100. Following the Blessed Sacrament.
i. 200 Days, to all who accompany the Blessed Sacrament carried to the sick. ii. 100 Days, for accompanying the Blessed Sacrament on any other occasion. (See Instructions.) 100 Pius IX July 18, 1877.

101. Following the Blessed Sacrament to the Sick.
i. Seven Years and Seven Quarantines, to all who accompany the Blessed Sacrament with a light, and pray according to the intention of the Pope. ii. Five Years and Five Quarantines, to those who accompany it without a light, praying as above. iii. Three Years and Three Quarantines, to those who, being legitimately hindered from going themselves, send some one in their stead to carry a light. iv. 100 Days, to those who cannot go, provided they say one Pater noster and one Ave Maria for the intention of the Pope, while it is being carried to the sick. (See Instructions.) 101 Innocent XII, Cons. January s, 1695.

102. Prayer to be said during the Elevation in the Mass.
60 Days, once a day. (See Instructions.) 102 Leo XIII, June 30, 1893.

SALVE, salutaris victima, pro me et omni Humano genere in patibulo crucis oblata. Salve, pretiose Sanguis, de vulneribus crucifixi DOMINI nostri JESU CHRISTI profluens, et peccata totius mundi abluens. Recordare, DOMINE, creaturæ tuæ, quam tuo pretioso sanguine redemisti.

HAIL, saving victim, offered upon the scaffold of the Cross, for me, and for the whole human race. Hail, Precious Blood streaming from the wounds of my crucified LORD JESUS CHRIST, washing away the sins of the whole world. Remember, O LORD, thy servant, the work of thy hands, whom Thou hast redeemed with thy Precious Blood.

103. Ejaculation.
i. 100 Days, before the tabernacle. T.Q. ii. 300 Days, at exposition. T.Q. iii. 100 Days, for making a reverence passing a church or chapel where the Blessed Sacrament is reserved. T.Q. (See Instructions.) 103 Pius X, July 3, 1908.

JESUS, my GOD, I adore Thee here present in the Sacrament of thy love.

104. Act of Spiritual Communion of Saint Alphonsus Liguori.
60 Days, once a day. (See Instructions.) 104 Leo III, June 30, 1893.
MY JESUS, I believe that Thou art in the Blessed Sacrament. I love Thee above everything, and I long for Thee in my soul. Since I cannot now receive Thee sacramentally, come at least spiritually into my heart. As though Thou wert already come, I embrace Thee and unite myself entirely to Thee; allow me not to be separated from Thee.

JESUS, my good, my sweet love,
Wound, inflame this heart of mine.
So that it may be always and all on fire for Thee.

105. Act of Homage to Christ, our God and our King.
i. Plenary, on Corpus CHRISTI, one day in the Octave, once during the forty hours, and on any two Thursdays in the year fixed by the Bishop. I, II, IV. ii. Seven Years and Seven Quarantines, on all other Thursdays. iii. 300 Days, once a day, for private recitation before the Blessed Sacrament. iv. 100 Days, once a day, for private recitation anywhere. (See Instructions.) 105 Leo XIII, February 15, 1895.
To be said by priest and people together during Exposition of the Blessed Sacrament.
O SWEET SAVIOUR and REDEEMER of mankind, JESUS CHRIST, who in the impenetrable designs of thine infinite wisdom bearest with the audacity of the impious and sufferest the violence of the wicked, reserving to thyself the sovereign right of judging the impious man and his perverse works, turn thy merciful regard upon thy children, who in the blindness of their hearts have turned from Thee in rebellion. With the eyes of a Father, and with the power of the sovereign King of the Universe, stretch forth thy hand to bless and regenerate modern society, which is rebelliously turning its back upon Thee, the King of Kings, LORD of Lords. Be moved to compassion for thy people, whom Thou hast purchased with thy Blood, regenerated with thy grace, and exalted with thy love. Thou hast given them true liberty, Thou hast called them to the inheritance of thy FATHER, Thou hast numbered them among thy brethren;

but in the delirium of their rebellion they have preferred the slavery of Satan, and live in abject misery, without joy, without hope.

O my LORD JESUS CHRIST, King of eternal glory, restorer of all things in heaven and on earth, supreme and omnipotent, who with infinite wisdom reunitest at thy feet things scattered and dispersed; enlighten the Kings of the earth, the rulers of nations; instil thy spirit into all civil institutions, into every form of government, into laws and armies; grant that all the powers of earth may recognize in Thee the majesty of the eternal GOD, the source from which all authority is derived; illuminate the nations that they may understand that Thou art the origin of rights and duties, that it is through Thee that the Kings of the earth rule, and that it is to Thee that Kings and people alike owe obedience. O most sweet JESUS, who hast deigned to descend into this valley of tears, and to dwell with us, suffering and dying for the salvation of us sinners, and who in an excess of charity hast set up thy abode in the midst of men, hidden under the sacramental species, and who in the fullness of the Godhead, corporally present in our tabernacles, makest thyself the food and life of our souls; oh, receive the humble but sincere and profound homage of our hearts, offered in reparation for the falling away of the rebellious. We firmly believe in Thee and all that the faith infused into our hearts by the HOLY SPIRIT has revealed to us about Thee. We see in Thee the beginning and the end of all existing things, we adore Thee as the one true GOD, we wish to live only for Thee and in thy service. Do Thou, O LORD, save our brethren, reunite the scattered members of modern society gone astray, that we as brethren may together be one with Thee, as Thou art one with thy FATHER in Heaven. May thy will be done by all and in everything-. May thy Majesty shine forth on the throne of thy earthly dominion, and the world confess Thee to be the true SON of GOD, through whom all things were created.

O JESUS, GOD of love, set free from his chains thy Vicar, the successor of Peter; re-establish him in the exercise of that liberty which Thou thyself didst give him, together with the supreme keys, that he might effectually carry on thy work of regenerating mankind; and so hasten on that longed-for day, in which Thou wilt be glorified by the return of Society to its paternal home. Gather together, O King of the nations, the sheep and the lambs under the care of the one shepherd. O LORD, do not abandon us; we are thy children, we love Thee; recognize us still as thy children, unworthy, yet ever thine; save us, and together with us, save Kings, Rulers, and Nations. Amen.

106. Hymn of St Thomas Aquinas.
100 Days, if said after Communion. (See Instructions.) 106 Leo XIII, Ind. June 15, 1895

ADORO te devote, latens DEITAS, Quæ sub his figuris vere latitas; Tibi se cor meum totum subjicit, Quia te contemplans, totum deficit. Visus, tactus, gustus, in te fallitur, Sed auditu solo tuto ere ditur; Credo quidquid dixit DEI FILIUS, Nil hoc verbo veritatis verius. In cruce latebat sola DEITAS, At hic latet simul et humanitas: Ambo tamen credens atque confitens, Peto quod petivit latro pœnitens. Plagas sicut Thomas non intueor, Deum tamen meum te confiteor: Fac me tibi semper magis credere, In te spem habere, te diligere. O memoriale mortis DOMINI, Panis vivus vitam præstans homini: Præta meæ menti de te vivere, Et te illi semper dulce sapere. Pie pelicane JESU DOMINE, Me immundum munda tuo sanguine, Cujus una stilla salvum face re Totum mundum quit ab omni scelere. JESUM quem velatum nunc aspicio Oro, fiat illud, quod tam sitio, Ut te revelata cernens facie, Visu sim beatus tuæ gloriæ. Amen.

O GODHEAD hid, devoutly I adore Thee, Who truly art within the forms before me; To Thee my heart I bow with bended knee, As failing quite in contemplating Thee. Sight, touch, and taste in Thee are each deceived; The ear alone most safely is believed: I believe all the SON of GOD has spoken, Than truth's own word there is no truer token. GOD only on the Cross lay hid from view; But here lies hid at once the manhood too: And I, in both professing my belief, Make the same prayer as the repentant thief. Thy wounds, as Thomas saw, I do not see: Yet Thee confess my LORD and GOD to be: Make me believe Thee ever more and more; In Thee my hope, in Thee my love to store. O Thou memorial of our LORD'S own dying! O living bread, to mortals life supplying! Make Thou my soul henceforth on Thee to live; Ever a taste of heavenly sweetness give. O loving Pelican! O JESU LORD! Unclean I am, but cleanse me in thy blood! Of which a single drop, for sinners spilt, Can purge the entire world from all its guilt. JESU! whom for the present veil'd I see, What I so thirst for, oh, vouchsafe to me: That I may see thy countenance unfolding, And may be blest thy glory in beholding. Amen.

107. Prayer.
300 Days, if said after Communion. (See Instructions.) 107 Leo XIII. June 3, 1896.
HOW full of delight is the sweetness of thy heavenly bread! How admirable is the tranquillity and how complete the peace of those who receive Thee, after detesting and sincerely confessing their sins. Be Thou blessed a thousand times, my JESUS! When I was in sin, I was unhappy. Now not only do I find my soul tranquil, but I seem to enjoy a very foretaste of the peace of Paradise. How true it is that our hearts are made for Thee, my beloved LORD, and that they rejoice only when they repose in Thee. I, then, render Thee thanks, and firmly purpose ever to fly sin and its occasions, to fix my abode in thy divine Heart, and thence to look for help to love Thee until death. Amen.

108. Ejaculation.
i. 100 Days, once a day. ii. 100 Days, three times a day on Thursdays, and during the Octave of Corpus CHRISTI. iii. Plenary, once a month. I, II, IV. iv. 100 Days, during- Mass, if said at each elevation. v. 100 Days, at the ringing- of the bell at the hours during the forty hours Exposition, or at other times, and at Benediction. (See Instructions.) 108 Pius VI, Mem. May 24, 1776. Pius VII, June 30, 1818 ; December 7, 1819
BLESSED and praised every moment Be the most holy and divine Sacrament.

109. Ejaculation after Mass.
Seven Years and Seven Quarantines. This indulgence holds good if the Prayer is said alternately with the priest. (See Instructions.) 109 Pius X, June 17, 1904; August 19, 1904.
MOST Sacred Heart of JESUS, have mercy on us. (Thrice.)

110. First Communicants and their Friends.
i. Plenary, to the third degree of relationship. I, II, IV. ii. Seven Years and Seven Quarantines to others present. (See Instructions.) 110 Pius X, July 12, 1905.

111. Prayer for the Increase of Daily Communion.
i. 300 Days, once a day. ii. Plenary, once a month. I, II, III, IV. (See Instructions.) 111 Pius X, June 3, 1905.
O SWEETEST JESUS, who earnest into this world to give to all the life of thy grace, and who, to preserve and sustain it, didst will to be the daily remedy of our daily infirmities, and our daily food; humbly we pray Thee, by thy heart, all on fire with love of us, to pour out thy HOLY SPIRIT upon all, so that those who are unhappily in mortal sin may be converted to Thee, and recover the life of grace which they have lost; and those who by thy gift still live this divine life, may every day, when they are able, approach devoutly to thy holy table, where, in daily communion, receiving every day the antidote to their daily venial sins, and nourishing the life of grace in their hearts, and purifying more and more their souls, they may come at last to the enjoyment with Thee of eternal beatitude. Amen.

112. Prayer to our Lady of the Blessed Sacrament.
300 Days. T.Q. (See Instructions.) 112 Pius X, January 23, 1907.
O VIRGIN Mary, our Lady of the Blessed Sacrament, glory of the Christian people, joy of the universal Church, salvation of the world; pray for us, and awaken in all the faithful devotion to the Holy Eucharist in order that they may render themselves worthy to receive it daily.

113. Prayer to our Lord in the Blessed Sacrament.
300 Days. T.Q. (See Instructions.) 113 Pius X, July 6, 1906.
OUR sins, O LORD, darken our minds, and we lose the benefit of loving Thee as Thou deservest. Enlighten us with a ray of thy bright light. Thou art Friend, REDEEMER, Father of all who turn repentant to thy Heart; and we return to Thee sorrowing. Save us, O JESUS; provide out of thy infinite bounty for our miseries. O JESUS, we hope in Thee because we know that our salvation cost Thee thy life sacrificed upon the Cross and induced Thee to dwell continuously in the Blessed Sacrament, in order to be united with us as often as we desire. We, O LORD, to thank Thee for the great love Thou bearest us, promise with the help of thy grace to receive Thee in the Blessed Sacrament as often as possible; to declare thy praises in church and in every place, without human respect. O LORD, confiding in thy Sacred Heart, we

beseech Thee, to preserve in thy love those who love Thee, and to invite all to receive Thee daily at the altar in accordance with thy burning desire.

114. Prayers during a Procession of the Blessed Sacrament.
300 Days. (See Instructions.) 114 Pius X , August 11, 1906.
PATER, Ave, Gloria. Then say ten times:
V/. Let us every moment praise the most holy Sacrament.
R/. May our GOD, present in the Sacrament, be now and ever praised.
Repeat PATER, Ave, etc., as often as needed.

115. Prayer to be said at the Beginning of Mass.
i. 300 Days. T.Q. ii. Plenary once a month, if said on every Sunday and holiday of obligation. I, II. (See Instructions.) 115 Pius X, Aft. July 8, 1904
ETERNAL FATHER, I unite myself with the intentions and affections of our Lady of Sorrows on Calvary, and I offer Thee the sacrifice which thy beloved SON JESUS made of himself on the Cross, and now renews on this holy altar: 1. To adore Thee and give Thee the honour which is due to Thee, confessing thy supreme dominion overall things, and the absolute dependence of everything upon Thee, Thou who art our one and last end. 2. To thank Thee for innumerable benefits received. 3. To appease thy justice, irritated against us by so many sins, and to make satisfaction for them. 4. To implore grace and mercy for myself, for . . . , for all afflicted and sorrowing, for poor sinners, for all the world, and for the holy souls in Purgatory.

116. Ejaculation.
i. Seven Years and Seven Quarantines.* T.Q. ii. Plenary, once a week, if used daily, II.* (See Instructions.) 116 Pius X, May 18, 1907.
DOMINUS meus, et DEUS meus. My LORD and my GOD.
These words are to be said with faith, piety, and love, while looking upon the Blessed Sacrament, either during the Elevation in the Mass, or when exposed on the altar.

VII. JESUS CRUCIFIED
117. The Stations of the Cross.
117 Clement XIV, Res. January 26, 1773; Pius IX, Br. August n, 1863; Leo XIII, January 19, March 15, 1884.
Those who perform devoutly the Stations of the Cross may gain all the Indulgences which have ever been granted by Popes to the faithful who visit in person the sacred places in Jerusalem. It is not permitted to specify definitely what these Indulgences are. All, however, who wish to gain them must bear in mind that the Stations must be erected by one who has Faculties, and that it is indispensably required of them to meditate, according to their abilities, on the Passion of our LORD and SAVIOUR JESUS CHRIST, and to go from one Station to the other, so far as the number of persons engaged in the devotion, and the space where the fourteen Stations are erected, will admit, and this is all that is required for the Indulgences. Those who are sick, in prison, or at sea, or in parlibus infidelium, or who are prevented in any other way from visiting the Stations erected in churches or public oratories, may gain the said Indulgences by reciting fourteen times Pater noster and Ave Maria, and at the end of these, Pater noster and Ave Maria and Gloria Patri five times, and one Pater, Ave, and Gloria besides, for the Pope, "holding in their hands the while a crucifix " blessed by the Father-General of the Order of the Friars Minor Observants at the Convent of Ara Cœli, or else by the Father-Provincial or any Father-Guardian, subject of the said Father-General, or any priest with Faculties from the said Father-General. These crucifixes, so indulgenced, after they have been blessed, cannot be sold or given away or lent for the purpose of enabling others to gain the Indulgences of the Stations.
Devotions which may be used for the Stations. *(The pious reader may use any other devotions which are more to his mind.)*
Begin with an act of contrition.

STATION I. JESUS condemned to death.
V/. Adoramuste, CHRISTE, et benedicimus tibi.
R/. Quia per sanctam Crucem tuam redemisti mundum.

V/. We adore Thee, O CHRIST, and we bless Thee.
R/. Because by thy holy Cross Thou hast redeemed the world.

My JESUS, oft have I signed thy death-warrant by my sins; save me by thy death from that death eternal I deserve. PATER, Ave.
V/. Miserere nostri, DOMINE.
R/. Miserere nostri.

V/. Have mercy on us, O LORD.
R/. Have mercy on us.

Passing on from one station to another, say, or sing,

> Holy Mother, pierce me through,
> In my heart each wound renew
> Of my SAVIOUR crucified.

or the Stabat Mater (p. 238).

STATION II. JESUS receives his cross.
V/. Adoramuste, CHRISTE, et benedicimus tibi.
R/. Quia per sanctam Crucem tuam redemisti mundum.

V/. We adore Thee, O CHRIST, and we bless Thee.
R/. Because by thy holy Cross Thou hast redeemed the world.

My JESUS, who by thine own will didst take on Thee the Cross which I made for Thee by my sins; oh, make me know the weight of them, and sorrow for them ever while I live. PATER, Ave.

V/. Miserere nostri, DOMINE.
R/. Miserere nostri.

V/. Have mercy on us, O LORD.
R/. Have mercy on us.

STATION III. JESUS falls the first time beneath the Cross.
V/. Adoramuste, CHRISTE, et benedicimus tibi.
R/. Quia per sanctam Crucem tuam redemisti mundum.

V/. We adore Thee, O CHRIST, and we bless Thee.
R/. Because by thy holy Cross Thou hast redeemed the world.

My JESUS, the heavy burden of my sins has made Thee fall down beneath the Cross. My JESUS, I loathe them, I detest them, I beseech Thee to pardon them; aided by thy grace, I will never commit them more. PATER, Ave.

V/. Miserere nostri, DOMINE.
R/. Miserere nostri.

V/. Have mercy on us, O LORD.
R/. Have mercy on us.

STATION IV. JESUS meets his Mother.
V/. Adoramuste, CHRISTE, et benedicimus tibi.
R/. Quia per sanctam Crucem tuam redemisti mundum.

V/. We adore Thee, O CHRIST, and we bless Thee.
R/. Because by thy holy Cross Thou hast redeemed the world.

JESUS, most suffering ! Mary, Mother most sorrowful ! if for the past by sin I have caused you pain and sorrow, yet by divine grace it shall be so no more, but I will love you faithfully until death. PATER, Ave.

V/. Miserere nostri, DOMINE.
R/. Miserere nostri.

V/. Have mercy on us, O LORD.
R/. Have mercy on us.

STATION V. Simon of Cyrene helps JESUS to carry the Cross.
V/. Adoramuste, CHRISTE, et benedicimus tibi.
R/. Quia per sanctam Crucem tuam redemisti mundum.

V/. We adore Thee, O CHRIST, and we bless Thee.
R/. Because by thy holy Cross Thou hast redeemed the world.

My JESUS, happy was that man of Cyrene who aided Thee to bear the Cross. Happy shall I be if I too aid Thee to bear the Cross, by suffering with patience and goodwill the crosses Thou shalt send me during life. My JESUS, give me grace to do so. PATER, Ave.

V/. Miserere nostri, DOMINE.
R/. Miserere nostri.

V/. Have mercy on us, O LORD.
R/. Have mercy on us.

STATION VI. JESUS and Veronica.
V/. Adoramuste, CHRISTE, et benedicimus tibi.
R/. Quia per sanctam Crucem tuam redemisti mundum.

V/. We adore Thee, O CHRIST, and we bless Thee.
R/. Because by thy holy Cross Thou hast redeemed the world.

JESUS most compassionate, who didst deign to print thy sacred countenance upon the cloth with which Veronica wiped the sweat from off thy brows; print in my soul deep, I pray Thee, the lasting memory of thy most bitter pains. PATER, Ave.

V/. Miserere nostri, DOMINE.
R/. Miserere nostri.

V/. Have mercy on us, O LORD.
R/. Have mercy on us.

STATION VII. JESUS falls a second time.
V/. Adoramuste, CHRISTE, et benedicimus tibi.
R/. Quia per sanctam Crucem tuam redemisti

V/. We adore Thee, O CHRIST, and we bless Thee.
R/. Because by thy holy Cross Thou hast redeemed

mundum.   the world.

My JESUS, oft have I sinned, and by sin often made Thee fall beneath the Cross. Help me to use such efficacious means of grace that I may never fall again into sin. PATER, Ave.

V/. Miserere nostri, DOMINE.   V/. Have mercy on us, O LORD.
R/. Miserere nostri.   R/. Have mercy on us.

STATION VIII. JESUS comforts the women of Jerusalem.
V/. Adoramuste, CHRISTE, et benedicimus tibi.   V/. We adore Thee, O CHRIST, and we bless Thee.
R/. Quia per sanctam Crucem tuam redemisti mundum.   R/. Because by thy holy Cross Thou hast redeemed the world.

My JESUS, who didst comfort the pious women of Jerusalem who wept to see Thee so tormented; comfort my soul with thy mercy, for in thy mercy alone is my trust; oh, may I never frustrate it! PATER, Ave.

V/. Miserere nostri, DOMINE.   V/. Have mercy on us, O LORD.
R/. Miserere nostri.   R/. Have mercy on us.

STATION IX. Again a third time JESUS falls.
V/. Adoramuste, CHRISTE, et benedicimus tibi.   V/. We adore Thee, O CHRIST, and we bless Thee.
R/. Quia per sanctam Crucem tuam redemisti mundum.   R/. Because by thy holy Cross Thou hast redeemed the world.

My JESUS, by all the bitter woe Thou didst endure when a third time Thou didst fall beneath the heavy Cross, oh, never, never let me fall away; but rather let me die than ever mortally sin again. PATER, Ave.

V/. Miserere nostri, DOMINE.   V/. Have mercy on us, O LORD.
R/. Miserere nostri.   R/. Have mercy on us.

STATION X. JESUS stripped and given gall to drink.
V/. Adoramuste, CHRISTE, et benedicimus tibi.   V/. We adore Thee, O CHRIST, and we bless Thee.
R/. Quia per sanctam Crucem tuam redemisti mundum.   R/. Because by thy holy Cross Thou hast redeemed the world.

My JESUS, who wast stripped of thy clothes and given gall to drink, strip me of love for things of earth, and make me loathe all that savours of the world and sin. PATER, Ave.

V/. Miserere nostri, DOMINE.   V/. Have mercy on us, O LORD.
R/. Miserere nostri.   R/. Have mercy on us.

STATION XI. JESUS nailed to the Cross.
V/. Adoramuste, CHRISTE, et benedicimus tibi.   V/. We adore Thee, O CHRIST, and we bless Thee.
R/. Quia per sanctam Crucem tuam redemisti mundum.   R/. Because by thy holy Cross Thou hast redeemed the world.

My JESUS, by those agonizing- pains Thou didst endure when the hard nails pierced thy tender hands and feet and fixed them to the Cross, oh, make me ever crucify my flesh with the spirit of true Christian penance. PATER, Ave.

V/. Miserere nostri, DOMINE.   V/. Have mercy on us, O LORD.
R/. Miserere nostri.   R/. Have mercy on us.

STATION XII. JESUS dies upon the Cross.
V/. Adoramuste, CHRISTE, et benedicimus tibi.   V/. We adore Thee, O CHRIST, and we bless Thee.
R/. Quia per sanctam Crucem tuam redemisti mundum.   R/. Because by thy holy Cross Thou hast redeemed the world.

My JESUS, three hours didst Thou hang in agony upon the Cross, and then didst die for me; let me die before I sin again, and if I live, may I live to love Thee and to serve Thee faithfully. PATER, Ave.

V/. Miserere nostri, DOMINE.   V/. Have mercy on us, O LORD.
R/. Miserere nostri.   R/. Have mercy on us.

STATION XIII. JESUS taken from the Cross and laid in Mary's bosom.
V/. Adoramuste, CHRISTE, et benedicimus tibi.   V/. We adore Thee, O CHRIST, and we bless Thee.
R/. Quia per sanctam Crucem tuam redemisti   R/. Because by thy holy Cross Thou hast redeemed

mundum. | the world.

Mary, Mother most sorrowful, the sword of grief went through thy soul when thou didst see thy dear Son JESUS lying lifeless in thy bosom ; ask for me hatred of sin, which was the cause of his death and made thee suffer so much; and then obtain for me grace to live a true Christian life, and save my soul. PATER, Ave.

V/. Miserere nostri, DOMINE.
R/. Miserere nostri.

V/. Have mercy on us, O LORD.
R/. Have mercy on us.

STATION XIV. JESUS laid in the tomb.
V/. Adoramuste, CHRISTE, et benedicimus tibi.
R/. Quia per sanctam Crucem tuam redemisti mundum.

V/. We adore Thee, O CHRIST, and we bless Thee.
R/. Because by thy holy Cross Thou hast redeemed the world.

My JESUS, beside Thee in the tomb I desire that I may ever remain as one dead ; and if I live, I wish to live only to Thee, that so one day I may come with Thee to taste of the bliss of heaven, fruit of thy Passion and most painful death. Amen. PATER, Ave.

V/. Miserere nostri, DOMINE.
R/. Miserere nostri.
Oremus.
DEUS, qui Unigeniti FILII tui pretioso sanguine vivificæ crucis vexillum sanctificare voluisti ; concede, quæsumus, eos, qui ejusdem sanctæ crucis gaudent honore, tua quoque ubi que protectione gaudere. Per eundem CHRISTUM DOMINUM nostrum. **R/.** Amen.

V/. Have mercy on us, O LORD.
R/. Have mercy on us.
Let us pray.
GOD, who by the Precious Blood of thy only-begotten SON didst sanctify the standard of the Cross; grant, we beseech Thee, that all those who rejoice in the glory of the same Holy Cross may at all times and places feel the gladness of thy protection. Through the same CHRIST our LORD. **R/.** Amen.

End with one PATER, Ave, and Gloria for the intention of the Sovereign Pontiff.

118. Chaplet of the Stations of the Gross.
Indulgences, the same as for the Stations, if hindered from making the Stations.
This Chaplet, invented by Louisa Borgiotti, co-founder of the Nazarene Sisters, consists of Pater, Ave, and Gloria, twenty times, one for each Station, five for the five wounds, and one for the intention of the Pope. The beads must be blessed by a Priest of the Missions. If several persons say the Chaplet together, it is sufficient if one has beads. A similar privilege attaches to Crucifixes blessed by the Friars Minor (Pius IX, August 8, 1859). 118 Pius X, November 2, 1906 ; December 1, 1907.

119. The "Scala Santa" in Rome.
i. Nine Years, for each of the twenty-eight steps of the Scala Santa. N.B. The two stairs on either side are similarly indulgenced on All Saints, during the Octave of All Souls, from Christmas to the Epiphany, and during Lent. The ascent must be made on the knees, with a contrite heart and meditation on the Passion of our LORD. ii. Plenary, as often as the ascent is made. I, II, IV. T.Q. (See Instructions.) 119 Pius VII, September 2, 1817: Leo XIII, July 23, 1898; Pius X, February 26, 1908.

120. Pious Exercise on Fridays.
100 Days, to all who when the church bell rings on Friday at three in the afternoon, or at any other hour fixed by custom, kneel and say five times Pater noster and Ave Maria, in memory of the Passion of our LORD, praying according to the intention of the Pope. (See Instructions.) 120 Benedict XIV, Br. December 13, 1740. Leo XIII, May 15, 1886.

121. Devotions in Honour of the Five Wounds.
100 Days, once a day. ii. Plenary, twice a year that is, on the two feasts, first, that of the Invention (May 3), and, secondly, that of the Exaltation of the Holy Cross (September 14) to all who shall say these prayers at least ten times a month. I, II. iii. Seven Years and Seven Quarantines, once a day, to those who say these prayers from Passion Sunday to Holy Saturday inclusive. iv. Plenary on Easter Day to those who have said the prayers daily during the period mentioned. I, II. (See Instructions.) 121 Pius VII, September 29, 1807.

Act of Contrition.

AS I kneel before Thee on the Cross, most loving SAVIOUR of my soul, my conscience tells me it was I who nailed Thee to that Cross with these hands of mine, as often as I have fallen into mortal sin, wearying Thee with my monstrous ingratitude. My GOD, my chief and most perfect Good, worthy of all my love, seeing Thou hast ever loaded me with blessings, I cannot now undo my misdeeds, as 1 would most willingly, but I can and will loathe them, grieving greatly for having offended Thee who art infinite Goodness. And now, kneeling at thy feet, I will try at least to compassionate Thee, to give Thee thanks, to ask of Thee pardon and contrition; wherefore with heart and lips I say:

To the First Wound of the Left Foot.

HOLY wound of the Left Foot of my JESUS, I adore Thee! I compassionate Thee, O my JESUS, for that most bitter pain which Thou didst suffer. I thank Thee for the love whereby Thou wast wearied in overtaking me on the way to ruin, and didst bleed amid the thorns and brambles of my sins. I offer to the Eternal FATHER the pain and love of thy most sacred humanity, in atonement for my sins, all which I detest with sincere and bitter contrition. PATER, Ave, Gloria.

Holy Mother, pierce me through;
In my heart each wound renew
Of my SAVIOUR crucified.

To the Second Wound, of the Right Foot.

HOLY wound of the Right Foot of my JESUS, I adore Thee! I compassionate Thee, O my JESUS, for that most bitter pain which Thou didst suffer. I thank Thee for the love which pierced Thee with such torture and shedding of blood in order to punish my wanderings and the guilty pleasures I have granted to my passions. I offer the Eternal FATHER all the pain and love of thy most sacred humanity, and I pray unto Him for grace to weep over my transgressions with burning tears, and to enable me to persevere in the good which I have begun, without ever swerving again from my obedience to the Commandments of my GOD. PATER, Ave, Gloria.

Holy Mother, pierce me through;
In my heart each wound renew
Of my SAVIOUR crucified.

To the Third Wound, of the Left Hand.

HOLY wound of the Left Hand of my JESUS, I adoreThee! I compassionate Thee, O my JESUS, for that most bitter pain which Thou didst suffer. I thank Thee for having, in thy love, spared me the scourges and eternal damnation which my sins have merited. I offer to the Eternal FATHER the pain and love of thy most sacred humanity, and I pray Him to teach me how to turn to good account my span of life, and bring forth in it worthy fruits of penance, and so disarm the angry justice of my GOD. PATER, Ave, Gloria.

Holy Mother, pierce me through;
In my heart each wound renew
Of my SAVIOUR crucified.

To the Fourth Wound, of the Right Hand.

HOLY wound of the Right Hand of my JESUS, I adore Thee! I compassionate Thee, O my JESUS, for that most bitter pain which Thou didst suffer. I thank Thee for thy graces lavished on me with such love, in spite of all my miserable obstinacy. I offer to the Eternal FATHER all the pain and love of thy most sacred humanity, and I pray Him to change my heart and its affections, and make me do all my actions in accordance with the will of GOD. PATER, Ave, Gloria.

Holy Mother, pierce me through;
In my heart each wound renew
Of my SAVIOUR crucified.

To the Fifth Wound, of the sacred Side.

HOLY wound in the side of my JESUS, I adore Thee! I compassionate Thee, O my JESUS, for the cruel insult Thou didst suffer. I thank Thee, my JESUS, for the love which suffered thy side and heart to be pierced, that so the last drops of blood and water might issue forth, making my redemption to abound. I offer to the Eternal FATHER this outrage, and the love of thy most sacred humanity, that my soul may enter once for all into that most loving Heart, eager and ready to receive the greatest sinners, and from it may never more depart. PATER, Ave, Gloria.

Holy Mother, pierce me through;
In my heart each wound renew
Of my SAVIOUR crucified.

To the most Holy Virgin, Mother of Sorrows.
MARY, Virgin Mother of GOD, Martyr of love and sorrow, in that thou didst witness the pains and torments of JESUS; truly didst thou concur in the great work of my redemption, first by thy innumerable afflictions, and then by the offering thou didst make to the Eternal FATHER of his and thy only-begotten for a holocaust and victim of propitiation for my sins. I thank thee for that love, well-nigh infinite, through which thou didst bereave thyself of the fruit of thy womb, very GOD and very Man, to save me, sinner that I am; let thy intercession, which never returneth to thee void, interpose with the FATHER and the SON for me; that I may steadily amend my evil ways, and never by further faults crucify afresh my loving SAVIOUR; that so, persevering in his grace until death, I may obtain eternal life through the merits of his painful Passion and Death upon the Cross. Ave Maria, thrice.

Let us pray.
O LORD JESUS CHRIST, who at the sixth hour of the day didst, for the redemption of the world, mount the scaffold of the Cross, and shed thy Precious Blood for the remission of sins; we humbly beseech Thee grant us that after our death we may joyfully enter the gates of Paradise. We beseech Thee, O LORD JESUS CHRIST, that now, and at the hour of our death, blessed Mary ever Virgin, thy Mother, may intercede for us, through whose most holy soul the sword passed in the hour of thy Passion. Through Thee, JESUS CHRIST, SAVIOUR of the world, who with the FATHER and the HOLY GHOST livest and reignest for ever and ever. Amen.

122. Devotion of the Seven Words.
Seven Years and Seven Quarantines. T.Q. (See Instructions.) 122 Leo XIII, Decembers, 1897.

V/. DEUS, in adjutorium meum intende.	V/. O GOD, come to my assistance.
R/. DOMINE, ad adjuvandum me festina.	R/. O LORD make haste to help me.
V/. Gloria PATRI, etc.	V/. Glory be to the FATHER, etc.

FIRST WORD: Father, forgive them ; for they know not what they do.

V/. Adoramuste, CHRISTE, et benedicimus tibi.	V/. We adore Thee, O CHRIST, and we bless Thee.
R/. Quia per sanctam Crucem tuam redemisti mundum.	R/. Because by thy holy Cross Thou hast redeemed the world.

JESUS, my love ! who for love of me didst hang in agony upon the Cross, there by thy pains to pay the penalty of my sins, and didst open thy divine mouth to obtain for me the pardon of them from Eternal Justice ; O JESUS, pity all the faithful who are now in their last agony, and pity me when I too shall be in mine. By the merits of thy most Precious Blood shed for our salvation, vouchsafe unto us all such lively sorrow for our sins that at our death we may breathe forth our souls into the bosom of thy infinite mercy. Gloria PATRI, thrice.

V/. Miserere nostri, DOMINE.	V/. Have mercy on us, O LORD.
R/. Miserere nostri.	R/. Have mercy on us.

My GOD, I believe in Thee, I hope in Thee, I love Thee. I repent of my sins, because by them I have offended Thee.

SECOND WORD : This day shalt thou be with Me in Paradise.

V/. Adoramuste, CHRISTE, et benedicimus tibi.	V/. We adore Thee, O CHRIST, and we bless Thee.
R/. Quia per sanctam Crucem tuam redemisti mundum.	R/. Because by thy holy Cross Thou hast redeemed the world.

JESUS, my love! who for love of me didst hang in agony upon the Cross, and with such readiness and bounty didst respond to the faith of the good thief, who in thy humiliations acknowledged Thee to be the SON of GOD, and didst assure unto him the Paradise prepared for him ; oh, pity all the faithful who are in their last agony, and pity me when I too shall be in mine. By the merit of thy most Precious Blood, wake up in our souls such firm and steadfast faith as shall never waver at any suggestion of the evil one ; that so we also may obtain the prize of holy Paradise. Gloria PATRI, thrice.

V/. Miserere nostri, DOMINE.   V/. Have mercy on us, O LORD.
R/. Miserere nostri.   R/. Have mercy on us.

My GOD, I believe in Thee, I hope in Thee, I love Thee. I repent of my sins, because by them I have offended Thee.

THIRD WORD: Behold thy Mother! Behold thy Son.

V/. Adoramuste, CHRISTE, et benedicimus tibi.   V/. We adore Thee, O CHRIST, and we bless Thee.
R/. Quia per sanctam Crucem tuam redemisti mundum.   R/. Because by thy holy Cross Thou hast redeemed the world.

JESUS, my love ! who for love of me didst hang in agony upon the Cross, and, unmindful of thine own sorrows, didst leave us thy own most holy Mother as the pledge of thy love, that through her intercession we might seek Thee with confidence in our greatest straits; have pity on all the faithful who are in their last agony, and pity me when I too shall be in mine. By the inward martyrdom of thy dear Mother, quicken in our hearts a firm hope in the infinite merits of thine own most Precious Blood, that so we may escape the sentence of eternal death, which we have merited by our sins. Gloria PATRI, thrice.

V/. Miserere nostri, DOMINE.   V/. Have mercy on us, O LORD.
R/. Miserere nostri.   R/. Have mercy on us.

My GOD, I believe in Thee, I hope in Thee, I love Thee. I repent of my sins, because by them I have offended Thee.

FOURTH WORD: My God, my God, why hast Thou forsaken Me ?

V/. Adoramuste, CHRISTE, et benedicimus tibi.   V/. We adore Thee, O CHRIST, and we bless Thee.
R/. Quia per sanctam Crucem tuam redemisti mundum.   R/. Because by thy holy Cross Thou hast redeemed the world.

JESUS, my love! who for love of me didst hang in agony upon the Cross, and, whilst suffering after suffering was heaped upon Thee, with all thy bodily pain didst bear with infinite patience the most afflicting desolation of spirit, being forsaken by thine Eternal FATHER; pity all the faithful who are in their last agony, and pity me when I too shall be in mine. By the merits of thy most Precious Blood, grant us all thy grace, that we may suffer with patience the pain and anguish of our last agony, and so, joining our pains with thine, be made partakers of thy glory in Paradise. Gloria PATRI, thrice.

V/. Miserere nostri, DOMINE.   V/. Have mercy on us, O LORD.
R/. Miserere nostri.   R/. Have mercy on us.

My GOD, I believe in Thee, I hope in Thee, I love Thee. I repent of my sins, because by them I have offended Thee.

FIFTH WORD : I thirst.

V/. Adoramuste, CHRISTE, et benedicimus tibi.   V/. We adore Thee, O CHRIST, and we bless Thee.
R/. Quia per sanctam Crucem tuam redemisti mundum.   R/. Because by thy holy Cross Thou hast redeemed the world.

JESUS, my love! who for love of me didst hang in agony upon the Cross, and who, insatiable in thy thirst for insults and sufferings, didst will yet more and more to suffer, that all men might be saved, showing thereby that all the torrent of thy Passion was not enough to quench the thirst of thy most loving Heart; pity all the faithful who are in their last agony, and pity me when I too shall be in mine. By the merits of thy most Precious Blood, kindle in our hearts such fire of charity, as may make them burn to be made one with Thee for all eternity. Gloria PATRI, thrice.

V/. Miserere nostri, DOMINE.   V/. Have mercy on us, O LORD.
R/. Miserere nostri.   R/. Have mercy on us.

My GOD, I believe in Thee, I hope in Thee, I love Thee. I repent of my sins, because by them I have offended Thee.

SIXTH WORD: It is consummated.

V/. Adoramuste, CHRISTE, et benedicimus tibi.   V/. We adore Thee, O CHRIST, and we bless Thee.
R/. Quia per sanctam Crucem tuam redemisti mundum.   R/. Because by thy holy Cross Thou hast redeemed the world.

JESUS, my love! who for love of me didst hang in agony upon the Cross, and from this pulpit of truth didst announce that the work of our redemption was finished that work through which, from children of wrath and perdition, we become GOD'S children and the heirs of heaven; pity all the faithful who are in their last agony, and pity me when I too shall be in mine. By the merits of thy most Precious Blood, detach us wholly from the world and from ourselves, and at the moment of our agony grant us grace to offer Thee with all our hearts the sacrifice of our life, in expiation for our sins. Gloria PATRI, thrice.

V/. Miserere nostri, DOMINE.	V/. Have mercy on us, O LORD.
R/. Miserere nostri.	R/. Have mercy on us.

My GOD, I believe in Thee, I hope in Thee, I love Thee. I repent of my sins, because by them I have offended Thee.

SEVENTH WORD: Father, into Thy hands I commend My spirit.

V/. Adoramuste, CHRISTE, et benedicimus tibi.	V/. We adore Thee, O CHRIST, and we bless Thee.
R/. Quia per sanctam Crucem tuam redemisti mundum.	R/. Because by thy holy Cross Thou hast redeemed the world.

JESUS, my love! who for love of me didst hang in agony upon the Cross, and who in accomplishment of the great sacrifice didst accept the will of thine Eternal FATHER, commending thy spirit into his hands, and so didst bow thy head and die; pity all the faithful who are in their last agony, and pity me when I too shall be in mine. By the merits of thy most Precious Blood, give us in our agony an entire conformity to thy divine will, that ready to live or die as it please Thee, we may desire nothing so much as that thine adorable will may ever find its full accomplishment in us. Gloria PATRI, thrice.

V/. Miserere nostri, DOMINE.	V/. Have mercy on us, O LORD.
R/. Miserere nostri.	R/. Have mercy on us.

My GOD, I believe in Thee, I hope in Thee, I love Thee. I repent of my sins, because by them I have offended Thee.

Prayer to the Holy Virgin, Mother of Sorrows.

MOST Holy Mother of sorrows, by that intense martyrdom which thou didst suffer at the foot of the Cross during the three hours of the agony of JESUS, deign to aid us all, children of thy sorrows, in our last agony, that by thy prayers we may pass from our bed of death to adorn thy crown in Paradise. Ave Maria, thrice.

Maria, mater gratiæ,	*Mother of mercy, Mother of grace,*
Mater misericordiæ,	*Mary, help a fallen race;*
Tu nos ab hoste protege,	*Shield us when the foe is nigh,*
Et mortis hora suscipe.	*And receive us when we die.*
V/. A subitanea et improvisa morte	V/. From sudden and unprepared death,
R/. Libera nos, DOMINE.	R/. Deliver us, O LORD.
V/. Ab insidiis diaboli,	V/. From the snares of the devil,
R/. Libera nos, DOMINE.	R/. Deliver us, O LORD
V/. A morte perpetua,	V/. From everlasting death,
R/. Libera nos, DOMINE	R/. Deliver us, O LORD.
Oremus.	**Let us pray.**
DEUS, qui ad humani generis salutem in dolorosissima FILII tui morte exemplum et subsidium constituisti; concede, quæsumus, ut in extreme mortis nostræ periculo tantæ charitatis effectum consequi et ipsius Redemptoris gloriæ consociari mereamur. Per eundem CHRISTUM DOMINUM nostrum. R/. Amen.	GOD, who for the salvation of the human race hast, in the most bitter death of thy SON, made for us both an example and a refuge; grant, we beseech Thee, that in the last peril, at the hour of our death, we may merit to obtain the full effect of his great charity, and be made partakers of our REDEEMER'S glory. Through the same JESUS CHRIST our LORD. R/. Amen.

End with the three ejaculations,

JESUS, Mary, and Joseph, I give you my heart and my soul.
JESUS, Mary, and Joseph, assist me in my last agony.
JESUS, Mary, and Joseph, may I breathe forth my soul with you in peace.

123. The Three Hours on Good Friday and any other Friday.

i. Plenary, on Holy Thursday or during Easter Week, to all who shall, either in public or private, practise this devotional exercise on Good Friday from noon to three o'clock, either by meditating 1 according" to their abilities on the suffering's of JESUS CHRIST during the three hours He hung on the Cross, and on the seven words He then uttered, or else, instead of meditation, by reciting psalms, hymns, or other prayers. I, II, IV.

ii. 200 Days, any Friday in the year, to every one who, in remembrance of, and out of devotion to, the agony of our Blessed LORD, shall spend some time in prayer, as above. IV.

iii. Plenary, once every month, on the last Friday, to everyone who has meditated and prayed every previous Friday in the month, in the way just mentioned. I, II, IV. (See Instructions.) 123 Pius VII, February 14, 1815.

124. Devotion for Lent.

i. 300 Days, for each of the seven Fridays in Lent. I, II, IV. ii. Plenary, on any one of these Fridays. I, II, IV. iii. 300 Days, to every one who shall make use of this devotion on any other Friday in the year. IV. iv. Plenary, if any one shall practise it on seven consecutive Fridays at any time in the year; to be gained on any one of those Fridays. IV. (See Instructions.) 124 Gregory XVI, August 4, 1837.

To all who visit a public church or chapel, and say before a representation of Jesus crucified, in memory of the Passion, Pater, Ave and Gloria seven times, praying according to the Pope s intention.

125. The Prayer, Deus, qui pro Redemptione, etc.

i. 300 Days, once a day. ii. Plenary, once a month, on one of the last three days. I, II, IV. (See Instructions.) 125 Pius VII, August 25, 1820

O GOD, who to redeem the world didst vouchsafe to be born amongst men, to be circumcised, rejected by the Jews, betrayed by the traitor Judas with a kiss, to be bound with cords, and as an innocent lamb to be led to the slaughter; who didst suffer thyself to be shamelessly exposed to the gaze of Annas, Caiphas, Pilate and Herod; to be accused by false witnesses, tormented by scourges and insults, crowned with thorns, smitten with blows, defiled with spittings, to have thy divine countenance covered, to be struck with a reed, to be stripped of thy clothes, nailed to and raised high upon a Cross between two thieves, to be given gall and vinegar to drink, and then pierced with a lance; do Thou, O LORD, by these most sacred sufferings, which I, unworthy as I am, yet dare to contemplate, by thy holy Cross and by thy bitter Death, free me from the pains of hell, and vouchsafe to bring me to Paradise, whither Thou didst lead the thief who was crucified with Thee, my JESUS, who with the FATHER and the HOLY GHOST livest and reignest GOD for ever and ever. Amen. PATER, Ave and Gloria five times.

126. Chaplet of the Five Wounds.

i. One Year, once a day. ii. Plenary, three times a year, that is, on any one Friday in March, on the Feasts of the Invention and Exaltation of the Holy Cross, or on any one day in the octaves of these feasts, to all who shall have practised the devotion of saying this Chaplet at least ten times each month. I, II, IV.

The Sovereign Pontiff Pius IX extended this Plenary Indulgence to the feasts of the Nativity, Circumcision and Epiphany of our LORD JESUS CHRIST, the feasts of His Most Holy Name, Easter Sunday, the Ascension, Corpus CHRISTI and the Transfiguration, or any one day in the octaves of these feasts. I, II, III, IV. iii. Seven Years and Seven Quarantines, daily, to all who shall say this Chaplet from Passion Sunday to Holy Saturday inclusive; Plenary, when they fulfil the Paschal precept.

This Chaplet consists of five sets of five beads each; and at each one of these beads, in memory of the Five Wounds of JESUS CHRIST, one Gloria Patri is to be said; and at the end of each set of five, one Ave Maria is added in honour of our Lady's sorrows.

The condition of gaining all these Indulgences is, that the Chaplets used should be blessed by the most reverend the Father-General of the Congregation of Discalced Clerics of the Passion (Passionists), or by some other priest of the Congregation to whom the General has communicated the faculty received by him; after they have been blessed, they cannot be sold or. lent, or given away to others, etc., for the purpose of communicating to them the Indulgences. (See Instructions.) 126 Leo XII, December 20, 1823; Pius IX, August 11, 1851.

127. Prayer, En Ego.
Plenary, when said before any representation of JESUS crucified. I, II, IV. (See Instructions.) 127 Pius IX, July 31, 1858.

EN EGO, O bone et dulcissime JESU, ante conspectum tuum genibus me provolvo, ac maximo animi ardore te oro atque obtestor ut meum in cor vividos fidei, spei, et charitatis sensus, atque veram peccatorum meorum pœnitentiam, eaque emendandi firmissimam voluntatem velis imprimere: dum mag-no animi affectu, et dolore tua quinque Vulnera mecum ipse considero, ac mente contemplor, illud præoculis habens, quod jam in ore ponebat tuo David propheta de te, O bone JESU: Foderunt manus meas et pedes meos; dinumeraverunt omnia ossa mea. (Ps. xxi, 17, 18.)

O GOOD and sweetest JESUS, before thy face I humbly kneel, and with the greatest fervour of spirit I pray and beseech Thee to vouchsafe to fix deep in my heart lively sentiments of faith, hope and charity, true contrition for my sins, and a most firm purpose of amendment; whilst I contemplate with great sorrow and affection thy five wounds, and ponder them over in my mind, having before my eyes the words which, long ago, David the prophet spoke in thy own person concerning Thee, my JESUS: They have pierced my hands and my feet; they have numbered all my bones. (Ps. xxi, 17,18.)

128. Prayers of St Pius V, with the Apostles Creed five times.
i. 60 Days, T.Q., provided that the faithful, while saying these prayers, known as the Five Credos of St Pius, intend to apply them according to the intention of the Pope. ii. Plenary, once a month. I, II, III, IV. (See Instructions.) 128 Pius IX, Pr. Ma. May 24, 1859.

I O MY LORD JESUS CHRIST crucified, Son of the most Blessed Virgin Mary, open thine ears, and listen to me as Thou didst listen to the Eternal FATHER on Mount Tabor. Credo,

II O MY LORD JESUS CHRIST crucified, Son of the most Blessed Virgin Mary, open thine eyes, and look upon me as Thou didst look from the tree of the Cross upon thy dear Mother sorrowing and afflicted. Credo.

III O MY LORD JESUS CHRIST crucified, Son of the most Blessed Virgin Mary, open thy blessed mouth, and speak to me as Thou didst speak to St John when Thou gavest him for son to thine own most beloved Mother. Credo.

IV O MY LORD JESUS CHRIST crucified, Son of the most Blessed Virgin Mary, open thine arms and embrace me as Thou didst open them upon the Cross to embrace the whole human race. Credo.

V O MY LORD JESUS CHRIST crucified, Son of the most Blessed Virgin Mary, open thy Heart and receive therein my heart, and hear me in all that I ask of Thee, if so be it be agreeable to thy most holy will. Credo.

129. Invocation of St Thomas Aquinas to the Cross.
300 Days, once a day. (See Instructions.) 129 Pius IX, Pr. Ma. January 21, 1874.

CRUX mihi certa salus. Crux est quam semper adoro. Crux DOMINI mecum. Crux mihi refugium.

THE Cross is my sure salvation. The Cross I ever adore. The Cross of my LORD is with me. The Cross is my refuge.

130. Prayers of St Clare of Assisi.
300 Days, once a day. (See Instructions.) 130 Leo XIII, November 21, 1885.

I. To the Wound in the Right Hand.
PRAISE be to Thee, O JESUS CHRIST, for the most sacred wound in thy Right Hand. By this adorable wound, and by thy most sacred Passion, pardon me all the sins I have committed against Thee in thought, word and deed, and all negligence in thy service, and all sensuality for which I have been to blame whether asleep or awake. Grant that I may be able to recall with devotion thy most pitiful death

and sacred wounds; grant me the grace to mortify my body, and so to offer a pledge of my gratitude to Thee, who livest and reignest world without end. Amen. PATER noster, Ave Maria.

II. To the Wound in the Left Hand.
PRAISE and glory be to Thee, O sweetest JESUS CHRIST, for the most sacred wound in thy Left Hand. By this adorable wound, have mercy on me, and deign to root out of my heart everything displeasing to Thee. Give me the victory over thy perverse enemies, so that with thy grace I may be able to overcome them; and by the merits of thy most pitiful death save me from all the dangers of my present and future life; and then, grant that I may share thy glory in heaven, who livest and reignest for ever and ever. Amen. PATER noster and Ave Maria.

III. To the Wound in the Right Foot.
PRAISE and glory be to Thee, O sweet JESUS CHRIST, for the most sacred wound in thy Right Foot; and by that adorable wound, grant me grace to do penance for my sins. And by thy most pitiful death I devoutly beg of Thee to keep me, thy poor servant, united, night and day, to thy holy will, and to remove afar off every misfortune of body and soul. And when the day of wrath shall come, receive me into thy mercy, and lead me to eternal happiness. Who livest and reignest world without end. Amen. PATER noster and Ave Maria.

IV. To the Wound in the Left Foot.
PRAISE and glory be to Thee, most merciful JESUS CHRIST, for the most sacred wound in thy Left Foot; and by this adorable wound, grant me the grace of a full pardon, that with thine aid I may deserve to escape the sentence of eternal reprobation. I pray Thee, moreover, by thy most holy death, O my loving REDEEMER, that I may be able before my death to receive the sacrament of thy Body and Blood, after confession of my sins, and with perfect repentance and purity of body and mind. Grant that I may merit also to receive the holy anointing, for my eternal salvation, O LORD, who liveth and reigneth world without end. Amen. PATER noster and Ave Maria.

V. To the Wound in the sacred Side.
PRAISE and glory be to Thee, most loving JESUS CHRIST, for the most sacred wound in thy Side, and by that adorable wound, and by thy infinite mercy, which Thou didst make known in the opening of thy Breast to the soldier Longinus, and so to us all, I pray Thee, O most gentle JESUS, that having redeemed me by baptism from original sin, so now by thy Precious Blood, which is offered and received throughout the world, deliver me from all evils, past, present and to come. And by thy most bitter death give me a lively faith, a firm hope, and a perfect charity, so that I may love Thee with all my heart, and all my soul, and all my strength; make me firm and steadfast in good works, and grant me perseverance in thy service, so that I may be able to please Thee always. Amen. PATER noster and Ave Maria.
V/. We adore Thee, O CHRIST, and we bless Thee.
R/. Because by thy death and Blood Thou hast redeemed the world.
Let us pray.
ALMIGHTY and everlasting GOD, who by the five wounds of thy SON, our LORD JESUS CHRIST, hast redeemed the human race, grant to thy suppliants that we who daily venerate those wounds may, by the shedding of his Precious Blood, be freed from sudden and everlasting death. Through the same CHRIST our LORD. Amen.

131. Hymn, Vexilla Regis.
100 Days, once a day. (See Instructions.) 131 Leo XIII, January 16, 1886.

VEXILLA Regis prodeunt:	FORTH comes the Standard of the King:
Fulget crucis mysterium,	All hail, thou Mystery ador'd!
Qua vita mortem pertulit,	Hail, Cross! on which the Life himself Died,
Et morte vitam protulit.	and by death our life restor'd.
Quæ vulnerata lanceæ	On which our SAVIOUR'S holy side,
Mucrone diro, criminum	Rent open with a cruel spear,
Ut nos lavaret sordibus,	Of blood and water pour'd a stream,
Manavit unda et sanguine.	To wash us from defilement clear.
Impleta sunt, quæ concinit	O sacred Wood! in thee Fulfill'd

David fideli carmine,	Was holy David's truthful lay!
Dicendo nationibus:	Which told the world, that from a Tree,
Regnavit a ligno DEUS.	The LORD should all the nations sway.
Arbor decora et fulgida,	Most royally empurpled o'er,
Ornata regis purpura,	How beautiful thy stem doth shine,
Electa digno stipite	How glorious was its lot to touch
Tam sancta membra tangere.	Those limbs so holy and divine!
Beata, cujus brachiis	Thrice blest, upon whose arms outstretched
Pretium pependit saeculi,	The SAVIOUR of the world reclined;
Statera facia corporis,	Balance sublime! upon whose beam
Tulitque praedam tartari.	Was weigh'd the ransom of mankind.
O Crux, ave spes unica,	Hail, Cross! thou only hope of man,
Gentis redemptæ gloria!	Sign of redemption's glorious day,
Piis adauge gratiam,	To saints increase the grace they have!
Reisque dele crimina.	From sinners purge their guilt away.
Te, fons salutis Trinitas,	Salvation's spring, blest Trinity,
Collaudet omnis spiritus:	Be praise to Thee
Quibus crucis victoriam	through earth and skies: Thou through the Cross the victory
Largiris, adde præmium. Amen.	Dost give; oh, also give the prize. Amen.

In Passiontide:
Hoc Passionis tempore
Hail, on this holy Passion day.
In Paschal Time:
Paschalequæfers gaudium,
That bearest Paschal joy this day.
On the Exaltation of Cross (September 14):
In hac triumphi gloria
Amid the triumph of this day.

132. Prayer to Our Lord scourged at the Pillar.
100 Days, once a day. (See Instructions.) 132 Leo XIII, Card. Vic. May 15, 1886.

MY divine SAVIOUR, what didst Thou become, when for love of souls Thou didst allow thyself to be bound to the column? Oh, how literally was then fulfilled the word of the prophet, that from head to foot Thou shouldst be all one wound, and such as not to be recognized for what Thou wast. What shame when they stripped Thee of thy clothes! What torment under the tempest of blows, multiplied without measure! What a profusion of blood from thy streaming- wounds! But it was neither the injustice of the Roman governor nor the cruelty of the soldiers that scourged Thee, but my sins. O miserable pleasures which have cost Thee such pains! O hardness of heart, when, knowing Thee to be tormented for my sake, I have gone on offending Thee!

From today, then, it shall be so no more. Bound to Thee with eternal bonds and fastened with Thee to the column, as long as my life endures, I will make satisfaction to thy offended justice. By the column to which Thou wast bound, by the scourges which furrowed thy innocent flesh, by the blood Thou didst shed in such abundance, have pity, O LORD, have pity, on me in my desolation. Release me this day from the snares of the tempter and preserve me from them for ever; and at the end of this exile, receive me in heaven. Amen.

133. Ejaculation.
100 Days, once a day. (See Instructions.) 133 Leo XIII, March 4, 1882.

ADORAMUS te, sanctissime DOMINE JESU CHRISTE, benedicimus tibi; quia per sanctam crucem tuam redemisti mundum.	WE adore Thee, most holy LORD JESUS CHRIST, we bless Thee; because by thy holy Cross Thou hast redeemed the world.

134. Invocation.
100 Days, once a day. (See Instructions.) 134 Leo XIII, May 21, 1892.

ECCE Crucem DOMINI fugite partes adversæ, vicit Leo de tribu Juda, radix David, Alleluia.

BEHOLD the Cross of the LORD, flee ye adversaries, the Lion of the tribe of Juda has conquered, the root of David. Alleluia.

135. Prayer to Our Lord on the Cross.
i. 300 Days, once a Day. ii. Plenary, twice a year. I, II. (See Instructions.) 135 Pius X, September 4, 1903.

JESU mi crucifixe, suscipe benignus precem quam nunc pro meæ mortis articulo tibi fundo, quando ilia jam appetente, omnes mei sensus deficient. Cum igitur, dulcissime JESU, mei oculi languidi et demissi te non amplius respicere poterunt, memento illius succensi aspectus, quem nunc tibi converto, et miserere mei. Cum labia mea arefacta non amplius tuas sacratissimas plagas osculari poterunt, memento illorum osculorum, quæ nunc tibi figo, et miserere mei. Cum manus meae frigidæ non amplius tuam crucem amplecti poterunt, memento sensus, quo nunc hoc ago, et miserere mei. Et cum tandem mea lingua tumens et immobilis non amplius loqui poterit, memento meæ invocationis hujus momenti. JESU, Joseph, Maria, vobis commendo animam meam.

MY crucified JESUS, mercifully accept the prayer which I now make to Thee for help in the moment of my death, when at its approach all my senses shall fail me. When therefore, O sweetest JESUS, my weary and downcast eyes can no longer look up to Thee, be mindful of the loving gaze which now I turn on Thee, and have mercy on me. When my parched lips can no longer kiss thy most sacred wounds, remember then those kisses which now I imprint on thee, and have mercy on me. When my cold hands can no longer embrace thy Cross, forget not the affection with which I embrace it now, and have mercy on me. And when, at length, my swollen and lifeless tongue can no longer speak, remember that I called upon Thee now. JESU, Joseph, Mary, to you I commend my soul.

136. Prayer to Jesus Dead.
300 Days, T.Q (See Instructions.) 136 Pius X, February 16, 1906.

O JESUS, who in thy bitter Passion didst become the reproach of men and the man of sorrows, I venerate thy sacred face on which shone the grace and sweetness of the Divinity, now for my sake changed into the likeness of a leper. But under this deformity I perceive thy infinite love, and I am overwhelmed with the desire of loving Thee and making Thee beloved by all men. The tears which stream from thy eyes seem as precious pearls, which I love to gather up, in order to purchase with their infinite value the souls of poor sinners. O JESUS, thy face is the only beauty which ravishes my heart. I am content not to see here below the sweetness of thy look, not to feel the ineffable delight of a kiss of thy mouth; but oh! I beseech Thee print on me thy divine likeness, and inflame me with thy love, so that it may rapidly consume me, and I may soon come to see thy glorious face in Heaven. Amen.

137. Prayer for a Happy Death.
100 Days, once a day. (See Instructions.) 137 Leo XIII, July 16, 1902.

O JESUS, while adoring thy last breath, I pray Thee to receive mine. In the uncertainty whether I shall have the command of my senses, when I shall depart out of this world, I offer Thee from this moment my agony and all the pains of my passing away. Thou art my FATHER and my SAVIOUR, and I give back my soul into thy hands. I desire that my last moment may be united to the moment of thy death, and that the last beat of my heart may be an act of pure love of Thee. Amen.

VIII. THE PRECIOUS BLOOD
138. Chaplet of the Precious Blood.
i. Seven Years and Seven Quarantines, once a day ii. Plenary, once a month, I, II, IV. (See Instructions.) 138 Pius VII, Res. October 18, 1815 ; Gregory XVI, July 5, 1843.

This Chaplet consists of seven Mysteries, in which we meditate upon the seven times in which JESUS CHRIST shed his Blood for us; at each Mystery except the last we say Pater noster five times, and Gloria Patri once; and at the last, Pater noster thrice, and Gloria Patri once ; thus making up the number of 33, by saying the Pater noster thirty-three times in remembrance of the thirty-three years of our LORD'S life. End with the prayer, "Most Precious Blood," etc.

N.B. These Indulgences can be gained by merely saying thirty-three Pater Nosters and, if the person is capable of meditating, reflecting on the Mysteries.

THE CHAPLET

V/. DEUS, in adjutorium meum intende.	V/. O GOD, come to my assistance.
R/. DOMINE, ad adjuvandum me festina.	R/. O LORD make haste to help me.
V/. Gloria PATRI, etc.	V/. Glory be to the FATHER, etc.
R/. Sicut erat, etc.	R/. As it was in the beginning, etc.

FIRST MYSTERY.

THE first time our loving SAVIOUR shed his Precious Blood for us was on the eighth day after his birth, when he was circumcised in order to fulfil the law of Moses. While, then, we reflect that JESUS did this to satisfy the justice of GOD for our lax ways, let us rouse ourselves to sorrow for them, and promise, with the help of his all-powerful grace, to be henceforth truly chaste in body and in soul. *PATER noster five times, and Gloria PATRI once.*

V/. Te ergo quæsumus tuis famulis subveni quos pretioso Sanguine redemisti.

V/. We beseech Thee, therefore, help thy servants, whom Thou hast redeemed with thy Precious Blood.

SECOND MYSTERY.

NEXT, in the Garden of Olives, JESUS shed his Blood for us in such quantity that it bathed the earth around. He did this at the sight of the ingratitude with which men would meet his love. Let us, then, repent sincerely that we have hitherto corresponded so ill with the countless blessings of GOD, and resolve to make good use of his graces and inspirations. *PATER noster five times, and Gloria PATRI once.*

V/. Te ergo quæsumus tuis famulis subveni quos pretioso Sanguine redemisti.

V/. We beseech Thee, therefore, help thy servants, whom Thou hast redeemed with thy Precious Blood.

THIRD MYSTERY.

NEXT, in his cruel scourging, JESUS shed his Blood when his flesh was so torn that streams of Blood flowed from every part of his body, all of which he offered all the time to his Eternal FATHER in payment of our impatience and our softness. How comes it, then, that we do not curb our anger and love of self? Henceforth we will try our best to bear our troubles well, and, despising self, take peacefully the injuries which men may do us. *PATER noster five times, and Gloria PATRI once.*

V/. Te ergo quæsumus tuis famulis subveni quos pretioso Sanguine redemisti.

V/. We beseech Thee, therefore, help thy servants, whom Thou hast redeemed with thy Precious Blood.

FOURTH MYSTERY.

AGAIN, from the sacred Head of JESUS, Blood poured down when it was crowned with thorns, in punishment of our pride and evil thoughts. Shall we, then, continue to nurture haughtiness, foster foul imaginations, and feed the wayward will within us? Henceforth let there be ever before our eyes our utter nothingness, our misery, and our weakness; and with generous hearts let us resist all the temptations of the devil. *PATER noster five times, and Gloria PATRI once.*

V/. Te ergo quæsumus tuis famulis subveni quos pretioso Sanguine redemisti.

V/. We beseech Thee, therefore, help thy servants, whom Thou hast redeemed with thy Precious Blood.

FIFTH MYSTERY.

WHAT streams of Precious Blood did not our loving LORD pour forth from his veins when laden with the heavy Cross on that most grievous journey to Calvary! The very streets and ways of Jerusalem, through which He passed, were watered with it! This He did in satisfaction for the scandals and bad example by which his own creatures had led others astray. Who can tell how many of us are of this unhappy number? Who knows how many he himself alone has, by his own bad example, brought down to hell? And what have we done to remedy this evil? Henceforth let us at least do all we can to save souls by word and by example, making ourselves a pattern to all of goodness and a holy life. *PATER noster five times, and Gloria PATRI once.*

V/. Te ergo quæsumus tuis famulis subveni quos pretioso Sanguine redemisti.

V/. We beseech Thee, therefore, help thy servants, whom Thou hast redeemed with thy Precious Blood.

SIXTH MYSTERY.

MORE, and still more Precious Blood did the REDEEMER of mankind shed in his barbarous Crucifixion; when, his veins being rent and arteries burst, there rushed forth in a torrent, from his hands and his feet, that saving balm of life eternal, to pay for all the crimes and enormities of a lost world. Who, after this, would continue in sin, and so renew the cruel crucifixion of the SON of GOD? Let us weep bitterly for our bad deeds done, and detest them before the feet of the sacred minister of GOD; let us amend our evil ways, and henceforth begin a truly Christian life, with the remembrance ever in our hearts of all the Blood which our salvation cost the SAVIOUR of men. *PATER noster five times, and Gloria PATRI once.*

V/. Te ergo quæsumus tuis famulis subveni quos pretioso Sanguine redemisti.

V/. We beseech Thee, therefore, help thy servants, whom Thou hast redeemed with thy Precious Blood.

SEVENTH MYSTERY.

LAST of all, after his death, when his sacred Side was opened by the lance, and his loving Heart was wounded, JESUS shed Blood, and with it there came forth water, to show us how his Blood was all poured out to the last drop for our salvation. Oh, the great goodness of our redeeming LORD! Who will not love Thee, SAVIOUR of my soul? What heart will not consume itself away for love of Thee, who hast done all this for our redemption? The tongue wants words to praise Thee; so let us invite all creatures upon earth, all angels and all saints in Paradise, and most of all our dear Mother Mary, to bless, praise, and celebrate thy most Precious Blood. Glory to the Blood of JESUS! Now and ever throughout all ages. Amen. *PATER noster thrice, and Gloria PATRI once.*

V/. Te ergo quæsumus tuis famulis subveni quos pretioso Sanguine redemisti.

V/. We beseech Thee, therefore, help thy servants, whom Thou hast redeemed with thy Precious Blood.

Prayer.

MOST Precious Blood of life eternal! price and ransom of the world! drink and bath of the soul! ever pleading the cause of man before the throne of Mercy; I adore Thee most profoundly; I would, if I were able, make Thee some compensation for the outrages and wrongs Thou dost ever suffer from men, and especially from those who dare in their rashness to blaspheme Thee. Who will not bless this Blood of value infinite? who does not feel himself on fire with the love of JESUS, who shed it all for us? What should I be but for this Blood, which hath redeemed me? And what drew Thee, Thou Precious Blood, from the veins of my LORD, even to the last drop? It was love. O boundless love, which gave to us this saving balsam! O balsam beyond all price, streaming forth from the fount of immeasurable love! Give to all hearts, all tongues, power to praise, celebrate, and thank Thee, now and ever, and throughout all eternity. Amen.

V/. Redemisti nos, DOMINE, in Sanguine tuo:
R/. Et fecisti nos DEO nostro regnum.

V/. Thou hast redeemed us, O LORD, with thy Blood,
R/. And hast made us a kingdom to our GOD.

Oremus.

OMNIPOTENS sempiterne DEUS, qui unigenitum FILIUM tuum mundi REDEMPTOREM constituisti, ac ejus Sanguine placari voluisti; concede nobis, quæsumus, salutis nostræ pretium ita venerari, atque a præsentis vitæ malis ejus virtute defendi in terris, ut fructu perpetuo lætemur in cœlis. Qui tecum vivit et regnat, etc. Amen.

Let us pray.

ALMIGHTY and everlasting GOD, who hast appointed thine only-begotten SON the SAVIOUR of the world, and hast willed to be appeased by his Blood; grant us, we beseech Thee, so to venerate this Blood, the price of our salvation, and so to be defended on earth by its power from the evils of this present life, that in heaven we may be made glad by its everlasting fruit. Who liveth and reigneth, etc. Amen.

139. Prayer.

300 Days, once a day. (See Instructions.) 139 Pius VII, Res. October 18, 1815.
Most Precious Blood, etc. (See previous)

140. Devout Aspirations.

100 Days, once a day. (See Instructions.) 140 Pius VII, Res. October 18, 1815.

GLORY be to JESUS!
Who in bitter pains
Pour'd for me the life-blood
From his sacred veins.
Grace and life eternal
In that Blood I find;
Bless'd be his compassion,
Infinitely kind!
Bless'd through endless ages
Be the precious stream,
Which from endless torment
Doth the world redeem.
There the fainting spirit
Drinks of life her fill;
There, as in a fountain,
Laves herself at will.
Oh, the Blood of CHRIST!
It soothes the FATHER'S ire,
Opes the gate of heaven,
Quells eternal fire.
Abel's blood for vengeance
Pleaded to the skies,
But the Blood of JESUS
For our pardon cries.
Oft as it is sprinkled
On our guilty hearts,
Satan in confusion
Terror-struck departs.
Oft as earth exulting
Wafts its praise on high,
Hell with terror trembles,
Heaven is filled with joy.
Lift ye, then, your voices;
Swell the mighty flood;
Louder still and louder,
Praise the Precious Blood!

141. Seven Offerings, in reparation for all the outrages received by Our Lord in the Precious Blood.

i. 300 Days. T.Q. ii. Plenary, once a month. I, II, IV. (See Instructions.) 141 Pius VII, Res. September 22, 1817.

I

ETERNAL FATHER! I offer Thee the merits of the Precious Blood of JESUS, thy well-beloved SON, my SAVIOUR and my GOD, for the propagation and exaltation of my dear Mother, thy Holy Church; for the safety and prosperity of her visible head, our chief pastor the Bishop of Rome; for the cardinals, bishops, and pastors of souls, and for all the ministers of the sanctuary. Gloria PATRI. Blessed and praised for evermore be JESUS, who hath saved us with his Blood,

II

ETERNAL FATHER! I offer Thee the merits of the Precious Blood of JESUS, thy well-beloved SON, my SAVIOUR and my GOD, for the peace and concord of Catholic kings and princes, for the humiliation of the enemies of our holy Faith, and for the welfare of all Christian people. Gloria PATRI. Blessed and praised, etc.

III

ETERNAL FATHER! I offer Thee the merits of the Precious Blood of JESUS, thy well-beloved SON, my SAVIOUR and my GOD, for the repentance of unbelievers, the uprooting of heresy, and the conversion of sinners. Gloria PATRI. Blessed and praised, etc.

IV

ETERNAL FATHER! I offer Thee the merits of the Precious Blood of JESUS, thy well-beloved SON, my SAVIOUR and my GOD, for all my relations, friends, and enemies; for the poor, the sick, and the afflicted, and for all those for whom Thou, my GOD, knowest that I ought to pray, or wouldst have me pray. Gloria PATRI. Blessed and praised, etc.

V

ETERNAL FATHER! I offer Thee the merits of the precious Blood of JESUS, thy well-beloved SON, my SAVIOUR and my GOD, for all who this day are passing to the other life; that thou wouldst save them from the pains of hell, and admit them quickly to the possession of thy glory. Gloria PATRI. Blessed and praised, etc.

VI

ETERNAL FATHER! I offer Thee the merits of the Precious Blood of JESUS, thy well-beloved SON, my SAVIOUR and my GOD, for all those who love this great treasure, for those who join with me in adoring-it and honouring it, and for those who strive to spread devotion to it. Gloria PATRI. Blessed and praised, etc.

VII

ETERNAL FATHER! I offer Thee the merits of the Precious Blood of JESUS, thy well-beloved SON, my SAVIOUR and my GOD, for all my wants, spiritual and temporal ; in suffrage for the holy souls in purgatory, and chiefly for those who were most devout lovers of this Blood, the price of our redemption, and of the sorrows and pains of our dear Mother, most holy Mary. Gloria PATRI. Blessed and praised, etc.

Glory be to the Blood of JESUS, now and for ever, and throughout all ages! Amen.

142. Act of Oblation in thanksgiving for blessings received.

i. 100 Days. T.Q. ii. Plenary, once a month. I, II, IV. (See Instructions.) 142 Leo XII, Res. October 25, 1823.

ETERNAL FATHER! we offer Thee the most Precious Blood of JESUS, shed for us with such great love and bitter pain from his Right Hand; and through the merits and the efficacy of that Blood, we entreat Thy Divine Majesty to grant us thy holy benediction, in order that we may be defended thereby from all our enemies, and be set free from every ill; whilst we say, May the blessing of Almighty GOD, FATHER, SON and HOLY SPIRIT descend upon us and remain with us for ever. Amen. PATER, Ave and Gloria.

143. Month consecrated to the Precious Blood

(which may begin on any day of the year).

i. Seven Years and Seven Quarantines daily to all who assist at the public devotions. ii. Plenary, to all who shall assist at public devotions at least ten times in the month; this they may gain in the course of the said month, or on one of the eight days immediately following it. I, II, III, IV. iii. 300 Days, daily, to those who shall practise this devotion in private, with devout prayers and acts in honour of the Precious Blood. iv. Plenary, to those who shall practise it in private for a month together; to be gained on the last day of the month, or one of the next eight days. I, II, III, IV (See Instructions.) 143 Plus IX, June 4, 1850.

144. Prayer to Jesus of Nazareth.

200 Days, once a day. (See Instructions.) 144 Leo XIII, June 26, 1894.

BEHOLD me at thy feet, O JESUS of Nazareth; behold the most miserable of creatures, who presents himself before Thee, humbled and penitent. Have mercy on me, O LORD, according- to thy great mercy. I sinned, and my sins were committed against Thee, O GOD of infinite bounty. O JESUS, hear my prayers, graciously hear, O loving FATHER, the requests I lay at thy feet: cast a favourable look on my soul, Thou who art the loving FATHER of men, the Supreme Judge, the King of Heaven and of earth, the true benefactor of the wretched. Come then to my assistance, O JESUS of Nazareth. Grant me the graces which I ask of Thee, kneeling at thy feet. My soul belongs to Thee, because Thou hast created and redeemed it with thy Precious Blood. May thy work not be in vain. Turn, O loving FATHER, thy regard upon me and bless me. O GOD of mercy, have pity on me; pardon me, who am thy son; deal not severely with me; give me tears of repentance; pardon me as Thou didst pardon the penitent thief; watch over me from the height of Heaven and bless me. Amen. End with the Apostles Creed.

145. Ejaculation.
i. 300 Days. T.Q. ii. Plenary, once a month. I, II, IV (See Instructions.) 145 Pius X, January 27, 1908.
To be said in reparation for blasphemies.
ETERNAL FATHER, by the most Precious Blood of JESUS CHRIST, glorify his most holy Name, according to the intention and the desires of his adorable Heart.

146. Offering.
100 Days. T.Q. (See Instructions.) 146 Pius VII, Res. September 22, 1817.
ETERNAL FATHER! I offer Thee the Precious Blood of JESUS CHRIST in satisfaction for my sins, and for the wants of Holy Church.

IX. THE SACRED HEART
147. Visit to a Representation of the Sacred Heart, exposed for public veneration.
Seven Years and Seven Quarantines. IV. (See Instructions.) 147 Pius VI, Res. January 2, 1709.

148. Act of Oblation to be made before a Representation of the Sacred Heart.
i. 100 Days, once a day. ii. Plenary, once a month. I, II, IV. (See Instructions.) 148 Pius VII, Mem. June 9, 1807.
MY loving JESUS, out of the grateful love I bear Thee, and to make reparation for my unfaithfulness to grace, I (N.N.) give Thee my heart, and I consecrate myself wholly to Thee; and with thy help I purpose never to sin

149. Acts of Devotion.
i. 300 Days, once a day. ii. Plenary, once a month. I, II, IV. (See Instructions.) 149 Pius VII, Res. February 12, 1808; Pius IX, June 18, 1876.

I. The Word was made Flesh and dwelt amongst us.
ETERNAL Word, made Man for love of us, humbly kneeling at thy feet we adore Thee with the deepest veneration of our souls; and in order that we may repair our ingratitude for this great benefit of thy Incarnation, we unite ourselves to the hearts of all those who love Thee, and together with them we offer Thee our humble loving thanksgiving-. Pierced by the excess of humility, goodness, and sweetness which we behold in thy Divine Heart, we beseech Thee to give us thy grace, that in our lives we too may imitate these virtues so dear to Thee. PATER, Ave, and Gloria.

II. He was crucified also for us; suffered under Pontius Pilate and was buried.
JESUS our loving SAVIOUR, humbly kneeling at thy feet we adore Thee with the deepest veneration of our souls; and, in order that we may give Thee proof of the sorrow w r e feel at our insensibility to the outrages and sufferings which thy loving Heart made Thee undergo for our salvation in thy painful Passion and Death, we here unite ourselves with the hearts of all those who love Thee, and together with them we give thanks unto Thee with our whole soul. We wonder at the boundless patience and generosity of thy divine Heart; and we entreat Thee to fill our hearts with such a spirit of Christian penance as may enable us courageously to embrace suffering, and to make thy Cross our great comfort and all our glory. PATER, Ave, Gloria.

III. Thou didst give them bread from heaven to eat, containing in itself all sweetness.
JESUS, who dost burn with love for us, humbly kneeling at thy feet we adore Thee with the deepest veneration of our souls; and, in order to make Thee reparation for the outrages which thy divine Heart daily receives in the most holy Sacrament of the Altar, we unite ourselves with the hearts of all those who love Thee, and give Thee tenderest thanks. We love in thy divine Heart this thy incomprehensible fire of love towards thy Eternal FATHER, and we entreat Thee to inflame our hearts with ardent charity towards Thee and towards our neighbour. PATER, Ave, and Gloria.
LASTLY, O most loving JESU, we pray Thee, by the sweetness of thy Divine Heart, convert the sinner, console the afflicted, help the dying, lighten the pains of the souls in purgatory. Make all our hearts one

in the bonds of true peace and charity, deliver us from sudden and unforeseen death, and grant us a death holy and peaceful. Amen.

V/. Heart of JESUS, burning- with love of us,
R/. Inflame our hearts with love of Thee.
Let us pray.
GRANT, we beseech Thee, Almighty GOD, that we who glory in the most Sacred Heart of thy well-beloved SON, and call to mind the chief benefits of his heavenly charity towards us, may be gladdened by the operation and the fruit of those graces in our souls. Through the same CHRIST, etc.

O Divine Heart of my JESUS! I adore Thee with all the powers of my soul; I consecrate them to Thee for ever, together with all my thoughts, my words, my works, and my whole self. I purpose to offer to Thee, as far as I am able, acts of adoration, love, and glory, like unto those which Thou dost offer to thine Eternal FATHER. I beseech Thee, be Thou the reparation for my transgressions, the protector of my life, my refuge and asylum in the hour of my death. By thy sighs, and by that sea of bitterness in which Thou wast immersed for me throughout the whole course of thy mortal life, grant me true contrition for my sins, contempt of earthly things, an ardent longing for the glory of heaven, trust in thy infinite merits, and final perseverance in thy grace.

Heart of JESUS, all love! I offer Thee these humble prayers for myself, and for all who unite with me in spirit to adore Thee; vouchsafe, of thy infinite goodness, to receive and to answer them, and especially for that one of us who shall first end this mortal life. Sweet Heart of my SAVIOUR, pour down upon him, in the agony of death, thine inward consolations; place him in thy sacred wounds; cleanse him from every stain in that furnace of love, that so Thou mayest open to him speedily the entrance into thy glory, there to intercede with Thee for all those who yet tarry in their land of exile.

Most Holy Heart of my most loving JESUS, I purpose to renew these acts of adoration and these prayers for myself, miserable sinner that I am, as well as for all who are associated with me to adore Thee, every moment while I live, down to the last instant of my life. I recommend to Thee, my JESUS, the Holy Church, thy well-beloved Spouse, our own true Mother, the souls that undergo thy justice, all poor sinners, those who are in affliction, the dying, and all mankind let not thy Blood be shed in vain for them; and, last of all, vouchsafe to receive my poor prayers for the relief of the souls in purgatory, and, above all, for those who in the course of their life were wont devoutly to adore Thee.

Most loving heart of Mary, which, amongst the hearts of all creatures of GOD, art at once the most pure, most inflamed with love for Jesus, and most compassionate towards us poor sinners, gain for us from the Heart of JESUS our REDEEMER all the graces which we ask of thee. Mother of mercies, one single throb, one beat of thy heart, all on fire with love towards the Heart of JESUS, has power to console us to the full. Only grant us this favour and the Heart of JESUS, out of that filial love It had and will ever have for thee, will not fail to hear and answer us. Amen.

150. Chaplet.
i. 300 Days.T.Q. ii. Plenary, once a month. I, II, IV. (See Instructions.) 150 Pius VII, March 20, 1815.
V/. O GOD, come to my assistance.
R/. O LORD, make haste to help me.
V/. Glory be, etc.
R/. As it was, etc.

I

MY most loving JESUS, when I ponder over thy most Sacred Heart, all tenderness and sweetness for sinners, then doth my heart rejoice, and I am filled with hope of thy kind welcome. But, ah me, my sins! how many and how great! With Peter and with Magdalen, I bewail and abhor them, because they are an offence to Thee, my Sovereign Good. Oh, grant pardon for them all. I pray thy Sacred Heart that I may rather die than offend Thee again, and may live only to love Thee. *PATER once, Gloria five times, in honour of the Sacred Heart, then :*

Sweet Heart of my JESUS,
Make me love Thee ever more and more,

II

MY JESUS, I bless thy most humble Heart; and I give thanks unto Thee, who in making It my model dost urge me with strong pleadings to imitate It, and also, at the cost of so many humiliations, dost vouchsafe thyself to point out and smooth for me the way to follow Thee. Fool and ungrateful that I am, how have I wandered far away from Thee! Pardon me, my JESUS! Take away from me all hateful pride and ambition, that with lowly heart I may follow Thee, my JESUS, amidst humiliations, and so gain peace and salvation. Strengthen me, Thou who canst, and I will ever bless thy Sacred Heart. *PATER once, Gloria five times, in honour of the Sacred Heart, then* :

Sweet Heart of my JESUS,
Make me love Thee ever more and more,

III

MY JESUS, I marvel at thy most patient Heart, and I give Thee thanks for all the wondrous examples of unwearied patience which Thou hast left us. It grieves me that these examples still have to reproach me for my excessive delicacy, shrinking from every little pain. Pour, then, into my heart, O dear JESUS, a fervent and constant love of suffering- and the cross, of mortification and of penance, that, following Thee to Calvary, I may with Thee attain the joys of Paradise. *PATER once, Gloria five times, in honour of the Sacred Heart, then:*

Sweet Heart of my JESUS,
Make me love Thee ever more and more,

IV

DEAR JESUS, beside thy most gentle Heart I set my own, and shudder to see how unlike mine is to thine. How am I wont to fret and grieve when a hint, a look, or a word thwarts me! Pardon all my violence and give me for the future grace to imitate in every contradiction thy unalterable meekness, that so I may enjoy an everlasting holy peace. *PATER once, Gloria five times, in honour of the Sacred Heart, then:*

Sweet Heart of my JESUS,
Make me love Thee ever more and more,

V

LET us sing praise to JESUS for his generous Heart, Conqueror of death and hell; for well It merits every praise. Still more than ever confounded am I, looking upon my coward heart, which dreads even a rough word or injurious taunt. But it shall be so with me no more. My JESUS, I pray Thee for such strength that, fighting and conquering self on earth, I may one day rejoice triumphantly with Thee in heaven. *PATER once, Gloria five times, in honour of the Sacred Heart, then:*

Sweet Heart of my JESUS,
Make me love Thee ever more and more,

NOW let us turn to Mary, and dedicating ourselves yet more and more to her, and trusting in her Mother s heart, we say to her: By all the virtue of thy most sweet heart obtain for me, great Mother of GOD, our Mother Mary, a true and enduring devotion to the Sacred Heart of JESUS, thy Son, that, bound up in every thought and affection in union with his Heart, I may fulfil each duty of my state, serving JESUS ever more with readiness of heart, and specially this day.

V/. Heart of JESUS, burning with love or us,
R/.. Inflame our hearts with love of Thee.
Let us pray.
LORD, we beseech Thee, let thy HOLY SPIRIT kindle in our hearts that fire of charity which our LORD JESUS CHRIST, thy SON, sent forth from his inmost Heart upon this earth, and willed that it should burn exceedingly. Who liveth and reigneth with Thee, in the unity of the same HOLY SPIRIT, GOD for ever and ever. Amen.

151. Visit to any Church or Public Oratory where the Feast of the Sacred Heart is being kept.
Plenary. I, II, IV. (See Instructions.) 151 Pius VII, Mem. July 7, 1815; Leo XIII, Rit. June 28, 1889.
The Indulgences granted for Corpus CHRISTI, in the case of the divine offices celebrated during solemn Exposition (see 82), may be gained on the Feast of the Sacred Heart, even if transferred. The Feast may be transferred with leave of the Ordinary.

152. Novena of the Sacred Heart.
i. 300 Days, each day. ii. Plenary, during the Novena or Octave. I, II, IV. (See Instructions.) 152 Pius IX, Res. January 5, 1849; November 26, 1876.

This Novena may be made for the Feast or the Sacred Heart, and once during the year as well, with any form of prayers approved by competent ecclesiastical authority.

153. Prayer for those in their agony.
i. 100 Days. T.Q. ii. Plenary, once a month, if said thrice daily, at three distinct intervals. I, II, III, IV. (See Instructions.) 153 Pi us IX, February 2, 1850.

O CLEMENTISSIME JESU, amator animarum; obsecro te, per agoniam cordis tui sanctissimi,et per Dolores Matris tuæ Immaculatæ, lava in sanguine tuo peccatores totius mundi, nunc positos in agonia et hodie morituros. Amen
Cor JESU, in agonia factum, miserere morientium.

O MOST merciful JESUS, Lover of souls: I pray Thee, by the agony of thy most Sacred Heart, and by the sorrows of thy Immaculate Mother, cleanse in thine own Blood the sinners of the whole world who are now in their agony and to die this day. Amen. Heart of JESUS, once in agony, pity the dying.

154. Month of June.
i. Seven Years and Seven Quarantines, each day. ii. Plenary, during 1 the month or first eight days of July. I, II, III, IV.
For i and ii any form of devotion, public or private, may be used. If it be in public, ten attendances suffice for the plenary Indulgence. If in private, the devotion must be practised daily throughout the month.
iii. Plenary, T.Q., on June 30, every time a visit is made to a church where the Month of the Sacred Heart has been solemnly observed. I, II, IV.
iv. 500 Days, to promoters of this devotion whenever they do any good work calculated to propagate or make better observed this Month of the Sacred Heart.
v. Plenary, to the same persons for every communion made in June. The privilege of the Gregorian altar is conferred on the preacher of the month and the Rector of the church where the month has been duly observed, available for their Masses on June 30. (See Instructions.) 154 Leo XIII, May 30, 1902; Pius X, January 26, 1908
N.B. The solemn observance of June contemplated in III, IV, and V implies discourses, either daily, or at least for eight days, after the manner of spiritual exercises. The Month may be concluded on the last Sunday of the month. It may be observed in the semi-public chapels or seminaries, communities, etc. It may be transferred to another month by leave of the bishop.

155. Acts of Homage to the Eucharistic Heart of Jesus.
200 Days, for each of the four Acts. T.Q. (See Instructions.) 155 Leo XIII, Br. February 6, 1890.
N.B. This Devotion does not substantially differ from the ordinary Devotion to the Sacred Heart. It merely emphasizes the Act of Supreme love of that Heart in bestowing the gift of the Holy Eucharist upon us.
I. Prayer.
HEART of JESUS in the Eucharist, sweet companion in our exile, I adore Thee.
Eucharistic Heart of JESUS,
Heart solitary, Heart humiliated,
Heart abandoned, Heart forgotten,
Heart despised, Heart outraged,
Heart ignored by men,
Heart, lover of our hearts,
Heart desirous of being loved,
Heart patient in waiting for us,
Heart eager to hear us,
Heart longing to be prayed to,
Heart source of new graces,
Heart wrapped in silence, desiring to speak to souls,
Heart, the sweet refuge of the hidden life,
Heart, teacher of the secrets of union with GOD,
Heart of him who sleeps, yet ever watches,
Eucharistic Heart of JESUS, have pity on us.
JESUS victim, I desire to console Thee.

I unite myself to Thee, and sacrifice myself with Thee
I annihilate myself in thy presence.
I would forget myself to be mindful of Thee.
I would be forgotten and despised for love of Thee.
And be neither understood nor loved, unless by Thee.
I will silence myself to listen to Thee,
I will abandon myself to lose myself in Thee.
Grant that I may thus appease thy thirst, the thirst for my sanctification and salvation, and that being purified I may bestow on Thee a pure and true love.
I would not longer weary thy patience; take possession of me, I give myself to Thee.
I offer Thee all my actions, my intellect to be illuminated by Thee, my heart to be guided by Thee, my will to be made strong, my soul and body to be nourished, my misery to be lightened.
Eucharistic Heart of my JESUS, whose blood is the life of my soul, may it be no longer I that live, but do thou alone live in me. Amen.

II. Act of Consecration.
JESUS, adorable LORD, hidden in thy Sacrament of love, Thou who abidest with us to sweeten our exile, should I not occupy myself in consoling Thee in thine? To Thee who givest me thy heart, how should I not offer Thee mine? Truly, to give myself to Thee is to benefit myself; it is to find an ineffable treasure, a heart, loving, disinterested, and faithful, such as I would wish my own to be. I cannot be for ever receiving, and giving nothing in return. Dear LORD, I could never vie with Thee in generosity, but I love Thee; deign to accept my poor heart, and though it is worthless, yet because Thou lovest it, it may become something by thy grace; make it good and take it into thy custody.
Eucharistic Heart of JESUS, I consecrate to Thee all the powers of my soul, and all the powers of my body; I desire to apply myself to the work of knowing Thee and loving Thee ever more and more, in order to make Thee better known and loved by others. I would do nothing except what tends to thy glory, nor a& in anything but as thy divine FATHER wills. I consecrate to Thee all the moments of my life in a spirit of adoration before thy real presence, in a spirit of thanksgiving for this incomparable gift, of reparation for our cruel indifference, and of incessant supplication, so that our prayers offered to Thee, with Thee, and in Thee may rise to the throne of divine mercy pure and efficacious, and for GOD'S eternal glory. Amen.

III. Ejaculation.
EUCHARISTIC Heart of JESUS, on fire with love of us, inflame our hearts with love of Thee.

IV. Act of Reparation.
EUCHARISTIC Heart of my GOD, living and beating under the veil of the sacred species, I adore Thee. Moved afresh with love for the immense benefit of the divine Eucharist, penetrated with sorrow for my ingratitude, I humble and annihilate myself in the still greater abyss of thy mercies.
Thou didst choose me from childhood; Thou didst not despise my infirmity; Thou didst descend into my poor heart, and giving it happiness and peace, didst invite it to mutual love; and I have lost all, by being unfaithful to Thee, O JESUS, my LORD. I have allowed my spirit to become dissipated and my heart to grow cold; I have listened to my own voice and have forgotten Thee. Thou wouldst have been my guide, my counsellor, protector of my life, and I, allowing my passions to destroy the sweet attraction of thy presence, have lost sight of Thee and forgotten Thee.
In the salutary trials of our probation, in times of joy and consolation, in my difficulties and necessities, instead of having recourse to Thee, I have gone after creatures and have forgotten Thee.
I have forgotten Thee in deserted tabernacles, where thy love languishes, in the churches of towns where Thou art outraged in the hearts of the indifferent and sacrilegious, and in my own sinful heart, O JESUS, as well when I approached to receive Thee, as after receiving Thee.
Eucharistic Heart of my SAVIOUR, the delight of my first Communion and of the days of my fidelity, I surrender to Thee. Return! Return! draw me to Thyself afresh. Pardon me yet again this time; and I shall hope everything in the strength of thy love.
Glorious Archangel St Michael and thou, O be loved disciple St John, offer to JESUS this my act of reparation, and be propitious to me. Amen.

156. Daily Act of Oblation.
100 Days, once a day. (See Instructions.) 156 Leo XIII, December 19, 1885.

O LORD JESUS CHRIST, in union with that divine intention with which Thou didst on earth offer praises to GOD through thy Sacred Heart, and now dost continue to offer them in all places in the Sacrament of the Eucharist, and wilt do so to the end of the world, I most willingly offer Thee, throughout this entire day without the smallest exception, all my intentions and thoughts, all my affections and desires, all my words and actions, that they may be conformed to the most sacred heart of the blessed Virgin Mary ever Immaculate.

157. Act of Consecration of B. Margaret Mary.
i. 300 Days, once a day. ii. Plenary, once a month. I, II, III, IV. (See Instructions.) 157 Leo XIII, January 13, 1898 ; Pius X, May 30, 1908.

I N.N., give and consecrate to the Sacred Heart , of our LORD JESUS CHRIST my person and my life, my actions, penances, and sufferings, not wishing to make use of any part of my being for the future except in honouring, loving, and glorifying that Sacred Heart.

It is my irrevocable will to be entirely his, and to do everything for his love, renouncing with my whole heart whatever might displease Him. I take Thee then, O most Sacred Heart, as the sole object of my love, as the protector of my life, as the pledge of my salvation, as the remedy of my frailty and inconstancy, as the repairer of all the defects of my life, and as my secure refuge in the hour of death.

Be then, O Heart of goodness, my justification before GOD the FATHER, and remove far from me the thunderbolts of his just wrath. O Heart of love, I place my whole confidence in Thee. While I fear all things from my malice and frailty, I hope all things from thy goodness.

Consume then in me whatever can displease or be opposed to Thee, and may thy pure love be so deeply impressed upon my heart that it may be impossible that I should ever be separated from Thee, or forget Thee.

I implore Thee, by all thy goodness, that my name may be written in Thee, for in Thee I wish to place all my happiness and all my glory, living and dying in very bondage to Thee. Amen.

158. Devotions for Fridays.
i. Plenary on the first Friday of the month. I, II, IV. ii. Seven Years and Seven Quarantines, on other Fridays. I, II, IV. (See Instructions.) 158 Leo XIII, September 7, 1897.

All that is required is that some time should be spent in meditating on the infinite goodness of the Sacred Heart.

159. Ejaculation.
100 Days, once a day. (See Instructions.) 159 Pius IX, Pr. Ma. September 23, 1860.

MAY the Heart of JESUS be loved everywhere.

160. Ejaculation.
300 Days. T.Q. (See Instructions.) 160 Pius IX, Pr. Ma. January 25, 1868; Pius X, September 15, 1905.

JESUS, meek and humble of heart, make my heart like unto thine.

161. Ejaculation.
100 Days, once a day. (See Instructions.) 161 Pius IX, Pr. Ma. February 29, 1868.

MAY the Heart of JESUS in the most Blessed Sacrament be praised, adored, and loved with grateful affection, at every moment, in all the Tabernacles of the world, even to the end of time. Amen.

162. Ejaculation.
i. 300 Days. T.Q. ii. Plenary, once a month. I, II, III, IV. (See Instructions.) 162 Pius IX, November 26, 1876.

Sweet Heart of my JESUS, Make me love Thee ever more and more!

163. Ejaculation.
300 Days, once a day. (See Instructions.) 163 Leo XIII, May 21, 1892.

DULCE cor JESU, sis amor meus.
SWEET Heart of JESUS be my love.

164. Ejaculation.

100 Days, once a day. (See Instructions.) 164 Leo XIII, July 16, 1893.
COR JESU flagrans amore nostri, inflamma cor nostrum amore tui.
HEART of JESUS burning with love of us, inflame our hearts with love of Thee.

165. Litany of the Sacred Heart.

300 Days, once a day. (See Instructions.) 165 Leo XIII, Rit. April 2, 1899

KYRIE eleison.	LORD, have mercy on us.
CHRISTE eleison.	CHRIST, have mercy on us.
KYRIE eleison.	LORD, have mercy on us.
CHRISTE, audi nos.	CHRIST, hear us.
CHRISTE, exaudi nos.	CHRIST, graciously hear us

PATER de cœlis DEUS, — GOD the FATHER of heaven,
FILI REDEMPTOR mundi DEUS, — GOD the SON, REDEEMER of the world,
SPIRITUS SANCTE DEUS — GOD the HOLY GHOST,
Sancta Trinitas, unus DEUS, — Holy Trinity, one GOD,

(miserere nobis. / have mercy on us.)

Cor JESU, FILII PATRIS æterni, — Heart of JESUS, SON of the eternal FATHER
Cor JESU, in sinu Virginis Matris a SPIRITU SANCTO formatum, — Heart of JESUS, formed in the womb of the Virgin Mother by the HOLY GHOST,
Cor JESU, Verbo DEI substantialiter uniturn, — Heart of JESUS, united substantially with the Word of GOD,
Cor JESU, majestatis infinitæ, — Heart of JESUS, of infinite majesty,
Cor JESU, templum DEI sanctum, — Heart of JESUS, holy temple of GOD,
Cor JESU, tabernaculum Altissimi, — Heart of JESUS, tabernacle of the Most High,
Cor JESU, domus DEI et porta cœli, — Heart of JESUS, house of GOD and gate of Heaven,
Cor JESU, fornax ardens caritatis, — Heart of JESUS, glowing furnace of charity,
Cor JESU, justitiæ et amoris receptaculum, — Heart of JESUS, vessel of justice and love,
Cor JESU, bonitate et amore plenum, — Heart of JESUS, full of goodness and love,
Cor JESU, virtutum omnium abyssus, — Heart of JESUS, abyss of all virtues,
Cor JESU, omni laude dignissimum, — Heart of JESUS, most worthy of all praise,
Cor JESU, rex et centrum omnium cordium, — Heart of JESUS, King and centre of all hearts,
Cor JESU, in quo sunt omnes thesauri sapientiæ et scientiæ, — Heart of JESUS, in which are all the treasures of wisdom and knowledge,
Cor JESU, in quo habitat omnis plenitude Divinitatis, — Heart of JESUS, in which dwelleth all the fullness of the Divinity,
Cor JESU, in quo PATER sibi bene complacuit, — Heart of JESUS, in which the FATHER is well pleased,
Cor JESU, de cujus plenitudine omnes nos accepimus, — Heart of JESUS, of whose fullness we have all received,
Cor JESU, desiderium collium æternorum, — Heart of JESUS, desire of the eternal hills,
Cor JESU, patiens et multæ misericordiæ, — Heart of JESUS, patient and rich in mercy,
Cor JESU, dives in omnes qui invocant te, — Heart of JESUS, rich to all who invoke Thee,
Cor JESU, fons vitæ et sanctitatis, — Heart of JESUS, fount of life and holiness,
Cor JESU, propitiatio pro peccatis nostris, — Heart of JESUS, propitiation for our sins,
Cor JESU, saturatum opprobriis, — Heart of JESUS, saturated with revilings,
Cor JESU, attritum propter scelera nostra, — Heart of JESUS, crushed for our iniquities,
Cor JESU, usque ad mortem obediens factum, — Heart of JESUS, made obedient unto death,
Cor JESU, lancea perforatum, — Heart of JESUS, pierced with a lance,
Cor JESU, fons totius consolationis, — Heart of JESUS, source of all consolation,
Cor JESU, vita et resurrectio nostra, — Heart of JESUS, our life and resurrection,
Cor JESU, pax et reconciliatio nostra, — Heart of JESUS, our peace and reconciliation,
Cor JESU, victima peccatorum, — Heart of JESUS, victim for our sins,
Cor JESU, salus in te sperantium, — Heart of JESUS, salvation of those who hope in Thee,
Cor JESU, spes in te morientium, — Heart of JESUS, hope of those who die in Thee,
Cor JESU, deliciæ Sanctorum omnium, — Heart of JESUS, delight of all saints,

(have mercy on us.)

AGNUS DEI, qui tollis peccata mundi, parce nobis DOMINE.	LAMB of GOD, who takest away the sins of the world, spare us, O LORD.
AGNUS DEI, qui tollis peccata mundi, exaudi nos DOMINE.	LAMB of GOD, who takest away the sins of the world, graciously hear us, O LORD.
AGNUS DEI, qui tollis peccata mundi, miserere nobis.	LAMB of GOD, who takest away the sins of the world, have mercy on us,
V/. JESU mitis et humilis corde.	V/. JESUS meek and humble of heart,
R/. Fac cor nostrum secundum cor tuum.	R/. Make our hearts like to thine.
Oremus.	**Let us pray.**
OMNIPOTENS sempiterne DEUS, respice in cor dilectissimi FILII tui et in laudes et satisfactiones, quas in nomine peccatorum tibi persolvit, iisque misericordiam tuam petentibus, tu veniam concede placatus in nomine ejusdem FILII tui JESU CHRISTI, qui tecum vivit et regnat in unitate SPIRITUS SANCTI DEUS, per omnia sæcula sæculorum. Amen.	ALMIGHTY and everlasting GOD, graciously regard the heart of thy well-beloved SON and the acts of praise and satisfaction which He renders Thee on behalf of us sinners, and through their merit grant pardon to us who implore thy mercy in the name of thy SON JESUS CHRIST, who liveth and reigneth with Thee in the unity of the HOLY SPIRIT, world without end. Amen.

166. Prayer to the Sacred Hearts of Jesus and Mary for the Conversion of Jews and Turks.

100 Days, once a day. (See Instructions.) 166 Leo XIII, Br. December 18, 1899

O MOST loving and beloved Heart of JESUS, prostrate before Thee we fervently beseech Thee to extend over the Church and throughout the world those streams of living- water, which flow from Thee as from an inexhaustible fountain springing up into eternal life. O JESUS, SON of David and SON of the living GOD, have compassion upon us, the children of thy pierced Heart. O take not from us the gift of thy most holy faith, though we deserve as much for our sins and ingratitude; hide not thyself from our eyes, Thou who art the true light and our one hope; but remain with us, O LORD, while the darkness of error grows thicker, and fill us with the fire of charity, which Thou earnest on earth to bring, and desirest to be enkindled in the hearts of all men.

O JESUS, sacrificed for us upon the altar of the Cross, draw us to Thee, and with us draw the Jews and Turks, for whom also Thou hast shed thy Blood to the last drop.

May this Blood, once invoked by some in malediction, descend in benediction upon their heads and save them. May this Blood, despised and profaned by other nations, give forth for these a cry for mercy and purify them. Succour, O LORD, we implore Thee, the poor sons of Isaac and Ishmael, for whom Thou wouldst again undergo thy dolorous Passion and death. We appeal on their behalf to those most holy wounds in thy Hands and Feet and Side, which Thou dost keep ever fresh and open, as the price of the world's redemption. To their powerful pleadings are united those which issue from the heart of thy most sweet Mother. That heart, transfixed with a sword of grief, plunged in a sea of suffering-, tormented with thine at the foot of the Cross, we offer to Thee, O JESUS, for the salvation of all those unhappy souls.

O sweet heart of Mary, do Thou speak to JESUS as we ourselves know not how to speak, and He will hear thee, so that even if a miracle be necessary to overcome the resistance of those for whom we pray, we ask it of thee, O Virgin Immaculate, by that immense love which Thou bearest to JESUS.

Only deign to appear to the Jews and Turks as Thou didst once appear to Ratisbonne, and, at a signal from thy right hand, like him they will be suddenly converted.

Oh! may the day soon come when the Holy Trinity shall reign through thee in all hearts, and all shall know, love and adore in spirit and in truth the blessed fruit of thy womb, JESUS, who, with the FATHER and the HOLY SPIRIT, liveth and reigneth world without end. Amen.

167. Prayer.

100 Days, once a day.

(See Instructions.) 167 Leo XIII, Br. March 13, 1901.

O DIVINE Heart of JESUS, grant, we beseech Thee, eternal rest to the souls in purgatory, the final grace to those who shall die today, true repentance to sinners, the light of the faith to pagans, and thy blessing to me and mine. To Thee, O most compassionate Heart of JESUS, I commend all these souls, and I offer to Thee on their behalf all thy merits, together with the merits of thy most holy Mother and of all the saints and angels, and all the sacrifices of the holy Mass, Communions prayers and good works, which shall be accomplished today throughout the Christian world.

168. Ejaculation.
50 Days, once a day. (See Instructions.) 168 Leo XIII, June 14, 1901.
All praise, honour and glory to the divine Heart of JESUS.

169. Little Office of the Sacred Heart.
200 Days, once a day. IV. Plenary, once a month. I, II, III, IV.
(See Instructions.) 169 Leo XIII, Br. December 12, 1901; Pius X, Br. March i, 1904.

The text of The Little Office of the Sacred Heart is published separately in Latin and English, and may be had from Burns & Oates, price 4d.

170. Prayer to the Eucharistic Heart.
i. 300 Days, during- Exposition. ii. Plenary, once a month. For daily recitation and half- hour's adoration once a week. I, II. 170 Leo XIII, Br. June 2, 1902.
O EUCHARISTIC Heart, O sovereign love of our LORD JESUS, who hast instituted the august Sacrament, in order to dwell here below with us and to give to our souls thy Flesh as food and thy Blood as drink, we confidently trust, O LORD JESUS, in the supreme love which instituted the most holy Eucharist; and here, in the presence of this Victim, it is just that we should adore, confess, and exalt this love, as the great store-house of the life of thy Church. This love is an urgent invitation for us, as though Thou didst say to us: "See how I love you! giving you my Flesh as food, and my Blood as drink; I desire by this union to excite your charity, I desire to unite you to myself, I desire to effect the transformation of your souls into my crucified Self, I who am the Bread of eternal life. Give me then your hearts, live in my life, and you shall live in GOD." We recognise, O LORD, that such is the appeal of thy Eucharistic Heart, and we thank Thee for it, and we desire earnestly to respond to it. Grant us the grace to be keenly alive to this supreme love, with which, before thy Passion, Thou didst invite us to receive and feed upon thy sacred Body. Print deeply on our souls the firm determination to respond faithfully to this invitation. Give us devotion and reverence whereby we may honour and receive worthily the gift of thy supreme love, and of thy Eucharistic Heart. Grant that we may thus be able, with thy grace, to celebrate profitably the remembrance of thy Passion, to make reparation for our offences and our coldness, to nourish and increase our love for Thee, and to keep ever living within our hearts this seed of a blessed immortality. Amen.

171. Prayer to the Sacred Heart.
i. 300 Days, once a day. ii. Plenary, once a month. I, II, IV.(See Instructions.) 171 Pius X, June 16, 1906
O MOST sacred Heart of JESUS, pour down thy blessings abundantly upon thy Church, upon the Supreme Pontiff, and upon all the clergy; give perseverance to the just, convert sinners, enlighten unbelievers, bless our parents, friends and benefactors, help the dying, free the souls in Purgatory, and extend over all hearts the sweet empire of thy love. Amen.

172. Consecration of the Family to the Sacred Heart.
Plenary, on the day of consecration, and every year on the day of renewal, II. 172 Pius X, June 15, 1908. (See Instructions.)
SACRED Heart of JESUS, who didst manifest to Blessed Margaret Mary the desire of reigning in Christian families, we today wish to proclaim thy most complete regal dominion over our own. We would live in future with thy life, we would cause to flourish in our midst those virtues to which Thou hast promised peace here below, we would banish far from us the spirit of the world which Thou hast cursed; and Thou shalt reign, over our minds in the simplicity of our faith, and over our hearts by the whole-hearted love with which they shall burn for Thee, the flame of which we shall keep alive by the frequent reception of thy divine Eucharist.

Deign, O divine Heart, to preside over our assemblings, to bless our enterprises, both spiritual and temporal, to dispel our cares, to sanctify our joys, to alleviate our sufferings. If ever one or other of us should have the misfortune to afflict Thee, remind him, O Heart of JESUS, that Thou art good and merciful to the penitent sinner. And when the hour of separation strikes, when death shall come to cast mourning into our midst, we will all, both those who go and those who stay, be submissive to thy eternal decrees. We will console ourselves with the thought that a day will come when the entire family, reunited in Heaven, can sing for ever thy glories and thy mercies.

May the immaculate heart of Mary and the glorious Patriarch, St Joseph, present this consecration to Thee, and keep it in our minds all the days of our life. All glory to the Heart of JESUS, our King and our FATHER.

173. Prayer to the Sacred Heart.
i. 200 Days. T.Q. ii. Plenary, on the Immaculate Conception, if said every day for a year. I, II, III, IV. (See Instructions.) 173 Pius X, Br. December 19, 1904.
LET us, with Mary Immaculate, adore, thank, pray to and console the most sacred and well-beloved Eucharistic Heart of JESUS.

174. Ejaculation.
100 Days. T.Q. (See Instructions.) 174 Pius X, Br. July 9, 1904.
Our Lady of the Sacred Heart, pray for us.

175. Ejaculation.
i. 300 Days. T.Q. ii. Plenary, once a month. I, II, IV. 175 Pius X, August 19, 1905; June 27, 1906. (See Instructions)
SACRED Heart of JESUS, I trust in Thee.

176. Ejaculation.
300 Days. T.Q. (See Instructions.) 176 Pius X, July 26, 1907; December 26, 1907.
EUCHARISTIC Heart of JESUS, have mercy on us.

177. Ejaculation.
300 Days. T.Q. (See Instructions.) 177 Pius X, September 11, 1907
COR JESU Eucharisticum, cordis sacerdotalis exemplar, miserere nobis.
EUCHARISTIC Heart of JESUS, model of the priestly heart, have mercy on us.

178. Ejaculation.
300 Days. T.Q. (See Instructions.) 178 Pi us X, May 4, 1906.
SACRED Heart of JESUS, thy Kingdom come!

179. Ejaculation.
300 Days. T.Q. (See Instructions.) 179 Pius X, November 6, 1906.
DIVINE Heart of JESUS, convert sinners, save the dying, set free the holy souls in Purgatory.

180. Ejaculation of B. Margaret Mary.
300 Days. T.Q. (See Instructions.) 180 Pius X, June 3, 1908.
O HEART of love, I place all my trust in Thee: for though I fear all things from my weakness, I hope all things from thy mercies.

X. MARY.
A. GENERAL.
181. The Rosary of St Bridget.
181 Leo X, Bl. July 10, 1515; Clement XI, Bl. September 22, 1714; Benedict XIV, Br. January 15, 1743; Leo XIII, Br. January 16, 1886, December 8, 1897.

This Chaplet is said in honour of the sixty-three years which, it is said, the most holy Mary lived on earth: it is composed of six divisions, each division consisting of the Pater once, Ave ten times, and Credo once; after these, one Pater more is said, and Ave thrice. Thus in all the Pater will be said seven times, to mark the number of Seven Dolours and Seven Joys; and the Ave sixty-three times, to make up the full number of sixty-three years. The following Indulgences may all (except II and VI) be gained by saying five out of the six decades.

It is requisite, in order to gain these Indulgences, that the Chaplet, being made either of six or of five decades, should be blessed by the superiors of the monastic houses or other priests of the Order of St Saviour, otherwise the Order of St Bridget, or by one with the necessary faculties.

i. 100 Days for each Pater, 100 Days for each Ave, and 100 Days for each Credo, for those who say at least five decades simultaneously with other indulgences.

ii. Seven Years and Seven Quarantines, for saying six decades.

N.B. Whenever this Rosary is said with others, each person may gain the Indulgences I and II precisely the same as when the said Rosary is said by one person alone.

iii. Plenary, to all who shall say at least five decades daily for a year, on any one day in the year. I, II, IV.

iv. Plenary, on the usual conditions, on the Feast of St Bridget (October 8), to all who say the said Rosary of five decades at least once a week. I, II, III, IV.

v. Plenary, to all who, having confessed and communicated, or being at least contrite, shall have been accustomed to say this Rosary, as in No. iv, when, in articulo mortis, recommending their souls to GOD, they say the holy name JESUS with their hearts, if unable to do so with their lips, I, II (if possible).

vi. Plenary, once a month, for saying five decades. I, II, III, IV.

vii. 40 Days, to all who carry this Rosary with them, if, at the tolling of the bell for a passing soul, they kneel down and pray for that soul.

viii. 20 Days, to all who carry this Rosary, whenever, in a contrite spirit, they make examination of conscience, and say thrice Pater and Ave.

ix. 100 Days, to all who carry this Rosary whenever they hear Mass, or assist at a sermon, or accompany the Most Holy Viaticum, or bring-back any sinner into the way of salvation or do any other good work in honour of our LORD JESUS CHRIST, the Blessed Virgin, or St Bridget, provided they say also the Pater and Ave thrice. (See Instructions.)

182. The Angelus and Regina Cœli.

i. Plenary, once a month, to all who, every day, at the sound of the bell, morning, noon, or evening, shall say on their knees the Angelus, I, II, IV.

ii. 100 Days, every time that they say the Angelus. (See Instructions.) 182 Benedict XIII, Br. September 14, 1724; December 5, 1727; Benedict XIV, Card. Vic. April 20, 1742; Pius VI, Prop. March 18, 1781. Leo XIII, April 3, 1884; May 20, 1896.

N.B. These Indulgences are not suspended in the Holy Year of the Jubilee. The Angelus is to be said standing, every Sunday in the year, beginning from first Vespers, that is, Saturday evening; in Paschal-tide (i.e., from Holy Saturday at midday to midday on Saturday before Trinity Sunday inclusive), the Regina cœli, etc., is said instead, standing, with its proper V/., R/., and prayer; those, however, who do not know the Regina cœli may obtain the same Indulgences by saying the Angelus as above. Religious of both sexes, or others who live in community, if they cannot say the Angelus nor Regina Cœli at the sound of the bell as aforesaid, by reason of their being engaged upon some work prescribed by their rule or constitution, may obtain the above-named Indulgences, provided that immediately on the conclusion of their respective duties they say the Angelus or Regina cœli. Moreover, the faithful who happen to be dwelling where there is no such bell, may obtain the above-named Indulgences if, at the hours specified or thereabouts, they say the Angelus or Regina Cœli, according to the season. These Indulgences may be gained by saying five Hail Marys, three times, by those who do not know and cannot read the proper prayers.

On Saturdays in Lent, at noon, the Angelus is to be said standing.

V/. Angelus DOMINI nuntiavit Mariæ.	V/. The angel of the LORD declared unto Mary.
R/. Et concepit de SPIRITU SANCTO. Ave Maria.	R/. And she conceived of the HOLY GHOST. Ave Maria.
V/. Ecce ancilla DOMINI,	

R/. Fiat mihi secundum verbum tuum. Ave Maria,
V/. Et Verbum caro factum est.
R/. Et habitavit in nobis. Ave Maria.
V/. Ora pro nobis, sancta DEI Genitrix.
R/. Ut digni efficiamur promissionibus CHRISTI.
Oremus.
GRATIAM tuam quæsumus, DOMINE, mentibus nostris infunde: ut qui, angelo nuntiante, CHRISTI FILII tui Incarnationem cognovimus, per Passionem ejuset Crucem ad resurrectionis gloriam perducamur. Per eundem CHRISTUM DOMINUM nostrum. R/. Amen.
REGINA cœli, lætare. Alleluia.
Quia quem meruisti portare. Alleluia.
Resurrexit sicut dixit. Alleluia.
Ora pro nobis DEUM. Alleluia.
V/. Gaude et lætare, Virgo Maria. Alleluia.
R/. Quia surrexit DOMINUS vere. Alleluia.
Oremus.
DEUS, qui per resurrectionem FILII tui DOMINI nostri JESU CHRISTI mundum lætificare dignatuses; præsta, quæsumus, ut per ejus Genitricem Virginem Mariam perpetuæ capiamus gaudia vitae. Per eundem CHRISTUM DOMINUM nostrum. R/. Amen.

V/. Behold the handmaid of the LORD.
R/. Be it done unto me according to thy word. Ave Maria.
V/. And the Word was made Flesh.
R/. And dwelt among us. Ave Maria.
V/. Pray for us, O Holy Mother of GOD.
R/. That we may be made worthy of the promises of CHRIST.
Let us pray.
POUR forth, we beseech Thee, O LORD, thy grace into our hearts; that we, to whom the Incarnation of CHRIST thy SON was made known by the message of an angel, may by his Passion and Cross be brought to the glory of his resurrection. Through the same CHRIST our LORD. R/. Amen.
QUEEN of Heaven, rejoice. Alleluia.
For He whom thou wast made worthy to bear. Alleluia.
Hath risen, as He said. Alleluia.
Pray for us to GOD. Alleluia.
V/. Rejoice and be glad, O Virgin Mary. Alleluia.
R/. For the LORD hath risen indeed. Alleluia.
Let us pray.
O GOD, who through the resurrection of thy SON our LORD JESUS CHRIST hast vouchsafed to give joy to the whole world; grant us, we beseech Thee, that, through the intercession of the Virgin Mary his Mother, we may obtain the joys of eternal life. Through the same CHRIST our LORD. Amen.

183. Invocation of the Name of Mary.
25 Days. T.Q. (See Instructions.) 183 Clement XIII, September 5, 1759.

184. The Salve Regina and Sub Tuum Præsidium.
To all the faithful who, being moved by a spirit of true religion to make some reparation for the injuries done to the honour of Mary, Mother of GOD, and to the saints, and to defend and propagate the worship and veneration of their sacred images and pictures, shall to this end say at morn the Salve Regina, etc., with the VV. Dignare me, etc., and Benedictus Deus in sanctis suis, and at even, Sub tuum præsidium, etc., with the same versicles.
i. 100 Days, once a day. ii. Seven Years and Seven Quarantines, on Sundays, iii. Plenary, twice a month, on any two Sundays in the
month. I, II, IV. iv. Plenary, on every Feast of our blessed Lady, and on the Feast of All Saints. I, II, IV.
v. Plenary, in articulo mortis, at the point of death, to all who have been accustomed during life to say the prayers, provided they have been to Confession and Communion, or are at least contrite in heart.
(See Instructions.) 184 Pius VI, April 5, 1786.

MORNING.
SALVE, Regina, Mater misericordiæ, vita, dulcedo, et spes nostra, salve. Ad te clamamus, exules filii Hevæ; ad te suspiramus, gementes et flentes in hac lacrymarum valle. Eia ergo, Advocata nostra, illos tuos misericordes oculos ad nos converte; et JESUM, benedictum fructum ventris tui, nobis post hoc exilium ostende, O clemens, O pia, O dulcis Virgo Maria.

Hail Holy Queen, Mother of Mercy, Hail our Life, our Sweetness, and our Hope! To thee do we cry, poor banished children of Eve; to thee do we send up our sighs, mourning and weeping in this vale of tears. Turn, then, most gracious Advocate, thine eyes of mercy towards us ; and after this our exile, show unto us the blessed Fruit of thy womb, JESUS, O clement, O loving, O sweet Virgin Mary.
V/. Make me worthy to praise thee, O Holy Virgin.

V/. Dignare me laudare te, Virgo sacrata.
R/. Damihi virtutem contra hostes tuos.
V/. Benedictus DEUS in sanctis suis.
R/. Amen

R/. Give me strength against thine enemies.
V/. Blessed be God in his saints.
R/. Amen

EVENING.

SUB tuum præsidium confugimus, Sancta DEI Genitrix; nostras deprecationes ne despicias in necessitatibus nostris, et a periculis cunctis libera nos semper, Virgo gloriosa et benedicta.
V/. Dignare me laudare te, Virgo sacrata.
R/. Damihi virtutem contra hostes tuos.
V/. Benedictus DEUS in sanctis suis.
R/. Amen

WE fly to thy patronage, O Holy Mother of God despise not thou our petitions in our necessities, but deliver us always from all dangers, O glorious and blessed Virgin.
V/. Make me worthy to praise thee, O Holy Virgin.
R/. Give me strength against thine enemies.
V/. Blessed be God in his saints.
R/. Amen

185. Prayers of St Alphonsus Liguori for everyday of the Week, with Ave Maria thrice.

i. 300 Days, once a day. ii. Plenary, once a month. I, II, IV. 185 Pius VII, June 21, 1808; Pius IX, June 18, 1876. (See Instructions.)

PRAYER FOR SUNDAY.

MOTHER of my GOD, look down upon a poor sinner, who has recourse to thee and puts his trust in thee. I am not worthy that thou shouldst even cast thine eyes upon me; but I know that thou, beholding JESUS thy Son dying for sinners, dost thyself yearn exceedingly to save them. O Mother of Mercy, look on my miseries and have pity upon me. Men say thou art the refuge of the sinner, the hope of the desperate, the aid of the lost; be thou, then, my refuge, hope, and aid. It is thy prayers which must save me. For the love of JESUS CHRIST be thou my help; reach forth thy hand to the poor fallen sinner who recommends himself to thee. I know that it is thy joy to aid the sinner when thou canst; help me now, thou who canst help. By my sins I have forfeited the grace of GOD and my own soul. I place myself in thy hands; oh, tell me what to do that I may regain the grace of GOD, and I will do it. My SAVIOUR bids me go to thee for help; He wills that I should look to thy pity; that so, not only the merits of thy Son, but thine own prayers too, may unite to save me. To thee, then, I have recourse: pray thou to JESUS for me; and make me experience how great good thou canst do for one who trusts in thee. Be it done unto me according to my hope. Amen.

Then say thrice Ave Maria to the Blessed Virgin Mary, in reparation for the blasphemies uttered against her.

PRAYER FOR MONDAY.

MOST holy Mary, Queen of Heaven, I who was once the slave of the Evil One now dedicate myself to thy service for ever; and I offer myself, to honour and to serve thee as long as I live. Accept me for thy servant and cast me not away from thee as I deserve. In thee, O my Mother, I place all my hope. All blessing- and thanksgiving be to GOD, who in his mercy giveth me this trust in thee. True it is, that in past time I have fallen miserably into sin; but by the merits of JESUS CHRIST, and by thy prayers, I hope that GOD has pardoned me. But this is not enough, my Mother. One thought appals me; it is, that I may yet lose the grace of GOD. Danger is ever nigh; the devil sleeps not; fresh temptations assail me. Protect me, then, my Queen; help me against the assaults of my spiritual enemy. Never suffer me to sin again, or to offend JESUS thy Son. Let me not by sin lose my soul, heaven, and my GOD. This one grace, Mary, I ask of thee; this is my desire; this may thy prayers obtain for me. Such is my hope. Amen. *Ave Maria thrice.*

PRAYER FOR TUESDAY.

MOST holy Mary, Mother of Goodness, Mother of Mercy, when I reflect upon my sins and upon the moment of my death, I tremble and am confounded. O my sweetest Mother, in the Blood of JESUS, in thy intercession, are my hopes. Comforter of the sad, abandon me not at that hour; fail not to console me in that affliction. If even now I am so tormented by remorse for the sins I have committed, the uncertainty of my pardon, the danger of a relapse, and the strictness of the Judgment, how will it be with me then? O my Mother, before death overtake me, obtain for me great sorrow for my sins, a true amendment, and constant fidelity to GOD for the remainder of my life. And when at length my hour is come, then do thou, Mary, my hope, be thyself my aid in those great troubles wherewith my soul will be encompassed. Strengthen me, that I may not despair when the enemy sets my sins before my face. Obtain for me at that moment grace to invoke thee often, so that with thine own sweet name and that of thy most holy Son upon my lips I may breathe forth my spirit. This grace thou hast granted to many of thy servants; this, too, is my hope and my desire. *Ave Maria thrice.*

PRAYER FOR WEDNESDAY.
MOTHER of GOD, most holy Mary, how often by my sins have I merited hell! Long ago, perhaps, judgment would have gone forth against my first mortal sin, hadst not thou in thy tender pity delayed the justice of GOD, and afterwards attracted me by thy sweetness to have confidence in thy prayers. And oh, how very often should I have fallen in the dangers which beset my steps hadst not thou, loving Mother that thou art, preserved me by the graces thou, by thy prayers, didst obtain for me. But oh, my Queen, what will thy pity and thy favours avail me, if after all I perish in the flames of hell? If there was once a time when I loved thee not, yet now, next to GOD, I love thee before all. Wherefore, henceforth and for ever, suffer me not to turn my back upon thee and upon my GOD, who through thee has granted me so many mercies. O Lady, most worthy of all love, let it not be that I, thy child, should be doomed to hate and to curse thee for ever in hell. Thou wilt surely never endure to see thy servant lost who loves thee. O Mary, say not that I ever can be lost! Yet lost I shall assuredly be if I abandon thee. But who could ever have the heart to leave thee? Who can ever forget thy love? No, it is impossible for that man to perish who faithfully recommends himself to thee, and has recourse to thee. Only leave me not, my Mother, in my own hands, or I am lost! Let me but cling to thee! Save me, my hope! save me from hell ; or, rather, save me from sin, which alone can condemn me to hell. *Ave Maria thrice.*

PRAYER FOR THURSDAY.
QUEEN of heaven, who sittest enthroned above all the choirs of the angels nighest to GOD, from this vale of miseries I, a poor sinner, say to thee, " Hail, Mary," praying thee in thy love to turn upon me those gracious eyes of thine. See, Mary, the dangers among which I dwell, and shall ever have to dwell whilst I live upon this earth. I may yet lose my soul, Paradise, and GOD. In thee, Lady, is my hope. I love thee; and I sigh after the time when I shall see thee and praise thee in Paradise. O Mary, how soon will the happy day come when I shall see myself safe at thy feet? When shall I kiss that hand, which has dispensed to me so many graces? Alas, it is too true, my Mother, that I have ever been very ungrateful during my whole life; but if I get to Heaven, then I will love thee there every moment of a whole eternity, and make thee reparation in some sort for my ingratitude by ever blessing and praising thee. Thanks be to GOD, for that He hath vouchsafed me this hope through the Precious Blood of JESUS, and through thy powerful intercession. This has been the hope of all thy true lovers; and no one of them has been defrauded of his hope. No, neither shall I be defrauded of mine. O Mary, pray to thine own Son JESUS, as I too pray to Him, by the merits of his Passion, to strengthen
and increase this hope. Amen. *Ave Maria thrice.*

PRAYER FOR FRIDAY.
OMARY, thou art the noblest, highest, purest, fairest creature of GOD, the holiest of all creatures! Oh, that all men knew thee, loved thee, my Queen, as thou deservest to be loved! Yet great is my consolation, Mary, in that there are blessed souls in the courts of heaven, and just souls still on earth, whose hearts thou leadest captive with thy beauty and thy goodness. But above all I rejoice in this, that our GOD Himself loves thee alone more than all men and angels together. I too, O loveliest Queen, I, miserable sinner, dare to love thee, though my love is too little; I would I had a greater love, a more tender love; this thou must gain for me, since to love thee is a great mark of predestination, and a grace which GOD grants to those who shall be saved. Moreover, O my Mother, when I reflect upon the debt I owe thy Son, I see He deserves of me an immeasurable love. Do thou, then, who desirest nothing so much as to see Him loved, pray that I may have this grace a great love for JESUS CHRIST. Obtain it, thou who obtainest what thou wilt. I covet not goods of earth, nor honours, nor riches, but I desire that which thine own heart desires most to love my God alone. Oh, can it be that thou wilt not aid me in a desire so acceptable to thee ? No, it is impossible ! Even now I feel thy help ; even now thou prayest for me. Pray for me, Mary, pray ;

nor ever cease to pray, till thou dost see me safe in Paradise, where I shall be certain of possessing and of loving my GOD and thee, my dearest Mother, for ever and for ever. Amen. *Ave Maria thrice.*

PRAYER FOR SATURDAY.
MOST holy Mary, I know the graces which thou hast obtained for me, and I know the ingratitude which I have shown thee. The ungrateful man is unworthy of favours, and yet for all this I will not distrust thy mercy. O my great Advocate, have pity on me. Thou, Mary, art the stewardess of every grace which GOD vouchsafes to give us sinners, and therefore did He make thee so mighty, rich, and kind, that thou mightest succour us. I will that I may be saved: in thy hands I place my eternal salvation, to thee I consign my soul. I will to be associated with those who are thy special servants: reject me not. Thou goest up and down seeking the wretched, to console them. Cast not away, then, a wretched sinner who has recourse to thee. Speak for me, Mary; thy Son grants what thou askest. Take me beneath thy shelter, and it is enough for me; for with thee to guard me I fear no ill no, not even my sins, because thou wilt obtain GOD'S pardon for them; no, nor yet evil spirits, because thou art far mightier than hell; no, nor my Judge JESUS CHRIST, for at thy prayer He will lay aside his wrath. Protect me, then, my Mother; obtain for me pardon of my sins, love of JESUS, holy perseverance, a good death, and heaven. It is too true, I merit not these graces; yet do thou only ask them of our GOD and I shall obtain them. Pray, then, to JESUS for me. Mary, my Queen, in thee I trust; in this trust I rest, I live; and with this trust I will that I may die. Amen. *Ave Maria thrice.*

186. Month of May.
i. 300 Days, for each day, to all who shall honour the Blessed Virgin, during the month of May (in public or in private), with prayer or other devotion.
ii. Plenary, once in the month (or on one of the first eight days of June), to all who keep up this devotion every day during the month. I, II, IV. 186 Pius VII, Mem. March 21, 1815 ; June 18, 1822
(See Instructions.)

187. Psalms in Honour of the Name of Mary.
i. Seven Years and Seven Quarantines. T.Q. ii. Plenary, once a month. I, II, IV. iii. Plenary, on the Sunday in the Octave of our Lady's
Nativity (the Feast of her Name), if said often during a year. I, II, IV. (See Instructions.) 187 Pius VII, June 13, 1815

M. Ant. Mariæ nomen.
Cantic. B.M.V. Luc. 1.
MAGNIFICAT * anima mea DOMINUM.
Et exultavit spiritus meus * in DEO salutari meo.
Quia respexit humilitatem ancillae suæ: * ecce enim ex hoc beatam me dicent omnes generationes.
Quia fecit mihi magna, qui potens est, * et sanctum nomen ejus.
Et misericordia ejus a progenie in progenies * timentibus eum.
Fecit potentiam in brachio suo: * dispersit superbos mente cordis sui.
Deposuit potentes de sede, * et exaltavit humiles.
Esurientes implevit bonis, * et divites dimisit inanes.
Suscepit Israel puerum suum, * recordatus misericordiæ suæ.
Sicut locutus est ad patres nostros, * Abraham et semini ejus in saecula.
Gloria PATRI, etc.
Ant. Mariae nomen cunctas illustrat ecclesias, cui fecit magna, qui potens est, et sanctum nomen ejus.

A. Ant. A solis ortu.
Psalm, cxix.
AD DOMINUM, cum tribularer, clamavi: * et exaudivit me.
Domine, libera animam meam a labiis iniquis,* et a lingua dolosa.
Quid detur tibi, aut quid apponatur tibi, * ad linguam dolosam?
Sagittæ potentis acutæ, * cum carbonibus desolatoriis.
Heu mihi, quia incolatus meus prolongatus est! habitavi cum habitantibus Cedar: * multum incola fuit anima mea.
Cum his, qui oderunt pacem, eram pacificus: * cum loquebar illis, impugnabant me gratis.

Gloria PATRI, etc.
Ant. A solis ortu usque ad occasum laudabile nomen DOMINI, et Mariæ matris ejus.

R. Ant. Refugium est.
Psalm, cxviii.
RETRIBUE servo tuo, vivifica me: * et custodiam sermones tuos.
Revela oculos meos, * et considerabo mirabilia de lege tua.
Incola ego sum in terra, * non abscondas a me mandata tua.
Concupivit anima mea desiderare justificationes tuas * in omni tempore.
Increpasti superbos: * maledicti qui declinant a mandatis tuis.
Aufer a me opprobrium, et contemptum, * quia testimonia tua exquisivi.
Etenim sederunt principes, et adversus me loquebantur: * servus autem tuus exercebatur in justificationibus tuis.
Nam et testimonia tua meditatio mea est: * et consilium meum justificationes tuae.
Adhæsit pavimento anima mea: * vivifica me secundum verbum tuum.
Vias meas enuntiavi, et exaudisti me: * doce me justificationes tuas.
Viam justificationum tuarum instrue me, * et exercebor in mirabilibus tuis.
Dormitavit anima mea præ tædio: * confirma me in verbis tuis.
Viam iniquitatis amove a me, * et de lege tua miserere mei.
Viam veritatis elegi: * judicia tua non sum oblitus.
Adhæsi testimoniis tuis, DOMINE: * noli me confundere.
Viam mandatorum tuorum cucurri, * cum dilatasti cor meum.
Gloria PATRI, etc.

Ant. Refugium est in tribulationibus Mariæ nomen omnibus illud invocantibus.
I. Ant. In universa terra.
Psalm, cxxv.
IN convertendo DOMINUS captivitatem Sion, * facti sumus sicut consolati.
Tunc repletum est gaudio os nostrum, * et lingua nostra exultatione.
Tunc dicent inter gentes: * magnificavit DOMINUS facere cum eis.
Magnificavit DOMINUS facere nobiscum: * facti sumus lætantes.
Converte, DOMINE, captivitatem nostram, * sicut torrens in austro.
Qui seminantin lacrymis,*in exultatione metent.
Euntes ibant, et flebant, * mittentes seminasua.
Venientes autem venient cum exultatione * portantes manipulos suos.
Gloria PATRI, etc.

Ant. In universa terra admirabile est nomen tuum, O Maria.
A. Ant. Annuntiaverunt.
Psalm, cxxii.
AD te levavi oculos meos, * qui habitas in cœlis.
Ecce sicut oculi servorum * in manibus dominorum suorum.
Sicut oculi ancillæ in manibus dominæ suæ: * ita oculi nostri ad DOMINUM DEUM nostrum, donec misereatur nostri.
Miserere nostri, DOMINE, miserere nostri, *quia multum repleti sumus despectione.
Quia multum repleta est anima nostra, * opprobrium abundantibus, et despectio superbis.
Gloria PATRI, etc.

Ant. Annuntiaverunt cœli nomen Mariæ, et viderunt omnes populi gloriam ejus.
V/. *Sit nomen Virginis Mariæ benedictum.*
R/. *Ex hoc nunc et usque in saeculum.*
Oremus.
CONCEDE, quæsumus, omnipotens DEUS, ut fideles tui, qui sub sanctissimæ Virginis Mariæ Nomine et protectione lætantur; ejus pia intercessione a cunclis malis liberentur in terris, et ad gaudia aeterna pervenire mereantur in caelis. Per CHRISTUM DOMINUM, etc.

188. Twenty-five Days Preparation for the Nativity, after the example of St Catharine of Bologna.

i. 100 Days, each day. ii. Plenary, to those who shall have practised it for at least twenty days, I,II, III, IV. (See Instructions.) 188 Pius VII, November 14, 1815.

Prayer to be said every day.

IN lowly reverence at thy feet we kneel, great Mother of our GOD, most holy Mary, advocate of sinners; humbly praying thee, by the merits of the Precious Blood of thy Divine Son, shed for us sinners, and by the intercession of thy well-beloved servant, Catharine, to gain for us by thy prayers true fervour of spirit in this holy exercise, and the grace to walk in the way of all thy virtues, after the example of St Catharine, to the honour and glory of JESUS CHRIST, thine only Son our SAVIOUR. Forget our monstrous ingratitude, look not upon our sins, but rather find for us a refuge in the depths of thy loving kindness ; and having regard to that love wherewith thou didst ever love thy faithful servant Catharine, obtain for us the remission of our sins, so that we may confidently hope to attain all that we desire for our spiritual wants. Amen.

FOR THE FIRST DAY.

IN imitation of St Catharine, we purpose now to praise the great Mother of our GOD, honouring her Sacred Delivery, and saying- to her forty Angelic Salutations and forty Benedictions, thereby to obtain her powerful aid at the hour of our death, and a true contrition for our sins, that so we may pass from this land of our pilgrimage to eternal joys.

FOR THE OTHER DAYS.

IN imitation of St Catharine, let us continue to praise the great Mother of our GOD, honouring her Sacred Delivery with forty Angelic Salutations and forty Benedictions, to obtain thereby her powerful aid at the hour of our death, and true contrition for our sins, that so we may pass from this land of our pilgrimage to eternal joys.

FOR THE LAST DAY.

IN imitation of St Catharine, today we end this exercise praising the great Mother of our GOD, and honouring her Sacred Delivery, with forty Angelic Salutations and forty Benedictions, to obtain thereby her powerful aid at the hour of our death, and true contrition for our sins, that so we may pass from this land of our pilgrimage to eternal joys.

FIRST DECADE.

WHILST saying for the first time Ave Maria ten times and the ten Benedictions, we meditate on the ineffable mystery of the Incarnation of the Eternal Word, and the great dignity of the Virgin who was elected to be the Mother of the Most High.

Ave Maria ten times, and after each Ave say,

Blessed be the hour, Mary, when thou didst become Mother of JESUS, SON of GOD.

SECOND DECADE.

WHILST saying for the second time Ave Maria ten times and the ten Benedictions, we meditate on the humility of the King of heaven, who chose for his birthplace a poor stable, and on the joy of Mary when she first saw the Only-begotten of the FATHER, the Fruit of her womb. Ave Maria ten times, and after each Ave,

Blessed be the hour, Mary, when thou didst bring forth JESUS the SON of GOD.

THIRD DECADE.

WHILST saying for the third time Ave Maria ten times and the ten Benedictions, we contemplate the exact carefulness of Mary, as she fulfilled perfectly the parts both of Martha and of Magdalen, contemplating her Son as her REDEEMER, and at the same time ministering to Him as her Child. Ave Maria ten times, and after each Ave,

Blessed be the hour, Mary, when thou didst nourish at thy breast JESUS, SON of GOD.

FOURTH DECADE.

WHILST saying for the fourth time Ave Maria ten times and the ten Benedictions, we meditate upon the great reverence with which Mary embraced and pressed to her very heart rather than to her bosom, kissed, and adored her GOD and ours, incarnate for love of us; and moved thereby with profound reverence and devout affection we say, Ave Maria ten times, and after each Ave,

Blessed be that hour, Mary, when thou didst embrace JESUS, SON of GOD.
Then say,
PRAISE be to our GOD, because in imitation of
ST. CATHERINE, we have begun (first day]
are continuing (other days]
have ended (last day]
We beseech the Queen of Angels that for these our thousand Angelic Salutations and thousand Benedictions which we are saying
have said (last day)

Mother may obtain of the Infant which is born of her these two special blessings, viz., the first, in life, grace truly to repent of our sins; the second, in death, certainty of salvation. Wherefore let everyone here present say heartily with St Catharine:
Turn, then, most gracious Advocate, thine eyes of mercy towards us ; and after this our exile show unto us the blessed Fruit of thy womb, JESUS, O clement, O loving, O sweet Virgin Mary. Then the Litany B. V.M. (see next page), and then,
V/. *Make me worthy to praise thee, Virgin ever blessed.*
R/. *Give me strength against thine enemies.*

Let us pray.
GOD, who by the message of an angel didst will that thy Divine Word should take to Himself human flesh in the womb of the Blessed Virgin Mary; grant unto us thy suppliants that we, who believe her to be verily and indeed Mother of GOD, may be aided by her intercession with Thee. Visit us, O LORD, we beseech Thee, and purify our hearts; that our LORD JESUS CHRIST thy SON may, when He comes with all his saints, find a dwelling-place prepared for Himself within us. Who with Thee liveth and reigneth for ever and ever. R/. Amen.

189. The Litany of Loreto.
i. 300 Days. T.Q.
ii. Plenary, to all who say it daily, on the Immaculate Conception, the Nativity, the Annunciation, the Purification, and the Assumption. I, II, III, IV. 189 Pius VII, September 30, 1817. (See Instructions.)

KYRIE eleison.		LORD, have mercy on us.
CHRISTE eleison.		CHRIST, have mercy on us.
KYRIE eleison.	*miserere nobis.*	LORD, have mercy on us.
CHRISTE, audi nos.		CHRIST, hear us.
CHRISTE, exaudi nos.		CHRIST, graciously hear us
PATER de cœlis DEUS,		GOD the FATHER of heaven,
FILI REDEMPTOR mundi DEUS,		GOD the SON, REDEEMER of the world,
SPIRITUS SANCTE DEUS		GOD the HOLY GHOST,
Sancta Trinitas, unus DEUS,		Holy Trinity, one GOD,

have mercy on us.

Sancta Maria,	Holy Mary,
Sancta DEI Genitrix,	Holy Mother of GOD,
Sancta Virgo virginum,	Holy Virgin of virgins,
Mater CHRISTI,	Mother of CHRIST,
Mater divinæ gratiæ,	Mother of divine grace,
Mater purissima,	Mother most pure,
Mater castissima,	Mother most chaste,
Mater inviolata,	Mother inviolate,
Mater intemerata,	Mother undefiled,
Mater amabilis,	Mother most amiable,
Mater admirabilis,	Mother most admirable,
Mater boni consilii,	Mother of Good Counsel,
Mater CREATORIS,	Mother of our CREATOR,
Mater SALVATORIS,	Mother of our SAVIOUR,
Virgo prudentissima,	Virgin most prudent,
Virgo veneranda,	Virgin most venerable,
Virgo prædicanda,	Virgin most renowned,
Virgo potens,	Virgin, most powerful,
Virgo clemens,	Virgin most merciful,
Virgo fidelis,	Virgin most faithful,
Speculum justitiæ,	Mirror of justice,
Sedes sapientiæ,	Seat of wisdom,
Causa nostræ laetitiæ,	Cause of our joy,
Vas spirituale,	Spiritual Vessel,
Vas honorabile,	Vessel of honour,
Vas insigne devotionis,	Vessel of singular devotion,
Rosa mystica,	Mystical Rose,
Turris Davidica,	Tower of David,
Turris eburnea,	Tower of ivory,
Domus aurea,	House of gold,
Fœderis arca,	Ark of the covenant,
Janua cæli,	Gate of heaven,
Stella matutina,	Morning-star,
Salus infirmorum,	Health of the sick,
Refugium peccatorum,	Refuge of sinners,
Consolatrix afflictorum,	Comforter of the afflicted,
Auxilium Christianorum,	Help of Christians,
Regina Angelorum,	Queen of Angels,
Regina Patriarcharum,	Queen of Patriarchs,
Regina Prophetarum,	Queen of Prophets,
Regina Apostolorum,	Queen of Apostles,
Regina Martyrum,	Queen of Martyrs,
Regina Confessorum,	Queen of Confessors,
Regina Virginum,	Queen of Virgins,
Regina Sanctorum omnium,	Queen of all saints,
Regina sine labe originali concepta,	Queen conceived without original sin,
Regina Sacratissimi Rosarii,	Queen of the most holy Rosary,

Ora pro nobis. — *Pray for us.*

AGNUS DEI, qui tollis peccata mundi, parce nobis DOMINE.	LAMB of GOD, who takest away the sins of the world, spare us, O LORD.
AGNUS DEI, qui tollis peccata mundi, exaudi nos DOMINE.	LAMB of GOD, who takest away the sins of the world, graciously hear us, O LORD.
AGNUS DEI, qui tollis peccata mundi, miserere nobis.	LAMB of GOD, who takest away the sins of the world, have mercy on us..

190. Prayer of St Alphonsus.
i. 300 Days, once a day. ii. Plenary, once a month. I, II, IV. (See Instructions.) 190 Pius VII, May 15, 1821.
Say the prayer for Wednesday (No.185) Then the Salve Regina thrice. (see p. 184)

191. Three Offerings.
i. 300 Days. T.Q.
ii. Plenary, once a month. I, II, IV. (See Instructions.) 191 Leo XII, Pr. Ma. October 21, 1823. Pius IX, June 18, 1876.
MOST Holy Virgin, I venerate thee with my whole heart above all angels and saints in Paradise, as the Daughter of the Eternal FATHER, and I consecrate to thee my soul with all its powers. Ave Maria.
MOST Holy Virgin, I venerate thee with my whole heart above all angels and saints in Paradise, as the Mother of the Only-begotten SON, and I consecrate to thee my body with all its senses. Ave Maria.
MOST Holy Virgin, I venerate thee with my whole heart above all angels and saints in Paradise, as the Spouse of the HOLY GHOST, and I consecrate to thee my heart and all its affections, praying thee to obtain for me from the ever-blessed Trinity all that is necessary for my salvation. Ave Maria.

192. Prayer, with Ave Maria, thrice, etc.
100 Days, once a day. (See Instructions.) 192 Leo XII, August ii, 1824.
VIRGIN most holy, Mother of the Word Incarnate, Treasurer of graces, Refuge of us poor sinners; we fly to thy maternal love with lively faith, and we ask thee to obtain for us grace ever to do the will of GOD and thine own. Into thy most holy hands we commit the keeping of our hearts; beseeching thee for health of soul and body, in the certain hope that thou, our most loving Mother, wilt hear our prayer. Wherefore with lively faith we say, Ave Maria thrice.
Let us pray.
DEFEND, O LORD, we beseech Thee, us thy servants, through the intercession of the Blessed Mary ever-Virgin, from all infirmity both of body and soul; and mercifully protect from the snares of enemies those who, with their whole heart, prostrate themselves before Thee. Through CHRIST our LORD. Amen.

193. Prayer, O Excellentissima.
i. 100 Days, once a day. ii. Plenary, once a month, on the last day, or one of eight succeeding- days. I, II, III, IV. (See Instructions) 193 Leo XII, January 30, 1828
O MOST excellent, glorious, most holy and ever inviolate blessed Virgin Mary, Mother of our LORD JESUS CHRIST, Queen of the world, and Mistress of all creatures! Thou who forsakest no one, despisest no one, who leavest in sadness none who seek help at thy hands with pure and lowly hearts; do not despise me because of the number and hatefulness of my sins, do not abandon me on account of my grievous iniquities nor on account of the hardness and uncleanness of my heart. Do not refuse me, thy servant, a share in thy favour and thy love. Hear me, a wretched sinner, who trusts in thy mercy and pity. Help me, O most loving Virgin Mary, in all my perils and needs, and obtain for me from thy beloved Son, Almighty GOD and our LORD JESUS CHRIST, the forgiveness of all my sins, the grace of the fear and love of thee, health and chastity of body, and deliverance from all the dangers which beset both soul and body.

In the last moments of my life be thou my kind helper, and save from eternal darkness, and from evil of every kind, my poor soul, and the souls of my parents, brothers, sisters, friends, relatives, and benefactors, together with the souls of all the faithful, both living and dead; through the grace of Him whom for nine months thou didst bear in thy most holy womb, and whom thou didst place with thy holy hands in the manger, JESUS CHRIST our LORD, to whom be all honour given for endless ages. Amen.

194. Prayer.
i. 100 Days, once a day. ii. Plenary, once a month, on last day of the month, or within eight days. I, II, III, IV. (See Instructions.) 194 Leo XII, January 30, 1828
VIRGIN Mother of GOD, most holy Mary, safe refuge of sinners! to thee, who art, after GOD, our hope and consolation in this place of exile, to thee I have recourse with sincere confidence, though most undeserving of thy patronage. I know, on the one hand, how much I stand in need of being converted from my very heart; yet, on the other, the heinousness of my crimes strikes me with terror. To thee, then, I betake myself to thee who art our sovereign mediator with thy dear Son JESUS, as He is with his Eternal

FATHER. To thee, after JESUS, must I look for my amendment. Vouchsafe then, O Mother of Mercy, to obtain for me the grace of a true and lasting conversion. I wish to change my life entirely. In this I am sincere; but my evil habits and the ill use I have made of so many saving inspirations, the multitude and heinousness of my sins, and the bonds by which the world holds me, while they render amendment difficult, call for thy special assistance. Grant it to me in spite of my unworthiness. In thee I trust; do thou not reject me. Although deserving- of eternal punishment, I throw myself at thy feet, sorrowful and repentant. My sins, I own, have taken from me the strength which grace imparts, have cast me out from among the adopted sons of GOD, have deprived me of the right to everlasting happiness, and drawn on me instead the wrath of heaven. Tell me what I must do to regain the friendship of thy Son JESUS. Beg of Him, by his Precious Blood, his bitter Passion, and cruel death on the Cross, to pardon my offences, and He will pardon them. Tell Him thy desire for my salvation, and He will save me. But as I can still fall into sin and lose the life of grace amid the dangers which encompass me, ever watch thou over me, and I shall surely triumph over the enemies who incessantly work for my ruin. Instil into my heart a lively faith, a firm hope, an ardent charity, and all the virtues suitable to my state of life; and obtain for me constancy in good, and final perseverance. In fine, be thou my loving Mother here below, and my advocate at the hour of death, that I may be of the number of those to whom thy divine Son shall say: "Come, ye blessed of my FATHER, possess the kingdom prepared for you." Amen.

195. The Crown of Twelve Stars.
i. 100 Days. T.Q. ii. Plenary, once a month. I,II, IV. (See Instructions.) 195 Gregory XVI, January 8, 1838; Pius IX, March 17, 1856; Leo XIII, July 23, 1898.

ALL praise and thanksgiving; be to the ever-blessed Trinity, who hath shown unto us Mary, ever-Virgin, clothed with the sun, with the moon beneath her feet, and on her head a mystic crown of twelve stars. R/. For ever and ever. Amen.

Let us praise and give thanks to God the FATHER, who elected her for his daughter. R/. Amen. PATER noster.

Praise be to GOD the FATHER, who predestined her to be the Mother of his SON. R/. Amen. Ave Maria.
Praise be to GOD the FATHER, who preserved her from all stain in her conception. R/. Amen. Ave Maria.
Praise be to GOD the FATHER, who on her birthday adorned her with his choicest gifts, R/. Amen. Ave Maria.
Praise be to GOD the FATHER, who gave her Joseph for her pure spouse and companion. R/. . Amen. Ave Maria and Gloria PATRI.
Let us praise and give thanks to GOD the SON, who chose her for his Mother. R/. Amen. PATER noster.
Praise be to GOD the SON, who became Incarnate in her womb, and abode there nine months. R/. Amen. Ave Maria.
Praise be to GOD the SON, who was born of her and was nourished at her breast. R/. Amen. Ave Maria.
Praise be to GOD the SON, who in his childhood willed that Mary should teach Him. R/. Amen. Ave Maria.
Praise is to GOD the SON, who revealed to her the mysteries of the redemption of the world. R/. Amen. Ave Maria and Gloria PATRI.
Let us praise and give thanks to GOD the HOLY GHOST who made her his spouse. R/. Amen. PATER noster.
Praise be to GOD the HOLY GHOST, who revealed to her first his name of HOLY GHOST. R/. Amen. Ave Maria.
Praise be to GOD the HOLY GHOST, through whose operation she became at once Virgin and Mother. R/. Amen. Ave Maria.
Praise be to GOD the HOLYGHOST, through whom she became the living temple of the Most Holy Trinity. R/. Amen. Ave Maria.
Praise be to GOD the HOLY GHOST, by whom she was exalted in Heaven high above all creatures. R/. Amen. Ave Maria and Gloria PATRI.
For the Holy Catholic Church, for the propagation of the faith, for peace among Christian princes, and for the uprooting of heresies, let us say Salve Regina, (see p. 184) etc.

196. The Memorare.
i. 300 Days. T.Q. ii. Plenary, once a month. I, II,III IV. (See Instructions.) 196 Plus IX, ii Dec., 1846.

MEMORARE, O piissima Virgo Maria, non esse auditum a sæculo quemquam ad tua currentem praesidia, tua implorantem auxilia, tua petentem suffragia, esse derelictum. Ego tali animatus confidentia, ad te, Virgo virginum, Mater, curro, ad te venio, coram te gemens peccator assisto; noli, Mater Verbi, verba mea despicere, sed audi propitia, et exaudi. Amen.	REMEMBER, O most gracious Virgin Mary, that never - was it known that anyone who fled to thy protection, implored thy, help, or sought thy intercession, was left unaided. Inspired with this confidence, I fly unto thee, O Virgin of virgins, my mother; to thee I come, before thee I stand, sinful and sorrowful; O Mother of the Word Incarnate, despise not my petitions; but in thy clemency hear and answer me. Amen.

197. Prayer, Ave Augustissima.
i. 300 Days. T.Q. ii. Plenary, once a month. I, II, III,, IV. (See Instructions.) 197 Pius IX, September 23, 1846.
HAIL, thou that art most venerable, Queen of Peace, most holy Mother of GOD; through the Sacred Heart of JESUS, thy Son, the Prince of Peace, procure for us the cessation of his anger, that so He may reign over us in peace. Remember, O most gracious Virgin Mary, that never was it known that any one who sought thy prayers was forsaken by GOD. Inspired with this confidence, I come unto Thee. Despise not my petitions, O Mother of the Incarnate Word; but in thy loving-kindness hear and answer me, O merciful, O sweet Virgin Mary.

198. The Tota Pulchra, etc.
i. 300 Days, once a day. ii. Plenary, on the Immaculate Conception, Nativity, Purification Annunciation, and Assumption. I, II, III, IV.(See Instructions.) 198 Pius X, 23 Mar. 1904.
Tota pulchra es Maria, etc.; with **V/.R/.** and Prayer.
Deus qui per immaculatam.(See 199).

199. Five Novenas for the Principal Feasts of Our Lady.
These Novenas maybe said in public or private, i. 300 Days, each day. ii. Plenary on the Feast or during the Octave. I, II, IV. (See Instructions.) 199 Pius VII, Res. August 4, 1808; Res. November 24, 1808; Res. January 11, 1809.
N.B. The prayers for the intention of the Pope are to be addressed to "God and to our Lady."

I. NOVENA FOR THE IMMACULATE CONCEPTION. Begins November 29.

VENI SANCTE SPIRITUS, reple tuorum corda fidelium, et tui amoris in eis ignem accende.	COME, O HOLY GHOST, fill the hearts of thy faithful and kindle in them the fire of thy love.
V/.. Emitte SPIRITUM tuum, et creabuntur.	**V/.** Send forth thy SPIRIT and they shall be created;
R/. Et renovabis faciem terræ.	**R/.** And Thou shalt renew the face of the earth.
Oremus.	**Let us pray.**
DEUS qui corda fidelium SANCTI SPIRITUS illustratione docuisti, da nobis in eodem SPIRITU recta sapere et de ejus semper consolatione gaudere. Per CHRISTUM DOMINUM nostrum. **R/.** Amen.	O GOD, who hast taught the hearts of the faithful by the light of the HOLY SPIRIT grant us by the same SPIRIT to relish what is right, and evermore to rejoice in his consolation. Through CHRIST our LORD. **R/.** Amen.

Preparatory Prayer to be said each day.
VIRGIN most pure, conceived without sin, all fair and stainless in thy Conception ; glorious Mary, full of grace, Mother of my GOD, Queen of Angels and of men, I humbly venerate thee as Mother of my SAVIOUR, who, though He was GOD, taught me by his own veneration, reverence, and obedience to thee, the honour and homage that are due to thee. Vouchsafe, I pray thee, to accept this Novena which I dedicate to thee. Thou art the safe refuge of the penitent sinner; it is very fitting, then, that I should have recourse to thee. Thou art the Mother of Compassion; then wilt thou surely be moved with pity for my many miseries. Thou art my best hope after JESUS; thou canst not but accept the loving confidence that I have in thee. Make me worthy to be called thy son, that so I may dare to cry unto thee : Show thyself a mother.
Ave Maria nine times, and Gloria PATRI once.

Prayer for the First Day.

BEHOLD me at thy sacred feet, O Immaculate Virgin. I rejoice with thee, because from all eternity thou wast elected to be the Mother of the Eternal Word, and wast preserved stainless from the taint of original sin. I praise and bless the Most Holy Trinity, who poured out upon thy soul in thy Conception the treasure of that privilege. I humbly pray thee to obtain for me grace effectually to overcome the sad effects produced in my soul by original sin; make me wholly victorious over them, that I may never cease to love my GOD. Then say or sing the Litany of the Blessed Virgin, No. 189, or else,

V/. Tota pulchra es Maria,
R/. Tota pulchra es Maria
V/. Et macula originalis non est in te
R/. Et macula originalis non est in te
V/. Tu gloria Jerusalem.
R/. Tu lætitia Israel.
V/. Tu honorificentia populi nostri.
R/. Tu advocata peccatorum.
V/. O Maria.
R/. O Maria.
V/. Virgo prudentissima.
R/. Mater clementissima.
V/. Ora pro nobis.
R/. Intercede pro nobis ad DOMINUM JESUM CHRISTUM.

V/. All fair art thou, O Mary.
R/. All fair art thou, O Mary.
V/. The original stain is not in thee.
R/. The original stain is not in thee.
V/. Thou art the glory of Jerusalem.
R/. Thou art the joy of Israel.
V/. Thou art the honour of our people.
R/. Thou art the advocate of sinners.
V/. O Mary.
R/. O Mary.
V/. Virgin most prudent.
R/. Mother most clement.
V/. Pray for us.
R/. Intercede for us with our LORD JESUS CHRIST.

After the Litany or Hymn as above, say,

V/. In Conceptione tua, Virgo, immaculata fuisti.
R/. Ora pro nobis PATREM, CUJUS FILIUM peperisti.
Oremus.
DEus qui per Immaculatam Virginis Conceptionem dignum FILIO tuo habitaculum præparasti : quæsumus ut qui ex morte ejusdem FILII tui prævisa eam ab omni labe præservasti, nosquo que mundos ejus intercessione ad te pervenire con cedas. Per CHRISTUM DOMINUM nostrum. Amen.

DEUS omnium fidelium pastor et rector, famulum tuum N., quem pastorem ecclesiæ tuæ præesse voluisti, propitius respice; da ei quæsumus, verbo et exemplo, quibus præest, proficere, ut ad vitam una cum grege sibi credito perveniat sempiternam.

DEUS refugium nostrum et virtus, adesto piis ecclesiæ tuæ precibus, auctor ipse pietatis; et præsta, ut quod fideliter petimus efficaciter consequamur. Per CHRISTUM DOMINUM nostrum, R/. Amen.

V/. In thy conception, O Virgin, thou wast immaculate.
R/. Pray for us to the FATHER, whose SON was born of thee.
Let us pray.
O GOD, who through the Immaculate Conception of a Virgin didst prepare a worthy dwelling place for Thy SON, we beseech Thee, who by the death of that SON, foreseen by Thee, didst preserve her from all stain of sin, to grant that by her intercession we also maybe purified, and so may come to Thee. Through CHRIST our LORD. Amen

O GOD, the Shepherd and Ruler of all the faithful, graciously look down upon thy servant N., whom Thou hast chosen to be the Pastor of thy Church; and grant him, we beseech Thee, both by word and example, so to direct those over whom Thou hast placed him, that together with the flock entrusted to his care, he may attain eternal life.

O GOD, our refuge and strength, who art the author of all holiness, listen to the pious prayers of thy Church, and grant that what we ask in faith we may effectually obtain, through CHRIST our LORD. R/. Amen.

The same order is to be observed on the other days of the Novena, the prayer for the day alone being changed.

Prayer for the Second Day, November 30.
MARY, unsullied lily of purity, I rejoice with thee, because from the first moment of thy Conception thou wast filled with grace, and hadst given unto thee the perfect use of reason. I thank and adore the ever blessed Trinity, who gave thee those high gifts. Behold me at thy feet overwhelmed with shame to see myself so poor in grace. O Thou who wast filled full of heavenly grace, grant me a portion of that same grace, and make me a partaker in the treasures of thy Immaculate Conception.

Prayer for the Third Day, December 1.
MARY, mystic rose of purity, I rejoice with thee at the glorious triumph thou didst gain over the serpent by thy Immaculate Conception, in that thou wast conceived without original sin. I thank and praise with my whole heart the ever blessed Trinity, who granted thee that glorious privilege; and I pray thee to obtain for me courage to overcome every snare of the great enemy, and never to stain my soul with mortal sin. Be thou always mine aid, and enable me with thy protection to obtain the victory over all the enemies of man's eternal welfare.

Prayer for the Fourth Day, December 2.
MARY Immaculate Virgin, mirror of holy purity, I rejoice exceedingly to see how from thy Immaculate Conception there were infused into thy soul the most sublime and perfect virtues with all the gifts of the most HOLY SPIRIT. I thank and praise the ever-blessed Trinity who bestowed upon thee these high privileges, and I beseech thee, gracious Mother, obtain for me grace to practise every Christian virtue, and so to become worthy to receive the gifts and graces of the HOLY GHOST.

Prayer for the Fifth Day, December 3.
MARY, bright moon of purity, I congratulate thee in that the mystery of thy Immaculate Conception was the beginning of salvation to the human race and was the joy of the whole world. I thank and bless the ever-blessed Trinity who did so magnify and glorify thy person. I entreat thee to obtain for me grace so to profit by the death and passion of thy dear Son, that his Precious Blood may not have been shed upon the Cross for me in vain, but that after a holy life I may be saved.

Prayer for the Sixth Day, December 4.
MARY Immaculate, brilliant star of purity, I rejoice with thee, because thy Immaculate Conception brought exceeding joy to all the angels of Paradise. I thank and bless the ever-blessed Trinity, who enriched thee with this privilege. Enable me also one day to take part in this heavenly joy, praising and blessing thee in the company of angels, world without end. Amen.

Prayer for the Seventh Day, December 5.
MARY Immaculate, rising morn of purity, I rejoice with thee, and I am filled with admiration at beholding thee confirmed in grace and rendered sinless from the first moment of thy Conception. I thank and praise the ever-blessed Trinity, who elected thee alone from all mankind for this special privilege. Holiest Virgin, obtain for me so entire and lasting- a hatred of sin, the worst of all evils, that I may rather die than ever again commit a mortal sin.

Prayer for the Eighth Day, December 6.
MARY, Virgin, sun without stain, I congratulate thee and I rejoice with thee, because GOD gave thee in thy Conception a greater and more abundant grace than He gave to all his angels and his saints together, even when their merits were most exalted. I thank and admire the immense beneficence of the ever-blessed Trinity, who hath dispensed to thee alone this privilege. Oh, enable me too to correspond with the grace of GOD, and never more to receive it in vain; change my heart, and help me to begin in earnest a new life.

Prayer for the Ninth Day, December 7.
IMMACULATE Mary, living light of holiness, model of purity, Virgin and Mother, as soon as thou wast conceived, thou didst profoundly adore thy GOD, giving him thanks, because by means of thee the ancient curse was blotted out, and blessing was again come upon the sinful sons of Adam. Let this blessing kindle in my heart love towards GOD; and do thou inflame my heart still more and more, that I may ever love Him constantly on earth, and afterwards eternally enjoy Him in heaven, there to thank and praise Him more and more fervently for all the wondrous privileges conferred on thee, and to rejoice with thee for thy high crown of glory.

II. NOVENA FOR OUR LADY'S NATIVITY (Beginning August 30).
Come, O HOLY GHOST, etc., see 199.

MOST holy Mary, elect and predestined from all eternity by the most Holy Trinity to be Mother of the only-begotten SON of the Eternal FATHER, foretold by the Prophets, expected by the Patriarchs, desired by all nations, Sanctuary and living- temple of the HOLY GHOST, sun without stain, conceived free from original sin, Mistress of Heaven and of Earth, Queen of Angels: humbly prostrate at thy feet we give thee our homage, rejoicing that the year has brought round again the memory of thy most happy Nativity; and we pray thee with all our hearts to vouchsafe in thy goodness now to come down again and be reborn spiritually in our souls, that, led captive by thy loveliness and sweetness, they may ever live united to thy most sweet and loving heart.

So now whilst we salute thee nine times, we will direct our thoughts to the nine months which thou didst pass enclosed in thy mother's womb; and we will devoutly say:

We hail thee, O Mary, who tracing thy descent from the royal house of David, didst come forth to the light of Heaven with high honour from the womb of holy Anna, thy most happy mother. Ave Maria.

We hail thee, heavenly babe, white dove of purity; who in spite of the serpent wast conceived free from original sin. Ave Maria.

We hail thee, bright morn; who, forerunner of the heavenly Sun of Justice, didst bring the first light to earth. Ave Maria.

We hail thee, Ele6l; who, like the untarnished Sun, didst burst forth in the dark night of sin. Ave Maria.

We hail thee, beauteous Moon; who didst shed light upon a world wrapped in the thickest darkness of paganism. Ave Maria.

We hail thee, dread warrior-child; who, in thyself a host, didst put to flight all hell. Ave Maria.

We hail thee, fair soul of Mary; who from eternity wast possessed by GOD. Ave Maria.

We hail thee, dear child, and we humbly venerate thy most holy infant body, the sacred swaddling-clothes wherewith they bound thee, the sacred crib wherein they laid thee, and we bless the hour and the day when thou wast born. Ave Maria.

We hail thee, much beloved infant, adorned with every virtue immeasurably above all saints, and therefore worthy Mother of the SAVIOUR of the world; who, having- been made fruitful by the HOLY SPIRIT, didst bring- forth the WORD Incarnate. Ave Maria.

Let us pray.
O MOST lovely infant, who by thy holy birth hast comforted the world, made glad the Heavens, struck terror into hell, brought help to the fallen, consolation to the sad, salvation to the weak, joy to all men living-; we entreat thee, with the most fervent love and gratitude, to be spiritually reborn in our souls by means of thy most holy love; renew our spirit in thy service, rekindle in our hearts the fire of charity, bid all virtues blossom there, that so we may find more and more favour in thy gracious eyes. Mary! be thou our Mary, and may we feel the saving power of thy sweetest name; may it ever be our comfort to call on that name in all our troubles; may it be our hope in dangers, our shield in temptation, and our last utterance in death.

Sit nobis nomen Mariæ mel in ore, melos in aure, et jubilus in corde. Amen. Let the name of Mary be honey in the mouth, melody in the ear, joy in the heart. Amen.

Here follows the Litany, 189. Then say:

V/. Nativitas tua, DEI Genitrix Virgo
R/. Gaudium annuntiavit universo mundo.
Oremus.
FAMULIS tuis, quæsumus Domine, cælestis gratiai munus impertire; ut quibus Beatæ Virginis partus extitit salutis exordium, nativitatis ejus votiva solemnitas pacis tribuat incrementum.
DEUS, omnium fidelium, and Deus refugium etc. (see prayer for the first day).

V/. The Nativity, O Virgin Mother of GOD.
R/. Hath brought joy to the whole world.
Let us pray.
GRANT to us thy servants, we beseech Thee, O LORD, the gift of heavenly grace; that to all those for whom the delivery of the Blessed Virgin was the beginning of salvation, this her votive festival may give increase of peace.
O GOD, the Shepherd, etc

III. NOVENA FOR THE ANNUNCIATION {Beginning March 16).
Come, O HOLY GHOST, etc.,

I VENERATE and I admire thee, most holy Virgin Mary, as the humblest of all the creatures of GOD on the very day of thy Annunciation, when GOD Himself exalted thee to the most sublime dignity of his own Mother. O mighty Virgin, enable me, wretched sinner that I am, to know the depths of my own nothingness, and at once with all my heart to humble myself before all men. Ave Maria.

Mary, most holy Virgin, when thou wast saluted by Gabriel the Archangel, and the message from GOD was conveyed to thee, and thou wast exalted by GOD above all the Choirs of the Angels, then thou didst humbly say, "Behold the handmaid of the LORD." Oh, obtain for me true humility and angelic purity, enabling me so to live on earth that I may ever be worthy of the blessing of GOD. Ave Maria.

O Virgin ever blessed, I rejoice with thee because solely by thy humble Fiat thou didst draw from the bosom of the Eternal FATHER the divine Word into thy own pure bosom. Draw then ever my heart to GOD; and with GOD draw grace into my heart, that I may ever bless thy Fiat, and cry with devotion, "O mighty Fiat! O efficacious Fiat! O Fiat to be venerated above all Fiats" (St Thomas of Villanova}. Ave Maria.

O Virgin Mary, on the day of thy Annunciation thou wast found by Gabriel the Archangel quick and ready to do GOD'S will, when it pleased the most Holy Trinity to await thy consent in order to redeem the world. Enable me in every good and bad fortune to turn to GOD with resignation and say: Be it done unto me according to thy word. Ave Maria.

Most holy Mary, I well understand that thy obedience made the union between thy GOD and thee more intimate than shall ever again be possible for any other creature: ("No creature could be in closer union with GOD." B. Albertus Magnus). I am confounded to see how sin has separated me from GOD. Help me then, kind Mother, truly to do penance for my sins, that thy own loving JESUS may yet once more live in me and I in Him. Ave Maria.

Most holy Mary, thou wast troubled by reason of thy modesty, when Gabriel the Archangel stood before thee in thy house; but I, when I come before thee, am troubled because of my great pride; wherefore do thou in thy incomparable humility, "which brought forth GOD for men, reopened Paradise, and set the captive souls free from hell beneath" (S. Aug. Sermo de Sanct.), draw me, I pray thee, out of the deep pit of my sins, and enable me to save my soul. Ave Maria.

Most holy Virgin, though I have an unhallowed tongue, I have the boldness to salute thee all hours of the day: "Hail, hail Mary, full of grace." I pray thee from my heart to replenish my soul with a little of that grace wherewith the HOLY SPIRIT, when He overshadowed thee, filled thee to the full. Ave Maria.

Most holy Mary, "The LORD is with thee"; I know by faith that the great GOD who has been ever with thee from thy Conception, is, by his Incarnation in thy purest womb, made still more closely one with thee; make it thy care, I pray thee, that I may ever be one in heart and soul with that same dear LORD JESUS, by means of his sanctifying grace. Ave Maria.

Most holy Mary, "Blessed art thou amongst women"; pour out upon my heart and soul thy heavenly blessing, as thou thyself wast ever blessed of GOD among all women; for I have this sure hope, that if, my dear Mother, thou wilt bless me while I live, then when I die I shall be blessed of GOD in the everlasting glory of Heaven. Ave Maria.

Then say the Litany, and then:

V/. Angelus DOMINI nuntiavit Mariæ.
R/. Et concepit de SPIRITU SANCTO. Ave Maria.
Oremus.
DEUS qui de beatæ Mariæ Virginis utero Verbum tuum, angelo nuntiante carnem suscipere voluisti: præsta supplicibus tuis, ut qui vere eam Genitricem DEI credimus, ejus apud te intercessionibus adjuvemur.
DEUS, omnium fidelium, and Deus refugium etc. (see prayer for the first day).

V/. The angel of the LORD declared unto Mary,
R/. And she conceived of the HOLY GHOST.
Let us pray.
O GOD, who by the message of an angel didst will that the divine Word should take flesh of the Blessed Virgin Mary; grant unto us thy suppliants that we, who believe her to be truly the Mother of GOD, maybe helped by her intercession with Thee.

IV. NOVENA FOR THE PURIFICATION (Beginning January 24).

Come, O HOLY GHOST, etc.,

MOST holy Virgin, bright mirror of all virtues, the forty days after thy delivery were no sooner passed than thou, though the purest of all virgins, didst will to be presented in the Temple to be purified; oh, help us then to keep our hearts unstained by sin, that so we too may be made worthy one day to be presented to our GOD in Heaven. Ave Maria.

Virgin most obedient, at thy presentation in the Temple, thou didst willingly offer the sacrifice customary among women ; enable us so to follow thy example, that we may make ourselves a living sacrifice to GOD by practising every virtue. Ave Maria.

Virgin most pure, thou didst despise the reproach of men, observing the precepts of the Law; ask for us grace always to keep our hearts pure, whatever the world may think of us. Ave Maria.

Virgin most holy, by offering thy Son, the Divine Word, to his Eternal FATHER, thou didst make Heaven glad; present our poor hearts to GOD, that by his grace they may be kept free from mortal sin. Ave Maria.

Virgin most humble, in consigning JESUS into the arms of the holy old man Simeon, thou didst fill his spirit full of heavenly joy; consign our hearts to GOD, that He may fill them full of his HOLY SPIRIT. Ave Maria.

Virgin most diligent, in ransoming thy Son JESUS according to the Law, thou didst co-operate in the salvation of the world; ransom our poor hearts from the slavery of sin, that they may be ever pure in the sight of GOD. Ave Maria.

Virgin most clement, on hearing the prophecy of Simeon foretelling thy woes, thou didst at once resign thyself to the good pleasure of thy GOD; make us always resigned to the dispositions of his Providence, and enable us to bear all troubles with patience. Ave Maria.

Virgin most compassionate, when thou didst fill the soul of Anna the prophetess with light, by means of thy Divine Son, thou didst make her magnify the mercies of GOD by recognizing JESUS as the REDEEMER of the world; enrich our spirits too with heavenly grace, that we may joyfully reap in full measure the fruits of our LORD'S Redemption. Ave Maria.

Virgin most resigned, although thou didst feel thine own soul transfixed with sorrow, foreseeing all the bitter Passion of thy Son, yet knowing the grief of Joseph thy spouse for all thy sufferings, thou didst console him with holy words ; pierce through and through our souls with true sorrow for our sins, that we may one day come to rejoice with thee in everlasting bliss, partakers of thy glory. Ave Maria.

Then say the Litany, and then:

V/. Responsum accepit Simeon a SPIRITU SANCTO.

R/. Non visurum se mortem nisi videret CHRISTUM DOMINI.

Oremus.

OMNIPOTENS sempiterne DEUS, majestatem tuam supplices exoramus, ut sicut unigenitus tuus cum nostræ carnis substantia in Templo est præsentatus, ita nos facias purificatistibi mentibus præsentari.

V/. Simeon received answer from the HOLY SPIRIT.

R/. That he should not see death till he had seen the CHRIST of the LORD.

Let us pray.

ALMIGHTY, everlasting GOD, we humbly pray thy Majesty that, as thine only-begotten SON was presented in the Temple in the substance of our flesh, so Thou wouldst enable us to present ourselves before thee with clean hearts.

DEUS, omnium fidelium, and Deus refugium etc. (see prayer for the first day).

V. NOVENA FOR THE ASSUMPTION (Beginning August 6).

First Day, August 6.
Come, O HOLY GHOST, etc.,

Hymn.

O GLORIOSA virginum	O QUEEN of all the virgin choir,
Sublimis inter sidera,	Enthroned above the starry sky;
Qui te creavit parvulum	Who with pure milk from thy own breast
Lactente nutris ubere.	Thy own CREATOR didst supply.
Quod Heva tristis abstulit	What man hath lost in hapless Eve,
Tu reddis almo germine:	Thy sacred womb to man restores;
Intrent ut astra flebiles,	Thou to the sorrowing here beneath

Cæli recludis cardines.	Hast opened heaven's eternal doors.
Tu regis alti janua,	Hail, O refulgent Hall of Light!
Et aula lucis fulgida:	Hail, Gate sublime of Heaven's high King!
Vitam datam per Virginem	Through Thee redeemed to endless life,
Gentes redemptæ plaudite.	Thy praise let all the nations sing.
JESU, tibi sit gloria,	O JESU, born of Virgin bright
Qui natus es de Virgine,	Immortal glory be to Thee;
Cum PATRE et almo SPIRITU	Praise to the FATHER infinite,
In sempiterna sæcula. Amen.	And HOLY GHOST eternally. Amen.

The glory of Mary in death, in that she was well prepared to die.
LET us meditate how glorious Mary was at the moment of her death, because in life she was so well prepared to die; first by reason of her ardent longing to see her GOD and to be again united to her Son; and next, by the unapproachable merit of her consummate perfection. Then, reflecting how different we are from Mary in our practice of preparation for our death, let us say:

MOST holy Virgin, who in order to prepare thyself for a holy death, didst live in continual desire of the beatific vision; oh, take from us all vain desires for the frail things of earth. Ave Maria thrice.
Most holy Virgin, who in order to prepare thyself for a holy death didst in life ever sigh to be united to thy Son JESUS ; obtain for us fidelity to JESUS even unto death. Ave Maria thrice.
Most holy Virgin, who, in preparation for a holy death, didst attain an unapproachable height of merit and of virtue; intercede for us that we may know that virtue and the grace of GOD alone will lead us to salvation. Ave Maria thrice.
Let us now give praise to Mary, so prudent in preparing for death; and whilst we exalt her glory, we will unite with the nine Choirs of Angels, who, on her Assumption into Heaven, escorted her, praising her with the first Choir:
Then say the Litany, and then:

V/. Exaltata est Sancta DEI Genitrix.	V/. The Holy Mother of GOD is exalted.
R/. Super Chores Angelorum ad cælestia regna.	R/. Into the heavenly kingdom above the Angel Choirs.
Oremus.	**Let us pray.**
FAMULORUM tuorum, quæsumus DOMINE, delictis ignosce: ut qui tibi placere de actibus nostris non valemus, Genitricis FILII tui DOMINI nostri intercessione salvemur.	WE beseech Thee, O LORD, to pardon the shortcoming's of thy servants; that we who by our own works are not able to please Thee, may be saved by the intercession of the Mother of thy Son, our LORD JESUS CHRIST.

DEUS, omnium fidelium, and Deus refugium etc. (see prayer for the first day).

Second Day, August 7.
Come, O HOLY GHOST, etc. O Queen of all, etc.,(hymn for the first day).
The glory of Mary in death, in that she was assisted by her Son Jesus and the Apostles.
Let us meditate how glorious Mary was at her death, in that, according to the teaching of holy writers, she was comforted not only by the apostles and saints, but also by her dear Son JESUS; and whilst we contemplate the unspeakable joy which filled her soul at this grace granted to her alone, let us entreat her for ourselves:

GLORIOUS Virgin, who for thy consolation didst merit to die in the blessed company of apostles and saints: obtain for us, that when we breathe forth our souls we may feel thy presence and that of our holy patrons, assisting us. Ave Maria thrice.
Glorious Virgin, who at the moment of thy death wast comforted by the sight of thy dear Son JESUS: oh, pray for us, that at that awful moment we too may be comforted by receiving JESUS in the most holy Viaticum. Ave Maria thrice.
Glorious Virgin, who didst surrender thy spirit into the arms of JESUS: assist us, that we also, in life and in death, may surrender our souls into the arms of JESUS, and that we may always desire that his most holy will be done. Ave Maria thrice.
Come then, let us magnify the glory of Mary, assisted at her death by her Son JESUS and his apostles, and join in jubilee at her triumph, with the second Choir of the heavenly host: Then say the Litany, and then:

V/. Exaltata est Sancta DEI Genitrix.
R/. Super Chores Angelorum ad cælestia regna.
Oremus.
FAMULORUM tuorum, quæsumus DOMINE, delictis ignosce: ut qui tibi placere de actibus nostris non valemus, Genitricis FILII tui DOMINI nostri intercessione salvemur.

V/. The Holy Mother of GOD is exalted.
R/. Into the heavenly kingdom above the Angel Choirs.
Let us pray.
WE beseech Thee, O LORD, to pardon the shortcoming's of thy servants; that we who by our own works are not able to please Thee, may be saved by the intercession of the Mother of thy Son, our LORD JESUS CHRIST.

Third Day, August 8.
Come, O HOLY GHOST, etc. O Queen of all, etc., (hymn for the first day).
The glory of Mary in death, in that she died in an ecstasy of love.
Let us meditate how glorious the holy Mary was in her death, because she died in a very ecstasy of the love of GOD; and desiring that we too may be strengthened by that holy fire of love, let us ask for her help.
MARY, most happy Virgin, who didst die of the vehemence of the love of GOD; make it thy care that in our hearts, as GOD wills, there be lit up this living fire of his love. Ave Maria thrice.
Mary, most happy Virgin, who dying of divine love didst teach us what our love of GOD ought to do; pray for us, that we may never abandon our GOD in life or death. Ave Maria thrice.
Mary, most happy Virgin, who in leaving this mortal life, by virtue of an ecstasy of love didst make known the fire which ever burnt in thy heart, obtain for us at least a spark of that same fire, to give us true sorrow for our sins. Ave Maria thrice.
Let us with the third Choir of Angels now exalt the ineffable glory of Mary inflamed with the love of her GOD:
Then say the Litany, and then:

V/. Exaltata est Sancta DEI Genitrix.
R/. Super Chores Angelorum ad cælestia regna.
Oremus.
FAMULORUM tuorum, quæsumus DOMINE, delictis ignosce: ut qui tibi placere de actibus nostris non valemus, Genitricis FILII tui DOMINI nostri intercessione salvemur.

V/. The Holy Mother of GOD is exalted.
R/. Into the heavenly kingdom above the Angel Choirs.
Let us pray.
WE beseech Thee, O LORD, to pardon the shortcoming's of thy servants; that we who by our own works are not able to please Thee, may be saved by the intercession of the Mother of thy Son, our LORD JESUS CHRIST.

Fourth Day, August 9.
Come, O HOLY GHOST, etc. O Queen of all, etc., (hymn for the first day).
The glory of Mary after death in her dead body.
Let us meditate how glorious Mary was in her dead body, because it was adorned with marvelous splendour and majesty, and spread around an odour of sanctity, which was the very fragrance of Paradise, and because innumerable miracles were wrought at the sight of it. Then, thinking on our own misery, let us pray:
O LADY, most pure, who by reason of thy virginal purity didst merit the glory of being so bright and so majestic in thy body after death; obtain for us the strength to detach ourselves from every foul spirit of impurity. Ave Maria thrice.
O Lady most pure, who by reason of thy rare virtue didst from thy dead body spread around the sweetness of Paradise; make it thy care that we may edify our neighbour by our life, and never more by our bad example become a stumbling block to others. Ave Maria thrice.
O Lady most pure, at the sight of whose holy body numberless bodily infirmities were cured; intercede for us, that by thy prayers all our spiritual ills may be healed. Ave Maria thrice.
Come, let us rejoice in the glory given to the dead body of Mary, magnifying her with the fourth Choir of Angels:
Then say the Litany, and then:
V/. Exaltata est Sancta DEI Genitrix.
R/. Super Chores Angelorum ad cælestia regna.
Oremus.

V/. The Holy Mother of GOD is exalted.
R/. Into the heavenly kingdom above the Angel Choirs.

FAMULORUM tuorum, quæsumus DOMINE, delictis ignosce: ut qui tibi placere de actibus nostris non valemus, Genitricis FILII tui DOMINI nostri intercessione salvemur.

Let us pray.
WE beseech Thee, O LORD, to pardon the shortcomings of thy servants; that we who by our own works are not able to please Thee, may be saved by the intercession of the Mother of thy Son, our LORD JESUS CHRIST.

Fifth Day, August 10.
Come, O HOLY GHOST, etc. O Queen of all, etc., (hymn for the first day).
The glory of Mary after death in the resurrection of her body.
Let us meditate how glorious Mary was after death, since by the power of the Highest her body, raised again to life, forthwith acquired the four gifts of brightness, agility, subtlety and impassibility; and filled with consolation at the excellence of her glory, let us invoke her:
OLADY exalted, who wast so gloriously raised to life again by thy GOD ; help us so to live on earth, that we also may rise again like unto thee in the last judgment day. Ave Maria thrice.
O Lady exalted, to whose risen body were given the gifts of brightness and subtlety, by reason of the bright example and humility of thy life on earth; pray for us, that all contemptuous affectation may be taken from us; that so our souls, being freed from all self-love, may be adorned with humility. Ave Maria thrice.
O Lady exalted, whose risen body was glorified by the gifts of agility and impassibility, by reason of thy spiritual zeal and patience while on earth ; obtain for us courage valiantly to mortify our bodies, and patiently to curb all our disordinate inclinations. Ave Maria thrice.
Then let us render due praise to Mary, and magnify the glory which adorned her risen body; while, with the fifth Choir, we exalt her:
Then say the Litany, and then:

V/. Exaltata est Sancta DEI Genitrix.
R/. Super Chores Angelorum ad cælestia regna.
Oremus.
FAMULORUM tuorum, quæsumus DOMINE, delictis ignosce: ut qui tibi placere de actibus nostris non valemus, Genitricis FILII tui DOMINI nostri intercessione salvemur.

V/. The Holy Mother of GOD is exalted.
R/. Into the heavenly kingdom above the Angel Choirs.
Let us pray.
WE beseech Thee, O LORD, to pardon the shortcomings of thy servants; that we who by our own works are not able to please Thee, may be saved by the intercession of the Mother of thy Son, our LORD JESUS CHRIST.

Sixth Day, August 11.
Come, O HOLY GHOST, etc. O Queen of all, etc., (hymn for the first day).
The glory of Mary after death in her Assumption into Heaven.

Let us meditate how gloriously Mary was taken up to Heaven, being escorted thither by many legions of the heavenly host and of blessed souls drawn by her merits out of Purgatory; and rejoicing in that majestic triumph, let us with all humility offer to her our supplications:
GREAT Queen, who wast assumed so royally into the Kingdom of eternal peace; obtain for us that all sordid, earthly thoughts be taken away from us, and our hearts be fixed upon the contemplation of the unchangeable happiness of Heaven. Ave Maria thrice.
Great Queen, who wast assumed to Heaven amidst a company of the Angelic Hierarchy; obtain for us strength to overcome the wiles of all our enemies, and that we may lend a docile ear to the counsels of that good angel who continually assists and governs us. Ave Maria thrice.
Great Queen, who wast assumed to Heaven most gloriously, in the company of souls drawn by thy merits out of Purgatory; free us from the slavery of sin and make us worthy to praise thee for all eternity. Ave Maria thrice.
Let us not cease to applaud the royal triumph of Mary; and uniting our homage with the sixth Choir of angels, let us honour the singular glory of her Assumption into Heaven:
Then say the Litany, and then:

V/. Exaltata est Sancta DEI Genitrix.
R/. Super Chores Angelorum ad cælestia regna.
Oremus.

V/. The Holy Mother of GOD is exalted.
R/. Into the heavenly kingdom above the Angel Choirs.

FAMULORUM tuorum, quæsumus DOMINE, delictis ignosce: ut qui tibi placere de actibus nostris non valemus, Genitricis FILII tui DOMINI nostri intercessione salvemur.

Let us pray.
WE beseech Thee, O LORD, to pardon the shortcomings of thy servants; that we who by our own works are not able to please Thee, may be saved by the intercession of the Mother of thy Son, our LORD JESUS CHRIST.

Seventh Day, August 12.
Come, O HOLY GHOST, etc. O Queen of all, etc., (hymn for the first day).
The glory of Mary after death in her exaltation as Queen of Heaven.
Let us meditate how glorious Mary is in Heaven, because she is enthroned there as Queen of the universe, "and is ever receiving homage and veneration from countless hosts of angels and of saints; and assisting at her royal throne, let us implore her aid: SOVEREIGN Queen of the universe, who for thy incomparable merit art raised to such high glory in the heavens; in thy pity look upon our miseries, and rule us with the gentle sway of thy protection, Ave Maria thrice.
Sovereign Queen of the universe, who art ever receiving worship and homage from all the heavenly host; accept, we pray thee, these our invocations, offered with such reverence as befits thy dignity and greatness. Ave Maria thrice.
Sovereign Queen of the universe, by that glory which thou hast by reason of thy high place in Heaven; vouchsafe to take us into the number of thy servants and obtain for us grace that with quick and ready will we may faithfully keep the precepts of GOD our LORD. Ave Maria thrice.
Let us take part in the joy of the angels praising Mary, and rejoice with the seventh Choir, because we know that she is raised to the dignity of Queen of the universe.
Then say the Litany, and then:

V/. Exaltata est Sancta DEI Genitrix.
R/. Super Chores Angelorum ad cælestia regna.
Oremus.
FAMULORUM tuorum, quæsumus DOMINE, delictis ignosce: ut qui tibi placere de actibus nostris non valemus, Genitricis FILII tui DOMINI nostri intercessione salvemur.

V/. The Holy Mother of GOD is exalted.
R/. Into the heavenly kingdom above the Angel Choirs.
Let us pray.
WE beseech Thee, O LORD, to pardon the shortcomings of thy servants; that we who by our own works are not able to please Thee, may be saved by the intercession of the Mother of thy Son, our LORD JESUS CHRIST.

Eighth Day, August 13.
Come, O HOLY GHOST, etc. O Queen of all, etc., (hymn for the first day).
The glory of Mary after death in the crown which decks her brow.
Let us meditate how glorious Mary is in Heaven by reason of the royal crown wherewith her divine Son has crowned her, and for the full knowledge which she now has of the deep mysteries of GOD, past, present and to come; and full of veneration for the incomparable honour bestowed upon our Queen, let us have recourse to her and say:
QUEEN unrivalled, who in Heaven above dost enjoy the high glory of being crowned by thy divine Son with a royal diadem; help us to share thy matchless virtues, and ask for us that, purified in heart, we may be made worthy to be crowned with thee in Paradise. Ave Maria thrice.
Queen unrivalled, in the full knowledge granted thee of all things on earth; for thy own glory's sake obtain pardon for our past evil deeds, that we may never offend again by froward tongue or wanton thought. Ave Maria thrice.
Queen unrivalled, whose desire it is to see men pure and clean of heart, that so they may be made worthy of thy GOD; obtain for us forgiveness of our sins, and help us, that all our looks, words and deeds may please his heavenly Majesty. Ave Maria thrice.
Let us then purify our hearts, in order that we may be worthy to give praise to Mary; and to the glory she possesses in that bright crown which decks her royal brow, let us add humble tokens of our love, rejoicing in union with the eighth Choir:
Then say the Litany, and then:

V/. Exaltata est Sancta DEI Genitrix.
R/. Super Chores Angelorum ad cælestia regna.
Oremus.

V/. The Holy Mother of GOD is exalted.
R/. Into the heavenly kingdom above the Angel Choirs.

FAMULORUM tuorum, quæsumus DOMINE, delictis ignosce: ut qui tibi placere de actibus nostris non valemus, Genitricis FILII tui DOMINI nostri intercessione salvemur.

Let us pray.
WE beseech Thee, O LORD, to pardon the shortcomings of thy servants; that we who by our own works are not able to please Thee, may be saved by the intercession of the Mother of thy Son, our LORD JESUS CHRIST.

Ninth Day, August 14.
Come, O HOLY GHOST, etc. O Queen of all, etc., (hymn for the first day).
The glory of Mary after death in her patronage of man.
Let us meditate how glorious Mary is in Heaven by reason of her patronage of man, and for the power she has to aid him with great watchfulness in all his necessities ; wherefore with lively confidence in the patronage of the very Mother of our GOD, let us implore her aid.
MARY, our most powerful patroness, whose glory it is in Heaven to be the advocate of man; oh! take us from the hands of the enemy and place us in the arms of our GOD and CREATOR. Ave Maria thrice.
Mary, our most powerful patroness, who being in Heaven the advocate of men wouldst that all men should be saved; make it thy care that none of us succumb at the thought of our past relapses into sin. Ave Maria thrice.
Mary, our most powerful patroness, who to fulfil thy office dost love to be continually invoked by men; obtain for us such true devotion that we may ever call upon thee in life, and above all at the awful moment of our death. Ave Maria thrice.
Now with all our hearts let us celebrate the glories of Mary; and consoled at having Mary for our advocate in Heaven, let us join in praising her with the ninth Choir of angels:
Then say the Litany, and then:

V/. Exaltata est Sancta DEI Genitrix.
R/. Super Chores Angelorum ad cælestia regna.
Oremus.
FAMULORUM tuorum, quæsumus DOMINE, delictis ignosce: ut qui tibi placere de actibus nostris non valemus, Genitricis FILII tui DOMINI nostri intercessione salvemur.

V/. The Holy Mother of GOD is exalted.
R/. Into the heavenly kingdom above the Angel Choirs.
Let us pray.
WE beseech Thee, O LORD, to pardon the shortcomings of thy servants; that we who by our own works are not able to please Thee, may be saved by the intercession of the Mother of thy Son, our LORD JESUS CHRIST.

200. Eleven Novenas in Honour of Our Lady.
At any time of the year, with any form of prayer approved by competent ecclesiastical authority,
i. 300 Days each day. ii. Plenary, once during the Novena or Octave. I, II, IV. (See Instructions.) 200 Pius IX. Res., January 5, 1849; Bps., January 28, 1850; Indul., November 26, 1876.
In honour of (1) the Immaculate Conception; (2) the Nativity B.V.M.; (3) the Presentation B.V.M.; (4) the Annunciation B.V.M.; (5) the Visitation B.V.M. ; (6) the Sacred Delivery of Mary and Birth of JESUS; (7) the Purification B.V.M.; (8) the Seven Dolours B.V.M.; (9) the Assumption B.V.M.; (10) the Sacred Heart of Mary and her Patronage; and (11) for the Feast of the Most Holy Rosary.

201. One Ave and Prayer, O Domina Mea! for Victory in Temptations, especially those against Chastity.
i. 100 Days, once a day, if said morning and evening, ii. Plenary, once a month, I, II, III, IV. (See Instructions.) 201 Pius IX, August 5, 1851.
Ave Maria.

O DOMINA mea! O Mater mea! Tibi me totum offero, atque ut me tibi probem devotum, consecro tibi hodie oculos meos, aures meas, os meum, cor meum, plane me totum. Quoniam ita que tuus sum, O bona Mater, serva me, defende me, ut rem ac possessionem tuam.

O My Queen! my Mother! I give thee all myself, and, to show my devotion to thee, I consecrate to thee this day my eyes, ears, mouth, heart, my entire self. Wherefore, O loving Mother, as I am thy own, keep me, defend me, as thy property and possession.

202. Prayer, O Beata Virgo.
50 Days. T.Q. (See Instructions) 202 Pius ix, Mem. May 19, 1854.

MARY, Virgin ever blessed ! who can worthily praise thee or give thanks to thee, who, by that wondrous assent of thy will, didst rescue a fallen world? What honours can the weakness of our human nature pay to thee, which by thy intervention alone has found the way to restoration? Accept, then, such poor thanks as we crave here to offer, though they are unequal to thy merits; and, receiving our vows, obtain by thy prayers the remission of our offences. Carry thou our prayers within the sanctuary of the heavenly audience, and bring forth from it the medicine of our reconciliation. Through thee may those sins become pardonable the release from which through thee we ask of GOD, and that be granted which we demand with confidence. Accept what we offer, grant us what we seek, spare us what we fear, for thou art the sole hope of sinners. Through thee we hope for the forgiveness of our faults, and in thee, most blessed Virgin, is the hope of our reward. Holy Mary, succour the wretched, help the faint-hearted, comfort the sorrowful, pray for the people, shield the clergy, intercede for all women consecrated to GOD, let all feel thy aid who keep thy holy commemoration. Be thou at hand, ready to aid our prayers, when we pray; and bring back to us the answers we desire. Make it thy care to intercede ever for the people of GOD thou who, blessed of GOD, didst merit to bear the REDEEMER of the world, who liveth and reigneth for ever and ever. Amen.

203. Prayer of St Alphonsus to be said before a representation of Our Lady.
i. 300 Days. T.Q. ii. Plenary, once a month. I, II, IV. (See Instructions.) 203 Pius IX, Pr. Ma. September 7, 1854

MOST holy Mary, Immaculate Virgin and Mother, to thee who art the Mother of my LORD, the refuge of sinners, I, who am the most miserable of all, have recourse to-day. I adore thee, O great Queen, and I thank thee for the many favours thou hast done me up to now, especially for having preserved me from hell, which I have so often deserved. I love thee, most dear Lady; and by the love I bear thee I promise to desire ever to serve thee and to do all I can to make thee loved by others. I place all my hopes in thee, all my salvation. Accept me for thy servant and shelter me under thy mantle, O thou Mother of mercy. And since thou art so powerful with GOD, free me from all temptations, or obtain for me strength to overcome them as long as I live. Of thee I ask true love of JESUS CHRIST. Through thee I hope to die a good death. O Mother, by the love thou bearest to GOD, I pray thee to help me always, but specially in the last moment of my life. Do not leave me until thou seest me safe in Heaven, there to bless thee and sing thy mercies for all eternity. This is my hope. Amen.

204. Prayer for a Good Death.
100 days, once a day. (See Instructions.) 204 Pius IX, Brs. March 11, 1856

O MARY, conceived without stain, pray for us who fly to thee. Refuge of sinners, Mother of those who are in their agony, leave us not in the hour of our death, but obtain for us perfect sorrow, sincere contrition, remission of our sins, a worthy reception of the most holy Viaticum, the strengthening-of the Sacrament of Extreme Unction, so that we may be able to stand with safety before the throne of the just but merciful Judge, our GOD and our REDEEMER. Amen.

205. Psalms and Prayers of St Bonaventure for every day in the week.
i. Seven Years and Seven Quarantines, once a day, for reciting-, in any language, the psalms and prayers for each day, according to the order of the days of the week, from the Book entitled, The Daily Tribute of Loving Prayers and Praises for each day in the week to the Immaculate Mother of God, etc.

ii. Plenary, on the accustomed conditions, on the Feast, of the Immaculate Conception and once during its Octave, on the Feast of St Joseph, St Bonaventure (July 14), and on any one day at pleasure during the month of May, to those of the faithful who for one month previous to these days shall have said daily the above Psalms and Prayers. I, II,III, IV. (See Instructions.) 205 Pius IX, Br. December 9, 1856.

206. Chaplet of the Twelve Privileges of Our Lady.
i. 300 Days, once a day. ii. Plenary, once a month. I, II, III, IV. (See Instructions.) 206 Pius IX, Br. June 26, 1860.

In the Name of the FATHER and of the SON and of the HOLY GHOST. Amen.

V/. O GOD, come to my assistance.

R/. O LORD, make haste to help me.

Glory be to the FATHER, etc.

HAIL to thee, purest, holiest Mother of JESUS. We humbly pray thee, by thy predestination, whereby thou wast even from all eternity elected Mother of GOD ; by thy Immaculate Conception, whereby thou wast conceived without stain of original sin; by thy most perfect resignation, whereby thou wast ever conformed to the will of GOD; and, lastly, by thy consummate holiness, whereby throughout thy whole life thou didst never commit one single fault : we pray thee to become our advocate with our LORD, that He may pardon our many sins, which are the cause of his wrath. And thou, O FATHER Almighty, by the merits of these privileges vouchsafed to this thy well-beloved Daughter, hear her supplications for us, and pardon us, her clients.

Spare, O LORD, spare thy people. PATER once, Ave four times, Gloria once.
By thy holy and Immaculate Conception deliver us, glorious Virgin Mary.

HAIL to thee, purest, holiest Mother of JESUS. We humbly pray thee, by the most holy Annunciation, when thou didst conceive the Divine Word in thy womb ; by thy most happy delivery, in which thou didst experience no pain ; by thy perpetual virginity, which thou didst unite with the fruitfulness of a mother; and, lastly, by the bitter martyrdom which thou didst undergo in our SAVIOUR'S death: we pray thee to become our mediatrix, that we may reap the fruit of the Precious Blood of thy Son. And Thou, O Divine Son, by the merit of these privileges granted to thy well-beloved Mother, hear her supplications, and pardon us, her clients.

Spare, O LORD, spare thy people. PATER once, Ave four times, Gloria once.
By thy holy and Immaculate Conception deliver us, glorious Virgin Mary.

HAIL to thee, purest, holiest Mother of JESUS. We humbly pray thee, by the joys which thou didst feel in thy heart at the Resurrection and Ascension of JESUS CHRIST; by thy Assumption into Heaven, whereby thou wast exalted above all the Choirs of the Angels ; by the glory which GOD has given thee to be Queen of all saints; and, lastly, by that most powerful intercession, where

by thou art able to obtain all that thou dost desire: we pray thee, obtain for us true love of GOD. And Thou, O HOLY SPIRIT, by the merits of these privileges of thy well-beloved Spouse, hear her supplications, and pardon us her clients. Amen.

Spare, O LORD, spare thy people. PATER once, Ave four times, Gloria once.
By thy holy and Immaculate Conception deliver us, glorious Virgin Mary.

Antiphon. Thy Conception, Virgin Mother of GOD, brought joy to the whole world, for of thee was born the Sun of Justice, CHRIST our GOD, who, loosing the curse, bestowed the blessing, and, confounding death, gave unto us eternal life.

V/. In thy Conception, Virgin Mary, thou wast Immaculate.

R/. Pray to the FATHER for us, whose SON JESUS, conceived by the HOLY GHOST, thou didst bring forth.

Let us pray.

GOD of mercy, GOD of pity, GOD of tenderness, who, pitying the affliction of thy people, didst say to the angel smiting them, "Withhold thy hand"; for the love of thy glorious Mother, at whose precious breast thou didst sweetly find an antidote to the venom of our sins, bestow on us the help of thy grace, that we may be freed from all evil, and mercifully protected from every onset of destruction. Who livest and reignest for ever and ever. Amen.

207. Prayer for the Conversion of Heretics and Schismatics.

300 Days, once a day. (See Instructions.) 207 Pius IX, Prop. December 30, 1868.

O MARY, Mother of mercy and Refuge of sinners, we beseech thee to look with pitying-eyes on heretical and schismatical nations. Do thou, who art the Seat of wisdom, illuminate their minds, wretchedly involved in the darkness of ignorance and sin, that they may know the Holy, Catholic, Apostolic, Roman Church to be the only true Church of JESUS CHRIST, out of which no sanctity or salvation can be found. Finally, complete their conversion by obtaining for them the grace to believe every truth of our holy Faith, and to submit to the Sovereign Roman Pontiff, the Vicar of JESUS CHRIST on earth, that thus, being soon united to us by the bonds of divine charity, they may make with us but one fold under one and the same pastor, and that we may thus, O glorious Virgin, all sing exultingly for ever, "Rejoice, O Virgin Mary! alone thou hast destroyed all heresies in the whole world." Amen. Ave Maria thrice.

208. Prayer for the Conversion of Greek Schismatic's.
i. 300 Days, once a day. ii. Plenary, once a month. I, II, III, IV. (See Instructions.) 203 Pius IX, Br. June ii, 1869

O IMMACULATE Virgin Mary, we thy servants, and sons of the holy Catholic and Roman Church, full of confidence in thy powerful protection, humbly beseech thee that thou wouldst deign to implore of the HOLY GHOST, by the honour and glory of his eternal Procession from the FATHER and the SON, the abundance of his gifts for our separated brethren, the Greek schismatics, that, enlightened by his vivifying grace, they may re-enter into the bosom of the Catholic Church, under the infallible guidance of her supreme pastor and teacher, the Sovereign Roman Pontiff; and that thus, sincerely re-united to us by the indissoluble bonds of the same faith and the same charity, they may, with us, glorify, by the practice of good works, the most august Trinity, and at the same time honour thee, O Virgin Mother of GOD, full of grace, now and through all ages. Amen. Ave Maria thrice.

209. Act of Reparation.
i. 300 Days, once a day. ii. Plenary, once a month. I, II, III, IV (See Instructions.) 209 Leo XIII March 21, 1885.

MOST glorious Virgin Mary, Mother of GOD, and our mother, look with pity upon us poor sinners, who, afflicted with so many miseries surrounding us in this life, feel ourselves cut to the heart by the many horrible insults and blasphemies which we are often constrained to hear uttered against thee, O Immaculate Virgin. Oh, how these impious sayings offend the infinite Majesty of GOD, and JESUS CHRIST his only begotten SON! How they provoke his anger, and give us cause to fear the terrible effects of his vengeance! If the sacrifice of our lives could avail against such outrages and blasphemies, very willingly would we make it, for we desire, most holy Mother, to love and honour thee with all our hearts, such being the will of GOD. And just because we love thee, we will do whatever lies in our power to make thee loved and honoured by all. And do thou, Mother of pity, supreme consoler of the afflicted, accept this act of reparation offered to thee, in our name and in the name of all our families, and on behalf of those who, not knowing what they say, impiously blaspheme thee; that so, by obtaining from GOD their conversion, thy glorious compassion, thy power, and thy great mercy may become more manifest, and they too may join with us in proclaiming thee blessed amongst women, the Immaculate Virgin, the most compassionate Mother of GOD. Ave Maria thrice.

210. Prayer.
100 Days, once a day. (See Instructions.) 210 Leo XIII, December 19, 1885.

O POWERFUL Virgin, who alone hast destroyed all heresies throughout the world, deliver the Christian world from the snares of the devil, and have compassion on the souls deceived by diabolical cunning, that laying aside all heretical guilt, the hearts of the erring may be converted and return to the unity of the Catholic Faith, through thy intercession with our LORD JESUS CHRIST thy Son, who liveth and reigneth with GOD the FATHER in the unity of the HOLY SPIRIT, GOD for ever and ever. Amen.

211. Prayer.
300 Days, once a day. (See Instructions) 211 Pius X , June 2, 1905.

O MARY, who, crowned with stars, hast for a footstool under thy feet the moon, and for thy throne the wings of angels ; turn thy eyes upon this valley of sorrows, and listen to the voice of one who puts his hope and refuge in thee. Thou dost now enjoy the infinite sweetness of Paradise, but in the midst of joy and splendour thou bearest always in thy inmost heart the recollection of what thou didst suffer in this life. Thou hast tried the needs of this exile, and therefore knowest how bitterly flow the days of those who live in sorrow.

Ever in thy remembrance rises up a mount covered with armed men and the dregs of the people ; thou hearest ever a voice, so well known by thee, which says to thee: "O Lady, behold, in my place, thy son." And these thoughts move thee to profound tenderness, and thou dost realize, O blessed one, that on that mountain and with those words thou wast destined to be the Mother of the living..

Without thee what would life be to the unhappy children of Adam. Each one of them has a sorrow which tries him, a grief which overwhelms, a wound which torments. And all have recourse to thee, as to a port of safety, to a fount of complete refreshment. When the waves lash themselves into fury, the wayfarer turns to thee and prays for calm. To thee has recourse the orphan who, like a flower in the wilderness, lies exposed to the whirlwind of life. To thee pray the poor who want their daily bread; and not one of them remains without help and consolation. But if all find in thee aid and refreshment, what shall we say, to whom thou art wont to appear, glorious as thou art in heaven.

O Mary, mother of all, enlighten our minds, soften our hearts, so that this most pure love which streams from thy eyes may be poured forth on every side, and produce those marvellous fruits which thy Son prepared for by shedding his Blood, whilst thou didst suffer the most cruel pangs at the foot of the Cross.

212. Office of the Blessed Virgin.

i. Seven Years and Seven Quarantines, once a day. ii. Plenary, once a month. I, II
iii. 300 Days, once a day, for Matins and Lauds only, iv. 50 Days, for each Little Hour, for Vespers, and for Compline. 212 Leo XIII, November 27, 1887 ; December 8, 1897 ; Pius X, August 28, 1903; December 18, 1906.

The Indulgences attached to this Office are extended to the recitation of it in the vernacular only in case of private recitation.

Private recitation includes recitation by communities in their private chapels or even in their churches, if the doors are closed to the public.

213. Hymn, Ave Maris Stella.

300 Days, once a day. (See Instructions.) 213 Leo XIII, January 27, 1888,

AVE maris Stella,	HAIL thou star of the ocean !
DEI Mater alma	Portal of the sky!
Atque semper virgo,	Ever Virgin Mother
Felix cæli porta.	Of the LORD most high!
Sumens illud Ave	Oh! by Gabriel's Ave,
Gabrielis ore,	Utter d long ago,
Funda nos in pace,	Eva's name reversing,
Mutans Evæ nomen.	Stablish peace below.
Solve vincla reis,	Break the captive's fetters ;
Prefer lumen cascis,	Light on blindness pour;
Mala nostra pelle,	All our ills expelling,
Bona cuncta posce.	Every bliss implore.
Monstra te esse matrem,	Show thyself a Mother
Sumat per te preces,	Offer Him our sighs,
Qui pro nobis natus,	Who for us incarnate
Tulit esse tuns.	Did not thee despise.
Virgo singularis,	Virgin of all virgins!
Inter omnes mitis,	To thy shelter take us :
Nos culpis solutos,	Gentlest of the gentle!
Mites fac et castos.	Chaste and gentle make us
Vitam præsta puram,	Still as on we journey,
Iter para tutum,	Help our weak endeavour;
Ut videntes JESUM,	Till with thee and JESUS
Semper collætemur.	We rejoice for ever.
Sit laus DEO PATRI,	Through the highest heaven,
Summo CHRISTO decus,	To the Almighty Three,
SPIRITUI SANCTO,	FATHER, SON, and SPIRIT,
Tribus honor unus. Amen.	One same glory be. Amen.

214. Reparation for Blasphemy against Our Lady.

300 Days. T.Q. (See Instructions.) 214 Pius X, March 21, 1905.

OMARY, bless this house, where thy name is ever held in benediction. All glory to Mary ever Immaculate, ever Virgin, blessed among- women, the Mother of our LORD JESUS CHRIST, Queen of Paradise.

215. The Magnificat.

i. 100 Days, once a day. ii. Seven Years and Seven Quarantines, once on Saturdays. (See Instructions) 215 Leo XIII, September 20, 1879 ; February 22, 1888

MAGNIFICAT :*anima mea DOMINUM. Et exultavit spiritus meus :* in DEO salutari meo	My soul doth magnify: the LORD. And my spirit hath rejoiced : in GOD my Saviour.
Quia respexit humilitatem ancillæ suæ: * ecce enim ex hoc beatam me dicent omnes generationes,	For He hath regarded the humility of his handmaid: for behold from henceforth all generations shall call me blessed.
Quia fecit mihi magna qui potens est: * et sanctum nomen ejus.	For He that is mighty hath done great things unto me : and holy is his name. And his mercy is from generation to generation: unto them that fear Him.
Et misericordia ejusa progenie in progenies: * timentibus eum. Fecit potentiam in brachio suo: * dispersit superbos mente cordis sui.	He hath shewed strength with his arm: He hath scattered the proud in the imagination of their heart.
Deposuit potentes de sede : * et exaltavit humiles	He hath put down the mighty from their seat : and hath exalted the humble.
Esurientes implevit bonis: * et divites dimisit inanes.	He hath filled the hungry with good things: and the rich He hath sent empty away.
Suscepit Israel puerum suum:*recordatus misericordiæ suæ.	He hath upholden his servant Israel: being mindful of his mercy.
Sicut locutus est ad patres nostros: * Abraham, et semini ejus in sæcula. Gloria PATRI, etc.	As He spake unto our fathers: to Abraham and his seed for ever. Glory be to the FATHER, etc.

216. Prayer of St Aloysius Gonzaga.
200 Days, once a day. (See Instructions.) 216 Leo XIII, March 15, 1890.
O HOLY Mary, my mistress, into thy blessed trust and special custody, and into the bosom of thy mercy I this day, everyday, and in the hour of my death, commend my soul and my body : to thee I commit all my anxieties and miseries, my life and the end of my life, that by thy most holy intercession and by thy merits all my actions may be directed and disposed according to thy will and that of thy Son. Amen.

217. Prayer for England.
i. 300 Days. T.Q. ii. Plenary, once a month. I, II, III,IV. (See Instructions.) 217 Leo XIII, Lit. Apos., April 15, 1895.
O BLESSED Virgin Mary, Mother of GOD, and our most gentle Queen and Mother, look down in mercy upon England thy Dowry, and upon us all who greatly hope and trust in thee. By thee it was that JESUS our SAVIOUR and our hope was given unto the world ; and He has given thee to us that we might hope still more. Plead for us thy children, whom thou didst receive and accept at the foot of the Cross, O sorrowful Mother. Intercede for our separated brethren, that with us in the one true fold they may be united to the supreme Shepherd, the Vicar of thy Son. Pray for us all, dear Mother, that by faith fruitful in good works we may all deserve to see and praise GOD together with thee in our heavenly home. Amen.

218. Prayer for Reunion.
300 Days, once a day. (See Instructions.) 218 Leo XIII, February i, 1896.
O IMMACULATE Virgin, who wast preserved by a singular privilege of grace from original sin, look with pity on our separated brethren, who are still thy children, and recall them to the centre of unity. They have, even from afar, preserved a most tender devotion towards thee, O Mother; do thou, who art so generous, reward them for it by obtaining for them the grace of conversion. Victorious over the infernal serpent from the first moment of thy being, renew, now that the necessity is more urgent, thy triumphant progress, as of old. If our unhappy brethren continue in separation from our common Father, it is the work of the enemy; do thou, then, unmask his wiles, put his forces to rout, and let his victims see that it is impossible to obtain salvation except in union with the successor of St Peter. Do thou, who from the first in the plenitude of thy gifts didst glorify Him who worked such great wonders in thee, glorify thy Son, bringing back into his one fold his strayed sheep, making them subject to the guidance of the universal Shepherd, his Vicar on earth ; and may it be thy glory, O Virgin, as well to have rooted out of the world all errors, as to have put an end to schisms, and so to have restored peace to the world.

219. Aspiration.
40 Days. T,Q. (See Instructions.) 219 Pius IX, August 5, 1851.

O DOMINA mea! O Mater mea! memento me esse tuum. Serva me, defende me, ut rem et possessionem tuam.	MY Lady and my Mother, remember I am thine; protect and defend me as thy property and possession.

220. Ejaculation.
100 Days, once a day. (See Instructions) 220 Leo XIII, Card. Vic. December 15, 1883.
MARY, Mother of GOD and Mother of mercy, pray for us, and for the departed.

221. Three Invocations with Ave thrice.
100 Days, once a day. (See Instructions.) 221 Leo XIII, May 20, 1893.

VIRGO ante partum, ora pro nobis. Ave Maria	THOU who wast a Virgin before thy delivery, pray for us. Ave Maria.
Virgo in partu, ora pro nobis. Ave Maria.	THOU who wast a Virgin in thy delivery, pray for us. Ave Maria.
Virgo post partum, ora pro nobis. Ave Maria.	THOU who wast a Virgin after thy delivery, pray for us. Ave Maria.

222. Ejaculation of St Philip Neri.
50 Days, once a day. (See Instructions) 222 Leo XIII, March 29, 1894.
MARY, Virgin Mother of GOD, pray to JESUS for me.

223. Chaplet of the Seven Joys of Our Lady.
i. All who, in churches of the Franciscans, join in the public recitation of this chaplet, gain all the indulgences granted to members of the Order.
ii. Plenary, on each of the Feasts of the Seven Joys, the greater Feasts of our Lady, or on any day within the Octaves, to all who recite the chaplet. I, II.
iii. Plenary, once a month, if said every Saturday. I, II.
iv. Plenary, in articulo mortis, at the point of death, to all who carry the beads about and say them frequently. I, n (if possible) or with at least contrition and resignation, and the invocation of the Holy Name, in the heart, if not with the lips.
v. 300 Years, on other Feasts of our Lady.
vi. 200 Years, on holidays of obligation,
vii. 70 Years and 70 Quarantines, on any day.
viii. 10 Years to all who do any good work for the glory of GOD and the benefit, spiritual or temporal, of their neighbour, or who say Ave seven times in honour of the Joys, if they carry the beads about and say them frequently.
N.B. The beads must be blessed by the Franciscan Minister-General, or a priest duly authorized by him (single decades may be said separately during the course of the day.) (See Instructions.) 223 Pius X. Br. September is, July 22, 1905.
(1) The Annunciation. (2) The Visitation. (3) The Nativity. (4) The Adoration of the Magi. (5) The Finding in the Temple. (6) The Resurrection. (7) The Assumption.

224. Ejaculation.
Before the Blessed Sacrament exposed. 300 Days. T.Q. (See Instructions.) 224 Pius X, January 10, 1906
OUR Lady of the most holy Sacrament, pray for us.

225. Ejaculation.
300 Days. T.Q. (See Instructions.) 225 Pius X January 8, 1906.
MARY, our hope, have pity on us.

226. Ejaculation.
300 Days. T.Q. (See Instructions.) 226 Pius X, June 27, 1906.
MARY sorrowing, Mother of all Christians, pray for us.

227. Ejaculation.

300 Days. TQ. (See Instructions.) 227Pius X, May 30, 1908.

MOTHER of love, of sorrow, and of mercy, pray for us.

228. Prayer to Our Lady.

300 Days, once a day. (See Instructions.) 228 Pius X, December 19, 1906.

O MOTHER of mercy, help of Christians, faithful handmaid of divine providence, treasurer of all graces, remember that never was it known that those who devoutly had recourse to thee were left without consolation. Wherefore, I prostrate myself humbly before thee, trusting in thy heart of pity and in thy most generous watchfulness, and beg of thee to hear my prayers.

Obtain for me holy prudence, and graces in all my spiritual needs, and also that temporal prudence necessary for spending my days in this vale of tears.

I commend most fervently to thy loving and maternal heart Holy Church, the Supreme Pontiff, the conversion of souls, the propagation of the Catholic Faith, as well as the chosen spouses of our LORD who are suffering in the cruel flames of Purgatory, that they may quickly be consoled with eternal refreshment. Amen.

229. Prayer to Our Lady.

300 Days. T.Q. (See Instructions.) 229 Pius X, January 9, 1907.

MARIA Mater misericordiæ, Mater et Filia illius qui Pater est misericordiarum et DEUS totius consolationis, **1** Dispensatrix thesaurorum Filii tui, **2** Ministra DEI, **3** Mater summi Sacerdotis CHRISTI, Sacerdos pariter et Altare, **4** Sacrariuni immaculatum Verbi DEI, **5** Magistra Apostolorum omnium et Discipulorum CHRISTI ; **6** protege Pontificem Maximum, intercede pro nobis et pro sacerdotibus nostris, ut Summus Sacerdos CHRISTUS JESUS conscientias nostras purificet, et digne ac pie ad sacrum convivium suum accedamus.

O Virgo Immaculata, quæ non modo dedisti nobis panem cælestem CHRISTUM in remissionem peccatorum, **7** sed es tu ipsa hostia acceptissima DEO litata, **8** et gloria sacerdotum, **9** quæque teste beatissimo famulo tuo S. Antonino, quamvis sacramentum ordinis non acceperis, quidquid tamen dignitatis et gratiæ in ipso confertur, de hoc plena fuisti ; unde merito Virgo Sacerdos **10** prædicaris; respice super nos et super sacerdotes Filii tui, purifica nos, salva nos, sanctifica nos, ut ineffabiles sacramentorum thesauros sancle suscipiamus, et æternam animarum nostrarum salutem consequi mereamur. Amen

Mater misericordiæ, ora pro nobis.

Mater æterni Sacerdotis CHRISTI JESU, ora pro nobis.

Regina cleri, ora pro nobis.

Maria Virgo Sacerdos, ora pro nobis.

MARY, Mother of mercy. Mother and daughter of Him who is the Father of mercies and the GOD of all consolation, **1** Dispenser of the treasures of thy Son, **2** Handmaiden of God, **3** Mother of the supreme High-Priest, CHRIST, at once Priest and Altar, **4** immaculate Treasure house of the Word of GOD, **5** Mistress of all the Apostles and Disciples of CHRIST; **6** protect the Supreme Pontiff, intercede for us and for our priests, that the High Priest JESUS CHRIST may purify our consciences, so that we may worthily and piously approach his holy banquet.

O Immaculate Virgin, who not only gavest us CHRIST, to be our bread from Heaven, for the remission of sins, **7** but art thyself a most acceptable victim offered to GOD, **8** and the glory of the priesthood, **9** who according to the testimony of thy most blessed servant St Antoninus, although thou didst not receive the Sacrament of Order, art filled with whatever of dignity and grace is conferred by it; wherefore deservedly art thou proclaimed Virgin Priest; **10** look down upon us and on the priests of thy Son; purify, sanctify, save us, that receiving the ineffable gifts of the sacraments, we may deserve to obtain the eternal salvation of our souls. Amen.

Mother of mercy, pray for us.

Mother of the eternal Priest, CHRIST JESUS, pray for us.

Queen of the clergy, pray for us.

Mary, Virgin Priest, pray for us.

1 Richard of St Laurence. **2** St Bernard. **3** Bernard de Busto. **4** St Epiphanius. **5** Blosius. **6** St Thomas of Villanova. **7** St Epiphanius. **8** St Andrew of Crete. **9** St Ephrem. **10** Br. of Pius IX, August 25, 1873.

B. MARY SORROWING
230. The Rosary of the Seven Dolours.

(See Instructions.) 230 Benedict XIII, Br. September 26, 1724; Clement XII, Br. December 12, 1734; Pius IX, July 18, 1877; Leo XIII, May 15, 1886; June 8, 1898

This Chaplet consists of seven divisions, in memory of our Lady's seven sorrows, on which we are to meditate, if we can, saying the Pater noster once and the Ave Maria seven times at each division, then ending with Ave thrice in honour of our Lady's tears.

To gain any of the following Indulgences beads must be used, though in the case of several persons saying the rosary together it is sufficient if the person leading the devotion uses them. They must have been blessed by a Servite Father or another with special faculties. To gain viii and ix the beads must have been blessed by a Servite Father.

For the benefit of those who for any reason are prevented from meditating on the mysteries of the Seven Dolours while they recite the Chaplet, i, ii, iii, vi, vii and viii can be gained by merely reciting the Paters and Aves. To gain iv, v and ix each mystery must be named and meditated on.

i. Seven Years and Seven Quarantines for the entire Chaplet. T.Q.

ii. 100 Days for each Pater and Ave, if the entire Chaplet is said.

iii. 200 Days for each Pater and Ave to every one who, having confessed, or at least made a firm resolution to confess, says this Chaplet in a Servite church, or says it anywhere on Fridays, or during Lent, or on the feast and during the octave of the Seven Dolours.

iv. 200 Years to those who shall say it after examination of conscience and confession and pray according to the intention of the Pope.

v. Plenary to all who say it four times a week, on any one day in the year when they say this Chaplet after Confession and Communion.

vi. Plenary once a month. I, II, IV.

vii. Ten Years to those who keep one of these Chaplets about them and are in the habit of saying it frequently, every time that after Confession and Communion they shall hear Mass, be present at a sermon, accompany the Blessed Sacrament to the sick, make peace between enemies, bring a sinner to repentance, recite devoutly Pater and Ave seven times or do any spiritual or temporal work of mercy in honour of our LORD, the Blessed Virgin, or their patron saint,

viii. 100 Years to all who say this Chaplet, having confessed or at least made a firm resolution to confess.

ix. 150 Years every Monday, Wednesday, Friday and feast of obligation for reciting this Chaplet after Confession to those who habitually carry it about with them.

WAY OF SAYING THE CHAPLET.
Act of Contrition.

O My LORD, Thou who alone art most worthy of my love, behold me standing before thy Divine Presence utterly overwhelmed by the thought of the many grievous injuries I have done Thee. I ask thy pardon for them with my whole heart, repenting of them purely for love of Thee, and at the thought of thy great goodness hating and loathing them above every evil of this life. As I would rather have died a thousand times than have offended Thee, so now I am most firmly resolved to die a thousand deaths rather than offend Thee again. My crucified JESUS, I firmly purpose to cleanse my soul as soon as possible by thy most Precious Blood in the Sacrament of Penance. And thou, most tender Virgin, Mother of mercy and Refuge of sinners, do thou obtain for me by virtue of thy bitter pains, the pardon of sin which I desire; whilst, praying according to the mind of so many holy Pontiffs in order to obtain the Indulgences granted to this thy holy Rosary, I hope thereby to obtain remission of all pains due to my sins.

With this confidence in my heart, I meditate on the First Sorrow, when Mary, Virgin Mother of my GOD, presented JESUS her only Son in the Temple, laid Him in the arms of holy and aged Simeon, and heard his prophetic word, "The sword of grief shall pierce thy soul," foretelling thereby the Passion and Death of her Son JESUS. PATER once, Ave seven times.

The Second Sorrow of the Blessed Virgin was when she was obliged to fly into Egypt by reason of the persecution of cruel Herod, who impiously sought to slay her well beloved Son. PATER once, Ave seven times.

The Third Sorrow of the Blessed Virgin was when, after having gone up to Jerusalem at the Paschal Feast with Joseph her spouse and JESUS her beloved Son, she lost Him on the way back to her poor house, and for three days bewailed the loss of her only Love. PATER once, Ave seven times.

The Fourth Sorrow of the Blessed Virgin was when she met her dear Son JESUS carrying to Mount Calvary on his tender shoulders the heavy Cross whereon He was to be crucified for our salvation. PATER once, Ave seven times.

The Fifth Sorrow of the Blessed Virgin was when she saw her Son JESUS raised upon the hard tree of the Cross, and blood flowing from every part of his sacred Body, and then beheld Him die after three hours agony. PATER once, Ave seven times.

The Sixth Sorrow of the Blessed Virgin was when she saw the lance pierce the sacred Side of JESUS, her beloved Son, the nails withdrawn, and his holy Body laid in her purest bosom. PATER once, Ave seven times.

The Seventh and last Sorrow of the Blessed Virgin, Queen and Advocate of us, her servants, miserable sinners, was when she saw the Holy Body of her Son buried in the grave. PATER once, Ave seven times.

Then say Ave thrice in veneration of the tears which Mary shed in her sorrows, to obtain thereby true sorrow for sins and the holy Indulgences attached to this pious exercise.
V/.. Pray for us, Virgin most sorrowful.
R/. That we may be made worthy of the promises of CHRIST.
Let us pray.
GRANT, we beseech Thee, O LORD JESUS CHRIST, that the most blessed Virgin Mary, thy Mother, may intercede for us before the throne of thy mercy, now and at the hour of our death, whose most holy soul was transfixed with the sword of sorrow in the hour of thine own Passion. Through Thee, JESUS CHRIST, SAVIOUR of the world, who livest and reignest, etc. Amen.

231. One Hour's Prayer.
Plenary, once in the year, to all the faithful, who, after Confession and Communion, on any one day should make one hour's prayer in honour of the sorrows of most holy Mary, meditating on them, or reciting prayers adapted to this devotion.
(See Instructions.) 231 Clement XII, February 4, 1736.

232. Devotions in honour of the Sorrowful Heart of Mary.
300 Days. T.Q. (See Instructions.) 232 Pius VII, Res. January 14, 1815.
V/. O GOD, come to my assistance.
R/. O LORD, make haste to help me.
Glory be to the FATHER, etc.

I COMPASSIONATE thee, sorrowing Mary, in the affliction of thy tender heart at the prophecy of the holy old man Simeon. Dear Mother, by thy heart then so afflicted, obtain for me the virtue of humility and the gift of holy fear of GOD. Ave Maria.
I COMPASSIONATE thee, sorrowing Mary, in the anxiety which thy sensitive heart underwent in the flight and sojourn in Egypt. Dear Mother, by thy heart then made so anxious, obtain for me the virtue of liberality, especially towards the poor, and the gift of pity. Ave Maria.
I COMPASSIONATE thee, sorrowing Mary, in the trouble of thy anxious heart, when thou didst lose thy dear Son JESUS. Dear Mother, by thy heart then so troubled, obtain for me the virtue of holy chastity and the gift of knowledge. Ave Maria.
I COMPASSIONATE thee, sorrowing Mary, in the shock thy maternal heart underwent when JESUS met thee carrying his Cross. Dear Mother, by thy loving heart then so overwhelmed, obtain for me the virtue of patience and the gift of fortitude. Ave Maria.
I COMPASSIONATE thee, sorrowing Mary, in the martyrdom thy generous heart bore so nobly whilst thou didst stand by JESUS in his agony. Dear Mother, by thy heart then so martyred, obtain for me the virtue of temperance and the gift of counsel. Ave Maria.

I COMPASSIONATE thee, sorrowing Mary, in the wound of thy tender heart when the sacred Side of JESUS was pierced with the lance. Dear Mother, by thy heart then so transfixed, obtain for me the virtue of fraternal charity and the gift of understanding. Ave Maria.

I COMPASSIONATE thee, sorrowing Mary, in the pang felt by thy loving 1 heart when the Body of JESUS was buried in the grave. Dear Mother, by all the bitterness of desolation thou didst then experience, obtain for me the virtue of diligence and the gift of wisdom. Ave Maria.

V/. Pray for us, Virgin most sorrowful.

R/. That we may be made worthy of the promises of CHRIST.

Let us pray.

GRANT, we beseech Thee, O LORD JESUS CHRIST, that the most blessed Virgin Mary, thy Mother, may intercede for us before the throne of thy mercy, now and at the hour of our death, whose most holy soul was transfixed with the sword of sorrow in the hour of thine own Passion. Through Thee, JESUS CHRIST, SAVIOUR of the world, who livest and reignest, etc. Amen.

233. Devotions for Holy Week and Fridays.

i. Plenary, to all who from three o'clock on Good Friday until mid-day on Holy Saturday, either in public or private, spend one hour, or at least half an hour, in honour of our Lady sorrowing, in meditation or vocal prayer having reference to her sorrows, the Indulgence to be gained when the Paschal precept is fulfilled. I, II.

ii. 300 Days, in any other week, between three o'clock on Friday and Sunday morning.

iii. Plenary, once a month, to all who practise this devotion weekly. I, II.

(See Instructions) 233 Pius VII, Mem. February 25, March 21, 1815, June 18, 1822.

234. Ave Maria, etc., seven times.

i. 300 Days, once a day. ii. Plenary, once a month. I, II, IV. (See Instructions.) 234 Pius VII, Br. December i, 1815; Pius IX, June 18, 1876

After each Ave, say:

SANCTA Mater, istud agas, Crucifixi fige plagas Cordi meo valide

HOLY Mother, pierce me through; In my heart each wound renew Of my SAVIOUR crucified.

235. Devotions during the Carnival.

i. 300 Days, each time, to those who shall assist at any devout exercise in honour of the Sorrows of most holy Mary, in order to make reparation for the sins committed during the Carnival, on the last ten days of the Carnival, in any church, or private or public chapel.

ii. Plenary, to those who shall assist at this pious exercise for at least five out of the ten days, I, II, IV.

(See Instructions, p. i.) 235 Pius VII, June 18,1822,

236. Stations of Our Lady's Dolours.

The Stations must be erected and blessed by the Prior-General of the Servites, his Vicars or other ecclesiastics duly authorized by him, in a church or public chapel.

To all who in public or in private, passing from one to the other, meditate on the Dolours, or recite prayers in honour of them:

i. Seven Years and Seven Quarantines, once a day. ii. Plenary, after making- the Stations on seven days. I, II, IV. (See Instructions) 236 Gregory XIV, Br. July 13, 1837; Leo XIII, Br. May 8, 1884, July 23, 1898.

237. The Month of September.

To those who daily practise some special devotion to our Lady Sorrowing

i. 300 Days, each day. ii. Plenary, during the month or succeeding eight days. I, II, IV. (See Instructions.) 237 Pius IX, Br. April 3, 1857, November 26, 1876; Leo XIII, Jan. 27, 1888.

238. Hymn, Stabat Mater.

100 Days, T.Q. (See Instructions.) 238 Pius IX, June 18, 1876.

STABAT Mater Dolorosa	AT the cross her station keeping,
Juxta crucem lacrymosa	Stood the mournful Mother weeping,
Dum pendebat Filius	Close to JESUS to the last:

Cujusanimam gementem,	Through her heart, his sorrow sharing,
Contristatam et dolentem,	All his bitter anguish bearing,
Pertransivit gladius	Now at length the sword had passed.
O quam tristis et afflicta	Oh, how sad and sore distressed
Fuit ilia benedicta	Was that Mother, highly blest,
Mater Unigeniti!	Of the sole begotten One!
Quag mœrebat, et dolebat,	CHRIST above in torment hangs;
Pia Mater dum videbat	She beneath beholds the pangs
Nati pœnas incliti.	Of her dying glorious Son.
Quis est homo qui non fleret	Is there one who would not weep,
Matrem CHRISTI si videret	'Whelmed in miseries so deep,
In tanto supplicio?	CHRIST'S dear Mother to behold?
Quis non posset contristari	Can the human heart refrain
CHRISTI Matrem contemplari	From partaking in her pain
Dolentem cum Filio.	In that Mother's pain untold?
Pro peccatis suæ gentis	Bruised, derided, cursed, defiled,
Vidit JESUM in tormentis,	She beheld her tender Child,
Et flagellis subditum.	All with bloody scourges rent;
Vidit suum dulcem Natum	For the sins of his own nation,
Moriendo desolatum,	Saw Him hang in desolation
Dum emisit spiritum.	Till his spirit forth He sent.
Eja Mater, fons amoris,	O thou Mother! fount of love!
Me sentire vim doloris	Touch my spirit from above,
Fac, ut tecum lugeam.	Make my heart with thine accord;
Fac, ut ardeat cor meum	Make me feel as thou hast felt;
In amando CHRISTUM DEUM	Make my soul to glow and melt
Ut sibi complaceam.	With the love of CHRIST my LORD.
Sancta Mater, istud agas,	Holy Mother, pierce me through;
Crucifixi fige plagas	In my heart each wound renew
Cordi meo valide.	Of my SAVIOUR crucified ;
Tui Nati vulnerati,	Let me share with thee his pain,
Tam dignati pro me pati,	Who for all my sins was slain,
Pœnas mecum divide.	Who for me in torment died.
Fac me tecum pie flere,	Let me mingle tears with thee,
Crucifixo condolere,	Mourning Him who mourned for me,
Donec ego vixero,	All the days that I may live:
Juxta crucem tecum stare	By the cross with thee to stay;
Et me tibi sociare	There with thee to weep and pray
In planctu desidero	Is all I ask of thee to give.
Virgo Virginum præclara,	Virgin of all virgins best,
Mihi jam non sis amara,	Listen to my fond request:
Fac me tecum plangere.	Let me share thy grief divine;
Fac, ut portem CHRISTI mortem,	Let me to my latest breath
Passionis fac consortem,	In my body bear the death
Et plagas recolere.	Of that dying Son of thine.
Fac me plagis vulnerari,	Wounded with his every wound,
Fac me cruce inebriari,	Steep my soul till it hath swooned
Et cruore Filii.	In his very Blood away;
Flammis ne urar succensus,	Be to me, O Virgin, nigh,
Per te, Virgo, sim defensus	Lest in flames I burn and die
In die judicii.	In his awful judgment day.
CHRISTE, cum sit hinc exire,	CHRIST, when Thou shalt call me hence,
Da per Matrem me venire	Be thy Mother my defence,
Ad palmam victoriæ.	Be thy Cross my victory:
Quando corpus morietur,	While my body here decays,
Fac ut animæ donetur	May my soul thy goodness praise
Paradisi gloria. Amen.	Safe in Paradise with Thee. Amen.

239. Prayer.
200 Days, once a day. (See Instructions.) 239 Leo XIII, March 26, 1887.

MARY, most holy Virgin and Queen of Martyrs, would that I could be transported to Heaven, there to contemplate the honours bestowed on thee by the Blessed Trinity and by all the heavenly court. But since I am still a pilgrim in this valley of tears, accept from me, thy unworthy and sinful servant, the most sincere homage and the most complete act of submission which a human being is capable of making to thee. In thy sacred heart, transfixed with so many swords of grief, I lay, once for all, my poor soul; receive me as the companion of thy sorrows, and do not allow me ever to be separated from that Cross on which thy only Son breathed forth his blessed Soul for me. With thee, O Mary, will I suffer all the trials, contradictions and infirmities with which it may please thy Divine Son to visit me in this life. I offer all to thee in memory of those sorrows which thou didst endure in thy life on earth; so that every thought of my mind, every beating of my heart, may henceforth be an a6l of compassion for thy sorrows and an act of rejoicing in the glories which thou dost now enjoy in Heaven. Therefore, dear Mother, while I now compassionate thee and rejoice to see thee thus glorified, do thou have compassion on me, and reconcile me with thy Son JESUS, so that I may be able to return and be thy true and faithful son. Come on my last day to assist me in my agony, as thou didst once assist at that of thy Divine Son, so that from this cruel exile I may come to share in thy glory in Heaven. Amen.

240. Prayer.
200 Days, once a day. (See Instructions.) 240 Pius X, February 3, 1906.

O MOST holy Virgin and Mother, whose soul a sword of grief went through in the Passion of thy Divine Son, and who in his glorious Resurrection wast filled with unending joy at his triumph ; intercede for us thy suppliants, that we may become so truly partakers in the adversities of the Church and the trials of the Supreme Pontiff, that we may deserve to share in the consolations they desire, in the charity and peace of the same CHRIST our LORD. Amen.

C. MARY IMMACULATE
241. Chaplet of the Immaculate Conception.
i. 300 Days. T.Q. ii. Plenary, once a month. I, II (See Instructions) 241 Pius IX, Br. June 22, 1855.

IN the name of the FATHER and of the SON and of the HOLY GHOST. Amen.
First Set of Beads.
Blessed be the Holy and Immaculate Conception of the most Blessed Virgin Mary. PATER once, Ave four times and Gloria once.
Second Set. Blessed, etc. , as before. PATER, etc., as before.
Third Set. Blessed, etc. , as before. PATER, etc., as before.

242. Seven Sundays in Honour of the Immaculate Conception.
i. Seven Years, on each of any seven consecutive Sundays. (Once a year.) ii. Plenary, on the seventh Sunday. I, II, III, IV. (See Instructions) 242 Pius IX, Prop. September 21, 1865 ; Leo XIII, July 23, 1898
Some special Prayer must be said.

243. The Little Office of the Immaculate Conception.
The Latin and English Text may be obtained in separate form from Messrs Burns and Oates, price id. 300 Days. T.Q. (See Instructions.) 243 Pius IX, Br. March 31, 1876.

244. Antiphon, Versicle and Prayer.
100 Days. T.Q. 244 Pius IX, Br. March 31, 1876.
(See Instructions.)

Ant. Hæc est virga in qua nec nodus originalis, nec cortex actualis culpæ fuit.

V/. In Conceptione tua, Virgo, immaculate fuisti
R/. Ora pro nobis PATREM, cujus FILIUM peperisti.

Ant. This is the rod in which was neither knot of original sin nor rind of actual guilt.

V/. In thy Conception, O Virgin, thou wast immaculate.
R/. Pray for us to the FATHER, whose SON thou

Oremus.
DEUS qui per Immaculatam Virginis Conceptionem dignum FILIO tuo habitaculum præparasti; quæsumus, ut qui ex morte ejusdem FILII tui prævisa eam ab omni labe præservasti, nos quoque mundos ejus intercessione ad te pervenire concedas. Per eumdem CHRISTUM DOMINUM nostrum. **R/.** Amen.

didst bring forth.
Let us pray.
O GOD, who, by the Immaculate conception of the Virgin, didst prepare a worthy habitation for thy SON; we beseech Thee that,: as in view of the death of that SON Thou didst preserve her from all stain of sin, so Thou wouldst enable us, being made pure by her intercession, to come unto Thee. Through the same CHRIST our LORD. **R/.** Amen

245. Ejaculation.
100 Days. T.Q. (See Instructions) 245 Pius VI, November 21, 1793.
In Conceptione tua, Virgo Maria,, immaculate fuisti. Ora pro nobis PATREM, cujus FILIUM JESUM de SPIRITU SANCTO conceptum peperisti.

In thy Conception, O Virgin Mary, thou wast immaculate. Pray for us to the FATHER, whose SON JESUS CHRIST conceived of the HOLY GHOST thou didst bring forth.

246. Ejaculation.
100 Days, once a day. (See Instructions.) 246 Pius IX, Prop. November 26, 1854.
TO thee, O Virgin Mother, who wast never defiled with the slightest stain of original or actual sin, I commend and entrust the purity of my heart.

247. Ejaculation.
100 Days, once a day. (See Instructions.) 247 Pius IX, Bfs. March 27, 1863.
O MARY, who didst enter the world free from stain, do thou obtain for me from GOD, that I may pass out of it free from sin.

248. Ejaculation.
300 Days. T.Q. (See Instructions.) 248 Leo XIII, Br. September 10, 1878.
BLESSED be the holy and Immaculate Conception of the most blessed Virgin Mary, Mother of GOD.

249. Invocation.
100 Days, once a day. (See Instructions) 249 Leo XIII, March 15, 1884.
O MARY, conceived without sin, pray for us who have recourse to thee.

250. Invocation.
100 Days, once a day. (See Instructions) 250 Leo XIII, December 20, 1890.
SANCTA Virgo Maria Immaculata, Mater DEI, Mater nostra, tu pro nobis loquere ad Cor JESU, qui tuus Filius est et frater noster.

MOST holy and Immaculate Virgin Mary, Mother of GOD and our Mother, speak on our behalf to the Heart of JESUS, who is thy Son and our Brother.

251. Devotion to the Grown of Living Stars.
100 Days. T.Q. (See Instructions.) 251 Pius X, September 9, 1904.
A contribution must be made during the year to the Institute of St Zita in Lucca for the rescue of Chinese and African children.
O MARY Immaculate! come to our aid, and help the little infidel children. Ave Maria.

252. Prayer to Our Lady Immaculate.
300 Days, once a day. (See Instructions) 252 Pius X, January 11, 1905.
MOST holy Virgin, who wast pleasing to the LORD and became his Mother, immaculate in body and spirit, in faith and in love, look kindly on the wretched who implore thy powerful patronage. The wicked serpent, against whom was hurled the first curse, continues fiercely to attack and ensnare the unhappy children of Eve. Do thou, then, O Blessed Mother, our Queen and advocate, who from the first instant of thy Conception didst crush the head of the enemy, receive the prayers which, united with thee in one single heart, we implore thee to present at the throne of GOD, that we may never fall into the snares

which are laid out for us, and may all arrive at the port of salvation; and, in so many dangers, may the Church and Christian society sing once again the hymn of deliverance, of victory, and of peace. Amen.

253. First Saturdays in Honour of the Immaculate Conception.
Plenary on each Saturday (or Sunday). I, II, IV. (See Instructions) 253 Pius X. July 1, 1905
Some time of the day must be devoted to prayer, vocal or mental, in honour of Mary Immaculate, and the practice must be kept up for twelve consecutive first Saturdays (or Sundays); otherwise the indulgences will not be gained.

254. Consecration to Our Lady by Blessed Louis Mary Grignon de Montfort.
Plenary if said on the Immaculate Conception and April 28. I, II, III, IV.
 (See Instructions) 254 Leo XIII, February 25, 1896; Pius X, January 22, 1908.
O ETERNAL and incarnate Wisdom, O most sweet and adorable JESUS, true GOD and true Man, only SON of the Eternal FATHER and of Mary ever Virgin, I adore Thee profoundly, in the bosom and in the splendour of thy FATHER through eternity, and in the virginal womb of Mary thy most perfect Mother during the time of thy Incarnation.

I return Thee thanks for that Thou didst annihilate thyself, taking upon Thee the form of a servant, to rescue me from the cruel slavery of the devil. I praise and glorify Thee, for that Thou didst willingly become subject to Mary thy holy Mother in all things, in order to make me through her thy faithful slave. But, alas! ungrateful and faithless that I am in not keeping the promises I solemnly made to Thee in my Baptism, I have not fulfilled any of my obligations. I do not deserve to be called thy child or thy slave, and since there is nothing in me which does not merit thy reprobation and thy wrath, I dare no longer approach alone thy holy and august Majesty. Therefore it is that I have recourse to the intercession of thy most holy Mother, whom Thou hast given me to be my intercessor with Thee, and it is by this means that I hope to obtain from Thee the grace of contrition, the pardon of my sins, and the gift of abiding wisdom.

I salute thee, then, O Mary Immaculate, living tabernacle of the Divinity, where the eternal Wisdom lies hidden to be adored by angels and men. I salute thee, O Queen of heaven and of earth, beneath whose sway are subject all things that are lower than GOD. I salute thee, O secure refuge of sinners, whose mercy fails no one ; graciously respond to the desires which I have for divine wisdom, and receive the vows and offerings which my nothingness makes to thee to obtain it.

I, N , a faithless sinner, renew and ratify this day at thy hands my baptismal vows. I renounce for ever Satan, his works and pomps, and I give myself wholly to JESUS CHRIST, the incarnate Wisdom, to carry my cross after Him all the days of my life, and, in order that I may be more faithful to Him than I have hitherto been, I choose thee this day, O Mary, in the presence of the heavenly court, for my Mother and Mistress.

I deliver and consecrate to thee, as a bond slave, my body and my soul, my possessions interior and exterior, and even the value of all my good actions, past, present and to come, leaving thee the entire and full right to dispose of me and of all that belongs to me without exception, according to thy good pleasure, to the greater glory of GOD, for time and eternity.

Receive, O loving Virgin, this offering of bondage which I make to thee, in honour of and in union with the subjection which the eternal Wisdom gave to thy Maternity, as an act of homage before the power which thou and thy Son have over me, a worm and miserable sinner, in thanksgiving for the privileges which the Holy Trinity has bestowed on thee. I protest that I desire henceforth, as thy veritable slave, to seek thy honour and obey thee in all things. O Mother most admirable, present me to thy dear Son as his eternal slave, so that, having redeemed me through thee, He may receive me from thee. O Mother of mercy, obtain for me from GOD the gift of true wisdom, and also, to that end, the grace to place myself among the number of those who love thee, and whom thou dost cherish and protect as thy children and slaves. O faithful Virgin, make me a perfect disciple in all things, imitator and slave of the eternal Wisdom JESUS CHRIST, thy Son, so that by thy intercession I may come to the plenitude of his years on earth and of his glory in heaven. Amen.

255. The Miraculous Medal and Ejaculation.
100 Days. T.Q. (Sec Instructions.) 255 Pius X, Br. June 6, 1904.
This indulgence may be gained by those only who wear the miraculous medal blessed by a duly authorized priest.
O MARY, conceived without sin, pray for us who have recourse to thee.

256. Prayer of St Alphonsus for Purity.
300 Days, twice a day, morning and evening. (See Instructions.) 256 Pius X, Br. December 5, 1904.
Ave Maria thrice, and after each:
PER tuam Immaculatam Conceptionem, O Maria, redde purum corpus meum et sanctam animam meam.
BY thy Immaculate Conception, O Mary, make my body pure, and my soul holy.

D. THE SACRED HEART OF MARY
257. Prayer and Act of Praise.
i. 60 Days, once a day. ii. Plenary, to those who say it every day for a year, on each of the following three feasts of our Lady, viz., the Nativity, Assumption, and her Sacred Heart, provided they visit a church or altar dedicated to the Blessed Virgin, and pray for the intention of the Sovereign Pontiff. I, II, III, IV.
iii. Plenary, in articulo mortis, at the point of death, to all who in life have said this prayer every day. I, II (or at least with contrition). (See Instructions.) 257 Pius VII, August 18, 1807; February i, 1816.
The Prayer.
HEART of Mary, Mother of GOD and our Mother, Heart most amiable, on which the adorable Trinity ever gazes with complacency, worthy of all the veneration and tenderness of angels and of men; Heart most like the Heart of JESUS, whose most perfect image thou art; Heart full of goodness, ever compassionate towards our miseries; vouchsafe to thaw our icy hearts, that they may be wholly changed to the likeness of the Heart of JESUS. Infuse into them the love of thy virtues, inflame them with that blessed fire with which thou dost ever burn. In thee let the Holy Church find safe shelter; protect it and be its sweet asylum, its tower of strength, impregnable against every inroad of its enemies. Be thou the road leading to JESUS; be thou the channel whereby we receive all graces needful for our salvation. Be thou our help in need, our comfort in trouble, our strength in temptation, our refuge in persecution, our aid in all dangers ; but especially in the last struggle of our life, at the moment of our death, when all hell shall be unchained against us to snatch away our souls: in that dread moment, that hour so terrible, whereon our eternity depends, ah, then, most tender Virgin, make us feel how great is the tenderness of thy maternal Heart, and how mighty thy power with the Heart of JESUS, opening to us a safe refuge in the very fount of mercy itself, that so we too may join with thee in Paradise in blessing that same Heart of JESUS for ever and for ever. Amen.
Act of Praise to the SS. Hearts of Jesus and Mary.
MAY the Divine Heart of JESUS and the Immaculate Heart of Mary be known, praised, blessed, loved, worshipped and glorified always and in all places! Amen.

258. Chaplet of the Immaculate Heart of Mary.
i. 300 Days, once a day. ii. Plenary, once a month. I, II, III, IV. (See Instructions.) 258 Pius IX, December 11, 1854.
V/. O GOD, come to our assistance.
R/.. O LORD, make haste to help us.
V/. Glory be to the FATHER, etc.

I
IMMACULATE Virgin, who, conceived without sin, didst direct every movement of thy pure heart to GOD, ever the object of thy love, and who wast ever most submissive to his will, obtain for me the grace to hate sin with my whole heart, and to learn of thee to live in perfect resignation to the will of GOD. PATER once, Ave seven times.
Heart of Mary, pierced with grief, set my heart on fire with the love of GOD.

II
Mary, I wonder at thy deep humility when thy blessed heart was troubled at the gracious message brought thee by Gabriel the Archangel how that thou wast chosen to be Mother of the SON of GOD Most High and didst still proclaim thyself his humble handmaid; in great confusion at my pride, I ask thee for the grace of a contrite and humble heart, that, knowing my own misery, I may obtain that crown of glory promised to those who are truly humble of heart. PATER once, Ave seven times; Heart of Mary, etc.

III

Sweetest Heart or Mary, precious treasury, wherein the Blessed Virgin kept the words of JESUS whilst she thought on the high mysteries which she had heard from the lips of her Son, and whereby she learned to live for GOD alone; how does the coldness of my heart confound me! Dearest Mother, obtain for me grace so to meditate within my heart upon the holy law of GOD, that I may strive to follow thee in the fervent practice of every Christian virtue. PATER once, Ave seven times; Heart of Mary, etc.

IV
Glorious Queen of Martyrs, whose sacred heart was cruelly transfixed in the bitter Passion of thy Son by the sword foretold by the holy old man, Simeon, obtain for my heart true courage and a holy patience to bear well the troubles and adversities of this miserable life, and, by crucifying my flesh with its desires in following the mortification of the Cross, to show myself truly thy son. PATER once, Ave seven times; Heart of Mary, etc.

V
O Mary, Mystic Rose, whose loving heart, burning with the living fire of charity, accepted us for thy children at the foot of the Cross, whereby thou didst become our most tender Mother; make me feel the sweetness of thy maternal heart, and thy power with JESUS in all the perils of this mortal life, and especially in the terrible hour of death, that so my heart, united with thine own, may love JESUS now and throughout all ages. Amen. PATER once, Ave seven times; Heart of Mary, etc.
Let us entreat the Most Sacred Heart of JESUS to inflame us with his holy love.
O DIVINE Heart of JESUS, I consecrate myself to Thee, full of deep gratitude for the many blessings I have received, and daily receive, from thy infinite charity. I thank Thee with my whole heart for having also vouchsafed to give me thine own Mother to be my Mother, consigning me to her in the person of the beloved Disciple. Grant unto me that my heart may ever burn with this love of Thee, and so may find in Thee its peace, its refuge and its happiness.

259. Ejaculation.
i. 300 Days. T.Q. ii. Plenary, once a month. I, n, in, iv. (See Instructions.) 259 Pius IX, September 30, 1852
SWEET Heart of Mary, be my salvation.

E. OUR LADY OF THE ROSARY
260. The Rosary blessed by Canons Regular of St Augustine of the Order of the Holy Cross.
One Pater noster or one Ave Maria said on a rosary blessed by the Master General or one of the Canons delegated by him, or by one having this special privilege. See N.B. opposite point. 261. 500 Days. T.Q. (See Instructions.) 260 Leo X. Br. August 20, 1516; Gregory XVI, Prop. July 13, 1845; Pius IX, Prop. January 9, .848; Leo XIII, March 14, 1884.

261. The Rosary of St Dominic.
261 Sixtus IV, Bl. May 12, 1479; Benedict XIII, April 13, August 13, 1726, May 26, 1727; Pius IX, May 12, 1851, January 22, 1858; Pius X, July 31, 1906; June 12, 1907.
This Devotion, called also the Psalter of Mary, consists of the continuous recitation of the Ave Maria, said 150 times (as many times as there are Psalms), divided into fifteen decades, each beginning with a Pater noster, while at the same time the principal mysteries of the life, death and resurrection of our LORD are meditated on.
To gain the following indulgences beads must be used, though in the case of several persons saying the Rosary together it is sufficient if the person leading the Devotion uses them. They must, except in the case of i, have been blessed by a Dominican Father or other priest duly authorized.
Persons incapable of meditating may gain the indulgences by merely saying the Rosary devoutly. Such persons should however endeavour, in some measure, to acquire the power of meditating.
i. Five Years and five Quarantines, for a third part, five decades, of the Rosary (blessed beads not necessary). T.Q.
ii. 100 Days, to all who say the fifteen, or at least five decades for every Pater and Ave.
iii. Plenary, to all who say five decades every day for a year, on any one day in the year, I, II, IV.
iv. Ten Years and ten Quarantines, once a day, to all who say five decades in company with others, either in public or in private.

v. Plenary, on the last Sunday of every month, to all who are in the habit of saying with others, at least three times a week, five decades, I, II, III, IV.

vi. 100 Years and 100 Quarantines, once a day, to all associates of the confraternity who devoutly carry a rosary about with them.

vii. Plenary, to all associates who say the Fifteen Mysteries in the course of the natural day, for the triumph of the Church. I, II, III.

N.B. The indulgences attached to beads blessed by the Canons Regular of the Holy Cross (see No. 193) can be gained simultaneously with the Dominican indulgences, i.e., while reciting the Rosary, provided the beads are blessed with the two blessings. (Pius X, June 12, 1907.)

Note. Indulgences vi and vii, with many others not recorded in the Raccolta, can be gained only by members of the Confraternity of the Holy Rosary. To enjoy the privileges of this confraternity it is only requisite that a persons name be entered on the Dominican Register, and that the beads should be blessed as above.

The Joyful Mysteries.
IN the First Joyful Mystery we meditate on the Annunciation made by the angel Gabriel to most holy Mary, that she was to conceive and bear a Son, our LORD JESUS CHRIST.

PATER once, Ave ten times (a Gloria is usually added; so also in all the Mysteries).

In the Second Joyful Mystery we meditate how, when Mary heard that Elizabeth had conceived, she went to her house to visit her, and stayed with her three months.

In the Third Joyful Mystery we meditate how, when the full time of Mary's delivery was come, she brought forth our SAVIOUR JESUS CHRIST at midnight, in the city of Bethlehem, and laid Him in a manger between two brute beasts.

In the Fourth Joyful Mystery we meditate how most holy Mary, on the day of her Purification, presented CHRIST our LORD in the Temple, and placed Him in the hands of the holy old man Simeon.

In the Fifth Joyful Mystery we meditate how the Virgin Mary lost her Son, when twelve years old, sought for Him three days, and at the end of the third day found Him in the Temple amid the doctors, hearing them and asking them questions.

The Sorrowful Mysteries.
IN the First Sorrowful Mystery we meditate how our LORD JESUS CHRIST prayed in the garden of Olives, and sweated blood.

In the Second Sorrowful Mystery we meditate how our LORD JESUS CHRIST was cruelly scourged in Pilate's house with innumerable blows.

In the Third Sorrowful Mystery we meditate how our LORD JESUS CHRIST was crowned with sharp thorns.

In the Fourth Sorrowful Mystery we meditate how JESUS was condemned to die, and, for his greater ignominy and pain, the heavy tree of the Cross was laid upon his shoulder.

In the Fifth Sorrowful Mystery we meditate how, when JESUS arrived at Calvary, He was stripped and nailed with iron nails to the Cross, and died thereon, before the eyes of his afflicted Mother.

The Glorious Mysteries.
IN the First Glorious Mystery we meditate how JESUS CHRIST our LORD rose again in glory, the third day after his Death and Passion, triumphant over death, never more to die.

In the Second Glorious Mystery we meditate how JESUS CHRIST, the fortieth day after his Resurrection, ascended into Heaven with great joy and triumph, in the presence of his most holy Mother and his disciples.

In the Third Glorious Mystery we meditate how JESUS CHRIST sat down on the right hand of the FATHER, and sent from thence the HOLY GHOST into the room where the Apostles and the most holy Virgin were assembled.

In the Fourth Glorious Mystery we meditate how, twelve years after our LORD JESUS CHRIST rose from the dead, his Mother herself passed from this mortal life, and was carried into heaven by the angels.

In the Fifth Glorious Mystery we meditate how, in Heaven, Mary was crowned by her Son; in this Mystery also we meditate upon the glory of the saints.

262. The Month of October.
i. Seven Years and Seven Quarantines daily, if five decades are said either in public or in private. ii. Plenary, on Rosary Sunday, or during the Octave, if five decades are said on all those days. I, II, III, IV. iii. Plenary, once during the month, if, after the Octave, five decades are said on any ten days. I, II, III, IV. (See Instructions.) 262 Leo XIII, Enc. September i, 1883 ; Rit. August 20, 1885 : Indul. July 23, 1898.

263. Prayer.
100 Days, once a day. (See Instructions.) 263 Leo XIII, Card. Vic. July 3, 1886.

O QUEEN of the most holy Rosary, in these times of brazen impiety, show forth thy power, with the signs which accompanied thy victories of old, and from the throne where thou art seated, dispensing pardon and grace, in pity watch over the Church of thy Son, his Vicar, and every order of the clergy and laity, suffering in grievous warfare. Hasten, O most powerful destroyer of heresy, hasten the hour of mercy, seeing that the hour of judgment is daily challenged by innumerable offences. Obtain for me, the lowest of men, kneeling suppliant in thy presence, the grace which may enable me to live a just life on earth, and reign with the just in Heaven, whilst with the faithful through out the world, O Queen of the most holy Rosary, I salute thee and cry out: Queen of the most holy Rosary, pray for us.

264. The Fifteen Saturdays.
i. Plenary, on one Saturday. I, II. ii. Seven Years and Seven Quarantines, on each of the others. I, II. (See Instructions) 264 Leo XIII, September 21, 1889; September 17, 1892.

On each day five decades must be said, or meditation in some other manner made on the mysteries. In case of lawful hindrance, Sundays may be substituted. In either case they must be consecutive, and may be at any time of the year.

265. Our Lady of the Rosary of Pompeii.
i. 100 Days, once a day. ii. Plenary, on May 8, and on Rosary Sunday. I, II, III, IV.(See Instructions.) 265 Leo XIII, June 21, 1890.

A visit must be made to a statue of our Lady of Pompeii, in any church or public chapel.

266. Prayer to Our Lady of the Rosary.
300 Days, once a day. (See Instructions.) 266 St. Pius X , March 15, 1907.

O VIRGIN Mary, grant that the recitation of thy Rosary may be for me each day, in the midst of my manifold duties, a bond of unity in my actions, a tribute of filial piety, a sweet refreshment, an encouragement to walk joyfully along the path of duty. Grant, above all, O Virgin Mary, that the study of thy fifteen mysteries may form in my soul, little by little, a luminous atmosphere, pure, strengthening and fragrant, which may penetrate my understanding, my will, my heart, my memory, my imagination, my whole being. So shall I acquire the habit of praying while I work, without the aid of formal prayers, by interior acts of admiration and of supplication, or by aspirations of love. I ask this of thee, O Queen of the Holy Rosary, through St Dominic, thy son of predilection, the renowned preacher of thy mysteries, and the faithful imitator of thy virtues. Amen.

F. VARIOUS TITLES OF OUR LADY
267. Prayer to Our Lady of Pity.
i. 100 Days, once a day. ii. Plenary, once a month. I, II, III, IV. (See Instructions.) 267 Pius IX, March 26, 1860.

KNEELING at thy holy feet, O gracious Queen of Heaven, we offer thee our deepest reverence. We confess that thou art the daughter of the Eternal FATHER, the Mother of the Divine Word, and the Spouse of the HOLY GHOST. Full of grace, of virtue and of heavenly gifts, thou art the chaste temple of the Holy Trinity. With thee are treasured GOD'S mercies, and thou, too, dost dispense them. And since thy loving heart is filled with charity, sweetness, and tender compassion for us poor sinners, we call thee Mother of Divine Pity. With the greatest trust, then, O most loving Mother, do I come to thee in my sorrow and distress. I beg thee to give me an assurance of thy love, by granting me _____ if it be GOD'S will, and for the welfare of my soul. Cast, then, thy most pure eyes upon me and upon all my kindred. Consider the cruel warfare which the devil, the world, and the flesh wage against our souls, and how many perish in it. Remember, O fondest of mothers, that we are thy children, purchased with the

Precious Blood of thy Divine Son. Pray without ceasing that the adorable Trinity may give us the grace to be victorious over the devil, the world, and our own unhallowed passions; that grace by which the just grow in holiness, sinners are converted, and heresy is destroyed; by which unbelievers are enlightened, and Jews brought to the true religion. Bestow on us this boon, O most pure Virgin, through the infinite bounty of the Most High, through the merits of thy most holy Son, by the milk with which thou didst nourish Him, by the devotion with which thou didst serve Him, by the love with which thou didst cherish Him, by thy tears and the anguish endured by thee in his holy Passion. Obtain for us the great favour that the whole world may be made one people and one Church, to give thanks, praise, and glory to the most Holy Trinity, and to thee who art our mediatrix.

May the power of the FATHER, the wisdom of the SON and the virtue of the HOLY GHOST grant us this blessing. Amen.

268. Prayers to Our Lady of Perpetual Succour.
100 Days, once a day, for each of the three prayers. (See Instructions.) 268 Pius IX, Rit. May 17, 1866.

I

BEHOLD at thy feet, O Mother of Perpetual Succour, a wretched sinner who has recourse to thee, and confides in thee. O Mother of mercy, have pity on me. I hear thee called by all, the refuge and the hope of sinners: be, then, my refuge and my hope. Assist me, for the love of JESUS CHRIST; stretch forth thy hand to a miserable fallen creature who recommends himself to thee, and who devotes himself to thy service for ever. I bless and thank Almighty GOD, who in mercy has given me this confidence in thee, which I hold to be a pledge of my eternal salvation. It is true that in the past I have miserably fallen into sin, because I had not recourse to thee. I know that, with thy help, I shall conquer. I know, too, that thou wilt assist me, if I recommend myself to thee; but I fear that, in time of danger, I may neglect to call on thee, and thus lose my soul. This grace, then, I ask of thee, and this I beg, with all the fervour of my soul, that, in all the attacks of hell, I may ever have recourse to thee. O Mary, help me. O Mother of Perpetual Succour, never suffer me to lose my GOD.

II

O MOTHER of Perpetual Succour, grant that I may ever invoke thy most powerful name, which is the safeguard of the living and the salvation of the dying. O purest Mary! O sweetest Mary! let thy name henceforth be ever on my lips. Delay not, O blessed Lady, to succour me, whenever I call on thee; for, in all my temptations, in all my needs, I shall never cease to call on thee, ever repeating thy sacred name, Mary! Mary! Oh, what consolation, what sweetness, what confidence, what emotion fills my soul when I utter thy sacred name, or even only think of thee! I thank the LORD for having given thee, for my good, so sweet, so powerful, so lovely a name. But I will not be content with merely uttering thy name. Let my love for thee prompt me ever to hail thee Mother of Perpetual Succour.

III

O MOTHER of Perpetual Succour, thou art the dispenser of all the gifts which GOD grants to us miserable sinners; and for this end He has made thee so powerful, so rich, and so bountiful, in order that thou mayest help us in our misery. Thou art the advocate of the most wretched and abandoned sinners who have recourse to thee: come to my aid; I commend myself to thee. In thy hands I place my eternal salvation, and to thee I entrust my soul. Count me among thy most devoted servants; take me under thy protection, and it is enough for me. For, if thou protect me, I fear nothing; not from my sins, because thou wilt obtain for me the pardon of them; nor from the devils, because thou art more powerful than all hell together; nor even from JESUS, my Judge, because by one prayer from thee He will be appeased. But one thing I fear: that in the hour of temptation, I may through negligence fail to have recourse to thee, and thus perish miserably. Obtain for me, therefore, the pardon of my sins, love for JESUS, final perseverance, and the grace ever to have recourse to thee, O Mother of Perpetual Succour.

269. Prayer to Our Lady of Good Counsel.
100 Days, once a day. (See Instructions.) 269 Leo XIII, Aff. Nov. 23, 1880.

MOST glorious Virgin, chosen by the Eternal Counsel to be the Mother of the Eternal WORD made Man, treasure-house of divine graces and advocate of sinners; I, the most unworthy of thy servants, have recourse to thee, begging of thee to be my guide and counsellor in this vale of tears. Obtain for me, through the most Precious Blood of thy Divine Son, forgiveness of my sins, and the salvation of my soul with all the means necessary to secure it. Obtain for Holy Church triumph over her enemies and the extension of the Kingdom of JESUS CHRIST over the whole earth. Amen.

270. Prayer to Our Lady of Mount Carmel.
200 Days, once a day. (See Instructions.) 270 Leo XIII, January 16, 1886.
O MOST blessed Virgin Immaculate, the beauty and splendour of Carmel, thou who regardest with eyes of special love those who wear thy blessed habit, look kindly upon me and spread over me the mantle of thy maternal protection. Strengthen my weakness with thy power, illuminate the darkness of my mind with thy wisdom, increase in me the virtues of Faith, Hope and Charity. Adorn my soul with such graces and virtues that it may be ever dear to thy divine Son and to thee. Assist me in life, console me in death, with thy dear presence, and present me to the Holy Trinity as thy child and devoted servant, eternally to praise and bless thee in Paradise. Amen. Ave thrice and Gloria once.

271. Prayer to Our Lady, Mother of Divine Providence.
200 Days, once a day. (See Instructions.) 271 Leo XIII, February 27, 1886.
O IMMACULATE Virgin Mary, Mother of Divine Providence, take possession of my soul with all the fullness of thy favour and protection. Govern thou my life and direct it along the way of virtue to the fulfilment of the divine will. Do thou obtain for me the pardon of my sins; be my refuge, my protection, my defence, my guide in the pilgrimage of this life; console me in afflictions, sustain me in dangers, and in the storms of adversity afford me the security of thy guardianship. Obtain for me, O Mary, the renewal of my heart within me, so that it may become the holy dwelling place of thy divine Son JESUS; remove far from me, weak and miserable as I am, every kind of sin, negligence, sloth, timidity and human respect; entirely expel from me pride, vain glory, self-love, and all other earthly affections which hinder the efficacy of thy patronage. O sweetest Mother of Providence, turn thy maternal regard upon me, and if through frailty or malice I have provoked the menaces of the eternal Judge and embittered the most Sacred Heart of my loving JESUS, do thou throw over me the mantle of thy protection, and I shall be safe. Thou art the watchful Mother, the Virgin of forgiveness, and my hope on earth; oh, grant that I may have thee for the Mother of Glory in Heaven. Ave Maria thrice.

272. Prayer to Our Lady of the Cœnaculum.
i. 100 Days, once a day, for the Prayer, ii. 50 Days, once a day, for the Ejaculation. (See Instructions.) 272 Leo XIII, December 14, 1889
MOST holy Virgin of the Cœnaculum and our Mother, Mary Immaculate, we humbly beg of thee to obtain for us the gifts of the HOLY SPIRIT; that living united in charity, and persevering- with one mind and heart in prayer, assisted by thee, our guide and mistress, we may, to the greater glory of GOD, be worthy to devote ourselves to work by example and deed for the salvation of souls, and so secure for ourselves eternal life. O blessed Lady of the Cœnaculum, favour and assist us in our present need, and succour us with thy power, that by thy prayers GOD, almighty and merciful, may be pleased to grant the grace we so urgently demand. Amen. *Ejaculation. Our Lady of the Cœnaculum, pray for us.*

273. Prayer to Our Lady Help of Christians.
100 Days, once a day. (See Instructions.) 273 Leo XIII, December 20, 1890
MARY, Immaculate Virgin, Mother of GOD and our Mother, thou seest how the Catholic Faith, in which we propose by the help of GOD to live and die, and so attain to eternal glory, is everywhere assailed by the devil and the world. Do thou, Help of Christians, renew thy victories as of old, for the salvation of thy children. To thee we entrust our firm purpose of never joining assemblies of heretics or sectaries. Do thou, all holy, offer to thy divine SON our resolutions, and obtain from him the graces necessary to enable us to remain steadfast in them to the end. Bring consolation to the visible head of the Church; support the Catholic Episcopate; protect the Clergy and the people who proclaim thee Queen ; hasten by the power of thy prayers the day when all nations shall be gathered together around the Supreme Pastor. Amen. Mary, help of Christians, pray for us.

274. Prayer to Our Lady Help of Christians.
200 Days, once a day. (See Instructions.) 274 Leo XIII, June 20, 1891.
MOST powerful Virgin, loving help of the Christian people, what thanks are not due to thee from us for the help thou didst give to our fathers, who, when threatened by the infidel Turk, invoked thy maternal aid by devoutly reciting the Rosary. From heaven thou didst behold their danger, thou didst hear their pitiful voices, thou didst lend a favourable ear to the humble prayer suggested by the great Pontiff, St

Pius V, and didst promptly run to their assistance. Grant, O dear Mother, that the present and long continued groanings of the holy Spouse of CHRIST may penetrate to thy throne; may they again move thy compassion and arouse thee afresh to free her from the powerful enemies who surround her. And so from every corner of the earth there rises to thy throne that precious prayer to make thee propitious now, as then, in our present calamity. Perchance our sins hinder, or at least retard, their effect. Therefore, dearest Mother, obtain for us true sorrow for them, and a firm purpose to be ready rather to face death than return to sin. Intolerable is the thought that through our fault the aid we so desperately need should be denied or delayed. Arise then, dear Mother, yielding to the prayers of the Catholic world, and beat down the pride of those wretched men who in their insolence outrage GOD, and would have that Church destroyed against which, by the infallible word of CHRIST, the gates of hell shall never prevail. Let it once more be seen that where thou dost arise to protect her the victory is assured, that though it may be delayed it is certain in the end; for so we are taught by the faith, which bids us hope through thee to be mercifully heard by GOD. Amen.

275. Prayer to Our Lady of Africa for the Conversion of the Mussulmans and other Infidels.
100 Days, once a day. (See Instructions) 275 Leo XIII, June 30, 1896.
O THOU, our Lady of Africa, whose stainless heart is full of mercy and maternal compassion; consider the deep misery of the Mussulmans and other infidels of Africa; remember that the souls of these poor infidels are the work of the hands of thy divine Son, that they have been created in his image and redeemed at the price of his Precious Blood. Do not allow, O Mother of mercy, that these unhappy people, who are, like us, thy children, should continue to fall into hell, despite the merits of JESUS CHRIST and the most cruel death he suffered for their salvation. Obtain for them knowledge of our holy religion, and the grace to love, to embrace, and to practise it faithfully. And since thou art the mistress and sovereign of Africa, O Queen of the Apostles, be pleased to choose and send legions of holy missionaries to these abandoned countries, to conquer them, to rescue them from death and Satan, and to bring them into the fold of Holy Church. So shall we be all united in one and the same hope and in one and the same love, in thy stainless heart, and in the adorable Heart of thy divine Son our LORD JESUS CHRIST, who was crucified and died for the salvation of all men, and who rose full of glory, and liveth and reigneth in the unity of the FATHER and the HOLY SPIRIT, world without end. Amen.

276. Invocation to be said Morning and Evening.
200 Days, once a day. (See Instructions) 276 Leo XIII. Br. February 8, 1900.
MY Mother, preserve me this day from mortal sin. Ave Maria thrice.

277. Prayer to Mary our Helper.
300 Days. T.Q. (See Instructions.) 277 Leo XIII, Br. March 10, 1900.
MOST holy and immaculate Virgin Mary, our most tender Mother, and powerful Help of Christians, we dedicate ourselves entirely to thy most sweet love and holy service. We consecrate our minds with all their thoughts, our hearts with all their affections, our bodies with all their senses and powers, and we promise to desire always to work for the greater glory of GOD and for the salvation of souls. Meanwhile do thou, O incomparable Virgin, who hast always been the Help of the Christian people, continue to show thyself such, especially in these days. Humble the enemies of our holy religion, and frustrate their evil purposes. Enlighten and strengthen bishops and priests, and keep them ever united in obedience to the Pope, their infallible master. Preserve incautious youth from irreligion and vice. Promote holy vocations and increase the number of thy sacred ministers, that by means of them the Kingdom of JESUS CHRIST may be preserved among us, and extended to the farthest boundaries of the earth.

We pray thee also, most sweet Mother, to look at all times with compassion upon the young and thoughtless, exposed to so many dangers, and upon poor sinners and the dying ; be for all a sweet hope, O Mary, Mother of Mercy and Gate of Heaven.

Also we pray thee for ourselves, O great Mother of GOD. Teach us to copy thy virtues and especially angelic modesty, profound humility, and ardent charity; so that by word and example we may, as far as is possible in our state of life, present in the midst of the world a living image of blessed JESUS thy Son, and may cause thee to be known and loved, and so may succeed in saving many souls.

Obtain for us, O Mary our Helper, that we may be all gathered under thy maternal mantle, that in temptation we may invoke thee promptly and confidently; in short, that the thought of thee, so good, so loving, and so dear, and the remembrance of the love which thou bearest to thy clients may be such a support to us, as to render us victorious over the enemies of our souls in life and in death, so that we may become thy crown in beautiful Paradise. Amen.

278. Prayer to Our Lady, Queen of Prophets.
100 Days, once a day. (See Instructions.) 278 Leo XIII, January 24, 1901.
TO thee, O Queen of Prophets, foreseen by them, Mother of GOD and of his people, to thee we have recourse in our necessities, confident that as thou thyself art the fulfilment of prophecy, so thou wilt desire the fulfilment of thy own words, bringing, out of all generations, N_____, to call thee blessed. Say to all the erring for whom we beseech thee, and especially to N_____, "Thy light has come." Say but one word to thy Son, and the glory of the LORD shall rise upon them, and the eyes of the blind shall be opened, and so they, wondering at the star, will follow into the house of bread, where, finding thy Child with thee, they will eat of the true bread and live for ever, possessing joy and gladness, while sorrow and sadness will disappear. O thou who art omnipotent in prayer, at whose request thy Son worked his first miracle, beg Him to say: *"I the LORD will do this suddenly in its time,"* and grant to those for whom we pray, that they may draw water with joy at the fountains of the SAVIOUR. May it be granted to us all to be united with thee, O Mother, in singing thy Magnificat to Him thy Son, our LORD JESUS CHRIST, who with the FATHER and the HOLY GHOST liveth and reigneth one GOD world without end. Ave Maria. Magnificat (p. 215).

279. Prayer to Our Lady, Mother of Confidence.
200 Days, once a day. (See Instructions.) 279 Leo XIII, January 26, 1901.
O IMMACULATE Mary, when we venerate thee under the gracious title of Mother of Confidence, how our hearts overflow with the sweetest consolation, how we are moved to hope for every good gift from thee ! That such a name should have been given to thee is a sign that none have recourse to thee in vain. Receive, then, with a mother's compassion these a6ls of homage, with which we earnestly pray thee to be propitious to us in every necessity. Above all we ask thee to make us live ever united to thee and thy divine Son JESUS.* Under thy escort we shall safely walk along the straight road; and so shall it be our lot to hear on the last day of our lives those consoling words : *Come, O faithful servant, enter into the joy of thy LORD*. Amen.
*N.B. Clerics, in order to gain this indulgence, must insert the following words: *"and since in his goodness thy Son has chosen us to labour in his mystical vineyard, do thou, who desirest a rich harvest, bestow thy special care on us miserable creatures, that our work may be abundantly fruitful."*

280. Prayer to Our Lady of Lourdes.
300 Days. T.Q. (See Instructions.) 280 Leo XIII, Br. June 23, 1902.
O HOLY Mary, Mother of GOD, who to reanimate the faith of the world and draw men to thy divine Son, JESUS CHRIST our LORD, didst design to appear at Lourdes; thou who, in order to render more manifest thy maternal tenderness, and to inspire our hearts with greater confidence, didst choose a simple little child as the confidant of thy mercy; thou who didst say: "I am the Immaculate Conception" to make us understand the priceless value of that innocence which is the pledge of the friendship of GOD; thou who by eighteen successive apparitions didst not cease by thy actions and words to urge men to prayer and penance, which alone can appease Heaven and ward off the blows of divine justice; thou who, by a moving appeal to the world, hast reunited before the miraculous grotto an innumerable multitude of thy children; behold us, Our Lady of Lourdes, prostrate at thy feet, and confident of obtaining blessings and graces from GOD by thy most powerful intercession.
Those who love thee, O Mother of JESUS CHRIST, Mother of men, desire above everything to serve GOD faithfully in this world, so as to have the happiness of loving Him eternally in Heaven. Listen to the prayers which we this day address to thee; defend us against the enemies of our salvation, and against our own infirmities; together with the pardon of our sins, obtain for us perseverance in the determination never to fall away again.
We implore thee also to take under thy protection our friends and benefactors, and of these in a very special manner those who have abandoned the practice of their Christian duties. May they be converted and become thy faithful servants.

We beseech thee also to bless our country. She has many failings, for which we must implore pardon ; but in the midst of her wanderings from the right path, she has never ceased to proclaim through the best of her sons that thou art for ever her Mother and her Sovereign.

Thou hast always shown her thy love, and we hope that thou wilt not abandon her after having heaped thy favours and benefits upon her.

While we pour forth our hearts in prayer at thy feet, O Virgin Immaculate, Our Lady of Lourdes, we cannot forget our Holy Father, the Supreme Pontiff, and in his person the whole Catholic Church, which thy divine Son has entrusted to him to lead along the paths of eternal salvation. He, too, places his whole trust in thee. Protect and bless him ; be his support and consolation in the midst of his trials, and help him to extend the Kingdom of GOD. O Mother of mercy, be for us all "the cause of our joy, " and show unto us" " JESUS CHRIST, as thy gift in this life and in eternity. Amen.

281. Ejaculation.
300 Days. T.Q. (See Instructions.) 281 Pius X, November 9, 1907.
OUR Lady of Lourdes, pray for us.

282. Prayer to Our Lady "Reparatrice."
200 Days, once a day. (See Instructions.) 282 Pius X, August 24, 1904.
IMMACULATE Virgin, the refuge of sinners, thou who, to repair the outrages committed against GOD, and the evil inflicted on man by sin, didst resign thyself to the death of thy divine Son, be ever propitious to us, and carry on thy work of zeal and love for us in heaven, where thou reignest so gloriously. We wish to be thy children, do thou show thyself a Mother to us; obtain from the divine Restorer, JESUS, that by applying to our souls the fruits of his Passion and Death, He may free us from the bonds of our iniquities. May He be our light in the darkness, our strength in weakness, our help in danger, so that after He has consoled us by his grace and love in time, He may permit us to see, possess and love Him in eternity. Amen.

283. Prayer to Our Lady of Lourdes for a Sick Person.
300 Days. T.Q. (See Instructions.) 285 Pius X, November 20, 1907.
O MARY, conceived without sin, our Lady of Lourdes, who dost draw from all parts thy children to the Grotto of the apparitions; thou never ceasest to encourage, by innumerable benefits, the filial confidence of those who have responded to thy invitation. Suffering in body and soul, I come in the company of thousands and thousands of poor sick people to throw myself at thy feet and implore thee to heal me. O Mother of goodness, and all-powerful with our LORD, grant that I may be delivered from my infirmities, and that I may be able to consecrate my renewed strength to the service of GOD and of my brethren. How sweet it would be for me to proclaim that I owe to thy intercession the restoration of my health, which, while bearing witness to thy goodness to me, might be also a motive of conversion for many a soul.

But I desire, above everything, to abandon myself into thy maternal hands. If it be the will of JESUS CHRIST, my divine SAVIOUR, to which thy will is ever united, that the chalice of my sufferings should not at present depart from me, I desire the grace to say, with resignation and love, that I, too, will the same. Cause me, then, to be penetrated to the depths of my heart with a full and perfect acceptance of that consoling and heaven-sent doctrine: that the GOD of goodness loves us infinitely, always and under all circumstances, but especially without doubt when he associates us with the sufferings of JESUS CHRIST and fastens us to his Cross.

O Immaculate Virgin, our Lady of Lourdes, Mother of a GOD who was a man of sorrows, thy divine Son wished thee to be at his side on Calvary, whilst He suffered and died for us. He loves thee as only GOD could love a mother, and yet He willed that thy soul should be pierced with a sword of grief, so that thy love for Him should be revealed, and expand by sharing in his inexpressible sufferings.

Obtain for me this grace, our Lady of Lourdes, consoler of the afflicted, health of the sick, that I may love GOD more and more, in proportion as He prolongs and aggravates my trials. This would be a miracle greater than my sudden and complete restoration. To restore my health a single word would suffice, spoken by thee in the name and with the power of Him who is thy Son, while He is also thy GOD; but that the grace of resignation in suffering should make me accept with joy my sickness and its many painful consequences, this I feel to be in an eminent degree the work of the Most High. I see that it is in some sort easier for GOD to heal my sufferings than to make me love them. But, if thou desirest it, my weakness will have for support a supernatural force which will render it victorious, and so manifest the extent of thy power.

Would that the pains of my malady, sanctified by submission to the divine will, could be united to the agony of my Divine SAVIOUR ; would that my tears, mixed with his tears and his blood, could effect the expiation of my past sins, and draw down the graces of resurrection on poor souls dying or dead in sin. May the abundance of thy gifts, O my GOD, be granted, I beseech Thee, in the name of thy Mother, especially to those who are united to me by ties of blood or friendship. Grant that my sufferings, until it shall please thee to put an end to them, may open for them a fountain of mercies.

O Mother of Sorrows and Mother of merciful bounty, who stood erect at the foot of the Cross, pray for us, that we may be made worthy of the promises of CHRIST. Amen.

284. Our Lady of Ransom.
Plenary. I, II, IV, T.Q. (See Instructions) 284 Pius X, August 10, 1904.

This Indulgence, after the manner of the Portiuncula, may be gained between first vespers and sunset on September 24, the Feast of Our Lady of Ransom, as many times as a person visits a church or public chapel of the Order of Ransom, whether of men or women, or of the Third Order, or of confraternities.

285. Seven Saturdays of Our Lady of Ransom.
Plenary, to all who take part in this devotion in public, on one of the seven Saturdays. I, II,III, IV. The church visited must, if possible, be a church or chapel of the Religious of the Order of Ransom, as above. (See Instructions.) 285 Pius X, Br. May 25, 1908

286. Ejaculation to Our Lady "del Pilar" of Saragossa.
300 Days. T.Q. (See Instructions.) 286 Pius X, January 23, 1907.

MOST blessed Virgin of the Pillar, pray for us.

287. Ejaculation.
200 Days, once a day. (See Instructions.) 287 Pius X, January 31, 1906.

OUR LADY, deliverer of slaves, pray for us.

288. Ejaculation.
300 Days, once a day. (See Instructions.) 288 Pius X, May 22, 1906.

OUR LADY of Good Studies, pray for us.

XI. THE HOLY ANGELS
ST MICHAEL ARCHANGEL
289. Hymn, Antiphon, etc.
i. 200 Days, once a day. ii. Plenary, once a month. I, II, IV. (See Instructions.) 289 Pius VII, May 6, 1817.

TE splendor et virtus PATRIS,	O JESU! life-spring of the soul!
Te vita JESU, cordium,	The FATHER'S Power and Glory bright!
Ab ore qui pendent tuo,	Thee with the Angels we extol;
Laudamus inter Angelos,	From Thee they draw their life and light.
Tibi mille densa millium	Thy thousand, thousand hosts are spread, [
Ducum corona militat:	Embattled o'er the azure sky;
Sed explicat victor crucem	But Michael bears thy standard dread,
Michael salutis signifer.	And lifts the mighty Cross on high.
Draconis hic dirum caput	He in that Sign the rebel powers
In ima pellit tartara,	Did with their Dragon Prince expel;
Ducemque cum rebellibus	And hurled them from
Cœlesti ab arce fulminat.	the Heaven's high towers,
Contra ducem superbiæ	Down like a thunderbolt to hell.
Sequamur hunc nos Principem,	Grant us with Michael still, O LORD,
Ut detur ex AGNI throno	Against the Prince of Pride to fight;
Nobis corona gloriæ.	So may a crown be our reward,
PATRI, simulque FILIO,	Before the LAMB'S pure throne of light.

Tibi que, SANCTE SPIRITUS, Sicut fuit, sit jugiter Sæclum per omne gloria Amen. **Ant.** Princeps gloriosissime, Michael Archangele, esto memor nostri: hic et ubique semper precare pro nobis FILIUM DEI **V/.** In conspectu angelorum psallam tibi, DEUS meus. **R/.** Adorabo ad templum sanctum tuum, et confitebor nomini tuo **Oremus.** DEUS, qui miro ordine angelorum ministeria, hominumque dispensas: concede propitius, ut a quibus tibi ministrantibus in cœlo semper assistitur, ab his in terra vita nostra muniatur. Per CHRISTUM DOMINUM, etc.	To GOD the FATHER and the SON, Who rose from death, all glory be; With Thee, O blessed PARACLETE, Henceforth through all eternity. Amen. **Ant.** Most glorious Prince, Michael the Archangel, be mindful of us: pray for us always both here and everywhere to the SON of GOD. **V/.** In the sight of the Angels I will sing psalms to Thee, O my GOD. **R/.** I will adore at thy holy temple and will confess to thy name. **Let us pray.** O GOD, who disposest the services of Angels and men in a wonderful order; mercifully grant that those who ever stand before Thee, ministering to Thee in Heaven, may themselves also protect our life here upon earth. Through CHRIST our LORD. Amen.

290. Novena of St Michael.

i. 300 Days, on each day. ii. Plenary, once during- the Novena. I, II, IV. (See Instructions.) 290 Pius IX, November 26, 1876.

N. B. The Novena may be made at any time of the year, and with any form of prayers sanctioned by competent ecclesiastical authority.

291. Angelical Crown.

i. Seven Years and Seven Quarantines. ii. 100 Days, daily, to anyone who carries this Chaplet about him, or kisses the medal with the representation of the Holy Angels appended to the said Chaplet. iii. Plenary, once a month. I, II, IV. iv. Plenary, I, II, IV, on:
1. The Feast of the Apparition of St Michael, May 8.
2. The Dedication of St Michael, September 29.
3. St Gabriel the Archangel, March 18.
4. St Raphael the Archangel, October 24.
5. Holy Angel Guardians, October 2.

(See Instructions.) 291 Pius IX, Rit. August 8, 1851.

To gain these indulgences special beads must be used, and they must have been blessed by a priest holding from the Holy See general faculties for blessing- rosaries, medals, etc.

V/. O GOD, come to my assistance.
R/. O LORD, make haste to help me.
Glory be to the FATHER, etc.

FIRST SALUTATION. PATER once, Ave thrice, to the First Angelic Choir.
AT the intercession of St Michael and the heavenly choir of the Seraphim, may it please GOD to make us worthy to receive into our hearts the fire of his perfect charity. Amen.

SECOND SALUTATION. PATER once, Ave thrice, to the Second Angelic Choir.
AT the intercession of St Michael and the heavenly choir of the Cherubim, may GOD grant us grace to abandon the ways of sin, and follow the path of Christian perfection. Amen.

THIRD SALUTATION. PATER once, Ave thrice, to the Third Angelic Choir.
AT the intercession of St Michael and the sacred choir of the Thrones, may it please GOD to infuse into our hearts a true and earnest spirit of humility. Amen.

FOURTH SALUTATION. PATER once, Ave thrice, to the Fourth Angelic Choir.
AT the intercession of St Michael and the heavenly choir of the Dominations, may it please GOD to grant us grace to have dominion over our senses, and to correct our depraved passions. Amen.

FIFTH SALUTATION. PATER once, Ave thrice, to the Fifth Angelic Choir.
AT the intercession of St Michael and the heavenly choir of the Powers, may GOD vouchsafe to keep our souls from the wiles and temptations of the devil. Amen.

SIXTH SALUTATION. PATER once, Ave thrice, to the Sixth Angelic Choir.
AT the intercession of St Michael and the choir of the admirable celestial Virtues, may our LORD keep us from falling into temptations and deliver us from evil. Amen.

SEVENTH SALUTATION. PATER once, Ave thrice, to the Seventh Angelic Choir.
AT the intercession of St Michael and the heavenly choir of the Principalities, may it please GOD to fill our souls with the spirit of true and hearty obedience. Amen.

EIGHTH SALUTATION. PATER once, Ave thrice, to the Eighth Angelic Choir.
AT the intercession of St Michael and the heavenly choir of Archangels, may it please GOD to grant us the gift of perseverance in the faith and in all good works, that we may thereby be enabled to attain unto the glory of Paradise. Amen.

NINTH SALUTATION. PATER once, Ave thrice, to the Ninth Angelic Choir.
AT the intercession of St Michael and the heavenly choir of Angels, may GOD vouchsafe to grant that the Holy Angels may protect us during life, and after death may lead us into the everlasting glory of heaven. Amen.

Then say PATER noster four times in conclusion, the first to St Michael, the second to St Gabriel, the third to St Raphael, the fourth to our Angel Guardian. Then end with the following Antiphon:

MICHAEL, glorious Prince, chief and champion of the heavenly host, guardian of the souls of men, conqueror of the rebel angels, who art set over the palace of GOD, our worthy captain under JESUS CHRIST, endowed with superhuman excellence and virtue; vouchsafe to free us from every evil, who with full confidence have recourse to thee; and by thy powerful protection enable us to make progress every day in the faithful service of our GOD.

V/. Pray for us, most blessed Michael, Prince of the Church of JESUS CHRIST.

R/. That we may be made worthy of his promises.

Let us pray.
ALMIGHTY and eternal GOD, who in thy own marvellous goodness and pity didst, for the common salvation of man, choose the glorious Archangel Michael to be the Prince of thy Church; make us worthy, we pray Thee, to be delivered by his beneficent protection from all our enemies, that at the hour of our death no one of them may approach to harm us, and that by the same Archangel Michael we may be introduced into the presence of thy high and heavenly Majesty. Through the merits of JESUS CHRIST our LORD, Amen.

292. Prayer to St Michael.

300 Days, once a day. (See Instructions.) 292 Leo XIII, Mot. Pr, September 23, 1888,

O GLORIOUS Archangel St Michael, Prince of the heavenly host, be our defence in the terrible warfare which we carry on against principalities and Powers, against the rulers of this world of darkness, spirits of evil. Come to the aid of man, whom GOD created immortal, made in his own image and likeness, and redeemed at a great price from the tyranny of the devil. Fight this day the battle of the LORD, together with the holy angels, as already thou hast fought the leader of the proud angels, Lucifer, and his apostate host, who were powerless to resist thee, nor was there place for them any longer in Heaven. That cruel, that ancient serpent, who is called the devil or Satan, who seduces the whole world, was cast into the abyss with his angels. Behold, this primeval enemy and slayer of men has taken courage. Transformed into an angel of light, he wanders about with all the multitude of wicked spirits, invading the earth in order to blot out the name of God and of his CHRIST, to seize upon, slay and cast into eternal perdition souls destined for the crown of eternal glory. This wicked dragon pours out, as a most impure flood, the venom of his malice on men of depraved mind and corrupt heart, the spirit of lying, of impiety, of blasphemy, and the pestilent breath of impurity, and of every vice and iniquity. These most crafty enemies have filled and inebriated with gall and bitterness the Church, the spouse of the immaculate Lamb, and have laid impious hands on her most sacred possessions. In the Holy Place itself, where has been set up the See of the most holy Peter and the Chair of Truth for the light of the world, they have raised the throne of their abominable impiety, with the iniquitous design that when the Pastor has been struck, the sheep may be scattered. Arise then, O invincible Prince, bring- help against the attacks of the lost spirits to the people of GOD, and give them the victory. They venerate thee as their protector and patron; in thee holy Church glories as her defence against the malicious power of hell; to thee has GOD entrusted the souls of men to be established in heavenly beatitude. Oh, pray to the GOD of peace that He may put Satan under our feet, so far conquered that he may no longer be able to hold men in captivity and harm the Church. Offer our prayers in the sight of the Most High, so that they may quickly conciliate

the mercies of the LORD; and beating down the dragon, the ancient serpent, who is the devil and Satan, do thou again make him captive in the abyss, that he may no longer seduce the nations. Amen.
V/. Behold the Cross of the LORD ; be scattered ye hostile powers.
R/. The Lion of the tribe of Juda has conquered, the root of David.
V/. Let thy mercies be upon us, O LORD.
R/. As we have hoped in thee.
V/. O LORD, hear my prayer.
R/. And let my cry come unto thee.
Let us pray.
O GOD, the FATHER of our LORD JESUS CHRIST, we call upon thy holy name, and as suppliants we implore thy clemency, that by the intercession of Mary, ever Virgin immaculate and our Mother, and of the glorious Archangel St Michael, thou wouldst deign to help us against Satan and all other unclean spirits, who wander about the world for the injury of the human race and the ruin of souls. Amen.

293. Antiphon.
100 Days, once a day. (See Instructions.) 293 Leo XIII, August 19, 1893.
ST MICHAEL the Archangel, defend us in the day of battle, that we may not be lost in the dreadful judgment.

ST GABRIEL AND ST RAPHAEL
294. Novena.
i. 300 Days, each day. ii. Plenary once during the Novena. I, II, IV. (See Instructions.) 294 Pius X, November 26, 1876.
A Novena to either of these Archangels may be made at any lime of the year with any form of prayer sanctioned by competent ecclesiastical authority.

295. Prayer.
100 Days, once a day. (See Instructions.) 295 Leo XIII, June 21, 1890
O GLORIOUS Archangel, St Raphael, great Prince of the heavenly court, illustrious for thy gifts of wisdom and grace, guide of those who journey by land or sea, consoler of the afflicted, and refuge of sinners; I beg thee to assist me in all my needs and in all the sufferings of this life, as once thou didst help the young Tobias on his travels. And because thou art the medicine of GOD, I humbly pray thee to heal the many infirmities of my soul, and the ills which afflict my body, if it be for my greater good. I specially ask of thee an angelic purity which may fit me to be the temple of the HOLY SPIRIT. Amen.

THE GUARDIAN ANGEL
296. Invocation.
i.100 Days. T.Q. ii. Plenary on October 2, Feast of the Guardian Angels, if said daily, morning and evening, for a year. I, II, III, IV. iii. Plenary, once a month, I, II, III, IV. iv. Plenary in articulo mortis (at the point of death) if frequently used.
(See Instructions.) 296 Pius VI, Br. October 2, 1795; June n, 1796; Pius VII, May 15, 1821.

ANGELE DEI, qui custos es mei, me tibi commissum pietate superna illumina, custodi, rege, et guberna. Amen.
Or:

O ANGEL of GOD, whom GOD hath appointed to be my guardian, enlighten and protect, direct and govern me. Amen.

ANGEL of GOD, my guardian dear,
To whom his love commits me here,
Ever this day be at my side,
To light and guard, to rule and guide. Amen.

297. Novena of the Guardian Angel.
i. 300 Days, each day. ii. Plenary, once during- the Novena. I, II, IV. 297 Pius IX, November 26, 1876.
The Novena may be made at any time and with any form of prayer sanctioned by competent ecclesiastical authority.

XII. ST JOSEPH
298. Responsory, Antiphon, etc.
One Year. T.Q. (See Instructions.) 298 Pius VII, Res. Card, Vic. September 6, 1804.

QUICUMQUE sanus vivere,
Cursumque vitæ claudere,
In fine lætus expetit,
Opem Josephi postulet.

TO all who would holily live,
To all who would happily die
St Joseph is ready to give,
Sure guidance, and help from on high.

Hic Sponsus almæ Virginis,
Paterque JESU creditus,
Justus, fidelis, integer,
Quod poscit, orans impetrat.

Of Mary the spouse undefil'd,
Just, holy, and pure of all stain,
He asks of his own foster Child,
And needs but ask to obtain.

Here the first stanza is repeated.

Quicumque, etc. To all, etc.

Fœno jacentem parvulum
Adorat, et post exulem
Solatur; inde perditum
Quærit dolens, et invenit.

In the manger that Child he adored
And nursed Him in exile and flight;
Him, lost in his boyhood, deplored,
And found with amaze and delight.

Quicumque, etc. To all, etc.

Mundi supremus artifex
Ejus labore pascitur,
Summi Parentis FILIUS
Obedit illi subditus.

The Maker of heaven and earth
By the labour of Joseph was fed;
The SON by an infinite birth
Submissive to Joseph was made.

Quicumque, etc. To all, etc.

Adesse morti proximus
Cum Matre JESUM conspicit,
Et inter ipsos jubilans
Dulci sopore solvitur.

And when his last hour drew nigh,
Oh, full of all joy was his breast,
Seeing JESUS and Mary close by,
As he tranquilly slumbered to rest.

Quicumque, etc. To all, etc.

Gloria PATRI, et FILIO, et SPIRITUI SANCTO.

All praise to the FATHER above;
All praise to his glorious SON;
All praise to the SPIRIT of love,
While the days of eternity run.

Quicumque, etc. To all, etc.

Ant. Ecce fidelis servus, et prudens, quem constituit DOMINUS super familiam suam.
V/. Ora pro nobis, beate Joseph.
R/. Ut digni efficiamur promissionibus CHRISTI.
Oremus.
DEUS qui ineffabili providentia beatum Joseph Sanctissimæ Genitricis tuæ Sponsum eligere dignatus es; præsta, quæsumus, ut quem protectorem veneramur in terris intercessorem habere mereamur in cælis, qui vivis et regnas in sæcula sæculorum. Amen.

Ant. Behold the faithful and prudent servant whom the LORD set over his house.
V/. Pray for us, holy Joseph.
R/. That we may be made worthy of the promises of CHRIST.
Let us pray.
O GOD, who in thy ineffable providence didst vouchsafe to choose blessed Joseph to be the spouse of thy most holy Mother, grant, we beseech Thee, that we may have him for our intercessor in Heaven, whom on earth we venerate as our most holy protector. Who livest and reignest, etc. Amen.

299. Psalms in honour of the Name of St Joseph.
i. Seven Years and Seven Quarantines. T.Q. ii. Plenary once a month. I, II, IV. iii. Plenary on the feast of the Patronage of St Joseph (third Sunday after Easter) to those who have frequently practised this devotion during- the year. I, II. (See Instructions.) 299 Pius VII Res. Card. Provicar. June 26, 1809; Indul. June 13, 1815.
Ant. Joseph vir Mariæ, de qua natus est JESUS, qui vocatur CHRISTUS.
J. Psalm, xcix.
JUBILATE DEO omnis terra : * servite DOMINO in lætitia.
Introite in conspectu ejus, * in exultatione.

Scitote, quoniam DOMINUS ipse est DEUS: * ipse fecit nos, et non ipsi nos.

Populus ejus, et oves pascuæ ejus: * introite portas ejus in confessione, atria ejus in hymnis; confitemini illi.

Laudate nomen ejus, quoniam suavis est DOMINUS, in aeternum misericordia ejus: * et usque in generationem et generationem veritas ejus.

Gloria PATRI, et FILIO, etc.

Ant. Joseph vir Mariæ, de qua natus est JESUS, qui vocatur CHRISTUS.

Ant. Joseph de domo David, et nomen Virginis Maria.

O. Psalm, xlvi.

OMNES gentes, plaudite manibus: * jubilate DEO in voce exultationis.

Quoniam DOMINUS excelsus, terribilis, * rex magnus super omnem terram.

Subjecit populos nobis, * et gentes sub pedibus nostris.

Elegit nobis haereditatem suam, speciem Jacob, quam dilexit.

Ascendit DEUS in jubilo, et DOMINUS in voce tubæ.

Psallite DEO nostro, psallite; *psallite regi nostro psallite.

Quoniam rex omnis terrae DEUS; * psallite sapienter.

Regnabit DEUS super gentes;* DEUS sedet supersedem sanctam suam.

Principes populorum congregati sunt cum DEO Abraham: * quoniam dii fortes terræ vehementer elevati sunt.

Gloria PATRI, et FILIO, etc.

Ant. Joseph de domo David, et nomen Virginis Maria.

Ant. Joseph vir ejus, cum esset Justus, et nollet eam traducere.

S. Psalm, cxxviii.

SÆPE expugnaverunt me a juventute mea: * dicat nunc Israel.

Sæpe expugnaverunt me a juventute mea: * etenim non potuerunt mihi.

Supra dorsum meum fabricaverunt peccatores: * prolongaverunt iniquitatem suam.

DOMINUS Justus concidit cervices peccatorum: * confundantur, et convertantur retrorsum omnes, qui oderunt Sion.

Fiant sicut fœnum tectorum, * quod priusquam evellatur, exaruit.

De quo non implevit manum suam, qui metit, * et sinum suum, qui manipulos colligit.

Et non dixerunt, qui praeteribant: Benedictio DOMINI super vos: * benediximus vobis in nomine DOMINI.

Gloria PATRI, etc.

Ant. Joseph vir ejus, cum esset Justus, et nollet eam traducere.

Ant. Joseph fili David, noli timere accipere Mariam conjugem tuam.

E. Psalm. lxxx.

EXULTATE DEO adjutori nostro:*jubilate DEO Jacob.

Sumite psalmum, et date tympanum, *psalterium jucundum cum cithara.

Buccinate in neomenia tuba, * in insigni die solemnitatis vestræ.

Quia prseceptum in Israel est,*et judicium DEO Jacob.

Testimonium in Joseph posuit illud, cum exiret de terra Ægypti: * linguam, quam non noverat, audivit.

Divertit ab oneribus dorsum ejus: * manus ejus in cophino servierunt.

In tribulatione invocasti me, et liberavi te: * exaudivi te in abscondito tempestatis; probavi te apud aquam contradictionis.

Audi, populus meus, et contestabor te: * Israel si audieris me, non erit in te DEUS recens, neque adorabis deum alienum.

Ego enim sum DOMINUS DEUS tuus, qui eduxi te de terra Ægypti; dilata os tuum, et implebo illud.

Et non audivit populus meus vocem meam: * et Israel non intendit mihi.

Et dimisi eos secundum desideria cordis eorum: * ibunt in adinventionibus suis.

Si populus meus audisset me, * Israel si in viis meis ambulasset:

Pro nihilo forsitan inimicos eorum humiliassem: *et super tribulantes eos misissem manum meam.

Inimici DOMINI mentiti sunt ei: * et erit tempus eorum in sæcula.

Et cibavit eos ex adipe frumenti; * et de petra melle saturavit eos.

Gloria PATRI.

Ant. Joseph fili David, noli timere accipere Mariam conjugem tuam.

Ant. Joseph, exurgens a somno, fecit sicut præcepit ei angelus.

PH. Psalm. lxxxvi.

FUNDAMENTA ejus in montibus sanctis: * diligit DOMINUS portas Sion super omnia tabernacula Jacob.

Gloriosa dicta sunt de te, * civitas DEI.

Memor ero Rahab et Babylonis * scientium me.

Eccealienigenæ, et Tyrus, et populus Æthiopum, * hi fuerunt illic.

Numquid Sion dicet: Homo, et homo natus est in ea, * et ipse fundavit eam altissimus?

DOMINUS narrabit in scripturis populorum, et principum: *horum, qui fuerunt in ea.

Sicut lætantium omnium * habitatio est in te.

Gloria PATRI.

Ant. Joseph, exurgens a somno, fecit sicut præcepit ei angelus.

V/. Constituit eum dominum domus suæ.

R/. Et principem omnis possessionis suæ.

Oremus.

DEUS, qui ineffabili providentia beatum Joseph sanctissimas Genitricis tuæ sponsum eligere dignatus es; praesta, qusesumus, ut quem protectorem veneramur in terris, intercessorem habere mereamur in cœlis. Qui vivis et regnas, etc.

HYMNUS.

DEI qui gratiæ impotes
Cœlestium dona expetunt,
Josephi nomen invocent,
Opemque poscant supplices.

Joseph vocato nomine
DEUS adest petentibus,
Auget piis quærentibus
Culpamque delet impiis.

Joseph piis quærentibus
Dantur beata munera,
Datur palma victoriæ
Agonis in certamine.

Amplexus inter Virginis,
Castæque prolis placido
Vitam sopore deserens,
Morientium fit regula.

Illo nihil potentius,
Cujus parentem nutibus,
Et subditum imperiis
DEUM viderunt æthera.

Illo nihil perfectius,
Qui sponsus almæ Virginis
Electus est, Altissimi
Gustos, parensque creditus.

O ter beata et amplius
Honor sit tibi, Trinitas,
PATER, VERBUM que, et SPIRITUS,
Sanctoque Joseph nomini. Amen.

Ant. Adjutor est in tribulationibus, et protector omnibus beatus Joseph nomen suum pie invocantibus.

V/. Sit nomen beati Joseph benedictum,

R/. Ex hoc, nunc, et usque in sæculum.

Oremus.

DEUS, qui, mirabilis in sanctis tuis, mirabilior in beato Joseph, eum caelestium donorum dispensatorem super familiam tuam constituisti; præsta, quæsumus, ut cujus nomen devoti veneramur, ejus precibus et meritis adjuti ad portum salutis feliciter perveniamus. Per CHRISTUM DOMINUM nostrum. Amen.

300. Seven Sorrows and Seven Joys.

i. 100 Days, once a day. ii. 300 Days, every Wednesday in the year, and every day of the two Novenas preceding the two feasts of St Joseph, i.e., his principal feast, March 19, and the feast of his Patronage (third Sunday after Easter). iii. Plenary, on each of these two feasts, to all who shall say the prayers. I, II. iv. Plenary, once a month. I, II. v. 300 Days, on each of the first six Sundays, to all the faithful who say the Prayers on any seven consecutive Sundays in the year. vi. Plenary, on each of the Seven Sundays. The same Indulgence is also granted to the illiterate, wherever this devotion is not publicly practised, provided only they say seven times Pater noster, Ave Maria and Gloria Patri instead of the Prayers which follow. I, II,III, IV. (See Instructions.) 300 Pius VII, Card. Vic. December 9, 1819 ; Gregory XVI, January 22, 1836 ; Pius IX, February i, 1847, March 22, 1847.

I PURE spouse of most holy Mary, glorious St Joseph, the trouble and anguish of thy heart were great when, being in sore perplexity, thou wast minded to put away thy stainless spouse; yet was thy joy inexpressible when the Archangel revealed to thee the sublime mystery of the Incarnation. By this thy sorrow and thy joy, we pray thee comfort our souls now and in their last pains with the consolation of a well-spent life, and a holy death like unto thy own, with JESUS and Mary at our side. PATER, Ave, Gloria,

II MOST blessed Patriarch, glorious St Joseph, chosen to the office of Father of the Word made Man, the pain was keen that thou didst feel when thou didst see the Infant JESUS born in abject poverty; but thy pain was changed into heavenly joy when thou didst hear the harmony of angel-choirs, and behold the glory of that night. By this thy sorrow and thy joy, we pray thee obtain for us that, when the journey of our life is ended, we too may pass to that blessed land where we shall hear the angel-chants, and rejoice in the bright light of heavenly glory. PATER, Ave, Gloria,

III OTHOU who wast ever most obedient in executing the law of GOD, glorious St Joseph, thy heart was pierced with pain when the precious Blood of the Infant SAVIOUR was shed at his Circumcision; but with the Name of JESUS new life and heavenly joy returned to thee. By this thy sorrow and thy joy, obtain for us that, being freed, while we still live, from every vice, we too may cheerfully die with the sweet Name of JESUS in our hearts and on our lips. PATER, Ave, Gloria.

IV MOST faithful Saint, glorious St Joseph, who wast admitted to take part in the redemption of man; the prophecy of Simeon foretelling the sufferings of JESUS and Mary caused thee a pang like that of death, but, at the same time, by his prediction of the salvation and glorious resurrection of innumerable souls, filled thee with great joy. By this thy sorrow and thy joy, help us with thy prayers to be of the number of those who, by the merits of JESUS and the intercession of his Virgin Mother, shall be partakers of the resurrection to glory. PATER, Ave, Gloria.

V MOST watchful Guardian, glorious St Joseph, who wast so intimately familiar with the Incarnate SON of GOD, greatly thou didst toil to nurture and to serve the SON of the Most High, especially in the flight thou madest with Him into Egypt; greatly also didst thou rejoice to have GOD Himself always with thee, and to see the overthrow of the idols of Egypt. By this thy sorrow and thy joy, obtain for us grace to keep far out of the reach of the enemy of our souls, by quitting all dangerous occasions, that so no idol of earthly affection may any longer occupy a place in our hearts, but that, being entirely devoted to the service of JESUS and Mary, we may live and die for them alone. PATER, Ave, Gloria.

VI ANGEL on earth, glorious St Joseph, who didst so wonder to see the King of Heaven obedient to thy bidding, the consolation thou hadst at his return from Egypt was disturbed by the fear of Archelaus, but nevertheless, being reassured by the angel, thou didst go back and dwell happily at Nazareth, in the company of JESUS and Mary. By this thy sorrow and thy joy, obtain for us that, having our hearts freed from idle fears, we may enjoy the peace of a tranquil conscience, dwelling safely with JESUS and Mary, and dying at last in their arms. PATER, Ave, Gloria.

VII EXAMPLE of holy living, glorious St Joseph, when through no fault of thine thou didst lose JESUS, the Holy Child, thou didst search for Him with great sorrow for three days, until with joy unspeakable thou didst find Him, who was thy Life, amidst the doctors in the Temple. By this thy sorrow and thy joy, we pray thee with our whole hearts so to interpose always in our behalf, that we may never lose JESUS by mortal sin, and if we are at any time so wretched as to lose Him, then we pray thee to aid us to seek Him with unwearied sorrow until we find Him, particularly in the hour of our death, that we may pass from this life to enjoy Him for ever in heaven, there to sing with thee his divine mercies without end. PATER, Ave, Gloria.

Ant. JESUS Himself was about thirty years old, being, as was supposed, the son of Joseph.

V/. Pray for us, holy Joseph.

R/. That we may be made worthy of the promises of CHRIST.

Let us pray.

O GOD, who in thine ineffable providence didst vouchsafe to choose blessed Joseph to be the spouse of thy most holy Mother; grant, we beseech Thee, that we may have him for our intercessor in heaven, whom on earth we venerate as our holy Protector. Who livest and reignest, world without end. Amen.

301. Novena of St Joseph.

i. 300 Days, once a day. ii. Plenary, during- the Novena. I, II, IV. (See Instructions.) 301 Pius IX, November 26, 1876.

This Novena may be made at any time of the year, and with any form of prayer sanctioned by competent ecclesiastical authority.

302. Month of March.

i. 300 Days, each day. ii. Plenary, on any one day. I, II, IV. (See Instructions.) 302 Pius IX, April 27, 1865 ; July 18, 1877

The month may be either that of March, or a month terminating on the feast of St Joseph, March 19. Persons legitimately hindered from practicing this devotion in March may substitute any other month. The devotion consists of any prayers or other pious practice in honour of the Saint.

303. Prayer.

300 Days, once a day. (See Instructions) 303 Pius IX, Br. June 26, 1863.

REMEMBER, most pure spouse of Mary ever Virgin, my loving protector, St Joseph, that never has it been heard that anyone ever invoked thy protection, or besought aid of thee, without being consoled. In this confidence I come before thee, I fervently recommend myself to thee. Despise not my prayer, foster-father of our REDEEMER, but do thou in thy pity receive it. Amen.

304. Prayer.

100 Days, once a day. (See Instructions.) 304 Pius IX, February 4, 1877.

VIRGINUM custos, et pater Sancte Joseph, cujus fideli custodiæ ipsa innocentia CHRISTUS JESUS, et Virgo virginum, Maria commissa fuit; te per hoc utrumque carissimum pignus, JESUM et Mariam, obsecro, et obtestor, ut me ab omni immunditia præservatum, mente incontaminata, puro corde et casto corpore JESU et Mariæ semper facias castissime famulari. Amen.

GUARDIAN of virgins, and holy father Joseph, to whose faithful custody CHRIST JESUS Innocence itself, and Mary, Virgin of virgins, were committed ; I pray and beseech thee, by these dear pledges, JESUS and Mary, that, being preserved from all uncleanness, I may with spotless mind, pure heart and chaste body, ever serve JESUS and Mary most chastely all the days of my life. Amen.

305. Prayer to St Joseph, Patron of the Universal Church.

100 Days, once a day. (See Instructions.) 305 Leo XIII, March, 1882.

O MOST powerful Patriarch, St Joseph, Patron of that universal Church which has always invoked thee in anxieties and tribulations; from the lofty seat of thy glory lovingly regard the Catholic world. Let it move thy paternal heart to see the mystical Spouse of CHRIST and his Vicar weakened by sorrow and persecuted by powerful enemies. We beseech thee, by the most bitter suffering thou didst experience on earth, to wipe away in mercy the tears of the revered Pontiff, to defend and liberate him, and to intercede with the Giver of peace and charity, that every hostile power being overcome and every error being destroyed, the whole Church may serve the GOD of all blessings in perfect liberty: ut destructis adversitatibus et erroribus universis Ecclesiæ secura DEO serviat libertate. Amen.

306. Prayer.
300 Days, once a day. (See Instructions.) 306 Leo XIII, July 18, 1885.

O GLORIOUS St Joseph, chosen by GOD to be the reputed father of JESUS, the most pure spouse of Mary ever Virgin, and the head of the Holy Family, and then elected by the Vicar of CHRIST to be the heavenly Patron and Protector of the Church founded by JESUS CHRIST; with the greatest confidence I implore at this time thy powerful aid for the entire Church militant. Protect in a special manner with thy truly paternal love the Supreme Pontiff and all the bishops and priests united to the See of St Peter. Defend all those who labour for souls in the midst of the afflictions and tribulations of this life, and obtain the willing submission of every nation throughout the world to the Church, the necessary means of salvation for all.

O dearest St Joseph, be pleased to accept the consecration which I make to thee of myself. I dedicate myself entirely to thee that thou mayest ever be my father, my protector, and my guide in the way of salvation. Obtain for me great purity of heart and a fervent love of the interior life. Grant that after thy example all my actions may be directed to the greater glory of GOD, in union with the divine Heart of JESUS and the immaculate heart of Mary, and with thee. Finally, pray for me that I may be able to share in the peace and joy of thy most holy death. Amen.

307. Prayers for those in their Agony.
300 Days, once a day. (See Instructions.) 307 Leo XIII, May 17, 1884.

ETERNAL FATHER, by the love which Thou bearest to St Joseph, chosen by Thee from among all men to represent Thee on earth, have pity on us and on poor souls in their agony. PATER, Ave, Gloria.

Eternal and divine SON, by the love which Thou bearest to St Joseph, thy most faithful guardian on earth, have pity on us and on all poor souls in their agony. PATER, Ave, Gloria.

Eternal and divine SPIRIT, by the love Thou bearest to St Joseph, who with so great solicitude watched over most holy Mary the Spouse of thy predilection, have pity on us and on all poor souls in their agony. PATER, Ave, Gloria.

308. Prayer.
i. Seven Years and Seven Quarantines, if said after the Rosary in October. ii. 300 Days, once a day, at other times (and in this case the words in italics are omitted). (See Instructions) 308 Leo XIII, Enc. August 15, 1889; Indul. September 21, 1889.

TO thee, O blessed Joseph, do we fly in our tribulation, and having implored the help of thy most holy spouse, we confidently crave thy patronage also. Through that charity which bound thee to the Immaculate Virgin Mother of GOD, and through the paternal love with which thou didst embrace the Child JESUS, we humbly beseech thee graciously to regard the inheritance which JESUS CHRIST hath purchased by his Blood, and with thy power and strength to aid us in our necessities.

O most watchful Guardian of the Divine Family, defend the chosen children of JESUS CHRIST; O most loving Father, ward off from us every contagion of error and corrupting influence; O our most mighty protector, be propitious to us and from Heaven assist us in this our struggle with the power of darkness; and, as once thou didst rescue the Child JESUS from deadly peril, so now protect GOD'S holy Church from the snares of the enemy and from all adversity: shield, too, each one of us by thy constant protection, so that, supported by thine example and thine aid, we may be able to live piously, to die holily, and to obtain eternal happiness in Heaven. Amen.

309. Prayer of St Bernadine of Siena.
100 Days, once a day. (See Instructions.) 309 Leo XIII, December 14, 1889.

MEMENTO nostri, beate Joseph; et tuæ orationis suffragio apud tuum putativum Filium intercede; sed et beatissimam Virginem Sponsam tuam nobis propitiam redde, quae mater est ejus, qui cum PATRE et SPIRITU SANCTO vivit et regnat per infinita sæcula sæculorum. Amen.	BE mindful of us, O blessed Joseph, and intercede on our behalf with thy reputed Son; and secure for us the favour of thy most holy Virgin Spouse, the Mother of Him who liveth and reigneth with the FATHER and the HOLY GHOST, world without end. Amen.

310. Invocation.
300 Days, once a day. (See Instructions.) 310 Leo XIII, March 18, 1882

FAC nos innocuam, Joseph, decurrere vitam, sitque tuo semper tuta patrocinio.

GRANT, O holy Joseph, that, ever secure under thy protection, we may pass our lives without guilt.

311. Invocation.
300 Days, once a day. (See Instructions.) 311 Leo XIII, Mot. Pr. May 15, 1891
ST JOSEPH, foster-father of our LORD JESUS CHRIST, and true spouse of Mary ever Virgin, pray for us.

312. Ejaculation.
100 Days, once a day. (See Instructions.) 312 Leo XIII, December 19, 1891
ST JOSEPH, model and patron of those who love the Sacred Heart of JESUS, pray for us.

313. Prayer for the Observance of Sundays and Feast Days.
300 Days. T.Q. (See Instructions.) 313 Pius X, December 1, 1905
MOST glorious Patriarch, St Joseph, obtain, we beseech thee, from our LORD JESUS CHRIST a most abundant blessing on all who keep festival days holy; obtain for us that those who profane them may know, in time, the great evil they commit, and the chastisements which they draw down upon themselves in this life and in the next, and may be converted without delay.

O most blessed St Joseph, thou who on the LORD'S day didst cease from every labour of thy craft, and with JESUS and Mary didst fulfil the duties of religion with most lively devotion, bless the pious work of the sanctification of feast-days, erected under thy most powerful patronage; cause it to spread to every home, office, and workshop, so that the day may soon come when all the Christian populace may on feast-days abstain from forbidden work, seriously attend to the salvation of their souls, and give glory to GOD, who liveth and reigneth, world without end. Amen.

314. Prayer to St Joseph.
100 Days, twice a day. (See Instructions.) 314 Pius X, November 26, 1906

O JOSEPH, virgo pater JESU, purissime sponse Virginis Mariæ, quotidie deprecare pro nobis ipsum JESUM FILIUM DEI, ut, armis suæ gratiæ muniti, legitime certantes in vita ab eodem coronemur in morte.

O JOSEPH, virgin father of JESUS, most pure spouse of the Virgin Mary, pray for us daily to the SON of GOD, that, armed with the weapons of his grace, we may fight as we ought in life, and be crowned by Him in death.

315. Prayer to St Joseph.
300 Days, once a day. (See Instructions.) 315 Pius X, March 15, 1907.
GLORIOUS St Joseph, model of all those who are devoted to labour, obtain for me the grace to work in a spirit of penance for the expiation of my many sins; to work conscientiously, putting the call of duty above my inclinations; to work with gratitude and joy, considering it an honour to employ and develop, by means of labour, the gifts received from GOD; to work with order, peace, moderation and patience, without ever recoiling before weariness or difficulties; to work, above all, with purity of intention, and with detachment from self, having always death before my eyes and the account which I must render of time lost, of talents wasted, of good omitted, of vain complacency in success, so fatal to the work of GOD. All for JESUS, all for Mary, all after thy example, O Patriarch Joseph. Such shall be my watchword in life and in death. Amen.

XIII. VARIOUS SAINTS
ST JOACHIM
316. Prayer.
300 Days, once a day. (See Instructions) 316 Leo XIII, March 20, 1886.
O GREAT and glorious patriarch St Joachim, how I rejoice to think that thou wast chosen from among all the Saints to co-operate in the divine mysteries, and enrich the world by bestowing on it the great Mother of GOD, most holy Mary! By this singular privilege thou hast become so powerful with the Mother and the SON as to obtain whatever graces may be necessary for us. With great confidence, then, I have recourse to thy most powerful protection, and I commend to thee all the wants of my family, both spiritual and temporal, as well as my own; and especially I appeal to thee for the particular grace which I desire and expect from thy paternal intercession. And since thou wast a perfect model of the interior life,

obtain for me interior recollection and a distaste for the fleeting goods of this earth, with a lively and persevering love of JESUS and Mary. Obtain for me, too, devotion and sincere obedience to Holy Church, and to the Supreme Pontiff who governs her, so that I may live and die in Faith, Hope, and perfect Charity, invoking the most holy names of JESUS and Mary, and may save my soul. Amen. PATER, Ave, Gloria, thrice.

317. Prayer.
300 Days, once a day. (See Instructions.) 317 Pius X, June 16, 1906.

O JOACHIM sancte, conjux Annæ, Pater almæ Virginis, hic famulis confer salutis opem.	O HOLY Joachim, husband of Anne, father of the Blessed Virgin, bestow on thy servants here help and salvation.

318. Prayer.
300 Days, once a day. (See Instructions.) 318 Leo XIII, Mot. Pr. August 16, 1890

O GREAT patriarch St Joachim, by that singular privilege by which thou wast chosen by Divine Providence to present to the world that Immaculate Queen in whom all nations should be blessed, and who should bear in her virginal bosom the salvation of the human race; we thy devout clients rejoice with thee over this beautiful privilege, and we implore thy special protection for ourselves and our families. Do not allow, O dear Saint, the devil or sin to have any place in our souls, nor the perverse maxims of the world to seduce us, nor permit us to live unmindful of that eternity for which we have been created. Obtain for us from GOD a firm faith, unshaken by the impieties and errors which are scattered abroad by sects hostile to the Church and to the Apostolic See, a sincere and constant affection for the Vicar of JESUS CHRIST, the Roman Pontiff, a generous and indomitable courage in refuting the calumnies uttered against everything that is most sacred and revered in our holy religion. Thou who art powerful through the love which thy holy daughter, Mary, bears thee, help on the cause of the Church, obtain for her the long-desired triumph, scatter the powers of darkness, humble their pride, and cause the light of truth and of the Faith to outshine every falsehood. Grant us, above everything, a tender and filial devotion to most holy Mary, thy dear daughter and our Mother, so that daily honouring her with devout homage we may deserve to be counted by her among the happy company of her children, and after the miseries of this exile to be brought by her to Paradise, there to praise the mercies of GOD for ever. Amen. PATER, Ave, Gloria, thrice.

ST ANNE
319. Prayer.
300 Days, once a day. (See Instructions.) 319 Leo XIII, March 20, 1886.

WITH deep and heartfelt veneration I prostrate myself before thee, O glorious St Anne. Thou art that creation of privilege and predilection, who through thy extraordinary virtues and sanctity wast worthy to receive from GOD the supreme grace of giving life to the treasure-house of all graces, blessed among women, Mother of the Word Incarnate, the most holy Virgin Mary. Deign, therefore, O most compassionate saint, for the sake of this lofty privilege, to receive me into the number of thy true followers, for such I protest I am and desire to remain so long as I may live. Surround me with thy powerful patronage, and obtain for me from GOD the grace to imitate those virtues with which thou wast so abundantly adorned. Grant that I may know and bitterly lament my sins. Obtain for me a most lively affection for JESUS and Mary, and fidelity and constancy in the practice of the duties of my state. Preserve me from every danger in life, and assist me in the moment of my death, so that, safe in Paradise, I may unite with thee, most blessed Mother, in praising the Word of GOD made man in the bosom of thy most pure child, the Virgin Mary. Amen. PATER, Ave, Gloria, thrice.

SS. PETER AND PAUL
320. Prayer.
i. 100 Days, once a day. ii. Plenary, once on any Feast of St Peter and St Paul, or on one of the nine days preceding or eight days following such feast. I, II, III, IV.
N.B. The visit must be made to a church or altar dedicated to these Saints, and there the prayer must be recited. (See Instructions) 320 Pius VI, Mem. July 28, 1778 ; Pius IX, June 18, 1876

O BLESSED Apostles Peter and Paul, I elect you this day for my special protectors and advocates with GOD. In all humility I rejoice with thee, blessed Peter, Prince of the Apostles, because thou art the rock whereon GOD hath built his Church; and I rejoice with thee, too, blessed Paul, because thou wast chosen of GOD for a vessel of election and a preacher of the truth throughout the world. Obtain for me, I beseech you both, a lively faith, firm hope, and perfect charity, entire detachment from myself, contempt of the world, patience in adversity, humility in prosperity, attention in prayer, purity of heart, right intention in my works, diligence in the fulfilment of all the duties of my state of life, constancy in my good resolutions, resignation to the holy will of GOD, perseverance in Divine grace unto death ; that, having overcome, by your joint intercession and your glorious merits, the temptations of the world, the flesh and the devil, I may be made worthy to appear before the face of the chief and eternal Shepherd of Souls, JESUS CHRIST our LORD, to enjoy Him and to love Him for all eternity, who with the FATHER and the HOLY GHOST, liveth and reigneth ever, world without end. Amen. PATER, Ave, Gloria.

321. Responsory of St Peter.

i. 100 Days, once a day. ii. Plenary, on the feast of St Peters Chair in Rome, January 18, and also on the feast of St Peter's Chains,
August I, II, III, IV (See Instructions) 321 Pius VI, June 22, 1782.
N.B. The visit must be to a Church or Altar dedicated to St Peter.

SI vis patronum quærere, Si vis potentem vindicem, Quid jam moraris? invoca Apostolorum principem
 O sancte cœli Claviger,
Tu nos precando subleva;
Tu redde nobis pervia
Aulae supernæ limina

Ut ipse multis pœnitens
Culpam rigasti lacrymis,
Sic nostra tolli poscimus
Fletu perenni crimina.
O sancte cœli, etc.

Sicut fuisti ab angelo
Tuis solutus vinculis,
Tu nos iniquis exue
Tot implicatos nexibus.
O sancte cœli, etc.

O firma Petra Ecclesiæ,
Columna flecti nescia,
Da robur et constantiam,
Error fidem ne subruat.
O sancte cœli, etc.

Romam tuo qui sanguine
Olim sacrasti, protege;
In teque confidentibus
Præsta salutem gentibus.
O sancte cœli, etc.

Tu rem tuere publicam,
Qui te colunt, fidelium,
Ne læsa sit contagiis,
Ne scissa sit discordiis.
O sancte cœli, etc.

Quos hostis antiquus dolos

SEEK ye a patron to defend Your cause? Then, one and all, Without delay upon the Prince Of the Apostles call.
Blest holder of the heavenly keys,
Thy prayers we all implore;
Unlock to us the sacred bars
Of heaven's eternal door.
By penitential tears thou didst
The path of life regain ;
Teach us with thee to weep our sins,
And wash away their stain.
Blest holder, etc.

The angel touch'd thee, and forthwith
Thy chains from off thee fell;
Oh, loose us from the subtle coils
That bind us fast to hell.
Blest holder, etc.

Firm rock, whereon the Church is based,
Pillar that cannot bend,
With strength endue us;
and the faith
From heresy defend.
Blest holder, etc.

Save Rome, which from the days of old
Thy blood hath sanctified;
And help the nations of the earth
That in thy help confide.
Blest holder, etc.

Oh, worshipp'd by all Christendom,
Her realms in peace maintain;
Let no contagion sap her strength,
No discord rend in twain.
Blest holder, etc.

The weapons which our ancient foe

Instruxit in nos, destrue;	Against us doth prepare,
Truces et iras comprime,	Crush thou; nor suffer us to fall
Ne clade nostra sceviat.	Into his deadly snare.
O sancte cœli, etc.	Blest holder, etc.

Contra furentis impetus	Guard us through life; and in that hour
In morte vires suffice,	When our last flight draws nigh,
Ut et supremo vincere	O'er death, o'er hell, o'er Satans power,
Possimus in certamine.	Gain us the victory.
O sancte cœli, etc.	Blest holder, etc.

Gloria PATRI et FILIO et SPIRITUI SANCTO.	Glory be to the FATHER and to the SON and to the HOLY GHOST.
O sancte cœli, etc.	Blest holder, etc.

Ant. Tu es Pastor ovium, Princeps Apostolorum ; tibi traditæ sunt claves regni cœlorum.

Ant. Thou art the Shepherd of the sheep, Prince of the Apostles; to thee were given the keys of the Kingdom of Heaven.

V/. Tu es Petrus.
R/. Et super hanc petram ædificabo ecclesiam meam.
Oremus.
APOSTOLICIS nos, DOMINE quæsumus, beati Petri Apostoli tui attolle præsidiisiut quanto fragiliores sumus, tanto ejus intercessione validioribus auxiliis foveamur; et jugiter apostolica defensione muniti, nec succumbamus vitiis, nec opprimamur adversis. Per CHRISTUM, etc.

V/. Thou art Peter
R/. And upon this rock will I build my Church.
Let us pray.
O LORD, we beseech Thee, raise us up by the Apostolic might of blessed Peter, thy Apostle; that, the weaker we are in ourselves, the more powerful may be the assistance whereby we are strengthened through his intercession; that thus, ever fortified by the protection of thy Apostle, we may neither yield to sin nor be overwhelmed by adversity. Through CHRIST our LORD. Amen.

322. Responsory of St Paul.

i. 100 Days, once a day. ii. Plenary, on January 25, the feast of the Conversion of St Paul, and on June 30, the feast of his Commemoration. I, II, III, IV. (See Instructions.) 322 Pius VII, Card. Vic., January 23, 1806.
N.B. The visit must be to a church or altar dedicated to this Saint.

PRESSI malorum pondere	ALL ye who groan beneath
Adite Paulum supplices,	A load of ills oppress'd,
Qui certa largus desuper	Entreat St Paul, and he will pray
Dabit salutis pignora.	The LORD to give you rest.
O grata cœlo Victima	**O victim dear to Heaven!**
Doctorque, amorque, gentium,	**O Paul, thou teacher true!**
O Paule, nos te vindicem,	**Thou love and joy of Christendom,**
Nos te patronum poscimus.	**To thee for help we sue.**
Nam tu beato concitus	Pierced by the flame of love,
Divino amoris impetu,	Descending from on high,
Quos insecutor oderas,	'Twas thine to preach the faith which once
Defensor inde amplecteris.	Thou soughtest to destroy.
O grata, etc.	O victim, etc.
Non te procellae, et verbera,	Nor toil, nor threatened death,
Non vincla, et ardor hostium, -	Nor tempest, scourge, nor chain,
Non dira mors deterruit,	Could from the assembly of the saints
Ne sancto adesses cœtui.	Thy loving heart detain.
O grata, etc.	O victim, etc.
Amoris eja pristini	Oh, by that quenchless love
Ne sis, precamur, immemor,	Which burnt in thee of yore,
Et nos supernæ languidos	Take pity on our miseries,
In spem reducas gratiæ.	Our fainting hope restore.
O grata, etc.	O victim, etc.
Te destruantur auspice	True champion of the LORD,

Sævæ inferorum machinæ,	Crush thou the schemes of hell,
Et nostra templa publicis	And with adoring multitudes
Petita votis insonent.	Thy sacred temples fill.
O grata, etc	O victim, etc.
Te deprecante floreat	Through thy prevailing prayer
Ignara damni charitas,	May charity abound;
Quam nulla turbent jurgia,	Sweet charity, which knows no ill,
Nec ullus error sauciet.	Which nothing can confound.
O grata, etc..	O victim, etc
Qua terra cumque diditur,	To earth's remotest shores
Jungatur uno fcedere,	May one same faith extend;
Tuisque semper affluat	And thy epistles through all climes
Salubre nectar litteris	Their blessed perfume send.
O grata, etc.	O victim, etc.
Det velle nos quod imperat,	Grant us the will and power
Det posse Summus Arbiter,	To serve Thee, GOD of might,
Ne fluctuantes horridæ	Lest, wavering still and unprepared,
Caligo noctis obruat.	We sink in depths of night.
O grata, etc.	O victim, etc.
Gloria PATRI, et FILIO,	Praise to the FATHER be ;
etc.	Praise to the SON who rose;
	Praise to the SPIRIT PARACLETE;
O grata, etc.	While age on ages flows.
	O victim, etc.

Ant. Vas Electionis est mihi iste, ut portet nomen meum coram gentibus, et regibus, et filiis Israel
V/. Ora pro nobis, sancte Paule Apostole.
R/. Ut digni efficiamur promissionibus CHRISTI.
Oremus.

OMNIPOTENS sempiterne DEUS, qui beato Apostolo tuo Paulo, quid faceret ut impleretur SPIRITU SANCTO, divina miseratione præcepisti; ejus dirigentibus monitis, et suffragantibus meritis concede, ut servientes tibi in timore et tremore, cœlestium donorum consolatione repleamur. Per CHRISTUM DOMINUM nostrum. Amen.

Ant. He is my Vessel of Election, to carry my Name among the gentiles and kings and the children of Israel.
V/. Pray for us, O blessed Apostle Paul.
R/. That we may be made worthy of the promises of CHRIST.
Let us pray.

ALMIGHTY and eternal GOD, who in thy divine compassion didst direct thy blessed Apostle Paul what to do that he might be filled with thy HOLY SPIRIT; grant that we may be so counselled by his teaching, and aided by the suffrage of his merits, that, serving Thee in fear and trembling, we may be filled with the consolation of thy heavenly gifts. Through CHRIST our LORD. Amen.

323. Veneration of St Peter's Statue.
i. 50 Days, to any one who shall, with contrite heart and devotion, kiss the foot of the bronze statue of this Apostle in St Peter's at Rome. IV. T.Q. ii. 50 Days, once a day, for kissing the foot of a copy of the said statue, blessed by the Sovereign Pontiff; available for all the members of the family dwelling in the house where the statue is kept. IV. (See Instructions.) 323 Pius IX, Br. May 15,1857; February 4, 1877; Leo XIII, Bfs. April 27, 1880.

324. Prayer to St Paul.
300 Days, once a day. (See Instructions) 324 Pius X, January 18, 1905.
O GLORIOUS St Paul, who from a persecutor of the Christian name didst become an Apostle of burning zeal, and who, in order that JESUS CHRIST might be known to the furthermost bounds of the earth, didst joyfully suffer imprisonment, scourging, stoning, shipwreck, and every kind of persecution, and who didst finally shed thy blood to the last drop; obtain for us the grace of accepting, as divine favours, the infirmities, torments and calamities of this life, so that we may not be drawn from the service of GOD by

the vicissitudes of this our exile, but on the contrary may prove ourselves more and more faithful and fervent. Amen.

ST JOHN, APOSTLE & EVANGELIST
325. Prayer.
200 Days, once a day. (See Instructions.) 325 Leo XIII, December 8, 1897.
O GLORIOUS Apostle, who, on account of thy virginal purity, wast so beloved by JESUS as to deserve to lay thy head upon his divine breast, and to be left, in his place, as son to his most holy Mother; I beg thee to inflame me with a most ardent love towards JESUS and Mary. Obtain for me from our LORD that I, too, with a heart purified from earthly affections, may be made worthy to be ever united to JESUS as a faithful disciple, and to Mary as a devoted son, both here on earth and eternally in heaven. Amen.

ST EMIGDIUS, BISHOP & MARTYR
326. Prayer.
200 Days, once a day. (See Instructions.) 326 Leo XIII, June 26, 1894.
O GOD of infinite goodness, who hast given the crown of glory and honour to the martyred Bishop St Emigdius, we humbly pray Thee through his merits for that spirit of active faith which he inspired by his word and commended by his example, at last confirming the truth with his blood. Deign, I beseech Thee, O LORD, to preserve me from ruin by earthquake, through the intercession of this same glorious saint, to whom Thou hast given special power to protect his clients from this fearful scourge. Amen.

327. Invocation.
100 Days, once a day. (See Instructions) 327 Leo XIII, June 26, 1894.
BY the intercession and merits of the holy Father Emigdius, from earthquake and all evil deliver us, O LORD.

ST CHALCEDONIUS, MARTYR
328. Prayer.
100 Days, once a day. (See Instructions.) 328 Leo XIII, September 17, 1892.
MOST glorious martyr St. Chalcedonius, I rejoice with thee and return thanks to GOD for the sublime glory to which He has raised thee in Heaven, and specially for the great power which He has conferred upon thee of obtaining graces on behalf of those who are devout to thee. Behold me, then, O blessed Chalcedonius, suppliant at thy feet, praying thee to come to the aid of me, a humble client, and to obtain from GOD the grace I ask of thee (here insert the grace required). Most blessed Saint, be ever my advocate and protestor; assist me in every approach of danger; succour me in all my necessities ; free me from every peril of soul and body; keep me under thy powerful patronage all my life long, and specially in the awful moment of my death ; that so, after having enjoyed thy most powerful protection here on earth, I may come to thank, praise, and enjoy GOD with thee above in heaven for all eternity. Amen.

ST GREGORY VII
329. Prayer.
300 Days, once a day. (See Instructions.) 329 Pius IX, February 4, 1873.
O INVINCIBLE defender of the liberty of the Church, by that fortitude which thou didst manifest, O glorious St Gregory, in maintaining her rights against the powers of earth and hell conspiring together, extend from heaven, we pray thee, thy powerful arm over the Church, to strengthen and defend her in the terrible warfare in which she is engaged at this very time. Above all, encourage in the bitter struggle the august Pontiff, who has inherited with thy episcopal chair some of the fearlessness of thine own heart, and obtain that he may see his pious efforts crowned by the triumph of the Church and the return of the wandering to the right path. By thy means let all the earth know, once for all, that it is in vain to do battle against that faith which has ever conquered and will ever conquer the world: "hæc est victoria quæ vincit mundum, fides nostra," "this is the victory which overcomes the world, our faith." This is the prayer which we with one mind and heart send up to thee, and we trust that after we have been heard on earth thou wilt summon us one day to join thee in heaven in the presence of the Eternal Pontiff, who with the FATHER and the HOLY SPIRIT liveth and reigneth for ever and ever. Amen.

ST PIUS V

330. Hymn.

i. 40 Days, once a day. ii. Plenary from First Vespers till sunset on the Feast, May 5, if said before an altar or relic of the Saint, or in a Dominican church. I, II, IV. (See Instructions.) 330 Pius VIII, October 2, 1830.

BELLI tumultus ingruit,
Cultus DEI contemnitur;
Ultrixque culpam persequens
Jam pœna terris imminet.

Quem nos in hoc discrimine
Cœlestium de sedibus
Præsentiorem vindicem,
Quam te, Pie, invocabimus?

Nemo, beate Pontifex,
Intensiore robore
Quam tu superni numinis
Promovit in terris decus.
Quem nos, etc.

Ausisve fortioribus
Avertit a cervicibus,
Quod Christianis gentibus
Jugum parabant barbari.
Quem nos, etc.

Tu comparatis classibus,
Votis magis sed fervidis
Ad insulas Echinadas
Fundis tyrannum Thraciæ.
Quem nos, etc.

Absensque eodem tempore
Hostis fuit quo perditus,
Vides, et adstantes doces
Pugnæ secundos exitus.
Quem nos, etc.

Majora qui cœlo potes,
Tu supplices nunc aspice,
Tu civium discordias
Compesce, et iras hostium.
Quem nos, etc.

Precante te, pax aurea
Terras revisat; ut DEO
Tuti queamus reddere
Mox laetiora cantica.
Quem nos, etc.

Tibi, beata Trinitas
Uni DEO sit gloria,
Laus, et potestas omnia
Per saeculorum sæcula. Amen.
V/. Ora pro nobis, beate Pie.
R/. Ut digni efficiamur promissionibus CHRISTI.

WARS and tumults fill the earth;
Men the fear of GOD despise;
Retribution, vengeance, wrath,
Brood upon the angry skies.

Holy Pius! Pope sublime!
Whom, in this most evil time
Whom, of saints in bliss, can we
Better call to aid than thee?

None more mightily than thou
Hath, by holy deed or word,
Through the spacious earth below
Spread the glory of the LORD.
Holy Pius, etc.

Thine it was, O pontiff brave!
Pontiff of eternal Rome!
From barbaric yoke to save
Terror-stricken Christendom.
Holy Pius, etc.

When Lepanto's gulf beheld,
Strewn upon its waters fair,
Turkey's countless navy yield
To the power of thy prayer:
Holy Pius, etc.
Who meanwhile with prophet's eye
Didst the distant battle see,
And announce to standers-by
That same moment's victory.
Holy Pius, etc.

Mightier now and glorified,
Hear the suppliant cry we pour;
Crush rebellions haughty pride;
Quell the din of rising war.
Holy Pius, etc.

At thy prayer may golden peace
Down to earth descend again:
Licence, discord, trouble cease;
Justice, truth and order reign.
Holy Pius, etc.

To the LORD of endless days,
One Almighty Trinity,
Sempiternal glory, praise,
Honour, might, and blessing be.
Holy Pius, etc.
V/.. Pray for us, blessed Pius.
R/. That we may be made worthy of the promises

Oremus.
DEUS, qui ad conterendos ecclesiæ tuæ hostes, et ad divinum cultum reparandum beatum Pium Pontificem Maximum eligere dignatus es: fac nos ipsius defendi præsidiis, et ita tuis inhærere obsequiis, ut omnium hostium superatis insidiis perpetua pace lætemur. Per CHRISTUM DOMINUM nostrum.
℟. Amen.

of CHRIST.
Let us pray.
GOD, who, to the destruction of the enemies of thy Church and for the restoration of thy holy worship didst vouchsafe to elect blessed Pius to be thy High Priest; grant us so to be defended by his protection, and so to remain stedfast in thy service, that, overcoming the snares of all our enemies, we may enjoy perpetual peace. Through CHRIST our LORD. Amen.

ST NICHOLAS OF MYRA AND BARI
331. Prayer.
50 Days, once a day. (See Instructions.) 331 Gregory XVI, December 22, 1832.

ST NICHOLAS, my special protector, from that bright throne where thou dost enjoy the vision of thy GOD, in pity turn thine eyes upon me ; obtain for me from GOD that grace and assistance of which, in my present necessities, spiritual and temporal, I am most in want, and especially the grace of N_____ , if such be expedient for my eternal welfare. Remember, moreover, O glorious and holy Bishop, our Sovereign Pontiff, the Holy Church, and this City of Rome. Bring back to the right way of salvation those who live steeped in sin or buried in the darkness of ignorance, error, and heresy. Comfort the sorrowing, provide for the needy, strengthen the weak-hearted, defend the oppressed, help the sick; let all experience the effects of thy powerful intercession with Him who is Supreme Giver of all good. Amen.
PATER, Ave, Gloria.
℣. Pray for us, blessed Nicholas.
℟. That we may be made worthy of the promises of CHRIST.
Let us pray.
O GOD, who hast honoured and ceasest not daily to honour thy glorious Confessor and Pontiff, blessed Nicholas, with innumerable miracles; grant, we beseech Thee, that by his merits and prayers we may be delivered from the fire of hell and from all other dangers. Through CHRIST our LORD Amen.

ST ALPHONSUS LIGUORI
332. Prayer.
200 Days, once a day. (See Instructions.) 332 Leo XIII, June 18, 1887.

O GLORIOUS Saint Alphonsus, my most beloved protector, thou who hast laboured and suffered so much to secure to men the fruits of Redemption, behold the miseries of my poor soul, and have pity on me. Through thy powerful intercession with JESUS and Mary, obtain for me true repentance, together with the pardon of my past faults, a great horror of sin, and strength always to resist temptation. Impart to me, I pray thee, a spark of that ardent charity with which thy heart was ever inflamed; and grant that, imitating thee, I may make the good pleasure of GOD the only rule of my life. Obtain for me, moreover, a fervent and constant love for JESUS CHRIST, and a tender and filial devotion to his Mother Mary, together with the grace to pray always, and to persevere in the service of GOD until my death; so that I may at length join with thee in praising GOD, and the most Blessed Virgin Mary, for all eternity. Amen.

ST LOUIS OF TOULOUSE
333. Prayer.
100 Days, once a day. (See Instructions.) 333 Leo XIII, June 12, 1894.

TO thee, St Louis, lily of virginity, brilliant star, and vessel of sanctity, we have recourse in prayer. Diffuse by thy intercession heavenly graces over the Catholic nations with which thou art united by ties of affinity, and over which thou hast been appointed protector by GOD. Implore of GOD and the Immaculate Virgin that the faith of our ancestors may again be revived among Christian people, that charity may burn, and virtuous living flourish. Obtain true peace for princes and their subjects, the triumph of our holy Mother the Church over her enemies, complete liberty for the Vicar of CHRIST on earth in his sacred government of souls, and for all of us who implore thine aid, eternal happiness in Heaven. Amen.

ST DOMINIC
334. Prayers.

i. 100 Days, once a day. ii. Plenary, once a month. I,II, III, IV. (See Instructions.) 334 Leo XIII, July 21, 1883.

I MY LORD JESUS CHRIST, who didst found the Church with thy Precious Blood, and by the preaching of the Apostles didst establish, propagate and extend it throughout the whole world, and thereafter didst commission the holy Patriarch Dominic to adorn, illustrate, and defend it with the splendour of his merits and doctrine; graciously hear the prayers which this Apostolic man incessantly offers to Thee for the increase of her treasures, both spiritual and temporal. PATER, Ave, Gloria.

II MOST merciful REDEEMER, who didst choose as thy fellow labourer for the salvation of souls St Dominic, who by his zeal, aided by thy grace, gained over to the Church so many heretics who had been lost to her, and so many sinners who had grieved her by their obstinacy; send, O my GOD, ever fresh labourers into thy vineyard to work for thy glory, and gather in the fruits of eternal life. PATER, Ave, Gloria.

III O GOOD JESUS, who didst delight to see St Dominic prostrate every night before thy altar, adoring Thee hidden in the most holy Sacrament with most lively faith, and offering- up, now groans, now prayers, now penances on behalf of the Church, at that time persecuted by her enemies and profaned by her servants; defend this thy Spouse through the intercession of St Dominic from the outrages and plots of the infernal enemy of mankind. PATER, Ave, Gloria.

V/. Pray for us, St Dominic.

R/. . That we may be made worthy of the promises of CHRIST.

Let us pray.

GRANT, we beseech Thee, Almighty GOD, that we who are weighed down by the burden of our sins may be raised up by the patronage of thy blessed Confessor Dominic. Through CHRIST our LORD. Amen.

ST FRANCIS OF ASSISI
335. The Five Sundays.

Plenary, on each of the five Sundays. I, II, III, IV. (See Instructions.) 335 Leo XIII, November 21, 1885.

To all who apply themselves to meditation, vocal prayer or other good works, on any five successive Sundays, in honour of the Sacred Stigmata. N.B. Once in the year only.

336. Hymn.

100 Days, once a day. (See Instructions.) 336 Leo XIII, September 13, 1893.

O DIVI amoris victima,
Quino cruenta vulnere,
Francisce, qui vivam crucis
CHRISTI refers imaginem.
Tu caritatis fervidis
Flammis adustus, sanguinem
CHRISTO daturus, barbara
Ter cogitasti littora.
Voti sed impos, non sinis
Languere flammas desides:
Et excitas cœlestia,
Flagrans amore incendia.
In prole vivens efferas
Pervadis oras; algida
Gelu soluto, ut ferveant
Ardore sancto pectora.
Sic pertimendis lividum
Armis Avernum conteris;
Virtutis et firmum latus
Templo labenti subjicis.
Adsis, PATER, precantibus,
Ignemque, late quo tua

Exarsit ingens caritas,
Accende nostris mentibus.
Sit laus PATRI et FILIO,
Sit inclyto PARACLITO,
Qui nos parentis optimi
Det æmulari spiritum. Amen.

337. Feast of St Francis.
i. Plenary, on the feast or during the octave. I, II, III, IV. ii. 300 Days, each day of public novena or month dedicated to the Saint. (See Instructions.) 337 Pius X, Br. February 28, 1904.

THE SEVEN HOLY FOUNDERS OF THE SERVANTS OF MARY
338. Prayer.
200 Days, once a day. (See Instructions.) 338 Leo XIII, February 22, 1888.

O MOST glorious Patriarchs, who by your sublime sanctity became worthy to be chosen by the Mother of GOD herself to propagate the devotion to her Dolours; at her bidding you separated from the world, and, hidden in the rough caves of Senario, chastised your bodies with unheard-of penances and fed your spirit with the continual contemplation of the great mysteries of the Faith, thus unconsciously preparing for the mission which was afterwards entrusted to you and your Order, namely to eradicate sin and iniquity from the hearts of men through compassion for the Dolours of the Blessed Virgin Mary. Then, bearing the Passion of JESUS and the sufferings of his Mother deeply engraven on your hearts, you strove everywhere to quell civil feuds, move sinners to repentance, and bring back heretics to the obedience of the Roman Pontiff. Deign, O glorious Saints, now that you are reigning in Heaven with CHRIST, deign from the thrones of your glory to look down upon us, unfortunate pilgrims, who have still to fight in this land of trial and combat. The devil with his suggestions, the world with its deceits, the flesh with its concupiscence, as so many roaring lions, are ever seeking to devour us. Have then compassion on us, and pour down into our hearts a portion at least of that tender devotion to the Dolours of Mary with which you were constantly penetrated, that the sight of our Mother so afflicted may enable us to resist the seductions of temptation, and preserve us from renewing by sin the Passion of our divine REDEEMER and Mary's sorrows. Obtain for us, we beseech you, O powerful protectors, docility and promptitude to answer the calls of GOD, detachment from the fallacious goods of this world, a true spirit of mortification and penance, that, following on earth your examples of perfection and sanctity, we may deserve to join you in heaven, to praise for ever the tender mercies of our crucified REDEEMER and the glories of the Queen of Martyrs. Amen.

339. Seven Prayers.
100 Days, once a day. (See Instructions.) 339 Leo XIII, April 21, 1888

I O GLORIOUS Patriarchs, who, even in the midst of the corruption of the world, ever kept the fire of divine love burning in your hearts, and fostered a most tender devotion to the Queen of Heaven, thus deserving to be invited by her to leave the world the better to serve GOD; obtain for us, we beseech you, that we too, being inflamed with the fire of charity, may please the Most High, and imitating the love and patience of our sorrowful Mother, may conform ourselves, in adversity as well as in prosperity, to the dispositions of divine Providence. PATER, Ave, Gloria.

II O BRIGHT models of perfection, who, having turned your backs on the world and renounced whatever it might offer you, did deserve, in answer to your wish of being entirely hidden from men, that Mary herself should point out to you Mount Senario as the place of your retreat and tranquillity; obtain for us, we beseech you, that, despising the false and contemptible pleasures of the earth, we may, after your example, embrace a life of penance to atone for our sins; and if we cannot, like you, serve our Lady in solitude, at least may we show her our sorrow for the grief we have caused her, when by our sins we have renewed the bitter Passion of her Divine Son. PATER, Ave, Gloria.

III O MOST humble dwellers among the wild rocks of Senario, who, in order the better to imitate the heroic humility of the Handmaid of the LORD, did not only forget the nobility of your birth and the grandeur of your station, but with generosity humbled yourselves so deeply as to go and beg your scanty food in the streets of your native town; obtain for us, we beseech you, that no human respect may deter us from serving GOD, and that, as you, by an unheard of prodigy, merited to be called, by infants still at the breast, "Servants of Mary," so we too may edify and be a light to guide our brethren along the road to heaven ; thus showing ourselves by our deeds to be devout servants of the august Mother of GOD. PATER, Ave, Gloria.

IV O FAITHFUL servants of the Queen of Heaven, who wept so bitterly over the Dolours she suffered during the life and in the Passion and Death of her beloved Son, and were rewarded for it by the miracle of a vine putting forth ripe clusters in the midst of winter, by which she foreshadowed the propagation of the Order of her Servants, whose mission it would be to spread in the Church compassion for her sorrows; obtain for us, we beseech you, a most tender devotion to our Lady of Sorrows, that we may, by this our compassion, move our neighbour to sincere sorrow for his sins ; thus becoming fruitful branches of the mystical vine of our LORD JESUS CHRIST. PATER, Ave, Gloria.

V O GLORIOUS Founders of the Order of the Servants of Mary, who were filled with such inexpressible sweetness, when you were made worthy to see the Queen of Martyrs herself, who, pointing to you the rule to follow and the habit to wear in memory of her Dolours, showed you also the palm which should be the reward of your merits; obtain for us, we beseech you, to be shown by our heavenly Lady in what manner we may best serve her Divine Son, and thus attain more surely to the possession of the eternal happiness which GOD in his mercy has prepared for us in heaven. PATER, Ave, Gloria.

VI O MOST austere penitents, who, by continually chastising your bodies, became so rich in merits and so dear to our LORD that to show how well pleased he was in you, he made your retreat of Mount Senario a place of wonders, now causing it to seem all girt about with fire, now showing it covered with flowers and lilies of exquisite beauty, which the angels gathered and presented to Mary; obtain for us, we beseech you, that the fire of divine love be kindled in our hearts, and that our souls, purified from all sin, may become to the Queen of Heaven a garden of delight, from which we may offer to her choice flowers of virtues as so many tokens of our devotion. PATER, Ave, Gloria.

VII O MOST blessed Patriarchs, angels of purity, seraphs of love, and martyrs of penance, who were all granted the privilege of a most happy death, one dying comforted by the presence of the Child JESUS, another audibly called by Mary herself to his eternal reward, this one taking his flight to Heaven under the appearance of flames, and that under the form of a dazzling- lily; obtain for us, we beseech you, that, when the last hour comes for us, we may in that dread moment, through your intercession, be protected by our Lady of Sorrows against the wiles of the infernal foe, and breathing our souls into her maternal hands, be brought by her to Heaven, there to enjoy for ever the possession of GOD, who is the eternal source of all glory and sanctity. PATER, Ave, Gloria.

ST JOHN OF MATHA
340. Prayer.
100 Days, once a day. (See Instructions.) 340 Leo XIII, March 16, 1897.

GLORIOUS St John of Matha, thou who wast inflamed with a great love of GOD and a tender compassion for thy neighbour, and wast divinely chosen to found the famous Order of the Holy Trinity, and didst spend thy days in glorifying that adorable mystery and in redeeming Christians from a miserable slavery; obtain for us, we beseech thee, the grace to pass our lives also in glorifying the most blessed Trinity, and in doing good to our neighbour, by works of Christian charity, so that it may be our happy portion to enjoy in Heaven the blessed vision of the FATHER, the SON, and the HOLY SPIRIT. Amen.

ST FRANCIS OF PAOLA
341. The Thirteen Fridays in honour of Christ and his Twelve Apostles.
i. Plenary, on any one of the Fridays. I, II, IV. ii. Seven Years and Seven Quarantines, on each of the other Fridays. I, II, IV. (See Instructions.) 341 Clement XII, Br. December 2, 1738; March 20, 1739.

This Devotion consists in visiting" on thirteen consecutive Fridays a church of the Minims; or in the case of those who dwell more than a mile from such a church, any church dedicated to St Francis, or an altar where there is a picture of the Saint, or in default of these the parish church.

ST IGNATIUS LOYOLA
342. The Ten Sundays.
Plenary, on each of the Sundays. I, II, IV. (See Instructions.) 342 Clement XIII, January 27, 1767; Gregory XVI, December 10, 1841.

This Devotion consists of meditation, vocal prayers, or good works performed for the glory of GOD and in honour of the Saint, with a visit to a Jesuit church, or in default of such, the parish church, on ten consecutive Sundays. N.B. Once in the year only.

343. Prayer.

200 Days, once a day. (See Instructions.) 343 Leo XIII, February 5, 1885

O GLORIOUS Patriarch St Ignatius, we humbly beseech thee to obtain for us from GOD freedom, above all things, from sin, the greatest of evils, and then escape from the deadly disease of cholera, one of those terrible scourges with which the LORD punishes the sins of the people. May thy example inflame our hearts with an efficacious desire to labour continually for the greater glory of GOD and the good of our neighbour; and obtain from the loving Heart of JESUS, our LORD, the crown of all other graces, the gift of final perseverance, and eternal beatitude.

ST PHILIP NERI
344. Prayers for every Day of the Week.

50 Days, once a day. (See Instructions.) 344 Pius IX, May 17, 1852.

FOR SUNDAY. Prayer to obtain the virtue of Humility.

ST PHILIP, my glorious patron, who on earth didst so love humility as to count the praise and even the good esteem of men as dross; obtain for me also this virtue by thy prayers. Thou knowest how haughty I am in my thoughts, how contemptuous in my words, how ambitious in my works. Ask for me humility of heart, that my mind may be freed from all pride, and impressed with the same low esteem of self which thou hadst of thy self, counting thyself the worst of all men, and for that reason rejoicing when thou didst suffer contempt, and seeking-out for thyself occasions of enduring it. Great saint, obtain for me a truly humble heart and the knowledge of my own nothingness; that I may rejoice when I am despised, and chafe not when others are preferred before me; that I may never be vain when I am praised, but may ever seek only to be great in the eyes of GOD, desiring to receive from Him alone all my exaltation. PATER, Ave, Gloria.

FOR MONDAY. Prayer to obtain the virtue of Patience.

ST PHILIP, my patron Saint, whose heart was ever so constant in time of trouble, and whose spirit was so loving under suffering that, when persecuted by the jealous, or calumniated by the wicked who thought to discredit thy sanctity, or, when tried by GOD with many long painful infirmities, thou didst always bear thy trials with wonderful tranquillity of heart and mind; pray for me that I may have a spirit of true courage in every adversity. Alas, how much I stand in need of patience! I shrink from every little trouble; I sicken under every light affliction; I fire up at and resent every trifling contradiction; never setting myself to learn that the road to Paradise lies amidst the thorns of tribulation. Yet was this the path our Divine Master deigned to tread, and this too, my saintly patron, was thy path also. Obtain for me, then, this courage, that with good hearty will I may embrace the crosses which every day I receive from GOD, and bear them all with the same endurance and ready will which thou didst manifest on earth; that so I may be made worthy to enjoy the blessed fruit of sufferings with thee in heaven above. PATER, Ave, Gloria.

FOR TUESDAY. Prayer to obtain the virtue of Purity.

ST PHILIP, who didst ever keep unsullied the lily of purity, so that the glory of this fair virtue dwelt in thy eyes, shone forth from thy hands, and cast its fragrance over thy whole body, causing it to emit so sweet a perfume that it gave consolation, fervour, and devotion to all who conversed with thee; obtain for me from the HOLY SPIRIT of GOD so true a love for that virtue that neither the words nor bad examples of sinners may ever make any impression upon my soul. Never permit me in any way to lose that lovely virtue ; and since avoidance of occasions, prayer, labour, humility, mortification of the senses, frequent use of the Sacraments, were the arms with which thou didst conquer the flesh, which is our worst enemy, so do thou obtain for me grace to use the same arms to vanquish the same foe. Take not away thy help from me; but be as zealous for me as thou wast during thy life for thy penitents, keeping them far removed from all infection of the senses. Do this for me, my holy patron; and be my protector and pattern in this fair virtue. PATER, Ave, Gloria.

FOR WEDNESDAY. Prayer to obtain the Love of GOD.
ST PHILIP, I am filled with wonder at the great miracle which was wrought in thee by the HOLY SPIRIT when He poured into thy heart such a flood of heavenly charity that, in order to contain it, two of thy ribs were broken by the power of Divine love; and I am confounded when I compare thy heart with my own. I see thy heart all burning with love, and mine all frozen and taken up with creatures. I see thine inflamed with a fire from heaven, which so filled thy body that it radiated like flames from thy countenance, while mine is full of earthly love. I love the world, which allures me and can never make me happy ; I love the flesh, which ever wears me with its cares and can never render me immortal; I love riches, which I can enjoy but for a moment. Oh, when shall I learn of thee to love nothing but GOD, my incomprehensible and only good. Help me, then, blessed patron, that by thy intercession I may begin at once: obtain for me an efficacious love, manifesting itself by works; a pure love, making- me love GOD most perfectly; a strong love, enabling me to surmount all obstacles hindering- my union with GOD in life, that so I may be wholly united to Him for ever after my death. PATER, Ave, Gloria.

FOR THURSDAY. Prayer to obtain the Love of our Neighbour.
GLORIOUS Saint, who didst devote thyself wholly to the good of thy neighbour, thinking well of all, sympathizing with all, helping all; who throughout thy whole life didst ever try to secure the salvation of all, never shrinking from labour or trouble, keeping for thyself no time or comfort, that thou mightest win all hearts to GOD; pray for me, that, together with the pardon of all my sins, I may have charity for my neighbour, and be henceforth more compassionate to him in his necessities; and obtain for me grace that I may love every man with pure unselfish love as my own brother, succouring each one, if I am unable to do it with temporal good, at least with prayers and good advice. And teach me too, on every occasion, to defend the honour of my neighbour, and never to say to him a hurtful or displeasing word ; but ever to maintain, even with my enemies, sweetness of spirit like thy own, whereby thou didst triumph over thy persecutors. Blessed Saint, ask of GOD for me also this lovely virtue, which already thou hast gained for so many of thy clients ; that so we may all one day come to praise our GOD with thee in an eternity of bliss. PATER, Ave, Gloria.

FOR FRIDAY. Prayer to obtain Detachment from Temporal Goods.
GREAT Saint, who didst prefer a poor and austere life to the comforts of thy home, despising the honour and glory of thy station ; obtain for me grace ever to keep my heart detached from the transitory goods of this life. St Philip, whose desire it ever was to become so poor as one day to beg thy bread, and not to find the charitable hand to offer thee a crumb wherewith to support life; ask of GOD for me such love of poverty that I may turn all my thoughts to goods which never fail. St Philip, who didst prefer to live unknown to promotion to the highest honours of the Holy Church ; intercede for me that I may never seek after dignities, but always content my self with that state where GOD has set me. My heart is too anxious for the empty fleeting things of this earth, but do thou obtain for me, that the great lesson contained in the words "And then?" whence followed so many wonderful conversions, may ever be deeply impressed upon my soul; that, despising the nothingness of earth, GOD alone may reign sole object of my affections and my thoughts. PATER, Ave, Gloria.

FOR SATURDAY. Prayer to obtain Perseverance in Good Works.
ST PHILIP, my holy patron, who, ever constant in good works and full of merit, didst receive from the Most High GOD the crown of glory in reward of all thy labours, obtain for me grace never to weary in his service. St Philip, who didst recompense those who loved thee by acquiring for them the gift of perseverance in good, ask of GOD this gift for me; stand by me, dear father, at the last moment of my life, and pray for me that I may depart this life strengthened with the grace of the Holy Sacraments. Meanwhile, intercede for me, that I may do penance for my sins, and deplore them bitterly all my days. St Philip, who from on high beholdest all my miseries, and the chains which yet bind me to my sins and to this earth ; pray for me that I may be liberated from them, and be constantly devoted to my GOD. Obtain for me an ardent desire to co-operate in my own salvation, and unshaken firmness in the good which I have begun; that so, by thy intercession, I may deserve to be for ever in thy company in an eternity of bliss. PATER, Ave, Gloria.

345. Prayer.
100 Days, once a day. (See Instructions.) 345 Leo XIII, April 22, 1887.

O GLORIOUS St Philip, who wast so favoured by GOD while consoling and helping thy spiritual children in the hour of their death; be to me an advocate and father at the awful moment of my passage to eternity. Obtain for me the grace that Satan may not overcome me, temptation oppress me, or fear unnerve me in that hour; but that, fortified by a lively faith, a firm hope, and a sincere charity, I may bear with patience and perseverance this last conflict; so that, full of trust in the mercy of GOD, the infinite merits of JESUS CHRIST, and the protection of most holy Mary, I may be worthy to die the death of the just, and to enter the blessed country of Paradise, there to love and enjoy GOD, together with thee and all the saints forever. Amen.

ST JOSEPH CALASANCTIUS
346. Prayer.
200 Days, once a day. (See Instructions.) 346 Leo XIII, Card. Vic. October 19, 1897.

O BLESSED St Joseph Calasanctius, protector of the young, great servant of our LORD, who didst perform such great and wondrous works on their behalf; thou who didst make thyself a mirror to them of most ardent charity, of invincible patience, of most profound humility, of angelic purity, and of every other heroic virtue; and who by thy holy words and example, full of the spirit of GOD, didst excite them to fly dangerous occasions, to abhor vice, to hate sin, to love piety and devotion, and so didst guide innumerable souls to Heaven; thou who didst obtain for them the blessing of the infant JESUS and his most blessed Mother, visibly bestowed ; O great advocate and most loving father, obtain for us too, thy humble and devout clients, a constant hatred of sin, victory over temptation, help in peril, and profit from study ; that so, by acquiring the fullness of true wisdom, which is the holy fear of GOD, we may attain to eternal life. Amen.

ST CAMILLUS OF LELLIS
347. The Seven Sundays.
i. Seven Years and Seven Quarantines on each Sunday, ii. Plenary, on the seventh Sunday. I, II,III, IV. (See Instructions.) 347 Pius IX, August 8, 1853.

This devotion consists of any prayer in honour of the Saint, recited on any seven consecutive Sundays.

348. Prayer.
200 Days, once a day. (See Instructions.) 348 Leo XIII, February 27, 1894.

GLORIOUS St Camillus, special protector of poor sick people, who for forty years, with a charity truly heroic, didst devote thyself to alleviating their spiritual and corporal miseries; be pleased to succour them still more generously, now that thou art happy in Heaven and that they have been confided by the Church to thy powerful protection. Obtain for them from GOD either that they may be healed of the evils from which they are suffering, or that by patience and Christian resignation they may be sanctified and strengthened in the hour of their death; and obtain also for us the grace to live and die, after thy example, in the practice of divine love. Amen. PATER, Ave.

ST VINCENT OF PAUL
349. Novena.
i. 300 Days, each day. ii. Plenary, during the Novena. I, II, IV. (See Instructions) 349 Pius IX, November 26, 1876.

This Novena in honour of the saint may be made at any time, and with any form of prayer sanctioned by competent ecclesiastical authority.

350. Prayer.
100 Days, once a day. (See Instructions) 350 Leo XIII, June 23, 1885

O GLORIOUS St Vincent, heavenly patron of all charitable associations and father of all the unfortunate, who in thy lifetime didst not reject anyone who had recourse to thee; see now by how many evils we are oppressed, and come to our assistance. Obtain from our LORD help for the poor, solace for the sick, consolation for the afflicted, protection for the abandoned, charity for the rich, conversion for sinners, zeal for priests, peace for the Church, tranquillity among nations, and salvation for all. May all feel the effects of thy merciful intercession, so that, sustained by thee in the miseries of this life, we may be able to join thee above, where there will be no more strife, lamentation or sorrow, but joy, exultation, and beatitude for ever. Amen.

ST PAUL OF THE CROSS
351. Prayer.
i. One Year, once a day. ii. Plenary, on the Feast (April 28) or within the octave, if said for a month preceding the Feast. I, II. (See Instructions.) 351 Pius IX. Pr. Ma. April 24, 1863 ; April 20, 1868

O GLORIOUS St Paul, thou who, while on earth, wast a mirror of innocence and a model of penance ! O hero of sanctity, specially chosen by GOD to meditate nig-ht and day on the most bitter Passion of his only-begotten SON, and to propagate the same devotion throughout the world, by word, by example, and by means of thy institute! O Apostle, powerful in word and work, who didst spend thy life in bringing back the wandering souls of wretched sinners to the feet of the Crucified, look graciously down from heaven upon my soul, and hear my prayers. Obtain for me so great a love of JESUS suffering that, ever meditating on his Passion, I may make his sufferings mine; that I may recognize in the deep wounds of my SAVIOUR the wickedness of my sins, and may draw from them, as from so many founts of salvation, the grace of lamenting them bitterly, and a firm will to imitate thee in penance, if I have not followed thee in innocence. Procure for me, O St Paul, the grace which here, at thy feet, I particularly and earnestly beg of thee (here mention the grace desired). Moreover, obtain for our holy Mother the Church victory over her enemies; obtain conversion of sinners, and a return to the Catholic Faith of all heretical nations, particularly England, for which thou didst pray so much. Finally, intercede for me with GOD that I may die a holy death, and come to enjoy Him with thee in heaven, for all eternity. Amen. PATER, Ave, Gloria.

352. Novena.
i. 300 Days, on each day. ii. Plenary, at the end of the Novena. I, II, IV. (See Instructions.) 352 Pius IX. Pr. Ma. October 17, 1867.

Any form of prayers may be used.

ST PETER FOURIER
353. Prayer.
300 Days, once a day. (See Instructions.) 353. Leo XIII, May 27, 1897.

O GLORIOUS St Peter, lily of purity, example of Christian perfection, model of priestly zeal; by that glory which as a reward of thy merits has been bestowed on thee in heaven, look upon us kindly, and come to our assistance before the throne of the Most High. On earth thou didst make this maxim specially thy own, having it ever on thy lips, "Injure no one, give joy to all," and, armed with this, didst spend thy whole life in succouring the wretched, counselling the doubtful, comforting the afflicted, bringing back the strayed to the path of virtue, restoring to JESUS CHRIST souls redeemed by his Precious Blood. Now that thou art so powerful in heaven, continue thy labour of helping all, and be to us a watchful protector, so that, freed by thy intercession from temporal evils, and confirmed in faith and charity, we may overcome the snares of the enemies of our salvation, and be able one day with thee to praise and bless our LORD in Paradise for ever. Amen.

ST THOMAS AQUINAS
354. Prayer to St Thomas, Patron of Schools.
200 Days, once a day. (See Instructions.) 354 Leo XIII, July 3,1885

DOCTOR angelice, Sancte Thoma, theologorum princeps et philosophorum norma, præclarum Christiani orbisdecus et ecclesiæ lumen, scholarum omnium Catholicarum coelestis patrone, qui sapientiam sine fictione didicisti et sine invidia communicas, ipsam Sapientiam, FILIUM DEI, de precare pro nobis, ut veniente in nos spiritus sapientiæ, ea quae docuisti intellectu, conspiciamus et quæ egisti imitatione compleamus; doctrinæ et virtutis, quibus in terris solis instar simper

ANGELIC Doctor St. Thomas, prince of theologians and model of philosophers, bright ornament of the Christian world and light of the Church; O heavenly patron of all Catholic schools, who didst learn wisdom without guile and dost communicate it without envy, intercede for us with the SON of GOD, Wisdom itself, that the spirit of wisdom may descend upon us, and enable us to understand clearly that which thou hast taught, and fulfil it by imitating thy deeds; to become

eluxisti, participes efficiamur; ac tandem earum suavissimis fructibus perenniter tecum delectemur in cœlis, Divinam Sapientiam collaudantes per infinita sæcula sæculorum. Amen.

partakers of that doctrine & virtue which caused thee to shine like the sun on earth; and at last to rejoice with thee for ever in their most sweet fruits in Heaven together praising the Divine Wisdom for all eternity. Amen.

355. Little Office of St Thomas Aquinas.
300 Days, once a day. (See Instructions) 355 Leo XIII, March 26, 1887.
The Latin and English text may be obtained in separate form from Messrs Burns & Oates.

356. The Six Sundays.
Plenary, on each of the Sundays. I, II. (See Instructions.) 356 Leo XIII, August 21, 1886.
This devotion consists in spending some time in meditation, vocal prayer, or other works of piety, on any six consecutive Sundays, in honour of St Thomas. N.B. These Indulgences can be gained only once in the year.

357. Invocation, before Lecture or Study.
100 Days, once a day. (See Instructions.) 357 Leo XIII, December 14, 1889.
O BLESSED Thomas, patron of schools, obtain for us from GOD an invincible faith, burning charity, a chaste life, and true knowledge, through CHRIST our LORD. Amen

ST ANTHONY OF PADUA
358. Responsory.
i. 100 Days. T.Q. ii. Plenary, once a month. I, II, III, IV. (See Instructions.) 358 Pius IX, January 25, 1866.

SI quæris miracula,
Mors, error, calamitas,
Dæmon, lepra fugiunt,
Ægri surgunt sani.
Cedunt mare, vincula;
Membra resque perditas
Petunt et accipiunt
Juvenes et cani.
Pereunt pericula,
Cessat et necessitas;
Narrent hi, qui sentiunt,
Dicant Paduani.
Cedunt mare, vincula etc.
Gloria PATRI et FILIO, Et SPIRITUI SANCTO.
Cedunt mare, vincula etc.
V/.. Ora pro nobis, beate Antoni.
R/. Ut digni efficiamur promissionibus CHRISTI.
Oremus.
ECCLESIAM tuam, DEUS, beati Antonii confessoris tui commemoratio votiva lætificet, ut spiritualibus semper muniatur auxiliis et gaudiis perfrui mereatur æternis. Per CHRISTUM DOMINUM nostrum. Amen.

IF then you ask for miracles,
Death, error, all calamities,
The leprosy and demons fly,
And health succeeds infirmities.
The sea obeys, and fetters break,
And lifeless limbs thou dost restore;
Whilst treasures lost are found again,
When young or old thine aid implore.
All dangers vanish at thy prayer,
And direst need doth quickly flee.
Let those who know thy power proclaim,
Let Paduans say These are of thee.
The sea obeys, etc.
To FATHER, SON, may glory be, And HOLY GHOST eternally.
The sea obeys, etc.
V/. Pray for us, blessed Anthony.
R/. That we may be made worthy of the promises of CHRIST.
Let us pray.
GOD, may the votive commemoration of the blessed Anthony, thy Confessor, be a source of joy to thy Church, that she may always be fortified with spiritual assistance, and deserve to enjoy eternal rewards. Through JESUS CHRIST our LORD. Amen.

359. Pater, Ave, and Gloria, thirteen times, in honour of the Saint.
100 Days, once a day. (See Instructions.) 359 Leo XIII, June 9, 1896.

360. St Anthonys Bread. Prayer.
100 Days, once a day. (See Instructions.) 360 Leo XIII, May 11, 1897.
TO thee we have recourse, most powerful worker of miracles, in whose breast burned a sublime fire of charity towards GOD and the poor. To thee, who wast deemed worthy to hold in thy arms the Infant JESUS, who chose to be born poor, to thee, full of confidence, we betake ourselves, that thou mayest pray the good JESUS to have compassion on us in our great tribulations. Oh! obtain for us the favour which we humbly implore (here state the favour needed). If thou dost obtain it for us, O glorious St Anthony, we will offer thee bread for the poor whom thou didst love so greatly on earth. PATER, Ave, Gloria.

361. St Anthony's Bread. Thanksgiving.
100 Days, once a day. (See Instructions.) 361 Leo XIII, July 13, 1896
O GLORIOUS worker of miracles, father of the poor, who, wondrously gifted with a heart full of compassion for the miseries of the unfortunate, didst by a miracle lay open the heart of a miser steeped in avarice; thou who dost offer our prayers to our LORD and obtain a hearing, accept as a proof of our gratitude the pence we lay at thy feet for the relief of misfortune. May it turn to the benefit of ourselves and of the suffering; hasten with thy usual kindness to help us in our temporal necessities, and still more to provide for our spiritual needs, now and at the hour of our death. Amen.

362. The Thirteen Tuesdays, or Sundays.
Plenary, on each Tuesday, or Sunday. I, II. (See Instructions.) 362 Leo XIII, Br. March i, 1898.
Some time must be devoted to meditation, vocal prayer or other works of piety, in consecutive weeks, and in honour of the Saint.
These Indulgences can be obtained only once in the year.

363. Prayer to St Anthony.
300 Days, once a day.(See Instructions.) 363 Leo XIII, May 6, 1899.
O WONDERFUL St Anthony, glorious on account of the fame of thy miracles, and through the condescension of JESUS in coming in the form of a little child to repose in thy arms; obtain for me of his bounty the grace which I ardently desire from the depths of my heart. Thou who wast so compassionate towards miserable sinners, regard not the unworthiness of those who pray to thee, but the glory of GOD, that it may be once again magnified by thee, to the salvation of my soul, in connection with the particular request which I now ask for with persevering earnestness. May this small offering of pence, which I make to thee in aid of the poor, be a pledge of my gratitude, and with them may it one day be granted to me, through the grace of JESUS CHRIST and thy intercession, to possess the kingdom of Heaven. Amen.

ST VINCENT FERRER
364. Prayer.
200 Days, once a day. (See Instructions.) 364 Leo XIII, September 17, 1887.
O GLORIOUS Apostle and worker of miracles, St Vincent Ferrer, new angel of the Apocalypse and our kind protector, receive our humble prayers and obtain for us a copious shower of divine favours. By that love with which thy heart was inflamed, obtain for us from the FATHER of mercies the pardon of all our sins, confirmation in the Faith, and perseverance in good works; so that by living as good and fervent Christians we may become worthy of thy powerful patronage. Extend thy patronage also to our bodies, and free us from our infirmities. Protect our lands from the violence of tempest and hail, and keep misfortune far from us. Thus, blessed by thee in the goods of soul and body, we shall be ever devout to thee, and one day see thee in Heaven, there with thee to praise GOD for ever and ever. Amen.

ST JOHN OF THE GROSS
365. Prayer.
i. 100 Days, once a day. ii. Plenary, once a month, on the last day, or within eight days. I, II,III, IV. (See Instructions.) 365 Leo XII, January 30, 1828.
O GLORIOUS St John, who, through a pure desire of being like unto JESUS crucified, didst long for nothing so eagerly, up to the last moment of thy holy life, as to be despised and made little of by all, and whose thirst after sufferings was so burning that thy noble heart rejoiced in the midst of the sorest torments and afflictions: vouchsafe, I beseech thee, O dear Saint, by the glory which thy many sufferings

have gained for thee, to intercede for me, and obtain for me of GOD a love of suffering, together with grace and strength to bear with firmness of mind all trials and adversities, which are the sure means to the happy attainment of that glorious crown which awaits me in Heaven. Dear Saint, from thy most happy throne of glory, whereon thou art now seated in majesty, hear, I beseech thee, my prayers; so that, after thy example, full of love for the Cross and for suffering, I may deserve to be thy companion in glory. Amen.

ST ANDREW AVELLINO
366. Prayers.
i. 300 Days. T.Q. ii. Plenary, once a month. I, II. (See Instructions.) 366 Pius IX, Br. June 25, 1869

I O MOST glorious Saint, whom GOD has made our protector against apoplexy, seeing that thou thyself didst die of that disease, we earnestly pray thee to preserve us from an evil so dangerous and so common. PATER, Ave, Gloria.

V/.. By the intercession of St Andrew, stricken with apoplexy.

R/. From a sudden and unprovided death deliver us, O LORD.

II O MOST glorious Saint, if ever by the just judgment of GOD we should be stricken with apoplexy, we earnestly beseech thee to obtain for us time enough to receive the last Sacraments and die in the grace of GOD. PATER, Ave, Gloria.

V/.. By the intercession of St Andrew, stricken with apoplexy.

R/. From a sudden and unprovided death deliver us, O LORD.

III O MOST glorious Saint, who didst endure, before dying, a terrible agony, through the assaults of the devil, from which the Blessed Virgin and St Michael delivered thee, we earnestly beseech thee to assist us in the tremendous moment of our death. PATER, Ave, Gloria.

V/.. By the intercession of St Andrew, stricken with apoplexy.

R/. From a sudden and unprovided death deliver us, O LORD.

ST MICHAEL DE SANTI
367. Prayer.
i. 300 days, once a day. ii. Plenary, on April 10 (the day of the Saint's death), on Corpus CHRISTI, and on July 5, his Feast, provided the prayer has been said at least ten times during the year. I, II, IV. (See Instructions.) 367 Pius IX, Pr. Ma. May 20 1862.

GLORIOUS Michael, Seraph inflamed with burning love of JESUS in the most holy Sacrament ; thou who, passing days and nights in his Royal Presence, didst find there those dear delights which, inundating not thy heart alone but thy whole body with surpassing sweetness, threw thee into an ecstasy of joy; and who, rapt in thy GOD, didst feel thyself faint for love, being unable to support the torrent of consolations; vouchsafe, I pray thee, powerful advocate, to obtain for me lively faith, firm hope, and burning- charity towards this priceless treasure, the precious pledge of everlasting glory; so that by thy intercession I may, through the whole course of my life, be numbered amongst the true worshippers of JESUS in the Holy Sacrament, and with thee hereafter enjoy Him face to face in an eternity of bliss. Amen. PATER, Ave, Gloria.

ST ANTHONY, ABBOT
368. Prayer.
100 Days, once a day. (See Instructions.) 368 Leo XIII, June 3, 1895.

O GLORIOUS St Anthony, who, on hearing one single precept of the Gospel while assisting at Mass, didst abandon riches and the comforts of home, and retire from thy country and the world into a desert; who, though burdened with years and wasted with penance, didst not hesitate to leave the desert, and make many journeys to Alexandria in Egypt to denounce publicly the impiety of the heretics and to strengthen wavering Christians in the Faith, eager, like a true confessor of JESUS CHRIST, to seize the palm of martyrdom, if only GOD had permitted it; obtain for us, we beseech thee, the grace to be ever zealous for the cause of JESUS CHRIST and his Church, and to persevere to the end of our days in believing the truths, observing the precepts, and practising the counsels of the Catholic Religion, and in imitating thy virtues; so that by faithfully following thy example here on earth we may rejoice in the participation of thy glory in Heaven through all eternity. PATER, Ave and Gloria thrice.

ST ALOYSIUS GONZAGA

369. Feast Day.
Plenary. I, II, IV. (See Instructions.) 369 Benedict XIII, November 22, 1729; Clement XII, November 21, 1737; Benedict XIV, April 12, 1742.

A visit must be made to an altar at which the Saint is being honoured.

N.B. The feast may be celebrated on any day, and in any place, with leave from the Bishop.

370. The Six Sundays.
Plenary, on each Sunday. I, II. (See Instructions.) 370 Clement XII, December 11, 1739; January 7, 1740

Some time must be spent in meditation, vocal prayer or other good works, in honour of the Saint, on six consecutive Sundays, either preceding the feast, June 21, or otherwise, at discretion.

371. Prayer.
100 Days, once a day. (See Instructions.) 371 Pius VII, March 6, 1802.

O BLESSED Aloysius, adorned with angelic virtues, I, thy most unworthy suppliant, recommend specially to thee the chastity of my soul and body, praying thee by thy angelic purity to plead for me with JESUS CHRIST, the Immaculate Lamb, and his most Holy Mother, Virgin of virgins, that they would vouchsafe to keep me from all grievous sin. Never suffer me to be denied with any stain of fleshly sin; but when thou dost see me in temptation, or in danger of falling, then remove far from my mind all bad thoughts and unclean desires, and awaken in me the memory of eternity to come and of JESUS crucified ; impress deeply in my heart a sense of the holy fear of GOD; and, kindling in me the fire of divine love, enable me so to follow thy footsteps here on earth that in heaven I may be made worthy to enjoy with thee the vision of our GOD for ever. Amen. PATER, Ave.

372. Act of Consecration.
i. 200 Days, once a day. ii. Plenary, on the Feast or during the Octave, if said every day in June. I, II,III, IV. (See Instructions.) 372 Leo XIII, June 12, 1894

O GLORIOUS St Aloysius, honoured by the Church with the title of Angelic Youth, for the eminent purity of thy life on earth, to thee I offer myself this day with all the devotion of my mind and heart, and to thee I consecrate myself entirely. O perfect example, O kind and powerful protector of youth, how much I have need of thee ! The world and the devil lay snares for me; I feel the fire of my passions, I know the weakness and inconstancy of my age. Who can protect me if not thou, O angelic saint, the glory, ornament, love and mainstay of the young? To thee, then, with all my mind and heart I have recourse; in thee I confide, to thee I consecrate myself. Therefore I firmly purpose and resolve to be specially devout to thee, to glorify thee for thy lofty virtues, and especially for thy angelic purity; to imitate thy example, to promote devotion to thee among my companions, and to invoke and bless to the end of my life thy dear and holy name. To thee I consecrate my soul, my senses, my heart, and all my being. O dear St Aloysius, lo ! today I am all thine, and thine I wish to remain for ever. Oh! protect, defend, and preserve me as thy possession, that through honouring thee I may be better able to serve and honour JESUS and Mary, and come one day with thee to see and bless my GOD for ever in Paradise. Amen.

ST STANISLAUS KOSTKA

373. Feast Day. Ten Sundays, etc.
i. Plenary, to all who, after First Vespers, visit a church or chapel where the feast (November 13) is being celebrated. I, II, IV.

ii. Seven Years and Seven Quarantines, on each of the ten Sundays before the Feast, to those who visit a church or public chapel where these Sundays are being kept. IV. iii. 100 Days, each day for assisting- at the Novena for the Feast, IV.

N. B. These three Indulgences may be gained if the Feast be transferred, with leave from the Bishop. iv. 100 Days, once a day, to those who say a Pater and Ave before a representation of the Saint, exposed in any church or chapel, public or private.

v. Plenary, once a month, for the above. I, II, IV.

N. B. In cases of lawful impediment, the Pater and Ave may be said anywhere.

vi. 100 Days, to all those who assist at the day's retreat known as " The Retreat of St Stanislaus." IV.

(See Instructions) 373 Leo XII, March 3, 1827.

374. Prayers.

i. 300 Days, once a day. ii. Plenary, once a month, I, II, III, IV. (See Instructions.) 374 Pius IX, Pr. Ma. March 21, 1847 ; Indul. July 10, 1854.

ST STANISLAUS, my most pure patron, angel of purity, I rejoice with thee at the extraordinary gift of virginal purity which graced thy spotless heart; I humbly pray thee, obtain for me strength to overcome all impure temptations, and inspire me with constant watchfulness in guarding the virtue of holy purity. PATER, Ave, Gloria.

ST STANISLAUS, my most loving patron, Seraph of charity, I rejoice with thee at the ardent fire of charity which kept thy pure and innocent heart always at peace and united to GOD; I humbly pray thee, obtain for me such ardour of divine love that it may consume away every other earthly affection, and kindle in me the fire of his love alone. PATER, Ave, Gloria.

ST STANISLAUS, my most tender and most mighty patron, Angel of purity and Seraph of charity, I rejoice with thee at thy most happy death, which arose from thy desire to contemplate our Lady in heaven, and was at length caused by the excess of thy love for her. I give thanks to Mary because she thus accomplished thy desires; and I pray thee, by the lustre of thy happy death, to be my advocate and patron in my death. Intercede with Mary for me, to obtain for me a death, if not all happiness like thine, yet calm and peaceful, under the protection of Mary my advocate, and thee, my special patron. PATER, Ave, Gloria.

ST JOHN BERCHMANS

375. The Five Sundays.

i. Seven Years and Seven Quarantines, on the first four Sundays. I, II, III, IV. ii. Plenary on the fifth. I, II, III, IV. (See Instructions.) 375 Leo XIII, May 17, 1890.

Some pious exercise must be performed in honour of the saint on the five Sundays preceding the feast, August 13.

ST BENEDICT JOSEPH LABRE

376. Prayer.

100 Days, once a day. (See Instructions) 376 Leo XIII, January 21, 1882.

O ADMIRABLE example of Christian perfection, St Benedict Joseph ! From the first use of reason till death thou didst preserve inviolate the immaculate stole of innocence, and abandoning all things, as a wanderer on the face of the earth, didst meet with nothing but suffering, privations and insults. I, a miserable sinner, prostrate at thy feet, return thanks to the infinite goodness of GOD for having impressed on thee so living an image of his crucified SON, while at the same time I am covered with confusion at the sight of my life, so different from thine. I beseech thee, dear Saint, have pity on me; present thy merits at the throne of GOD, and obtain for me the grace that, following thy example and regulating my actions by the precepts and teaching of thy divine Master, I may come to love his suffering and humiliations, and may hold in contempt the pleasures and honours of the world, so that neither the fear of the one nor the desire of the other may ever induce me to transgress his holy laws. And so may I merit one day to be acknowledged and numbered among the blessed of his FATHER. PATER, Ave, Gloria.

V/.. Pray for us, St Benedict Joseph.

R/. That we may be made worthy of the promises of CHRIST.

Let us pray.

O GOD , who hast caused blessed Benedict Joseph, thy Confessor, by practising humility and loving poverty, to cling to Thee alone; grant through the power of his merits that we may despise all earthly things and ever seek after the things of Heaven. Through CHRIST our LORD. Amen.

ST LUCY, VIRGIN AND MARTYR

377. Prayers.

200 Days, once a day. (See Instructions.) 377 Leo XIII, February 27, 1886.

WE contemplate with wonder, O glorious virgin and martyr, St Lucy, that light of living faith which GOD in his mercy was pleased to infuse into thy fair soul. By the light of this faith thou didst know how to despise the vain and fleeting things of this miserable world, and to keep thy eyes fixed on heaven, for which alone we were created. The honours, riches, and pleasures of this seductive world did not obscure thy mind, much less corrupt thy heart, to the injury of thy faith and of divine grace; so that far from consenting to the wicked proposals of the unjust judge, thou didst fearlessly and resolutely encounter even death rather than be unfaithful to thy celestial LORD. What shame for us, who, illumined also by faith and strengthened by grace, know not at all how to resist our guilty passions, despise the perverse maxims of the world, or frustrate the wiles of our enemy the devil! Therefore we beseech thee, dear Saint, to obtain for us greater light from GOD, to understand better that we are not made for earthly things, but for the things of heaven. PATER, Ave, Gloria.

O VICTORIOUS martyr, St Lucy, admirable was thy virtue of hope, which kept alive in thee the desire of heaven and nourished that filial confidence in GOD, our most loving FATHER, which possessed thy heart. Animated with this virtue, while praying fervently for thy mother at the tomb of St Agatha, thou didst obtain for her health in sickness. Full of trust in GOD, in order to become more completely detached from the things of this earth, thou didst willingly distribute to the poor whatever still remained to thee of earthly treasure; and if courage and strength never failed thee in resisting the tyrant, and in standing firm in the faith in the midst of unspeakable torments, it was solely because thou didst place thy hope in Him who has promised never to abandon us in dangers, but to be to us a shield of defence, ready to work even miracles, such as actually happened in thy glorious martyrdom. Let us then freely confess that too great an attachment to things here below and too little confidence in GOD harden our hearts, and so deprive us of courage that we often miserably succumb to occasions of danger. Obtain for us, we beseech thee, O blessed St Lucy, a more firm trust in our LORD and GOD, that we may deserve in every untoward event of our lives to have Him for our helper and consoler. PATER, Ave, Gloria.

O GLORIOUS martyr of JESUS CHRIST, St Lucy, thy living faith and firm hope could not be separated from the fire of most ardent charity which inflamed thy heart, and made thee so ready to shed thy blood and sacrifice thy life for thy spouse JESUS. No wonder the flame of material fire which was applied to thy body by order of the tyrant could not penetrate it or reduce it to ashes. This fire was too weak beside that which burnt in thy breast ; and so the impious prefect, seeing that his efforts were vain, ordered that thy throat should be completely severed with a sharp sword. Then it was that thy beautiful soul took its flight to heaven, there to repose on the breast of thy JESUS, and enjoy his heavenly delights for ever. Alas! we love creatures, and so weary ourselves on their account that we find our poor hearts not only void of consolation, but overwhelmed with bitterness. Obtain for us, dear Saint, we beseech thee, that we may be persuaded, once for all, that our true happiness should begin on this earth, in the love of that GOD who will be the true and the sole object of our perfect and eternal beatitude in heaven. PATER, Ave, Gloria.

FULL of confidence in thy powerful intercession, O glorious martyr St Lucy, we beseech thee to intercede with thy divine spouse JESUS, that it may please Him to keep ever healthy the light of our bodily eyes, giving us at the same time the grace to make good use of them, so that on the day of the general resurrection they may become radiant with that heavenly light which will fit them to
behold the ineffable beauties of the country of the blessed. Amen.

V/.. Pray for us, St Lucy.

R/. That we may be made worthy of the promises of CHRIST.

Let us pray.

HEAR our prayers, O GOD our SAVIOUR, that as we rejoice in the constancy in the faith of the blessed St Lucy, virgin and martyr, so we may be filled with pious and devout affections. Through CHRIST our LORD. Amen.

378. Prayer to St Lucy.

300 Days, once a day. (See Instructions.) 378 Pius X, December 29, 1907

O SAINT, named from the light, full of confidence we present ourselves before thee, to ask of thee a holy light, which may render us cautious in avoiding the ways of sin and escaping the darkness of error. We beg also, through thy intercession, for the preservation of the light of our eyes, together with abundant grace to use it always in accordance with the will of GOD and without injury to our souls. Grant, O blessed Lucy, that, after venerating and thanking thee for thy powerful patronage on earth, we may come at last to rejoice with thee in the paradise of the eternal light of the divine Lamb, thy sweet spouse JESUS. Amen.

ST AGNES, V.M.

379. Prayer.

100 Days, once a day. (See Instructions.) 379 Pius IX. Pr. Ma. October 30, 1854.

SWEETEST LORD JESUS CHRIST, Source of all virtue, Lover of virgins, most powerful Conqueror of demons, most severe Extirpator of vice, deign to cast thy eyes upon my weakness, and through the intercession of Mary most blessed, Mother and Virgin, and of thy beloved spouse, St Agnes, glorious virgin and martyr, grant me the aid of thy heavenly grace, in order that I may learn to despise all earthly things, and to love what is heavenly; to oppose vice, and to be proof against temptation; to walk firmly in the path of virtue, not to seek honours, to shun pleasures, to bewail my past offences, to keep far from the occasions of evil, to keep free from bad habits, to seek the company of the good, and persevere in righteousness, so that, by the assistance of thy grace, I may deserve the crown of eternal life, together with St Agnes and all the saints, for ever and ever, in thy kingdom. Amen.

380. Prayers.

200 Days, once a day. (See Instructions.) 380 Leo XIII, January 16, 1886.

O SINGULAR example of virtue, glorious St Agnes, by that lively faith which animated thee from thy most tender years, and rendered thee so acceptable to GOD that thou didst merit the crown of martyrdom; obtain for us the grace to preserve entire in our hearts the Catholic Faith, and sincerely to profess ourselves Christians not only in word but also in deed; so that while we confess JESUS openly in the face of men, JESUS may give favourable testimony of us before his Heavenly FATHER. PATER, Ave, Gloria.

O INVINCIBLE martyr, St Agnes, by that hope which thou hadst in the divine aid, when being condemned by the impious prefect to see the lily of thy purity stained and trampled under foot, thou wast wholly undismayed, firmly trusting in the GOD who gives his angels charge over those who trust in Him ; we beseech thee to obtain for us by thy intercession the grace to guard this virtue jealously in our hearts, so that to the many sins which we commit we may never add that most hateful sin of distrust in the mercy of GOD. PATER, Ave, Gloria.

O BRAVE child, most pure St Agnes, by that ardent charity which enflamed thy heart and secured thee from being injured by the flames of passion or of the stake at which the enemies of JESUS CHRIST sought to destroy thee ; obtain for us from GOD that every fire may be extinguished in us except that which JESUS CHRIST came on earth to enkindle; so that after passing- a spotless life in the exercise of this beautiful virtue we may be allowed to share in that glory which is the crown of thy purity of heart and of thy martyrdom. PATER, Ave, Gloria.

ST BARBARA, VIRGIN

381. Prayer for a Happy Death.

100 Days, once a day. (See Instructions.) 381 Leo XIII, Br. March 21, 1879

O GOD, who didst choose St Barbara to bring consolation to the living and the dying; grant that through her intercession we may live always in thy divine love, and place all our hopes in the merits of the most sorrowful Passion of thy SON; so that a sinners death may never overtake us, but that, armed with the Sacraments of Penance, the Holy Eucharist, and Extreme Unction, we maybe able to pass without fear to everlasting glory. We implore this of Thee through the same JESUS CHRIST our LORD. Amen.

ST JULIANA FALGONIERI

382. Prayer.

200 Days, once a day. (See Instructions.) 382 Leo XIII, July 20, 1889

O FAITHFUL spouse of JESUS CHRIST and most humble servant of the Virgin Mary, Mother of Sorrows, glorious St Juliana; at the end of a life entirely spent in the exercise of heroic virtues, thou didst undergo one last trial, in that thou couldst not be united in holy Viaticum, to thy Beloved by reason of bodily infirmity. But this trial was so acceptable to thy heavenly Spouse, JESUS, that He deigned Himself to reward it with an extraordinary miracle; for at thy request JESUS in the Blessed Sacrament was placed on thy virginal breast, and He instantly entered within, leaving outwardly impressed the image of Himself crucified, while with a sweet smile thou didst breathe forth thy soul in his holy embrace. O great Saint and my special patroness, obtain from GOD, I beseech thee, that like thee I may live a good life and die a holy death; and that being so prepared for the last passage, fortified with the holy Sacraments, and invigorated by divine grace, I may finish my days in holiness and be preserved from eternal death.

ST THERESA, VIRGIN
383. Prayer of St Alphonsus.
100 Days, once a day. (See Instructions.) 383 Leo XIII, April 22, 1898

O SERAPHIC virgin, St Theresa, beloved spouse of the Crucified, thou who didst burn with such great love of GOD while on earth, and now burnest with a still purer and brighter flame in Heaven; thou who didst so greatly desire to see Him loved by all men, obtain for me too, I pray thee, a spark of that holy fire, whereby I may oppose the world, creatures, and myself; and grant that all my thoughts, desires and affections may be ever employed in pursuing, whether in the midst of joys or of sufferings, the will of the Supreme Good, who deserves our unbounded love and obedience. Oh, obtain for me this grace, thou who art so powerful with GOD, that, like thee, I may be all on fire with divine love. Amen.

ST MARY SALOME
384. Prayer.
100 Days, once a day. (See Instructions.) 384 Leo XIII, February 27, 1894

O BELOVED disciple and true lover of JESUS CHRIST, St Mary Salome; I thy humble client thank the Blessed Trinity for the glory bestowed on thee, making thy family truly a family of saints. By thy generosity in devoting to the apostolate thy sons and thyself, obtain for me that through out my whole life, whatever be the cost, I may labour efficaciously in promoting the glory of GOD and the salvation of souls. And when my end shall come, O my dear protectress, assist me with that loving pity with which thou didst assist our dying LORD on Calvary; and grant that in that terrible hour He may address to me also those consoling words which He spoke on the Cross to the penitent thief: "This day thou shalt be with Me in Paradise."

ST ELIZABETH OF HUNGARY
385. Prayer.
300 Days, once a day. (See Instructions.) 385 Pius IX, Br. August 9, 1861.

BLESSED Elizabeth, vessel elect of exalted virtues, thou dost show forth to the world by thy example what the virtues of Faith, Hope, and Charity are able to do in a Christian soul.

Thou didst employ all the powers of thy heart to love thy GOD alone. Thou didst love Him with a love so pure and fervent that it rendered thee worthy to taste upon earth beforehand those favours and those sweetnesses of Paradise which are communicated to souls invited to the nuptials of the Divine adorable LAMB of GOD.

Thou, illuminated by supernatural light and faith immovable, didst show thyself to be a true daughter of the Holy Gospel, by seeing in the person of thy neighbour the Person of our LORD JESUS CHRIST, sole object of thy affections; and therefore didst thou place all thy delight in holding converse with the poor, in serving them, in drying their tears and comforting their spirits, in assisting them with every pious good office, in the midst of pestilence and the miseries to which our human nature is subject.

Thou didst make thyself poor in order to succour thy neighbour in his poverty poor in the good things of earth, to enrich thyself with the goods of heaven.

Thou wast so humble that, after thou hadst exchanged a throne for a poor hovel, and a royal mantle for the modest habit of St Francis, thou didst subject thyself, innocent though thou wast, to a life of privation and of penance, and with holy joy didst embrace the cross of thy Redeemer, with goodwill accepting with Him insults and the most unjust persecution: thus didst thou forget the world and thyself, to remember thy GOD alone.

Dearest Saint, who wast so beloved by GOD, vouchsafe to be the heavenly friend of our souls, and help them to become ever more and more acceptable to JESUS. Cast down upon us from the height of heaven one of those tender looks which, when thou wast upon earth, healed the most distressing infirmities. In this our age, so depraved and corrupt, and at the same time so cold and indifferent to the things of GOD, we have recourse to thee with confidence, in order that we may receive from our LORD light for the understanding and strength for the will, and thence obtain peace of soul.

Whilst we bless the LORD for having glorified his name in this world with the splendour of thy heroic virtues and the eternal reward accorded to them, do thou bless them, O dear St Elizabeth, from that blessed throne which thou dost occupy close to the Saint of Saints; protect us in our dangerous pilgrimage; obtain for us the pardon of our sins, and open for us the way to enter and share with thee the Kingdom of GOD. Amen.

ST MARGARET OF CORTONA
386. Prayer.
100 Days, once a day. (See Instructions.) 386 Leo XIII, January 12, 1897.

O MOST glorious Margaret, true gem wrested by GOD with so much love out of the hands of the infernal robbers who had seized thee, that by the example of thy wonderful conversion, holy life and most precious death all sinners might be moved to abandon sin and every approximate occasion of evil, and practise virtue; obtain for us thy clients, we beseech thee, from the lofty throne of thy glory, to which thy tears and penances have raised thee, the grace of a sincere conversion of heart and of a lively sorrow for our sins, and, after a holy life passed like thine in the love of JESUS crucified for us, a happy death, and the crown of glory in the bosom of the Eternal Beatitude. Amen. PATER, Ave, Gloria.

387. Prayer to St Blaise.
300 Days, once a day. (See Instructions.) 387 Leo XIII, May 13, 1903.

O GLORIOUS St Blaise, who with a short prayer didst restore to perfect safety a child at the point of death from a fish-bone fixed in its throat, grant that we may all feel the power of thy patronage in every malady of the throat, and may have the special grace to mortify the dangerous sense of taste by observing faithfully the precepts of the Church. Thou also, who in thy martyrdom hast left to the Church the testimony of a glorious faith, grant that we may keep this divine gift intact, and that in these times we may be enabled, by word and deed, without fear of man, to defend the truths of faith, so grievously obscured and attacked.

ST STEPHEN
388. Antiphon and Prayer.
i. 300 Days, once a day. ii. Plenary, on August 3 and December 26, or during the Octaves, if said for nine days preceding the feast. I, II, III, IV. (See Instructions.) 388 Pius X, January 23, and June 8, 1904.

Antiphon.

ELEGERUNT Apostoli Stephanum Levitam plenum fide et SPIRITU SANCTO, quem lapidaverunt Judæi orantem et dicentem: DOMINE JESU, accipe spiritum meum, et non statuas illis hoc peccatum.

V/. Meritis et precibus beati Stephani.

R/. Propitius esto, DOMINE, populo tuo.

Oremus.

OMNIPOTENS, sempiterne DEUS, qui primitias Martyrum in beati Levitæ Stephani sanguine dedicasti: tribue, quæsumus, ut pro nobis intercessor existat, qui pro suis etiam persecutoribus exoravit DOMINUM nostrum JESUM CHRISTUM FILIUM tuum, qui vivit et regnat in sæcula sæculorum. Amen.

THE APOSTLES chose the Levite Stephen, full of faith and the HOLY SPIRIT, whom the Jews stoned while he prayed, saying: LORD JESUS, receive my spirit, and lay not this sin to their charge.

V/. By the merits and prayers of the blessed Stephen.

R/. Be merciful, O LORD, to thy people.

Let us pray.

ALMIGHTY and everlasting GOD, who didst consecrate the first fruits of the Martyrs in the blood of the blessed Levite Stephen, grant, we beseech Thee, that he may become our advocate, who even for his persecutors besought our LORD, thy SON JESUS CHRIST, who liveth and reigneth world without end. Amen.

ST JOHN THE BAPTIST
389. Prayers.
i. 200 Days, once a day. ii. 300 Days, once a day, during- a triduo or novena. iii. Plenary, once during the Triduo or Novena, or within eight days. I, II, IV. (See Instructions.) 389 Pius X, Jan. ii, 1904.

O GLORIOUS St John the Baptist, of those born of women the greatest of prophets (Luke vii, 28); thou, though sanctified from thy mothers womb and most innocent, didst nevertheless will to retire into the desert, there to practise austerities and penance; obtain for us from our LORD the grace to be detached, at least in the affections of our hearts, from all earthly treasure, and to practise Christian mortification with interior recollection and a spirit of holy prayer. PATER, Ave, and Gloria.

O MOST zealous Apostle, who, without working any miracle on others, but solely by the example of thy life of penance and the power of thy words, didst draw after thee crowds, in order to prepare them to worthily receive the MESSIAH, and listen to his heavenly teaching; grant that it may be given to us also, by the example of a holy life and the practice of good works, to lead many souls to GOD, and, above all, those who have been enveloped in the darkness of error and ignorance, and led astray by vice. PATER, Ave, Gloria.

UNCONQUERED martyr, who for the honour of GOD and the salvation of souls, didst, with heroic constancy, and at the cost of life itself, with stand the impious Herod, reproving him openly for his bad and dissolute life ; obtain for us a brave and generous heart, so that, overcoming all human respect, we may boldly profess our faith, and follow the teaching of our divine master JESUS CHRIST. PATER, Ave, Gloria.

V/. Pray for us, St John the Baptist.
R/. That we may be made worthy of the promises of CHRIST.
Let us pray.
O GOD, who hast made this day worthy of honour in the nativity (commemoration) of St John, grant to thy people the grace of spiritual joys, and dire6l the minds of all the faithful into the way of eternal salvation. Through CHRIST our LORD. Amen.

ST FRANCIS XAVIER
390. Novena in honour of the Saint.
i. 300 Days, each day. ii. Plenary, within eight days of the completion. I, II, IV. (See Instructions.) 390 Pius X, March 23, 1904

The following- prayer must be said each day or Pater, Ave and Gloria five times. (N. B.- Twice a year only.)

O GREAT St Francis, well beloved and full of charity, with thee I reverently adore the divine Majesty; and since I specially rejoice in the singular gifts of grace, bestowed on thee in life, and of glory after death, I give thanks to GOD, and beg of thee, with all the affections of my heart, that by thy powerful intercession thou mayest obtain for me above all things the grace to live a holy life and die a holy death. Moreover, I beg of thee to obtain for me (here insert some special spiritual or temporal favour) , but if what I ask does not tend to the glory of GOD and the greater good of my soul, do thou, I beseech thee, obtain for me what will more certainly attain these ends. Amen.

ST PAUL OF THE CROSS
391. Prayer.
300 Days, once a day. (See Instructions.) 391 Pius X, September 17, 1904

O GLORIOUS St Paul of the Cross, thou who in meditating on the Passion of JESUS CHRIST didst attain to such a high degree of sanctity on earth and of happiness in Heaven, and didst, by preaching the same holy Passion, offer to the world a most efficacious remedy for all its evils; obtain for us that we may ever have that Passion so deeply engraven on our hearts, that we may gather similar fruits in time and in eternity. Amen. PATER, Ave, Gloria.

ST RITA
392. Prayer.
300 Days, once a day. (See Instructions.) 392 Pius X, August 11, 1906.

O GLORIOUS St Rita, thou who didst miraculously share in the sorrowful Passion of our LORD JESUS CHRIST, obtain for me that I may bear with resignation the sufferings of this life, and protect me in all my necessities.

ST JOHN DE LA SALLE
393. Prayer.
i. 300 Days, once a day. ii. Plenary, once a month. I,II, III, IV. (See Instructions.) 393 Pius X, November 28, 1906.

O GLORIOUS John Baptist de la Salle, Apostle of infancy and of youth, and, from the height of Heaven, our guide and our protector, intercede for us, help us, that, preserved from all the defilement of error and corruption, we may live always faithful to JESUS CHRIST and to the infallible Head of his Church. Grant that, practising the virtues of which thou wast so admirable an example, we may one day partake of thy glory in the heavenly country. Amen.

SS. BRIDGETT AND CATHARINE OF SWEDEN
394. Prayers.
300 Days, once a day, for either   (See Instructions.) 394 Pius X, July 5, 1905.

I. To St Bridgett, Queen of Sweden.
WITH confident hearts we fly to thee, blessed Bridgett, and ask, in these times of darkness and unbelief, thy intercession on behalf of those who are separated from the Church of JESUS CHRIST. By the clear knowledge which thou hadst of the cruel sufferings of our crucified SAVIOUR, the price of our redemption, we beg of thee to obtain for those who are outside the one fold the grace of faith, so that the scattered sheep may return to the one true Shepherd. Through CHRIST our LORD. Amen.
St Bridgett, fearless servant of GOD, pray for us.
St Bridgett, patient in suffering s and humiliations, pray for us.
St Bridgett, wonderful in thy love towards JESUS and Mary, pray for us. PATER, Ave, Gloria.

II. To St Catharine, Virgin.
O GOD, who didst adorn blessed Catharine in an especial manner with the virtues of humility, charity, and angelic purity, we humbly beseech Thee, by her merits and example, to make us so firm in faith and so ardent in charity that we may obtain the rewards of eternity. Through JESUS CHRIST our LORD. Amen. St Catharine, lily of purity, pray for us. St Catharine, model of humility, pray for us. St Catharine, admirable in the love of JESUS and Mary, pray for us. PATER, Ave, Gloria.

ST CATHARINE OF ALEXANDRIA
395. Prayers for the Promotion of Studies.
100 Days, once a day for each prayer. (See Instructions.) 395 Pi us X, April 29, 1907.
I LORD JESUS CHRIST, the Way, the Truth and the Life, Thou who so lovest souls, and who, not content with giving us an example, hast made such magnificent promises to those who shall teach the truth ; fill with thy spirit of wisdom, knowledge, and fear, all those who teach ; fill with thy grace those who are taught, so that, instructed in a profitable and useful manner, their minds may receive the truth, their hearts cling to what is right, and their lives be full of good works; and may thy holy Name be glorified in everything. O JESUS, teacher, who, moved to compassion for thy children, like sheep without a shepherd, didst say to thy disciples, Pray to the Lord of the harvest that He send labourers ; deign, we beseech Thee, to multiply worthy instructors of youth ; sanctify them in truth, and increase in them faith, hope and charity.
O good JESUS, who hast said, Suffer little children to come unto Me, let not one of these little ones, purchased with thy Precious Blood, perish; remove them from all scandal of impiety, of vice, and error; we ask this from Thee in the name of thy holy Passion, of the sorrows of thy holy Mother, and by the intercession of the angels and saints. Amen.

II PRAYER TO ST CATHARINE OF ALEXANDRIA, PATRONESS OF STUDIES.
O GLORIOUS Virgin and Martyr, St Catharine, who by thy admirable learning, thy zeal for the Faith, and by thy glorious martyrdom didst gain so many souls for JESUS CHRIST; thou whose patronage has been so often claimed by the most learned, we choose thee for the patroness and protector of our studies and our teaching.
Obtain for us who are thy clients a generous love for JESUS CHRIST our SAVIOUR, an ardent zeal to make Him known and loved, an inviolable fidelity to the Catholic Faith and to the teaching of Holy Church.
May our LORD deign, through thy intercession, to grant to all who teach, the plenitude of the gifts of the HOLY SPIRIT. May they join to true knowledge sure and effective methods, purity of faith, integrity of life, and a humble distrust of themselves.
Beg of JESUS, thy Spouse, that He take pity on all those who are taught; that He preserve them from impious or indifferent masters, and perverse or erroneous doctrines; that He give them an upright character, and docile heart, and the grace to make progress in their studies according to the designs of his sovereign wisdom.

And lastly, O glorious Saint, beg the FATHER of lights for such an outpouring of grace on the instruction of youth that, after having studied, loved and practised the divine law, all masters and disciples may together come to the holy Mount, which is JESUS CHRIST. Amen.

III ANOTHER PRAYER TO ST CATHARINE.
O GLORIOUS St Catharine, wise and prudent virgin, who didst place the knowledge of JESUS CHRIST above all knowledge, obtain for us the grace to live inviolably attached to the Catholic Faith, and to seek in our studies and teaching but one thing, to extend in ourselves and in others the kingdom of JESUS CHRIST our SAVIOUR, and of his holy Church. Amen.

396. BLESSED FRANGUS, Carmelite Confessor.
Plenary, on the feast, from First Vespers, to those who visit a Carmelite church or public chapel. I, II, III, IV. (See Instructions.) 396 Pius X, Br. February 11, 1905.

XIV. BLESSED CROSSES, CRUCIFIXES, ROSARIES, MEDALS, etc., FROM THE HOLY LAND
397.
397 Ven. Innocent XI, Br. January 28, 1688; Innocent XIII, June 4, 1721 ; Leo XIII, August 19, 1895.
The following indulgences may be gained by persons who possess blessed objects which have touched the holy places and sacred relics of the Holy Land.
i. Plenary, in articulo mortis, at the point of death. I, II. Should Confession and Communion be impossible, the invocation of the holy Name of JESUS with contrition, at least in the heart, suffices.
ii. Plenary, on Christmas Day, the Epiphany, Easter Day, Ascension Day, Pentecost, Trinity Sunday, Corpus Christi, the Purification, Annunciation, Nativity B.V.M., Nativity of St John Baptist, SS. Peter and Paul, Andrew, James, John, Thomas, Philip and James, Bartholomew, Matthew, Simon and Jude, Matthias, and All Saints, to those who say at least once a week a Chaplet of our LORD, or of our Lady, the Rosary or a third part thereof, the Divine Office, or the Office of the B.V.M. or of the Dead, the Penitential or Gradual Psalms; or whose custom it is to teach the Catechism, visit prisoners, or the sick in hospitals, or help the poor, or hear Mass, or say Mass. I, II, III.
iii. Seven Years and Seven Quarantines, for the above pious exercises on other feasts of our LORD or of our Lady.
iv. Five Years and Five Quarantines, for the same on any Sunday or feast in the year.
v. 100 Days, for the same, on any day of the year.
vi. 200 Days, to those who visit prisoners, or the sick in hospitals, or teach the Catechism in church, or at home to their own children, relations or servants, or who are accustomed to say at least once a week, the Chaplet or Rosary, or Office B.V.M or of the Dead, or Vespers of the Dead, or one Nocturn with Lauds of the same, or who shall say the Penitential Psalms with the Litanies and Prayers,
vii. 100 Days, to those who at the sound of the bell say the Angelus or not knowing it, a Pater and Ave, or in like manner say the De Profundis at night, or not knowing it, a Pater and Ave, or who every Friday meditate on the Passion and Death of our LORD and say the Pater and Ave thrice, or who with contrition and purpose of amendment examine their consciences and say Pater and Ave thrice, or who say the Pater and Ave thrice in honour of the Holy Trinity, or the Pater and Ave five times in memory of the Five Wounds of our LORD.
viii. 50 Days, to those who say any prayer in preparation before saying Mass or receiving Holy Communion, or before saying the Divine Office or the Office B.V. M.
ix. 50 Days, to those who pray for the dying, saying for them at least the Pater noster and Ave Maria. (See Instructions.)
N.B. Indulgences following the same lines and practically identical with the above are attached to similar objects blessed by the Pope or a priest with the requisite faculties. The list of these indulgences, with slight variations, is published anew by successive Pontiffs. The following conditions, however, must be observed :
i. The blessed object must be carried about on the person, or kept in the bedroom, or other suitable place, and reverently used for the prescribed devotions.
ii. It must not be made of fragile material,
iii. Pictures, whether printed or painted, are not admissible, and images must be of saints canonized or inscribed in approved martyrologies.

See also Decisions, No. 38, p. xiv. For precise particulars, cf. Acta S. Sedis xxxvi, 125.

XV. THE DYING AND THE APOSTOLIC BLESSING

398. Praying for the Dying.
100 Days. (See Instructions.) 398 Pius X, December 10, 1907.
This may be gained by priests saying Mass, or the laity assisting thereat, who commend to GOD all the sinners of the world who are "at that moment in their agony, or who are to die that day."

399. Offering of Masses for the Dying.
300 Days. T.Q. (See Instructions) 399 Pius X, December 18, 1907.
MY GOD, I offer Thee all the Masses which are being celebrated today throughout the whole world, for sinners who are in their agony and who are to die this day. May the Precious Blood of their REDEEMER, obtain mercy for them.

400. The Apostolic Blessing.
Plenary Indulgence, at the point of death to those who receive the blessing given by the Pope, or those who have the necessary faculties, who must in all cases use the prescribed form. (See Ritual.) 400 Benedict XIV, Con. April 5, 1747; Indul. September 23, 1775; February 5; 1841; March 22, 1879.
N.B. The dying person must renew his sorrow for sin and fervent love of GOD; and especially he must accept death from the hands of GOD with resignation and in conformity to the divine pleasure, invoking the holy Name of JESUS in his heart, if unable to do so with his lips. This Indulgence is not suspended in the year of Jubilee.

401. Plenary Indulgence in Articulo Mortis.
To all who, with sincere love towards GOD, after Confession and Communion, made on any day they may choose, say the following prayer:
O LORD my GOD, I now, at this moment, readily and willingly accept at thy hand whatever kind of death it may please Thee to send me, with all its pains, penalties, and sorrows.
401 Pius X, March 9, 1904.

XVI. THE FAITHFUL DEPARTED

402. The Office of the Dead.
i. 100 Days, on days prescribed by the Rubrics, ii. 50 Days, at other times. (See Instructions.) 402 St Pius V, Bl. July 9, 1568 ; Bl. April 5, 1571.

403. The Heroic Act.
This heroic act of charity in behalf of the souls in purgatory consists in a voluntary offering, made by any one of the faithful in their favour, of all works of satisfaction done by him in this life, as well as of all suffrages which shall be offered for him after his death ; by this act he deposits all these works and suffrages into the hands of the Blessed Virgin, that she may distribute them in behalf of those holy souls whom it is her good pleasure to deliver from the pains of purgatory, at the same time that he declares that by this personal offering he only forgoes in their behalf the special and personal benefit of these works of satisfaction, so that, if he is a priest, he is not hindered from applying the Holy Sacrifice of the Mass according to the intention of those who give him alms for that purpose.
This heroic act of charity, called also a vow of oblation, was instituted by F. Caspar Oliden, a Theatine. It was he who propagated it, and it was at his prayer that it was enriched with many Indulgences.
i. An Indult of a privileged altar, personally, every day in the year to all priests who have made this offering.
ii. Plenary, daily, applicable only to the departed, II, III, IV.
iii. Plenary, every Monday to all who hear Mass in suffrage for the souls in purgatory, II, III, IV. (See Instructions.) 403 Benedict XIII, August 23, 1728; Pius VI, December 12, 1788; Pius IX, September 30, 1852, November 20, 1854; Pius X, February 20, 1907.
N.B. All Indulgences granted, or to be granted and gained by the faithful who have made this offering, are applicable to the holy souls in purgatory.

For all the faithful who cannot hear Mass on Monday, the Mass heard on Sundays is available for gaining Indulgence No. iii. In the case of those who are not yet communicants, or who are hindered from communicating, their respective ordinaries may authorize confessors to commute the works enjoined.

Lastly, although this act of charity is denominated a vow in some printed tracts, in which also is given a formula for making the offering, no inference is to be drawn therefrom that this offering binds under sin.; neither is it necessary to make use of the said formula, since, in order to share in the said Indulgences, no more is required than a hearty act of our will.

N.B. This act, or offering-, may be at any time revoked.

404. The De Profundis.

i. 100 Days, to all the faithful, every time that, at the sound of the bell at nightfall, they say devotedly on their knees the Psalm De profundis or Pater, Ave and Requiem æternam.

ii. Plenary, once a year, if said daily. I, II, IV.

N.B. In places where no bell is rung, these Indulgences may be gained by reciting the above at nightfall.

iii. 50 Days, three times a day to all who say the De profundis with V/. and R/. Requiem æternam. (See Instructions) 404 Clement XII, Br. August n, 1736; Pius VI, Prop. March 18, 1781; Pius IX, July 18, 1877; Leo XIII, February 3, 1888.

Psalm, cxxix.

DE profundis clamavi ad te, DOMINE : * DOMINE, exaudi vocem meam. Fiant aures tuæ intendentes * in vocem deprecationis meæ. Si iniquitates observaveris, DOMINE: * DOMINE, quis sustinebit? Quia apud te propitiation est : * et propter legem tuam sustinui te, DOMINE

Sustinuit anima mea in verbo ejus : speravit anima mea in DOMINO.

A custodia matutina usque ad noctem * speret Israel in DOMINO. Quia apud DOMINUM misericordia, * et copiosa apud eum redemptio. Et ipse redimet Israel * ex omnibus iniquitatibus ejus.

V/. Requiem æternam * dona eis, DOMINE.

R/. Et lux perpetua luceat eis.

Psalm, cxxix.

OUT of the depths I have cried unto Thee, O LORD: LORD, hear my voice, Let thine ears be attentive : to the voice of my supplication. If Thou, O LORD, shalt mark our iniquities: O LORD, who can abide it? For with Thee there is mercy : and by reason of thy law I have waited on Thee, O LORD.

My soul hath waited on his word : my soul hath hoped in the LORD.

From the morning watch even unto night: let Israel hope in the LORD. For with the LORD there is mercy: and with Him is plenteous redemption.

And He shall redeem Israel: from all his iniquities.

V/. Eternal rest give to them, O LORD.

R/. And let perpetual light shine upon them.

405. Holy Week.

Seven Years and Seven Quarantines, on Holy Thursday, Good Friday, and Holy Saturday. (See Instructions.) 405 Benedict XIV, April 10, 1745 ; April 3, 1751.

To those who, on Thursday, Friday and Saturday in Holy Week make one hours mental or vocal prayer, or who assist at the functions and services of Holy Week by way of suffrage for the holy souls, seeing that on these days they are deprived of the benefit of holy Mass.

406. Pater and Ave five times, etc.

i. 300 Days, once a day, to all who, devoutly meditating on the Passion, shall say for the departed the Pater and Ave five times with the following versicle or ejaculation, etc. ii. Plenary, once a month. I, II, IV. (See Instructions.) 406 Pius VII, Br. February 6, 1817

V/. TE ergo quæsumus, tuis famulis subveni, quos pretioso sanguine redemisti.

V/. WE therefore beseech Thee, help thy servants, whom Thou hast redeemed with thy Precious Blood.

Ejaculation.

Eternal FATHER, by the Precious Blood of JESUS, Mercy!

Eternal rest give unto them, O LORD, and let perpetual light shine upon them.

407. All Souls Day.

Plenary Indulgence, T.Q. I,II, IV (See Instructions.) 407 Pius X, February 27, 1907; September 2 & 11, 1907. This Indulgence, like that of the Portiuncula, may be gained as often as a person visits a church or public chapel of the Benedictines, whether monks or nuns, between first Vespers on November i and sunset on November 2. I, II, IV. Communities and those dwelling with them may use a semi-public chapel.

Those who wear a duly blessed medal of St Benedict, and are hindered from visiting a church or public chapel of the Benedictines by infirmity, enclosure or distance (more than a mile), may gain the same indulgence by visiting- any church or public chapel. I, II, IV.

408. Prayers.
100 Days, once a day. IV (See Instructions.) 408 Leo XII, November 18, 1826.
FOR SUNDAY.
OLORD GOD ALMIGHTY, I pray Thee, by the Precious Blood which thy Divine SON JESUS shed in the garden, deliver the souls in purgatory, and especially that soul amongst them all which is most destitute of spiritual aid; and vouchsafe to bring it to thy glory, there to praise and bless Thee for ever. Amen. PATER, Ave, De profundis. (404)
FOR MONDAY.
O LORD GOD ALMIGHTY, I pray Thee, by the Precious Blood which thy Divine SON JESUS shed in his cruel scourging, deliver the souls in purgatory, and that soul especially amongst them all which is nearest to its entrance into thy glory; that so it may forthwith begin to praise and bless Thee for ever. Amen. PATER, Ave, De profundis.
FOR TUESDAY.
O LORD GOD ALMIGHTY, I pray Thee, by the Precious Blood which thy Divine SON JESUS shed in his bitter crowning with thorns, deliver the souls in purgatory, and in particular that one amongst them all which would be the last to depart out of those pains, that it may not tarry so long a time before it come to praise Thee in thy glory and bless Thee for ever. Amen. PATER, Ave, De profundis.
FOR WEDNESDAY.
O LORD GOD ALMIGHTY, I pray Thee, by the Precious Blood which thy Divine SON JESUS shed in the streets of Jerusalem, when He carried the Cross upon his sacred shoulders, deliver the souls in purgatory, and especially that soul which is richest in merits before Thee; that so, in that throne of glory which awaits it, it may magnify Thee and bless Thee for ever. Amen. PATER, Ave, De profundis.
FOR THURSDAY.
O LORD GOD ALMIGHTY, I pray Thee, by the Precious Body and Blood of thy Divine SON JESUS, which He gave with his own hands upon the eve of his Passion to his beloved Apostles to be their meat and drink, and which He left to his whole Church to be a perpetual sacrifice and the life-giving food of his own faithful people, deliver the souls in purgatory, and especially that one which was most devoted to this mystery of infinite love, that it may with the same thy Divine SON, and with thy HOLY SPIRIT, ever praise Thee for thy love therein in eternal glory. Amen. PATER, Ave, De profundis.
FOR FRIDAY.
O LORD GOD ALMIGHTY, I pray Thee, by the Precious Blood which thy Divine SON shed on this day upon the wood of the Cross, especially from his most sacred hands and feet, deliver the souls in purgatory, and in particular that soul for which I am most bound to pray; that no neglect of mine may hinder it from praising Thee in thy glory and blessing Thee for ever. Amen. PATER, Ave, De profundis.
FOR SATURDAY.
O LORD GOD ALMIGHTY, I beseech Thee, by the Precious Blood which gushed forth from the side of thy Divine SON JESUS, in the sight of, and to the extreme pain of his most holy Mother, deliver the souls in purgatory, and especially that one amongst them all which was the most devout to her; that it may soon attain unto thy glory, there to praise Thee in her, and her in Thee, world without end. Amen. PATER, Ave, De profundis.

409. Prayers for Nine or Seven Days.
i. 300 Days, each day. ii. Plenary, during- the period. I, II, IV. (See Instructions.) 409 Pius IX, Res. Januarys, 1849: Dps. January 28, 1850; November 26, 1876
Any form of prayers for the Holy Souls, sanctioned by competent ecclesiastical authority, may be used.

410. League of Perpetual Suffrage.
200 Days, once a day, to all who say thrice daily the versicle below. (See Instructions.) 410 Leo XIII, August 19, 1880.

REQUIEM æternam dona eis DOMINE, et lux perpetua luceat eis. Requiescant in pace, Amen

ETERNAL rest give unto them, O LORD, and let perpetual light shine upon them. May they rest in peace. Amen.

411. Month of November.
i. Seven Years and Seven Quarantines, each day. ii. Plenary, once during- the month. I,II, III, IV. (See Instructions.) 411 Leo XIII, January 17, 1888.
Any daily devotions for the Holy Souls, public or private, will suffice.

412. Devotion to the Five Wounds.
200 Days, once a day. (See Instructions.) 412 Leo XIII, September 15, 1888.
GO before our actions, we beseech Thee, O LORD, with thy inspiration, and follow after them with thy help, that every prayer and work of ours may begin from Thee and through Thee be likewise ended. Through CHRIST our LORD. Amen.
Eternal rest give unto them, O LORD, and let perpetual light shine upon them.
I WE offer unto Thee, O eternal FATHER, Father of mercies, for those souls so dear to Thee in purgatory, the most Precious Blood shed on Calvary from the wound in the left foot of JESUS thy SON, our SAVIOUR, and the sorrow of Mary his most loving Mother in beholding it. PATER, Ave, Requiem æternam.
II. We offer unto Thee, O eternal FATHER, Father of mercies, for those souls so dear to Thee in purgatory, the most Precious Blood shed on Calvary from the wound in the right foot of JESUS thy SON, our SAVIOUR, and the sorrow of Mary his most loving Mother in beholding it. PATER, Ave, Requiem æternam.
III. We offer unto Thee, O eternal FATHER, Father of mercies, for those souls so dear to Thee in purgatory, the most Precious Blood shed on Calvary from the wound in the left hand of JESUS thy SON, our SAVIOUR, and the sorrow of Mary his most loving Mother in beholding it. PATER, Ave, Requiem æternam.
IV. We offer unto Thee, O eternal FATHER, Father of mercies, for those souls so dear to Thee in purgatory, the most Precious Blood shed on Calvary from the wound in the right hand of JESUS thy SON, our SAVIOUR, and the sorrow of Mary his most loving Mother in beholding it. PATER, Ave, Requiem æternam.
V. We offer unto Thee, O eternal FATHER, Father of mercies, for those souls so dear to Thee in purgatory, the most Precious Blood and water flowing on Calvary from the pierced side of JESUS thy SON, our SAVIOUR, and the sorrow of Mary his most loving Mother in beholding it. PATER, Ave, Requiem æternam.
Let us pray.
AND now to give greater value to our feeble prayers, turning to Thee, most loving JESUS, we humbly pray Thee thyself to offer to the eternal FATHER the sacred wounds of thy feet, hands and side, together with thy most precious Blood, and thy agony and death; and do thou also, Mary, Virgin of sorrows, present, together with the most sorrowful Passion of thy well-beloved Son, the sighs, tears and all the sorrows suffered by thee through his sufferings, so that through their merits the souls who suffer in the most ardent flames of purgatory may obtain refreshment, and, freed from this prison of torment, may be clothed with glory in heaven, there to sing the mercies of GOD for ever. Amen.
Absolve, O LORD, the souls of all the faithful departed from every bond of sin, so that by thy aid they may deserve to escape the judgment of wrath, and come to the enjoyment of beatitude in eternal light.
V/. . Eternal rest give unto them, O LORD.
R/. And let perpetual light shine upon them.
V/. From the gate of hell.
R/. Deliver their souls, O LORD.
V/. May they rest in peace. R/. Amen.
V/. O LORD, hear my prayer.
R/. And let my cry come unto Thee.
V/. The LORD be with you.
R/. And with thy spirit.
Let us pray.
O GOD, the CREATOR and REDEEMER of all the faithful, grant to the souls of thy servants departed the remission of all their sins, that through pious supplications they may obtain the pardon they have always desired. Who livest and reignest world without end. Amen. Eternal rest, etc.

413. Prayers.
100 Days, once a day. (See Instructions.) 413 Leo XIII, December 14, 1889.

MY JESUS, by that copious sweat of blood with which Thou didst bedew the ground in the garden, have mercy on the souls of my nearest relations who are suffering in purgatory. PATER, Ave, Requiem æternam.

MY JESUS, by that cruel scourging which Thou didst suffer, bound to the column, have pity on the souls of my other relations and friends who are suffering in purgatory. PATER, Ave, Requiem æternam.

MY JESUS, by that crown of sharpest thorns which pierced thy sacred temples, have mercy on that soul which is most neglected and least prayed for, and on that soul which is furthest from being released from the pains of purgatory. PATER, Ave, Requiem æternam.

MY JESUS, by those sorrowful steps which Thou didst take with the Cross on thy shoulders, have mercy on that soul which is nearest to its departure from purgatory; and by the pains which Thou didst suffer together with thy most holy Mother Mary, when Thou didst meet her on the road to Calvary, deliver from the pains of purgatory those souls who were devout to this beloved Mother. PATER, Ave, Requiem æternam.

MY JESUS, by thy most holy body stretched on the Cross, by thy most holy hands and feet pierced with hard nails, by thy most cruel death, and by thy most holy side laid open with a lance, have pity and mercy on those poor souls ; free them from the awful pains they suffer, call and admit them to thy most sweet embrace in Paradise. PATER, Ave, Requiem æternam.

O HOLY souls, tormented in most cruel pains, as one truly devoted to you, I promise never to forget you, and continually to pray to the Most High for your release. I beseech you to respond to this offering which I make to you, and obtain for me from GOD, with whom you are so powerful on behalf of the living, that I may be freed from all dangers of soul and body ; I beg both for myself and for my relations and benefactors, friends and enemies, pardon for our sins, and the grace of perseverance in good, whereby we may save our souls.

Set us free from all misfortunes, miseries, sicknesses, trials and labours. Obtain for us peace of heart; assist us in all our actions; succour us promptly in all our spiritual and temporal needs; console and defend us in our dangers. Pray for the supreme Pontiff, for the exaltation of holy Church, for peace between nations, for Christian princes, and for tranquillity among peoples ; and obtain that we may one day all rejoice together in Paradise. Amen.

414. Prayer for the Dead.
50 Days. T.Q. Applicable only to the dead. (See Instructions.) 414 Leo XIII, Br. March 22, 1902.

V/. Requiem æternam * dona eis, DOMINE.
R/. Et lux perpetua luceat eis.

V/. Eternal rest give to them, O LORD.
R/. And let perpetual light shine upon them.

415. VV. & RR. for the Dead.
300 Days. T.Q. Applicable only to the dead. (See Instructions.) 415 Pius X, February 13, 1908.

V/. Requiem æternam * dona eis, DOMINE.
R/. Et lux perpetua luceat eis.
V/. Requiescant in pace. R/. Amen.

V/. Eternal rest give to them, O LORD.
R/. And let perpetual light shine upon them.
V/. May they rest in peace. R/. Amen.

XVII. MISCELLANEOUS
416. Visits to the Churches of the Stations.
i. 40 Years and as many Quarantines, to all the faithful, every time that during Lent, with contrite hearts and devotion, they visit the Churches of the Stations in the manner prescribed in the book printed for the purpose in Rome. ii. Plenary, to all persons who shall have made the visit as above three times, each visit on a different day. I, II, III, IV. 416 Pius VI, July 9, 1777; Leo XII, February 28, 1827.

The method prescribed to be used is as follows: First, to visit some church, and say there the prayers appointed in the book to the Blessed Sacrament, to the Blessed Virgin, and to the holy martyrs; then to go to the Church of the Station, saying on the way the Psalm Miserere, Paler, Ave, and Gloria, five times, and then the Steps of the Passion of our Lord Jesus Christ; and lastly, whilst at the Church itself, to say the Litanies of the Saints, with the versicles and prayers assigned, and at the end the Psalm De profundis, etc. All unlearned persons, however, and others who do not possess this book of the Stations, may gain the same Indulgences by saying at the two churches which they visit such prayers as their own devotion suggests to them, and as are suitable to their capacity; and while they go from one church to the other they are to say a third part of their Rosary with the Litanies, and on leaving the Church of the Station to end their visit with the Psalm De profundis, or else with one Pater noster, one Ave Maria and a Requiem æternam for the holy souls in purgatory.

N.B. Nuns and others dwelling in monasteries and communities may participate in the benefit of these Indulgences, provided that they keep the method prescribed and visit their own churches; these Indulgences may also be gained by the sick and prisoners, provided they supply what they are unable to perform by doing some good work enjoined them by their own confessor.

To gain the specific Indulgence attached to the churches and days specified below, a simple visit is all that is required for partial Indulgences; Confession and Communion must be made for Plenary Indulgences.

These Indulgences may be gained in certain churches and chapels out of Rome, to which this special privilege has been granted.

Days and Churches of the Stations in Rome.

January 1. Circumcision of our Lord Jesus Christ. Station, St Mary beyond the Tiber. Thirty Years and Thirty Quarantines. The same Indulgence for the next four Stations.

January 6. The Epiphany of our Lord. St Peter on the Vatican.

Septuagesima Sunday. St Laurence outside the Walls.

Sexagesima. St Paul outside the Walls.

Quinquagesima. St Peter on the Vatican.

Ash Wednesday. St Sabina in St Alexius, and St Mary in Cosmedin, called Bocca della Verità. Fifteen Years and Fifteen Quarantines.

Thursday after Ash Wednesday. St George in Velabro, and the Church of JESUS and Mary. Ten Years and Ten Quarantines. The same Indulgence is granted for all the following days till the fourth Sunday in Lent.

Friday after Ash Wednesday. SS. John and Paul, and St Gregory on the Celian Hill.

Saturday. St Tryphon and St Augustine.

First Sunday in Lent. St John Lateran.

Monday. St Peter s Chains and St John della Pigna.

Tuesday. St Anastasia.

Wednesday (Ember Day). St Mary Major.

Thursday. St Laurence in Panisperna.

Friday (Ember Day). The Twelve Holy Apostles.

Saturday (Ember Day). St Peter on the Vatican.

Second Sunday in Lent. St Mary in Domnica, called the Church of the Navicella, and St Gregory on the Celian.

Monday. St Mary Major and St Clement.

Tuesday. St Balbina.

Wednesday. St Cecilia beyond the Tiber.

Thursday. St Mary beyond the Tiber.

Friday. St Vitalis.

Saturday. SS. Marcellinus and Peter, near the Lateran Basilica.

Third Sunday in Lent. St Laurence outside the Walls.

Monday. St Mark.

Tuesday. St Pudentiana.

Wednesday. SS. Sixtus, Nereus and Achilleus.

Thursday. SS. Cosmas and Damian, in the Forum.

Friday. St Laurence in Lucina.

Saturday. SS. Caius and Susanna, and St Mary of the Angels at the Baths.

Fourth Sunday in Lent. The Holy Cross in Jerusalem. Fif teen Years and Fifteen Quarantines.

Monday. The Four Saints crowned with Martyrdom. Ten Years and Ten Quarantines. The same Indulgences for all the Stations following till Palm Sunday.

Tuesday. St Laurence in St Damasus, and St Andrew della Valle.

Wednesday. St Paul outside the Walls.

Thursday. SS. Martin and Silvester on the Hills, and St Silvester in Capite.

Ftiday. St Eusebius and St Bibiana.

Saturday. St Nicholas in Carcere.

Passion Sunday. St Peter on the Vatican, and St Lazarus.
> Monday. St Chrysogonus beyond the Tiber.
> Tuesday. St Cyriacus in St Mary in Viâ Latâ, and SS. Quiricus and Julitta on the Hills.
> Wednesday. St Marcellus.
> Thursday. St Apollinaris.
> Friday. St Stephen on the Celian.
> Saturday. St John before the Latin Gate, and St Cæsareus.

Palm Sunday. St John Lateran. Twenty-five Years and Twenty-five Quarantines.
> Monday in Holy Week. St Praxede. Ten Years and Ten Quarantines, also for next three days.
> Tuesday in Holy Week. St Prisca, and St Mary at the Gate of the People.
> Wednesday in Holy Week. St Mary Major.
> Thursday in Holy Week. St John Lateran. Plenary. I, II.
> Good Friday. Holy Cross in Jerusalem. Thirty Years and Thirty Quarantines.
> Holy Saturday. St John Lateran. The same Indulgence.

Easter Day. St Mary Major. Plenary. I, II.

Easter Monday. St Peter on the Vatican, and St Onuphrius -Thirty Years and Thirty Quarantines. The same till Ascension Day.

Easter Tuesday. St Paul outside the Walls.

Wednesday in Easter Week. St Laurence outside the Walls.
Thursday in Easter Week. The Twelve Holy Apostles.
Friday in Easter Week. St Mary of the Martyrs, called La Rotonda.
Saturday in Easter Week. St John Lateran.
Low Sunday. St Pancratius and St Mary della Scala.
April 25. Feast of St Mark the Evangelist. St Peter on the Vatican.
Rogation Monday. St Mary Major.
Rogation Tuesday. St John Lateran.
Rogation Wednesday. St Peter on the Vatican.
Ascension Day. St Peter on the Vatican. Plenary. I, II.
Saturday, Vigil of Pentecost. St John Lateran. Ten Years and Ten Quarantines.
Whit Sunday. St Peter on the Vatican. Thirty Years and Thirty Quarantines. The same to Saturday in Whitsun Week.
Whit Monday. St Peters Chains.
Whit Tuesday. St Anastasia.
Wednesday in Whitsun Week (Ember Day). St Mary Major.
Thursday in Whitsun Week. St Laurence outside the Walls.
Friday in Whitsun Week (Ember Day). The Twelve Holy Apostles.
Saturday in Whitsun Week (Ember Day). St Peter on the Vatican.
Wednesday in September (Ember Day). St Mary Major. Ten Years and Ten Quarantines. The same to Third Sunday in Advent.
Friday in September (Ember Day]. The Twelve Holy Apostles.
Saturday in September (Ember Day]. St Peter on the Vatican.
First Sunday in Advent. St Mary Major.
Second Sunday in Advent. Holy Cross in Jerusalem.
Third Sunday in Advent. St Peter on the Vatican. Fifteen Years and Fifteen Quarantines.
Wednesday in December (Ember Day]. St Mary Major. Ten Years and Ten Quarantines. The same up to Christmas Eve.
Friday in December (Ember Day]. The Twelve Holy Apostles.
Saturday in December (Ember Day]. St Peter on the Vatican. Fourth Sunday in Advent. The Twelve Holy Apostles.
December 24. Christmas Eve. St Mary Major. Fifteen Years and Fifteen Quarantines. The same up to the Third Mass on Christmas Day.
December 25. Christmas Day. First Mass. The Altar of the Holy Crib, in St Mary Major.
Second Mass. St Anastasia.
Third Mass, and the rest of the day. St Peter on the Vatican, and St Mary Major. Plenary. I, II.
December 26. St Stephen the first Martyr. St Stephen on the Celian. Thirty Years and Thirty Quarantines. The same on two following days.

December 27. St John the Apostle and Evangelist. St Mary Major.
December 28. Holy Innocents, Martyrs. St Paul outside the Walls.

417. Visit to the Seven Churches and the Seven Privileged Altars.

The custom of visiting the seven principal Churches in Rome is of most ancient institution. They are as follows : St Peter on the Vatican ; St Paul and Sebastian outside the Walls; St John Lateran; the Holy Cross in Jerusalem; St Laurence outside the Walls; and St Mary Major. Whoever between first Vespers and sunset of the day following, shall visit these Seven Churches, may gain the many Indulgences with which these Churches have been enriched for every day in the year, and a Plenary Indulgence. I, II, III.

Most ancient also is the custom of visiting in these Churches, but especially in St Peter on the Vatican, the seven privileged Altars. The seven Altars in St Peters are:
1. The Altar of Our Lady, commonly called the " Gregoriana";
2. Of SS. Processus and Martinianus ;
3. Of St Michael the Archangel;
4. Of St Petronilla, Virgin ;
5. Of Our Lady, commonly called "of the Pillar";
6. Of the Holy Apostles SS. Simon and Jude;
7. Of St Gregory the Great.

Any of the faithful who shall visit devoutly these seven Altars may obtain the numerous Indulgences granted to these seven Altars by successive Pontiffs.

The same Indulgences may be gained outside Rome in churches to which the privileges of the Seven Churches or the Seven Altars have been extended. 417 Pius IX, Br. January 26, 1866.

418. The Portiuncula.

Plenary, to all as often as they visit any one of the churches of the three Orders of St Francis, and many other churches and chapels having this privilege, between first Vespers on August i and sunset on August 2. I, II, IV. T.Q. (See Instructions.) 418 Honorius III, 1223; Gregory XV, Br. July 4, 1622; Ven. Innocent XI, Br. January 12, 1687; Pius IX, July 12, 1847; Leo XIII, July 14, 1894
N.B. The time for Confession is extended to July 30.

419. The Gradual or Penitential Psalms.

50 Days, on the days prescribed by the Rubric of the Roman Breviary. (See Instructions.) 419 Pius V, Bl. July 9, 1568; April 15, 1571.

420. Christian Doctrine.

i. Seven Years to all masters of schools who, on feast days, shall take their scholars to be instructed in Christian Doctrine, and shall themselves instruct them in it.
ii. 100 Days, to those masters who, on working days, explain Christian Doctrine in their schools.
iii. 100 Days, to fathers and mothers, every time they instruct their children and servants in Christian Doctrine.
iv. 100 Days, to all the faithful, every time they employ themselves for half an hour in studying the Catechism.
v. Seven Years and Seven Quarantines, to adults every time they assist at public Catechism, in church or chapel.
vi. Plenary, on Christmas Day, Easter Day and SS. Peter and Paul, to adults who make a practice of assisting at public Catechism. I. II, IV.
vii. Three Years, on all feasts of our Lady, to those of every age who make a practice of assisting in school or church at instruction in Christian Doctrine. I.
viii. Seven Years, for the same. I, II
(See Instructions) 420 Paul V, Br. October 6, 1607; Clement XII, Br. May 16, 1736; Pius IX, July 18, 1877.

421. Mental Prayer.

i. Plenary, once a month, to all the faithful who make mental prayer devoutly for half an hour, or at least a quarter of an hour, a day. I,II, IV.
ii. Plenary, once a month, to those who frequently teach or learn how to make mental prayer. I, II, IV.

iii. Seven Years and Seven Quarantines, every time, for teaching- or learning, in public or private, how to make mental prayer, I,II. (See Instructions.) 421 Benedict XIV, Br. December 16, 1746

422. Explanation of the Gospel.
i. Seven Years, to all who assist at the same in their parish church on Sundays and festivals.
ii. Plenary, on Christmas Day, Epiphany, Easter Day, Pentecost, and SS. Peter and Paul, to those who make a practice of assisting at the same. I, II. (See Instructions.) 422 Benedict XIV, July 31, 1756; Pius VI, December 12, 1784.

423. Prayer after saying Office.
The remission, in the case of persons under obligation to say office, of temporal punishment due for defects and faults committed through human frailty in the recital of Office, whether the Divine Office or that of our Lady. The prayer must be said kneeling, except in cases of inability. (See Instructions.) 423 Leo X; Pius IX, July 26, 1855.

SACROSANCTÆ et Individuæ Trinitati, Crucifixi DOMINI nostri JESU CHRISTI humanitati, beatissimæ et gloriosissimæ semperque Virginis Mariæ fœcundæ integritati, et omnium Sanctorum universitati sit sempiterna laus, honor, virtus, et gloria ab omni creatura, nobisque remissio omnium peccatorum, per infinita sæcula sæculorum. Amen.

V/. Beata viscera Mariæ Virginis, quæ portaverunt æterni PATRIS FILIUM.
R/. Et beata ubera quæ lactaverunt CHRISTUM DOMINUM. PATER noster, Ave Maria.

424. Prayers to be said after the Sacrosanctæ
i. 300 Days, once a day, for each prayer. ii. Plenary, once a month (I, II, IV) for each prayer. (See Instructions.) 424 Pius X, December 2, 1905

I

O CLEMENTISSIME JESU, gratias ago tibi ex toto corde meo. Propitius esto mihi vilissimo peccatori. Ego hanc actionem offero divino Cordi tuo emendandam atque perficiendam, ad laudem et gloriam sanctissimi Nominis tui et beatissimæ Matris tuæ, ad salutem animæ meæ totiusque ecclesiæ tuæ. Amen.

II

BENEDICTUM sit Cor amantissimum et dulcissimum Nomen DOMINI nostri JESU CHRISTI et gloriosissimæ Virginis Mariæ Matris ejus in æternum et ultra.

425. Prayer for the Conversion of the Dutch.
i. 200 Days. ii. Plenary, once a month. Any form of prayer may be used. (See Instructions.) 425 Pius X, March 14, 1906.

426. The Divine Praises.
i. One Year. T.Q. ii. Two Years, when said publicly after Mass or Benediction. iii. Plenary, once a month. I, II, III, IV (See Instructions.) 426 Pius VII, Card. Vic. July 23, 1801 ; Pius IX, August 8, 1847; Leo XIII, February 2, 1897.

BLESSED be GOD.
Blessed be his holy Name.
Blessed be JESUS CHRIST, true GOD and true Man.
Blessed be the Name of JESUS.
Blessed be his most Sacred Heart.
Blessed be JESUS in the most holy Sacrament of the Altar.
Blessed be the great Mother of GOD, Mary most holy.
Blessed be her holy and immaculate Conception.
Blessed be the name of Mary, Virgin and Mother.
Blessed be GOD in his Angels and in his Saints.

427. Ejaculations for a Happy Death.
i. 300 Days. T.Q. ii. 100 Days, for saying one of the same. (See Instructions.) 427 Pius VII, April 28. 1807

JESUS, Mary, Joseph, I give you my heart and my soul.
JESUS, Mary, Joseph, assist me in my last agony.
JESUS, Mary, Joseph, may I breathe forth my soul in peace with you.

428. Beati Mortui, etc.
300 Days. T.Q. (See Instructions.) 428 Pius X, January 12, 1906

BEATI mortui, qui in DOMINO moriuntur.	BLESSED are the dead who die in the LORD.
O mi DEUS, moriendum mihi est certo, sed nescio quando, quomodo, ubi moriar; hoc unum scio, me in æternum periturum, si in peccato lethali expirem.	O my GOD, I have certainly to die, but I know not when, how, or where I shall die; this only I know: that if I die in mortal sin, I shall be lost forever.
Beatissima Virgo Maria, Mater DEI Sancta ,ora pro me peccatore, nunc et in hora mortis meæ. Amen.	Most blessed Virgin Mary, holy Mother of GOD, pray for me a sinner, now and at the hour of my death. Amen.

429. Prayer for those in their Agony.
i. 300 Days, T.Q. ii. Plenary, once a month. I,II,IV (See Instructions.) 429 Pius VII, Card. Pro-Vic., April 18, 1809.
Pater noster thrice in memory of the Passion of Christ, and Ave Maria thrice in memory of the Sorrows of Mary assisting at the same. They are to be said kneeling unless physical infirmity makes it impossible.

430. Visiting the Sick in Hospitals.
100 Days, each visit. (See Instructions.) 430 Pius VI, Card. Vic., February 28, 1778.

431. Almsgiving.
i. Seven Years and Seven Quarantines, ii. Plenary, on the day itself, I, II, IV. iii. 100 Days, to members of the family and servants assisting at least by their presence. (See Instructions.) 431 Pius VII, June 13, 1815.
This Devotion consists in giving food to three poor persons in honour of JESUS, Mary and Joseph.

432. Prayer for Deaf-Mutes.
100 Days, T.Q. (See Instructions, p. i.) 432 Pius X, December 5, 1906.
OMOST merciful JESUS, who didst show such tenderness towards little children, who enjoyed the privilege of being caressed by thy divine hands, and didst say that whoever received one such innocent child, received Thee; extend, we pray Thee, the hand of thy providence over the little ones who, through being deprived of hearing and speech, are exposed to so many dangers of soul and body. Diffuse the spirit of thy ardent charity into Christian hearts, that they may come to their aid, and send down abundant graces on those who help in providing for this portion of thy flock a refuge where their innocence can be secure, and they can find food and affection. Amen.

433. Propagation of the Faith.
i. 100 Days, T.Q. ii. Plenary, on or during the Octaves of the Immaculate Conception, the feast of St Joseph, and that of St Francis Xavier. I, II, IV. (See Instructions.) 433 Pius IX, Prop., April 26, 1857
This Devotion consists in giving help, by contributions or personal service to the Missions, or by exhorting others to help them, together with the recital of the Ave Maria thrice.

434. Against an Unprovided Death.
i. 100 Days. T.Q. ii. Plenary, on Holy Thursday and Good Friday, and on the two feasts of the Holy Cross, May 3 and September 14, to those who, having made the Devotion every day for a year, visit the Holy Sepulchre, or the Blessed Sacrament in Church. I, II, III, IV. (See Instructions.) 434 Pius VII, March 2, 1816.
HEAR us, O GOD of our salvation, and issue not the decree for the completion of our days before Thou forgivest us our sins; and because penance avails not in hell, and there is no room for amendment in the pit, therefore we humbly pray and beseech Thee here on earth that, giving us time to pray for pardon, Thou wouldst give us also forgiveness of our sins. Through CHRIST our LORD. Amen.
Take away, merciful LORD, all errors from thy faithful people, avert from them the sudden destruction of the wasting- pestilence; and those whose wanderings Thou dost justly chastise, do Thou mercifully pity when corrected. Through CHRIST our LORD. Amen.

Ant. Sin no longer, O my soul; think upon the sudden change from sin to endless torments. There, in hell, penance is not accepted, and tears profit not. Turn, then, whilst thou hast time; cry out and say, Have mercy upon me, O my GOD.

Ant. In the midst of life we are in death; but to whom can we look to be our helper save Thee, O LORD, who art justly angry with us because of our sins? O holy GOD, holy and strong-, holy and merciful SAVIOUR, deliver us not over to a bitter death.

V/. Lest, overtaken by the day of death, we seek time for penance, and be unable to find it:
R/. Hearken, O LORD, and have mercy on us, for we have sinned against Thee.

WE beseech Thee, ALMIGHTY GOD, receive in thy fatherly pity thy people who flee unto Thee from thine anger; that those who fear to be chastised by the rod of thy majesty through sudden death, may be made worthy to rejoice in thy pardon. Through CHRIST our LORD. Amen.

We beseech Thee, ALMIGHTY GOD, graciously incline thine ear to the assembly of thy Church, and let thy mercy to us prevent thine anger, for if Thou shouldst mark iniquities there shall no creature be able to stand before Thee; and in that same admirable charity whereby Thou didst create us, pardon us sinners, and destroy not the work of thy own hands by sudden death. Through CHRIST our LORD. Amen.

Hear our prayers, O LORD, and enter not into judgment with thy servants; for, knowing that there is no justice in us on which we can dare to presume, we acknowledge no other fount of mercy whereby we can be washed from our sins, delivered from our infirmities, and especially from sudden death, but only Thee, O GOD. Through CHRIST our LORD. Amen.

O GOD, in whose sight every heart trembles and every conscience is awed ; show forth thy mercy upon us, thy suppliants, that we, who trust not in the excellence of our own merit, may never experience thy judgments by suddenness of death, but may receive Thy pardon. Through CHRIST our LORD. Amen.

Prayer.
MOST merciful LORD JESUS, by thy agony and bloody sweat, and by thy death, deliver me, I beseech Thee, from sudden and unprepared death. O most gentle LORD JESUS, by thy cruel and ignominious scourging and crowning with thorns, by thy Cross and bitter Passion, and by thy own great goodness, I humbly pray Thee let me not die unprepared and pass from this life without the Holy Sacraments. JESUS, my best be loved, my LORD! by all thy travails and all thy sorrows, by thy Precious Blood, and by thy most holy wounds, and by those last words spoken by Thee upon the Cross "My GOD, my GOD, why hast Thou forsaken Me?" and again, "FATHER, into thy hands I commend my spirit" most ardently I pray Thee, free me from sudden death. Thy hands, O my REDEEMER, have wholly made and formed me; oh, suffer not death to take me unawares; grant me, I beseech Thee, time for penance; vouchsafe me a happy passage when I am in thy grace, that in the world to come I may love Thee with my whole heart, and praise and bless Thee for ever and for ever. Amen.

PATER and AVE five times, in memory of the Passion of our Lord Jesus Christ, and Ave thrice, to the Blessed Virgin, Mother of Sorrows.

435. Ejaculation.
50 Days. T.Q. (See Instructions.) 435 Pius X, June 9, 1906.
Nos, JESU, Maria, et Joseph bone, Benedicite nunc et in mortis agone.

436. In Honour of the Blessed Trinity, etc.
100 Days, on every Sunday. (See Instructions.) 436 Pius VII, July 2, 1816.

I. THE BLESSED TRINITY.

WITH our whole hearts and lips we acknowledge, praise and bless Thee, O FATHER unbegotten; Thee, O only begotten SON; Thee, O HOLY SPIRIT and PARACLETE; O holy and undivided Trinity; to Thee be glory for ever.

V/. Let us bless the FATHER, SON, and HOLY SPIRIT.
R/. Let us praise and exalt Him for ever.

Let us pray.
O ALMIGHTY and everlasting GOD, who hast granted to thy servants in the confession of the true faith to acknowledge the glory of the eternal Trinity, and in the power of thy Majesty to adore the Unity; we beseech Thee that by the strength of the same faith we may ever be defended from all adversity; through CHRIST our LORD. Amen.

II. ALL ANGELS AND SAINTS.

ANGELS, Archangels, Thrones and Dominations, Principalities and Powers, and Virtues of Heaven, Cherubim and Seraphim, Patriarchs and Prophets, holy Doctors of the Law, Apostles, all Martyrs of CHRIST, holy Confessors, Virgins of the LORD, Anchorites, and all Saints, intercede for us.
V/. All ye holy men and women, saints of GOD.
R/. Intercede for us.

Let us pray.
ALMIGHTY and everlasting GOD, who hast willed that we should profit by the merits of all thy saints, we beseech Thee that, as our intercessors are multiplied, so thou wouldst bestow upon us that abundance of mercy which we desire. Through CHRIST our LORD. Amen.

437. Spiritual Canticles.
i. One Year, to all the faithful every time they promote the singing of the Spiritual Canticles. ii. 100 Days, every time anyone practises this devotion, iii. Plenary, once a month, for promoting" and practising this exercise, during the month. I, II, IV.
(See Instructions.) 437 Pius VII, Mem. January 16, 1817.

438. Prayer, with Ejaculation.
i. 40 Days, once a day. ii. Plenary, once a month. I, II, III, IV. (See Instructions.) 438 Pius VII, April 21, 1818
O FATHER of mercies, and source of every good! I humbly beg Thee, through the most sacred and most loving Heart of JESUS, thy well-beloved SON, our LORD and REDEEMER, in whom Thou art always well pleased, vouchsafe to grant me the grace of a lively faith, a firm hope, and an ardent charity for Thee and for my neighbour. Grant me, besides, the grace of a true sorrow for all my sins, together with a most firm purpose of never offending Thee in the future, that I may always live according to thy divine good pleasure, fulfil thy most holy will in all things with a generous and willing heart, and persevere in thy love unto the end of my life. Amen.
O MOST blessed Virgin Mary, Mother of my LORD and REDEEMER, I entreat thee and beseech thee to effect by thy mercy that, in all the dangers and necessities of my soul, I may flee to thee, pray to thee, and call upon thee for help.

439. Prayers for a Happy Death.
i. 100 Days, once a day. ii. Plenary, once a month. I, II, III, IV. (See Instructions.) 439 Leo XII, August 11, 1824.
O LORD JESUS, GOD of goodness, and FATHER of mercies, I draw nigh to Thee with a contrite and humble heart; to Thee I recommend the last hour of my life, and that judgment which awaits me afterwards.
When my feet, benumbed with death, shall admonish me, that my course in this life is drawing to an end, merciful JESUS, have mercy on me.
When my hands, cold and trembling, shall no longer be able to clasp the crucifix, and shall let it fall against my will on my bed of suffering, merciful JESUS, have mercy on me.
When my eyes, dim and troubled at the approach of death, shall fix themselves on Thee, my last and only support, merciful JESUS, have mercy on me.
When my lips, cold and trembling, pronounce for the last time thy adorable Name, merciful JESUS, have mercy on me.
When my face, pale and livid, shall inspire the beholders with pity and dismay; when my hair, bathed in the sweat of death, and stiffening on my head, shall forebode my approaching end, merciful JESUS, have mercy on me.
When my ears, soon to be for ever shut to the discourse of men, shall be open to that irrevocable decree which is to fix my doom for all eternity, merciful JESUS, have mercy on me.
When my imagination, agitated by dreadful spectres, shall be sunk in an abyss of anguish; when my soul, affrighted with the sight of my iniquities and the terrors of thy judgments, shall have to fight against the angels of darkness, who will endeavour to conceal thy mercies from my eyes, and plunge me into despair, merciful JESUS, have mercy on me.
When my poor heart, oppressed with suffering and exhausted by its continual struggles with the enemies of its salvation, shall feel the pangs of death, merciful JESUS, have mercy on me.

When the last tear, the forerunner of my dissolution, shall drop from my eyes, receive it as a sacrifice of expiation for my sins; grant that I may expire the victim of penance; and then, in that dreadful moment, merciful JESUS, have mercy on me.

When my friends and relations, encircling my bed, shall be moved with compassion for me, and invoke thy clemency in my behalf, merciful JESUS, have mercy on me.

When I shall have lost the use of my senses, when the world shall have vanished from my sight, when I shall groan with anguish in my last agony and the pangs of death, merciful JESUS, have mercy on me.

When my last sighs shall force my soul to issue from my body, accept them as born of a loving impatience to come to thee; merciful JESUS, have mercy on me.

When my soul, trembling on my lips, shall bid adieu to the world, and leave my body lifeless, pale and cold, receive this separation as a homage which I willingly pay to thy Divine Majesty, and in that last moment of my mortal life, merciful JESUS, have mercy on me.

When at length my soul, admitted to thy presence, shall first behold the immortal splendour of thy Majesty, reject it not, but receive me into the loving embrace of thy mercy, where I may for ever sing thy praises; merciful JESUS, have mercy on me.

Let us pray.

O GOD, who hast doomed all men to die, but hast concealed from all the hour of their death, grant that I may pass my days in the practice of holiness and justice, and that I may be made worthy to quit this world in the embrace of thy love, through the merits of our LORD JESUS CHRIST, who liveth and reigneth with Thee in the unity of the HOLY SPIRIT. Amen.

440. Invocations and Petitions.

i. 300 Days, once a day. IV. ii. Plenary, once a month on any of the three last days of the month, I ,II, III, IV. (See Instructions.) 440 Leo XII, March 3, 1827.

O FATHER ! O SON! O HOLY GHOST ! O Holy Trinity! O JESUS! O Mary! O ye blessed Angels of GOD, all ye Saints of Paradise, men and women, obtain for me these graces, which I ask through the Precious Blood of JESUS CHRIST:

1. Ever to do the holy will of GOD.
2. Ever to live in union with GOD.
3. Not to think of anything but GOD.
4. To love GOD alone.
5. To do all for GOD.
6. To seek only the glory of GOD.
7. To sanctify myself solely for GOD.
8. To know well my own utter nothingness.
9. Ever to know more and more the will of my GOD.
10. (Here ask for any special grace.)

MARY most holy, offer to the Eternal FATHER the most Precious Blood of JESUS CHRIST for my soul, for the holy souls in purgatory, for the needs of Holy Church, for the conversion of sinners, and for all the world.

Then say Gloria PATRI thrice to the most holy Blood of Jesus Christ, Ave Maria once to most holy Mary sorrowing, and Requiem æternam once for the holy souls in purgatory.

441. Prayers in Times of Calamity.

40 Days, once a day. (See Instructions.) 441 Gregory XVI, August 21, 1837.

MERCY of our GOD, encompass us, and deliver us from every plague. Gloria PATRI.

ETERNAL FATHER, sign us with the Blood of the Immaculate Lamb, as Thou didst sign the dwellings of thy people. Gloria PATRI.

MOST precious Blood of JESUS our Love, cry for mercy for us from thy Divine FATHER, and deliver us. Gloria PATRI.

WOUNDS of my JESUS, mouths of love and mercy, speak for us in pity to the Eternal FATHER ; hide us within yourselves and deliver us. Gloria PATRI.

ETERNAL FATHER, JESUS is ours; ours his Blood, ours his infinite merits ; to Thee we offer ourselves wholly: then, if Thou lovest Him, and boldest precious this gift we make Thee, Thou oughtest to deliver us : for this we hope with fullest confidence. Gloria PATRI.

ETERNAL FATHER, Thou desirest not the death of a sinner, but rather that he should be converted and live: in thy mercy grant that we may live before Thee and be for ever thine. Gloria PATRI.

SAVE us, CHRIST our SAVIOUR, by the virtue of thy holy Cross ; Thou who didst save Peter in the sea, have mercy upon us.

MARY, Mother of .mercy, pray for us, and we shall be delivered; Mary, our advocate, speak for us, and we shall be saved.

The LORD justly scourgeth us for our sins ; but do thou, Mary, plead for us, for thou art our most tender Mother.

Mary, in thy JESUS, and in thee, have we put our hope ; oh, let us never be confounded. Salve Regina (see p. 184).

442. Prayers for the Conversion of Japan.

i. 40 Days. T.Q. ii Plenary, twice a year, on any days they choose, to those who have prayed for this intention at least once a week, or have frequently exhorted others to do so. I, II, III, IV. (See Instructions.) 442 Pius IX, Prop. November 14, 1847

Prayer for this intention must be said at the visit.

443. Prayer in any Plague or Trouble.

100 Days. T.Q. (See Instructions.) 443 Pius IX, November 8, 1849.

HELP us, O GOD of our salvation, and for the glory of thy name deliver us : be merciful to our sins for thy name's sake.

Psalm liii.

SAVE me, O LORD, in thy name; and judge me in thy strength.

GOD, hear my prayer; give ear to the words of my mouth ;

For strangers have risen up against me, and the mighty have sought after my soul, and they have not set GOD before their eyes.

For, behold, GOD is my helper, and the LORD is the protector of my soul.

Turn away evil from me upon my enemies, and scatter them in thy truth.

I will freely sacrifice to Thee; and will give praise, O GOD, to thy name, because it is good.

For Thou hast delivered me out of all my trouble, and mine eye hath looked down upon mine enemies. Gloria PATRI.

V/. For the glory of thy name, deliver us.

R/. And deal mercifully with our sins for thy name's sake.

Let us pray.

LORD, we beseech Thee, in thy pity hear the prayers of thy people; that we who suffer justly for our sins may, for the glory of thy name, mercifully be delivered. Through CHRIST our LORD. **R/.** Amen.

We beseech Thee, therefore, help thy servants, whom Thou hast redeemed with thy Precious Blood.

444. Three Offerings.

i. 300 Days. T.Q. ii. Plenary, once a month. I, II,III, IV. (See Instructions.) 444 Pius IX, Pr. Ma. June 18, 1854.

ETERNAL FATHER, in union with the most holy and Immaculate Virgin, all the blessed in heaven and all the elect upon earth, I offer to Thee the most Precious Blood of JESUS CHRIST, in thanksgiving for the gifts and privileges with which Thou hast enriched Mary, thy most obedient daughter, particularly in her Immaculate Conception. I offer to Thee also this Precious Blood for the conversion of poor sinners, for the propagation and exaltation of thy Holy Church, for the safety and prosperity of our chief pastor, the Bishop of Rome, and according to his intentions. Gloria PATRI.

ETERNAL and Incarnate Word! in union with the most holy and Immaculate Virgin, all the blessed in heaven, and all the elect upon earth, I offer to thee thine own most Precious Blood, in thanksgiving for the gifts and privileges with which Thou hast enriched Mary, thy most loving Mother, particularly in her Immaculate Conception. I offer to thee also this Precious Blood for the conversion of poor sinners, for the propagation and exaltation of thy Holy Church, for the safety and prosperity of our chief pastor, the Bishop of Rome, and according to his intentions. Gloria PATRI.

HOLY and Eternal Spirit! in union with the most holy and Immaculate Virgin, all the blessed in Heaven, and all the elect upon earth, I offer to Thee the most Precious Blood of JESUS, in thanksgiving for the gifts and privileges with which Thou hast enriched Mary, thy most faithful Spouse, particularly in her Immaculate Conception. I offer to Thee also this Precious Blood for the conversion of poor sinners, for the propagation and exaltation of thy Holy Church, for the safety and prosperity of our chief pastor, the Bishop of Rome, and according to his intentions. Gloria PATRI.

PRAYER TO THE MOST HOLY VIRGIN.

MARY, Mother of GOD, most holy and Immaculate Virgin, by the love thou dost ever bear to GOD, by the gratitude thou hast towards Him for the manifold graces and favours with which thou wast enriched by Him, particularly for the privilege of Immaculate Conception granted to thee alone, and by the infinite merits of JESUS CHRIST, thy Divine Son our LORD, we pray thee most earnestly to obtain for us a most perfect and constant devotion towards thyself, and a full trust that through thy most mighty intercession we shall receive all the graces which we ask. Certain henceforth of obtaining them from thy great goodness, with hearts overflowing with joy and thankfulness, we venerate thee, and say the salutation which the holy archangel Gabriel made to thee. Ave Maria.

445. Prayer of St Benedict Joseph Labre for Times of Necessity.

100 Days. T.Q. (See Instructions) 415 Pius IX, Card. Vic. August 5, 1854.

JESUS CHRISTUS, Rex gloriæ, venit in pace	JESUS CHRIST, the King of Glory, hath come in peace.
DEUS homo factus est.	GOD was made man.
Verbum caro factum est.	The Word was made flesh.
CHRISTUS de Maria Virgine natus est.	CHRIST was born of Mary the Virgin.
CHRISTUS per medium illorum ibat in pace.	CHRIST went thro the midst of them in peace.
CHRISTUS crucifixus est.	CHRIST was crucified.
CHRISTUS mortuus est.	CHRIST died.
CHRISTUS sepultus est.	CHRIST was buried.
CHRISTUS resurrexit.	CHRIST rose from the dead.
CHRISTUS ascendit in cœlum.	CHRIST ascended into heaven.
CHRISTUS vincit.	CHRIST is victorious
CHRISTUS regnat.	CHRIST reigns.
CHRISTUS imperat.	CHRIST is LORD of all.
CHRISTUS ab omni malo nos defendat.	May CHRIST defend us from all evil.
JESUS nobiscum est.	JESUS is with us
PATER, Ave, Gloria.	PATER, Ave, Gloria.

ETERNAL FATHER, by the Blood of JESUS have mercy; sign us with the Blood of the Immaculate Lamb JESUS CHRIST, as Thou didst sign the people of Israel, in order to deliver them from death: and do thou, Mary, Mother of Mercy, pray to GOD and appease Him for us, and obtain for us the grace we ask. Gloria PATRI.

ETERNAL FATHER, by the Blood of JESUS have mercy; save us from the shipwreck of the world, as Thou didst save Noe from the universal deluge: and do thou, Mary, Ark of salvation, pray to GOD and appease Him for us, and obtain for us the grace we ask. Gloria PATRI.

ETERNAL FATHER, by the Blood of JESUS have mercy; deliver us from the plagues which we have deserved for our sins, as Thou didst deliver Lot from the flames of Sodom. And do thou, Mary, our Advocate, pray to GOD and appease Him for us, and obtain for us the grace we ask. Gloria PATRI.

ETERNAL FATHER, by the Blood of JESUS have mercy; comfort us under our present necessities and troubles, as Thou didst comfort Job, Anna and Tobias in their afflictions. And do thou, Mary, Comforter of the afflicted, pray to GOD and appease Him for us, and obtain for us the grace we ask. Gloria PATRI.

ETERNAL FATHER, by the Blood of JESUS have mercy ; Thou who wouldst not the death of a sinner, but rather that he should be converted and live, grant us through thy mercy time for penance; that, filled with contrition and penance for our sins, which are the cause of all our evils, we may live in the holy faith, hope, charity and peace of our LORD JESUS CHRIST. And do thou, Mary, Refuge of sinners, pray to GOD and appease Him for us, and obtain for us the grace we ask. Gloria PATRI.

PRECIOUS Blood of JESUS, our Love, cry unto the Divine FATHER for mercy, pardon, grace and peace for us, for N., and for all the world. Gloria PATRI.

MARY, our Mother and our Hope, pray to GOD for us, for N., and for all, and obtain for us the grace we ask. Gloria PATRI.

ETERNAL FATHER, I offer Thee the Blood of JESUS CHRIST in discharge of all my debt of sin, for the wants of Holy Church, and for the conversion of sinners. Gloria PATRI.

MARY Immaculate, Mother of GOD, pray to JESUS for us, for N., and for all. JESU, Mary, mercy !
St Michael Archangel, St Joseph, SS. Peter and Paul, protectors of all the faithful in the Church of GOD, and all ye Angels and Saints of Paradise, men and women, pray to GOD, and by your intercession obtain grace and mercy for me, for N., and for all. Amen.

446. Prayers for Purity.
i. 300 Days. T.Q. ii. Plenary, once a month. I, II. (See Instructions.) 446 Pius IX, Penit. February 26, 1862.
O JESUS, SON of the living GOD, brightness of eternal light, who from all eternity wast begotten most pure in the bosom of the Eternal FATHER, and w r ho in time didst will to be born of a most pure and immaculate Virgin, I, thy Creature full of infirmity, beg of Thee, with all my heart, to preserve me pure in mind and body; and do Thou cause to be renewed most abundantly in thy holy Church the virtue of holy Purity for thy greater glory and the salvation of the souls Thou hast redeemed.
O most pure and ever-immaculate Virgin Mary, Daughter of the Eternal FATHER, Mother of the Eternal SON, and Spouse of the HOLY GHOST, august and living temple of the most adorable Trinity, lily of purity and mirror without stain, obtain for me, dear Mother, I beseech thee, from the good JESUS, purity of mind and body, and beg of Him to cause this beautiful virtue to flourish more and more among all classes of the faithful.
O most chaste Spouse of Mary Immaculate, glorious St Joseph, who didst merit to receive from GOD the singular privilege of being the reputed Father of Innocence itself, JESUS CHRIST, and spotless guardian of the Virgin of virgins, obtain for me, I beseech thee, the love of JESUS, my SAVIOUR and GOD, and the special protection of Mary my most blessed Mother; grant, O blessed Joseph, protector of all chaste souls, that this thy beloved virtue of holy purity may be better loved by me and by all men.
And thou who didst so deeply love JESUS, Mary and Joseph, St Bernadine, my special advocate and example, model of Christian modesty, restorer in our times of piety and holy living, present my prayers, I beseech thee, to the Holy Family, and implore that, together with piety and the fear of GOD, holy purity of soul and body may reign in all Christian families and in all children of our Mother, the holy Roman Church. Amen.

447. Temperance Pledge.
300 Days. (See Instructions.) 447 Pius X, Br. March 29, 1904.
O GOD, my FATHER, to show my love for Thee, to make reparation to thy wounded honour, to obtain the salvation of souls, I firmly purpose to take this day neither wine, nor beer, nor any intoxicating drink. I offer Thee this act of mortification in union with the sacrifice of thy SON JESUS CHRIST, who daily offers Himself a victim on the altar for thy greater glory. Amen.

448. Salutation and Answer.
50 Days. T.Q. (See Instructions.) 448 Pius IX, September 26, 1864.
PRAISED be JESUS and Mary. Now and for ever.

449. For the Sovereign Pontiff.
i. 300 Days, once a day. ii. Plenary, once a month, I ,II, III, IV. (See Instructions.) 449 Pius IX, November 26, 1876.

V/. Oremus pro Pontifice nostro N.
R/. DOMINUS conservet eum, et vivificet eum, et beatum faciat eum in terra, et non tradat eum in an imam inimicorum ejus.
PATER noster. Ave Maria.

V/. Let us pray for our Pontiff N.
R/. The LORD preserve him and give him life, and make him blessed upon earth, and deliver him not up to the will of his enemies. PATER noster. Ave Maria.

450. Prayer for Pope Pius X.
COMPOSED BY H.E. CARDINAL CAPECELATRO, ARCHBISHOP OF CAPUA.
300 Days. T.Q. (See Instructions.) 450 Pius X, March 1, 1908.
O JESUS, Divine REDEEMER, Father of the great family called the Catholic Church, in these days of fear and bitter trial come to our aid. We pray Thee for all the Church, but especially for him who holds thy place here on earth, Pope Pius X. He loves Thee fervently, and desires to restore all things to Thee. Now having completed his fifty years of the priesthood, he strives with all his might to imitate Thee in his life,

praying, loving and sacrificing himself for the salvation of souls. O JESUS, mercifully hear the prayers which we offer to Thee for thy Vicar, true apostle of faith and charity. Respond to the ardent desire which he has to see our lives and the lives of all our brethren in the Church reformed. Give ever more and more light of supernatural wisdom to his intellect, and inflame more and more in him that burning charity which Thou hast diffused into his heart by the HOLY SPIRIT. Grant that he may have the longed-for consolation of seeing accomplished in his day that strict union of the sons of the Church for which Thou didst pray shortly before thy death, saying : *Grant, O FATHER, that all my followers -may be one with Me, as I am one with Thee.* Unite then, O JESUS, around the shepherd of shepherds, thy Vicar, all the flock of the Church in the unity of faith and love. Grant that each of her children may remember that Thou didst empty thyself, becoming obedient unto death, even the death of the Cross. Thus will all who glory in the name of Catholic be humble, obedient and devoted to thy Vicar. Grant him, O LORD, this consolation, so earnestly desired by him, and by us all. O LORD, LORD JESUS, we hope in Thee. Grant us (in this year of Jubilee) to sing the hymn of thy peace, that hymn of peace which the angels sing in Heaven. Amen.

451. For the Conversion of Africa.
i. 300 Days. T.Q. ii. Plenary, once a month, I, II, III, IV. (See Instructions) 451 Leo XIII, June 23, 1885 ; March 29, 1889.

N.B. Persons unable to read or otherwise hindered may substitute Pater, Ave and Gloria twice.

LET us pray also that for the most unhappy peoples of Africa, that Almighty GOD may at length remove the curse of Cham from their hearts, and give them that blessing which can only be obtained in JESUS CHRIST, our GOD and LORD.

Let us pray.

LORD JESUS CHRIST, the one and only SAVIOUR of the whole human race, "who reignest from sea to sea and from the river unto the boundaries of the world," open thy most Sacred Heart in mercy to those wretched souls in Africa who still sit in darkness and in the shadow of death, that through the intercession of the Blessed Virgin Mary, thy immaculate Mother, and of blessed Joseph her most glorious spouse, they may abandon their idols, and prostrating themselves before Thee, be admitted into thy holy Church, who livest and reignest, etc. PATER, Ave, Gloria.

452. Praises to Jesus Christ and most Holy Mary.
100 Days, once a day. (See Instructions.) 452 Leo XIII, July 18, 1885

PRAISED be JESUS CHRIST, SON of GOD;
May JESUS be ever praised.
true GOD and true man;
author of life ;
eternal Wisdom ;
infinite goodness;
GOD of peace ;
Good Shepherd;
most loving FATHER;
our SAVIOUR;
our Hope;
our Love ;
our Life;
our beginning;
our end;
MOST HOLY MARY.
PRAISED be Mary, daughter of the Eternal FATHER; May Mary be ever praised.

Mother of the Word Incarnate;
Spouse of the Divine SPIRIT;
co-redemptress of the world ;
Immaculate Queen;
full of grace;
refuge of sinners ;
Mother most merciful ;
consoler of the sorrowful ;
refuge of the afflicted ;
star of promise in the midst of evil ;
safe harbour for travellers; .
our comfort in life ;
our hope in death ;

453. Christian Acts.
i. 300 Days, once a day. ii. Plenary, once a month, on a Sunday. I, II, III, IV (See Instructions.) 453 Leo XIII, November 21, 1885.
The prayer must be repeated thirty-three times, with a Gloria after each eleven.
MY GOD, I believe in Thee, I hope in Thee, I love Thee above all things with all my soul, with all my heart, with all my strength: I love Thee because Thou art infinitely good and worthy to be loved; and because I love Thee, I repent with my whole heart for having offended Thee; be merciful to me a sinner. Amen.

454. Assisting at a First Mass.
i. Plenary, for blood relations to the third degree. I, II, IV ii. Seven Years and Seven Quarantines for others. IV. (See Instructions.) 454 Leo XIII, January 16, 1886.

455. Prayer of St Thomas Aquinas for grace to lead a holy life.
Three Years, once a day. (See Instructions) 455 Leo XIII, January 17, 1888,

CONCEDE mihi, misericors DEUS, quæ tibi sunt placita, ardenter concupiscere, prudenter investigare, veraciter agnoscere et perfecte adimplere ad laudem et gloriam nominis tui. Ordina, DEUS meus, statum meum: et quod a me requiris, ut faciam, tribue ut sciam; et da exequi sicut oportet et expedit animæ meæ.

Da mihi, DOMINUS DEUS meus, inter prospera et adversa non deficere, ut in illis non extollar, et in istis non deprimar. De nullo gaudeam vel doleam nisi quod ducat ad te, vel abducat ate. Nulli placere appetam, vel displicere timeam nisi tibi.

Vilescant mihi DOMINE, omnia transitoria, et cara mihi sint omnia æterna. Tædeat me gaudii quod est sine te, nec aliud cupiam quod est extra te. Delectet me DOMINE, labor, qui est pro te; et tædiosa sit mihi omnis quies, quæ est sine te.

Da mihi, DEUS meus, cor meum ad te dirigere, et in defectione meacum emendationis proposito constanter dolere.

Fac me, DOMINE DEUS meus, obedientem sine contradictione, pauperem sine dejectione, castum sine corruptione, patien tem sine murmuratione; humilem sine fictione, hi larem sine dissolutione, maturum sine gravidine, agilem sine levitate, timentem te sine desperatione, veracem sine duplicitate, operantem bona

O MERCIFUL GOD, grant that I may eagerly desire, carefully search out, truthfully acknowledge, and ever perfectly fulfil all things which are pleasing to Thee. Order, O my GOD, all my state and grant me to know what Thou dost require me to do, and give me to do it as is fitting and profitable to my soul.

Grant, O LORD my GOD, that I may not fail either in prosperity or adversity, that I be not lifted up by the one or cast down by the other. Let me joy in nothing but what leads to Thee, nor grieve for anything but what leads away from Thee; let men either seek to please, nor fear to displease any but Thee alone.

May all transitory things grow vile in my eyes, O LORD, and may all that is eternal be dear to me. May all joy be irksome to me that is without Thee, nor may I desire anything that is apart from Thee. May all labour and toil delight me which is for Thee, and all rest be weariness which is not in Thee.

Grant me, O LORD, continually to lift up my heart towards Thee, and to bring sorrowfully to mind my many short comings with full purpose of amendment.

Make me, O LORD, obedient without demur, poor without repining, chaste without stain, patient

Sine præsumptione, proximum corripere sine elatione, ipsum ædificare verbo et exemplo sine simulatione.

Da mihi, DOMINE DEUS, cor pervigil, quod nulla abducat a te curiosa cogitatio: da nobile, quod nulla deorsum trahat indigna affectio: da rectum, quod nulla seorsum obliquet sinistra intentio: da firmum, quod nulla fran quod nulla sibi vindicet gat tribulatio : da liberum, violenta affectio.

Largire mihi, DOMINE DEUS meus, intellectum te cognoscentem, diligenti am te quærentem, sapientiam te invenientem, conversationem tibi placentem, perseverantiam fidenter te expectantem, et fiduciam te finaliter amplectentem. Da tuis pœnis hie affligi per pœnitentiam, tuis beneficiis in via uti per gratiam, tuis gaudiis in patria perfrui per gloriam. Qui vivis et regnas DEUS per omnia sæcula sæculorum. Amen,

without murmur, humble without pretence, joyous without frivolity, fearful without abjectness, truthful without disguise, given to good works without presumption, faithful to rebuke my neighbour without arrogance, and ever careful to edify him by word and example without pretension.

Give me, O LORD, an ever watchful heart, which no subtle speculation may lure from Thee. Give me a noble heart, which no unworthy affection can draw downwards to the earth, Give me an upright heart, which no insincere intention can warp aside. Give me a firm heart, which no tribulation can crush or quell. Give me a free heart, which no perverted or impetuous affection can claim for its own.

Bestow on me, O LORD, my GOD, understanding to know Thee, diligence to seek Thee, wisdom to find Thee, a life and conversation which may please Thee, perseverance in waiting patiently for Thee, and a hope which may embrace Thee at the last. Grant me to be pierced with compunction by thy sorrows through true repentance, to improve all thy gifts and benefits during this my pilgrimage through thy grace, and so in glory to rejoice together with Thee in the heavenly country. Who livest and reignest GOD, for ever and ever. Amen.

456. Prayer in Times of Calamity.
100 Days, once a day. (See Instructions.) 456 Leo XIII, June 22, 1888.
O LORD JESUS CHRIST, true GOD and true Man, GOD of Sanctity, GOD of Majesty, GOD Everlasting, have pity on us and upon the whole human race; now and always purify us from our sins and infirmities with thy Precious Blood, so that we may be able to live in thy holy peace and charity, now and for ever. Amen.

457. Prayer for the Christian Family.
200 Days, once a day. (See Instructions.) 457 Leo XIII, January 19, 1889.
GOD of bounty and of mercy, to thy almighty protection we commend our home, our family and all we possess. Bless us all, as Thou didst bless the Holy Family at Nazareth.
O JESUS, our most blessed SAVIOUR, by the love with which Thou didst become man for our salvation, by thy mercy in dying- for us on the Cross, bless, we beseech thee, our home, our family and our household; preserve us from every evil and from the snares of men; protect us from lightning and hail, from fire, flood and tempest; preserve us from thy wrath, from the hatred and the evil designs of our enemies, from pestilence, famine and war. Let not any one of us die without the holy Sacraments ; grant us thy blessing, that we may bravely confess that faith by which we are sanctified, that we may preserve our hope in sorrow and in affliction, and that we may redouble our love of Thee and our charity towards our neighbour.
O JESUS, bless and protect us.
O Mary, mother of grace and of mercy, bless us, defend us against the evil spirit, lead us by the hand across this vale of tears, reconcile us with thy Son, and commend us to Him that we may be made worthy of his promises. O holy Joseph, reputed father of our SAVIOUR, guardian of his most blessed Mother, head of the Holy Family, intercede for us, and bless and protect our habitation at all times.
St Michael, defend us against all the malice of hell.
St Gabriel, make us ever to seek the holy will of GOD.
St Raphael, preserve us from sickness and all danger of death.
Ye holy angels, our guardians, keep us day and night in the way of salvation.

Ye holy saints, our patrons, pray for us before the throne of GOD.

Bless this our home, O GOD the FATHER, who hast created us; O GOD the SON, who hast suffered for us on the Cross ; O GOD the HOLY SPIRIT, who hast sanctified us in baptism. May GOD in his three divine Persons preserve our bodies, purify our souls, guide our hearts and lead us to eternal life.

Glory be to the FATHER, glory be to the SON, glory be to the HOLY GHOST. Amen.

458. Prayers to the Holy Family.

300 Days, once a day. (See Instructions) 458 Leo XIII, May 17, 1890.

JESUS, Mary and Joseph, bless us and grant us the grace to love the Church, as we ought, above every other earthly thing, and always to show forth our love by deeds. PATER, Ave, Gloria.

JESUS, Mary and Joseph, bless us and grant us the grace without fear or human respect openly to profess, as we ought, the faith which was given to us in baptism. PATER, Ave, Gloria.

JESUS, Mary and Joseph, bless us and grant us the grace to share, as we ought, in the defence and propagation of the Faith, when duty calls, whether by word or by the sacrifice of our fortunes and our lives. PATER, Ave, Gloria.

JESUS, Mary and Joseph, bless us and grant us the grace to love one another, as we ought, and to live together in perfect harmony of thought, will and action, under the rule and guidance of our pastors. PATER, Ave, Gloria.

JESUS, Mary and Joseph, bless us and grant us the grace to conform our lives, as we ought, to the precepts of GOD and of the Church, so as to live always in that charity which they set forth. PATER, Ave, Gloria.

459. Prayer for Benefactors.

50 Days, twice a day. (See Instructions.) 459 Leo XIII, December 17, 1892.

RETRIBUERE dignare DOMINE, omnibus nobis bona facientibus propter nomen tuum vitam æternam. Amen.

REWARD, O LORD, with eternal life all those who do us good for thy name's sake. Amen.

460. Prayer of St Alphonsus.

To be said before retiring to rest. 60 Days, once a day. (See Instructions) 460 Leo XIII, June 30, 1893.

JESUS CHRIST, my GOD, I adore Thee and I thank Thee for the many favours Thou hast bestowed on me this day. I offer Thee my sleep and all the moments of this night, and I pray Thee to preserve me from sin. Therefore I place myself in thy most sacred side, and under the mantle of our blessed Lady my Mother. May the holy angels assist me and keep me in peace, and may thy blessing be upon me.

461. Prayer for the Conversion of the Jews.

100 Days, once a day. (See Instructions.) 461 Leo XIII, July 15, 1893

GOD of goodness and FATHER of mercies, we beseech Thee, by the immaculate heart of Mary, and by the intercession of the Patriarchs and holy Apostles, to look with compassion upon the remnant of Israel, so that they may come to a knowledge of our only SAVIOUR JESUS CHRIST, and share in the precious graces of Redemption. Amen.

462. Prayer for the Propagation of Faith and Piety.

i. Seven Years and Seven Quarantines, once a day. ii. Plenary, once a month. I, II, IV. (See Instructions, p. i.) 462 Leo XIII, January 23, 1894.

ETERNAL FATHER, by thy infinite mercy and by the infinite merits of thy divine SON JESUS, make thyself known and loved by all souls, since it is thy will that all should be saved. Gloria PATRI.

Through the sacred mysteries of human redemption send, O LORD, labourers into thy harvest, and spare thy people.

Eternal Word incarnate, Redeemer of the human race, convert all souls to thyself, since for them Thou wast obedient even to the death of the Cross. Gloria PATRI.

Through the merits and intercession of thy most holy Mother, and of ail the Angels and Saints, send, O LORD, labourers into thy harvest, and spare thy people.

O HOLY SPIRIT of GOD, by the infinite merits of the Passion and Death of JESUS CHRIST, diffuse thy most ardent and all-powerful charity in all hearts, that there may be one Fold and one Shepherd throughout the world, and that all may come to sing thy divine mercies in Heaven for ever. Amen. Gloria PATRI.

Queen of Apostles, and all ye Angels and Saints, pray the LORD of the harvest to send labourers into his harvest and spare his people, that we may all rejoice with Him and the FATHER and the HOLY SPIRIT for ever and ever. Amen.

Immaculate Mother of GOD, Queen of Apostles, I know that the divine precept, by which I am bound to love my neighbour as myself, obliges me to procure by every possible means not only my eternal salvation, but also that of my neighbour. But I confess that through my sins I am not worthy of the grace to labour effectually and constantly for the eternal salvation of my soul and of the souls of my relations and neighbours; much less am I worthy of the grace to promote good works and increase the means, both spiritual and temporal, of restoring Faith and rekindling Charity among Catholics, and propagating the truth throughout the world. Do thou then, O Mother, obtain for me this grace through the mercy of GOD and the infinite merits of JESUS CHRIST; and in union with the heavenly court and all the just, who are or will be in the Church of GOD, from henceforth I intend to offer these same merits of JESUS as a thanksgiving in anticipation of this grace obtained by thee for us and for all, as thou didst obtain it for the holy Apostles. And so, I, N.N., trusting in thy powerful intercession, resolve from henceforth to use whatever I have from GOD of power, talents, learning, riches, position, health, sickness or sorrow, for the greater glory of GOD and the salvation of my soul, and that of my neighbour, more especially by working for the propagation of piety and the holy faith throughout the world. And when all other means to this end fail me, I will never cease to pray, that there may be one Fold and one Shepherd. By so doing I hope to reach Paradise, there to enjoy the fruit of the Apostolate of JESUS CHRIST for all eternity. Amen. Ave Maria thrice, Gloria PATRI once.

463. Prayer for the Sanctification of Priests.

i. Seven Years and Seven Quarantines. T.Q. ii. Plenary, once a month. I, II, III, IV. (See Instructions.) 463 Pius X, November 9, 1907.

O JESUS, eternal pastor of souls, hear our prayer on behalf of our priests and hear in it thy own eternal desire. Are not priests the object of thy most tender and exquisite care, that profound love in which are summed up all thy affections for souls? Let us confess our unworthiness to have good priests. But thy mercy is infinitely greater than our folly and wickedness.

O JESUS, grant that only those ascend to thy priesthood who are called by Thee; enlighten pastors in their choice, inspire directors with a spirit of counsel, and teachers in the cultivation of vocations. Give us priests who are angels of purity, models of humility, seraphs of holy love, heroes of self-sacrifice, apostles of thy glory, and saviours and sanctifiers of souls.

Have pity on the ignorant who should be enlightened, on the sons of toil who call for someone to save them from error and redeem them in thy name, on all the children and youths who cry for such as may save them and bring them to Thee, on so many who suffer and have need of a heart which will find them consolation in thine. What a number of souls would arrive at perfection through the ministry of holy priests! Then, O JESUS, have compassion again on the crowds who hunger and thirst. Grant that thy priesthood may bring to Thee fainting humanity, and let the earth be once again renewed, the Church exalted, and the reign of thy Heart established in peace.

Immaculate Virgin, Mother of the Eternal Priest, and thou thyself a priest at the altar, who hadst for thy first son of adoption St John, the beloved priest of JESUS, who didst preside in the cœnaculum, mistress and queen of the Apostles; deign to utterwith thy sacred lips this our humble prayer; do thou make its accents to penetrate to the Heart of thy divine Son, and, all-powerful in thy supplication, obtain for the Church of thy Son JESUS a perennial renewal of Pentecost. Amen.

464. Two Prayers for the Increase and Preservation of the Clergy.

300 Days for each.* (See Instructions.) 464 Pius X, March 30, 1908.

I. FOR THE INCREASE OF LABOURERS.

Ant. Quid statis tota die otiosi? Ite in vineam meam.	Ant. Why stand ye all the day idle, go ye into my vineyard
V/. Rogate DOMINUM messis.	V/. Ask the LORD of the harvest.
R/. Ut mittat operarios in vineam suam.	R/. That He send labourers into his vineyard.
Oremus	**Let us pray**

DEUS qui non vis mortem peccatoris, sed magis ut convertatur et vivat, da, quæsumus, per intercessionem beatæ Mariæ semper Virginis et omnium sanctorum, operarios Ecclesiæ tuæ, qui sunt cooperatores CHRISTI, ut se impendant et superimpendant pro animabus. Per eundem DOMINUM, etc. Amen.

GOD who willest not the death of the sinner, but rather that he be converted and live; grant, by the intercession of blessed Mary ever Virgin and of all the saints, labourers for thy Church, fellow labourers with Christ, to spend and consume themselves for souls. Through the same JESUS CHRIST, etc. Amen.

II. FOR THE PRESERVATION OF THE CLERGY.

Ant. Nemo mittens manum suam ad aratrum et respiciens retro aptus est regno DEI.
V/. Nemo militans DEO implicat se negotiis sæcularibus.
R/. Ut ei placeat, cui se probavit.
Oremus
DEUS infirmitatis humanæ singulare præsidium, exaudi, quæsumus, preces quas pro fratribus in discrimine positis humiliter fundimus, ut famulos tuos ab omni eruas peccatorum nequitia et in tua protectionis securitate constituas. Per DOMINUM, etc. Amen.

Ant. No one putting his hand to the plough and looking back is fit for the Kingdom of GOD.
V/. No soldier of GOD involves himself in worldly affairs.
R/. That he may please Him to whom he has approved himself.
Let us pray
GOD, the sole protection of human weakness, hear, we beseech Thee, the prayers which we humbly address to Thee for our brethren who are in danger, and do Thou rescue them from all evil of sin, and establish them in the security of thy protection. Through JESUS CHRIST our LORD. Amen.

465. For Clerics and Students putting on a Cotta.

300 Days. T.Q. (See Instructions.) 405 Pius X, December 1, 1907.
Make the Sign of the Cross and say:
INDUE me, DOMINE, novum hominem, qui secundum DEUM creatus est, in justitia et sanctitate veritatis. Amen

CLOTHE me, O LORD, with the new man, who was created according to GOD, in justice and the sanctity of truth. Amen.

FOR SPECIAL CLASSES
I. FOR PRIESTS
466. Intention before Mass.

50 Days. (See Instructions.) 466 Gregory XIII.
EGO volo celebrare Missam, et conficere Corpus et Sanguinem DOMINI nostri JESU CHRISTI, juxta ritum sanctæ Romanæ Ecclesiæ, ad laudem omnipotentis DEI, totiusque curiae triumphantis, ad utilitatem meam, totiusque curias militantis, pro omnibus, qui se commendaverunt orationibus meis in genere et in specie, et pro felici statu sanctæ Romanæ Ecclesiæ. Amen.
GAUDIUM cum pace, emendationem vitæ, spatium veræ pœnitentiæae, gratiam et consolationem SANCTI SPIRITUS, perseverantiam inbonis operibus, tribuat nobis omnipotens et misericors DOMINUS. Amen.

467. Prayer after Mass.

Three Years. (See Instructions.) 467 Pius IX, December 11, 1846.
OBSECRO te dulcissime, DOMINE JESU CHRISTE, ut passio tua sit mihi virtus qua muniar, protegar, atque defendar: vulnera tua sint mihi cibus potusque, quibus pascar, inebrier atque delecter: aspersio sanguinis tui sit mihi gloria sempiterna. In his sit mihi refectio, exsultatio, sanitas et dulcedo cordis mei: qui vivis et regnas in sæcula sæculorum. Amen.

468. Prayer to St Joseph, before Mass.

100 Days. (See Instructions.) 468 Pius IX, February 4, 1877.
OFELICEM virum beatum Joseph, cui datum est DEUM, quern multi reges voluerunt videre, et non viderunt, audire, et non audierunt, non solum videre et audire, sed portare, deosculari, vestire et custodire.

V/. Ora pro nobis, beate Joseph.
R/. Ut digni efficiamur promissionibus CHRISTI.

Oremus.
DEUS, qui dedisti nobis regale sacerdotium, præsta quæsumus, ut sicut beatus Joseph unigenitum FILIUM tuum natum ex Maria Virgine, suis manibus reverenter tractare meruit et portare, ita nos facias cum cordis munditia et operis innocentia tuis sanctis altaribus deservire, ut sacrosanctum FILII tui Corpus et Sanguinem hodie digne sumamus, et in future saeculo prgemium habere mereamur æternum. Per eumdem CHRISTUM DOMINUM nostrum. Amen.

469. Prayer to our Lady before Mass.
100 Days. (See Instructions.) 469 Leo XIII, February 17, 1883.
O MATER pietatis et misericordiæ, beatissima Virgo Maria, ego miser et indignus peccator ad te confugio toto corde et affectu, et precor pietatem tuam: ut sicut dulcissimo Filio tuo in crucependenti astitisti,itaet mihi misero peccatori, et sacerdotibus omnibus hic et in tota Sancta Ecclesia hodie offerentibus, clementer assistere digneris, ut tua gratia adjuti, dignam et acceptabilem hostiam in conspectu summæ et individual Trinitatis offere valeamus. Amen.

470. Preparation and Thanksgiving.
i. One Year, for the Antiphon, Psalms, Versicles and Prayers contained in the *Præparatio ad Missam*, together with one of the seven prayers of St Ambrose.
ii. One Year for the Antiphon, Canticle, Psalm, Versicles and Prayers contained in the *Gratiarum Actio post Missam*, together with the prayers of St Thomas and St Bonaventure.
iii. 100 Days, for each of the other prayers, to be said in Preparation and Thanksgiving (see Table below).
iv. Plenary, once a month, for saying daily all the Psalms, Prayers, etc., given below (see Table). (See Instructions.) 470 Leo XIII, December 20, 1884.
TABLE OF INDULGENCED PSALMS, PRAYERS, ETC., TO BE SAID IN PREPARATION FOR MASS OR IN THANKSGIVING:
Preparation:
1. Antiphon Ne reminiscaris, Psalms lxxxiii, lxxxiv, Ixxxv, cxv, cxxix, with **V/. V/.** , **R/. R/.** and Prayers.
2. Prayers of St Ambrose for every day of the week.
3. Prayer of St Thomas Aquinas, Gratias tibi ago.
4. Prayer of St Ambrose, Ad mensam dulcissimi.
5. Prayer to the Angels and Saints, Angeli, Archangeli.
6. Prayer when about to offer the Mass in honour of a Saint or Beatus.
Thanksgiving:
1. Antiphon, Trium puerorum ; Canticle, Benedicite; Psalm cl. **V/. V/.** , **R/. R/.** and Prayers.
2. Prayer of St Thomas Aquinas, Gratias tibi ago.
3. Prayer of St Bonaventure, Transfige dulcissime.
4. Adoro te devote.
5. Prayers of St Alphonsus for every Day of the Week.
6. Prayer to our Lady, O Maria, Virgo et Mater.
N.B. All these are to be found in Missals, Breviaries and other books used by Priests.

471. Prayer before Hearing Confessions.
100 Days, once a day. (See Instructions) 471 Pius IX, March 27, 1854.
DA mihi, DOMINE, sedium tuarum assistricem sapientiam, ut sciam judicare populum tuum in justitia, et pauperes tuos in judicio. Fac me ita tractare claves regni cælorum, ut nulli aperiam, cui claudendum sit, nulli claudam, cui aperiendum sit. Sit intentio mea pura, zelus meus sincerus, caritas mea patiens, labor meus fructuosus. Sit in me lenitas non remissa, asperitas non severa, pauperem ne despiciam, diviti ne aduler. Fac me ad alliciendos peccatores suavem, ad interrogandos prudentem, ad instruendos peritum. Tribue, quæso, ad retrahendos a malo solertiam, ad confirmandos in bono sedulitatem, ad promovendos ad meliora industriam, in responsis maturitatem, in consiliis rectitudinem, in obscuris lumen, in implexis sagacitatem, in arduis victoriam, inutilibus colloquiis ne detinear, pravis ne contaminer, alios salvem, meipsum non perdam. Amen.

472. Prayers before and after Confession.
200 Days. (See Instructions.) 472 Leo XIII, August 19, 1882.
Before.
SUSCIPE Confessionem meam, piissime ac clementissime DOMINE JESU CHRISTE, unica spes salutis animæ meæ, et da mihi, obsecro, contritionem cordis, et lacrimas oculis meis, ut defleam diebus ac noctibus omnes negligentias meas cum humilitate et puritate cordis. DOMINE DEUS meus, suscipe preces meas. SALVATOR mundi, JESU bone, qui te crucis morti dedisti, ut peccatores salvos faceres, respice me miserum peccatorem invocantem nomen tuum, et noli sic attendere malum meum ut obliviscaris bonum tuum ; et si commisi unde me damnare potes, tu non amisisti unde salvare soles. Parce ergo mihi qui es SALVATOR meus, et miserere peccatrici animæ meæ. Solve vincula ejus, sana vulnera. Emitte igitur, piissime DOMINE, mentis purissimæ et immaculatæ semper Virginis Genitricis tuæ Mariæ, et Sanctorum tuorum, lucem tuam, veritatem tuam in animam meam, quæ omnes defeclus meos in veritate mihi ostendat, de quibus confiteri me oportet, atque juvet et doceat ipsos plene et contrite corde explicare. Qui vivis et regnas DEUS, per omnia sæcula sæculorum. Amen.
After.
SIT tibi DOMINE, obsecro, mentis beatæ semper Virginis Genitricis tuæ Mariæ et omnium Sanctorum, grata et accepta ista confessio mea; et quid quid mihi defuit nunc et alias de sufficientia contritionis, de puritate et integritate confessionis, suppleat pietas et misericordia tua, et secundum illam digneris me habere plenius et perfectius absolutum in cælo : Qui vivis et regnas DEUS per omnia sæcula sæculorum. Amen.

473. First Mass.
Plenary, for the Celebrant. I, III, IV. (See Instructions.) 473 Leo XIII, January 16, 1886

II. FOR PRIESTS AND OTHERS IN SACRED ORDERS
474. Prayer to our Lord.
300 Days, once a day. (See Instructions.) 474 Leo XIII, August 14, 1884.
JESU dilectissime, qui ex singular! benevolentia me præ millenis hominibus ad tui sequelam et ad eximiam Sacerdotii dignitatem vocasti, largiri mihi, precor, opem tuam divinam ad officia mea obeunda. Oro te, DOMINE JESU, ut resuscites hodie et semper in me gratiam tuam, quæ fuit in me per impositionem manuum episcopalium. O potentissime animarum medice, sana me taliter, ne revolvar in vitia; et cuncta peccata fugiam tibique usque ad mortem placere possim. Amen.

475. Ejaculation.
100 Days, once a day. (See Instructions.) 475 Leo XIII, August 16, 1884.
BONE JESU, rogo te per dilectionem, qua diligis Matrem tuam, ut sicut vere earn diligis et diligi vis, ita mihi des, ut vere eam diligam.

476. Prayer for the Preservation of Chastity.
100 Days, once a day. (See Instructions.) 476 Leo XIII, March 16, 1889.
DOMINE JESU CHRISTE, sponse animæ meæ, deliciæ cordis mei, imo cor meum et anima mea, ante conspectum tuum genibus me provolvo, et maximo animi ardore te oro et obtestor, ut mihi des servare fidem a me tibi solemniter datam in receptione Subdiaconatus. Ideo O dulcissime JESU, abnegem omnem impietatem, sim semper alienus a carnalibus desideriis et terrenis concupiscentiis, quæ militant adversus animam, et castitatem te adjuvante intemerate servem.
O sanctissima et immaculata Maria, Virgo Virginum et Mater nostra amantissima, munda in dies cor meum et animam meam, impetra mihi timorem DOMINI et singrilarem mei diffidentiam.
Sancte Joseph, custos Virginitatis Mariæ, custodi animam meam ab omni peccato.
Omnes sanctæ Virgines divinum Agnum quocunque sequentes, estote mei peccatoris semper sollicitæ, ne cogitatione, verbo aut opere delinquam et a castissimo Corde JESU unquam discedam. Amen.

III. FOR YOUNG STUDENTS
477. Consecration of Studies to Mary Immaculate.
100 Days, once a day. (See Instructions.) 477 Leo XIII, November 18, 1882.

SUB patrocinio tuo, Mater dulcissima, et invocato Immaculatæ Conceptionis tuæ mysterio, studia mea laboresque litterarios prosequi volo: quibus me protestor hunc maxime ob finem incumbere, ut melius divino honori tuoque cultui propagando inserviam. Oro te igitur, Mater amantissima, sedes sapientiæ, ut laboribus meis benigne faveas. Ego vero, quod justum est, pie libenterque promitto, quidquid boni mihi inde successerit, id me tuæ apud DEUM intercessioni totum acceptum relaturum. Amen.

478. Prayer in Choosing a State of Life.

300 Days, once a day. (See Instructions.) 478 Pius X, May 6, 1905.

O My GOD, Thou who art the GOD of wisdom and of counsel, Thou who readest in my heart the sincere will to please Thee alone, and to govern myself with regard to my choice of a state of life, entirely in conformity with thy most holy desire; grant me, by the intercession of the most blessed Virgin, my Mother, and of my holy patrons, specially of St Joseph and St Aloysius, the grace to know what state I ought to choose, and when known to embrace it, so that in it I may be able to pursue and increase thy glory, work out my salvation, and merit that heavenly reward which Thou hast promised to those who do thy holy will. Amen.

479. Prayer for one aspiring to the Priesthood.

200 Days, once a day. (See Instructions.) 479 Leo XIII, Off. February 8, 1901

O My GOD, I am unworthy, most unworthy, to serve in the ministry of the priesthood, through which is offered on thy altars the Body and Blood of thy SON JESUS CHRIST. I am in no way worthy of this honour, being a miserable sinner, a mere nothing, even less than nothing by reason of my malice, fit for nothing but to commit sin. But while I feel within me an impulse drawing me to the ecclesiastical state, and of myself cannot tell whether it be presumption on my part or an inspiration from Thee, I humble myself before Thee, and I pray Thee to enlighten me to know if it be in accordance with thy good pleasure, for I would do nothing contrary to thy will. Do Thou, therefore, who art the Light of the world, shine forth in my heart, and if this thought is a call from Thee, give me the grace to obey it promptly, and worthily to correspond with it. But if, O LORD, Thou dost not call me to the priestly ministry, or Thou seest that as a member of it I should not be a good priest, but rather a disedification and a scandal to the Church, never permit me to enter a state which would be my damnation.

Most holy Virgin, Mother of GOD, and Mother of good counsel, do thou support my poor prayer, and may I have the grace from our LORD by thy merits and intercession in all things to regulate my actions, not by my own, but by thy holy Will. PATER, Ave, Gloria.

480. Prayer to Our Lady.

300 Days, once a day. (See Instructions) 480 Leo XIII, May 9, 1895.

O GREAT Queen of Heaven, most pure Virgin, look, I beseech thee from thy throne with eyes of pity upon my tender age. How many insidious and seductive maxims are abroad, to rob me of the holy faith, which was infused into my soul in Baptism, in order to enlighten my understanding and render my will upright and holy! In how many ways do the evil examples of men, the various arts and endless displays strive with their alluring images to destroy the precious germs of virtue in my tender heart! O thou who wast chosen by the GOD of mercy to give to the world the REDEEMER of the human race, which had fallen victim to the insidious promises of the rebellious and crafty Lucifer, protect me from the malicious snares which he is ever laying for the regenerate children of Adam. O thou who didst receive me on Calvary as thy son, let me not succumb to the suggestions of evil passions, or fall a victim to the crafty enemies of my eternal salvation; let not the ministers of Satan, proud of the laurels they have already gained, acquire fresh courage and strength for bolder and more fatal schemes. O sweet and powerful Mother Mary, may I never be guilty of renewing by my sins the Passion of thy Son, my most loving REDEEMER, and of piercing thy most loving heart with sharp swords. May all my actions, O dear Mother, thanks to thy patronage, be ever directed to the glory of GOD and the salvation of my soul. Amen. Ave Maria thrice.

481. Prayer for Children in Purgatory.

i. 100 Days, once a day, for children who say this prayer. ii. Plenary, on All Saints Day, to those who recite it daily for at least half the year. I, II, III, IV.

N.B. Bishops can authorize confessors to commute the Communion in case of children who have not made their first Communion. (See Instructions) 481 Leo XIII, May 15, 1886.

SWEET SAVIOUR JESUS, who during thy life didst show such great love for children; we who as children share with them thy blessing, beseech Thee to open the gate of Heaven to our companions who are lamenting in the place of sorrow and penance. Grant also their protection to us, to our relations, and to our common Father, the supreme Pontiff.

Holy Virgin, good Mother, pray for us and for the children who suffer. Ave Maria.

APPENDIX

482. Prayer for the Conversion of Freemasons.

100 Days, once a day. (See Instructions.) 482 Leo XIII, Br. August 16, 1898

O LORD JESUS CHRIST, who showest forth thy omnipotence most manifestly when Thou sparest and hast compassion; Thou who didst say, "Pray for those who persecute and calumniate you," we implore the clemency of thy Sacred Heart on behalf of souls, made in the image of GOD, but most miserably deceived by the treacherous snares of Freemasons, and going more and more astray in the way of perdition. Let not the Church, thy spouse, any longer be oppressed by them; but, appeased by the intercession of the blessed Virgin thy Mother and the prayers of the just, be mindful of thy infinite mercy; and, disregarding their perversity, cause these very men to return to Thee, that they may bring consolation to the Church by a most abundant penance, make reparation for their misdeeds, and secure for themselves a glorious eternity; who livest and reignest world without end. Amen.

483. Pious Reading of the Gospel.

i. 300 Days, once a day. ii. Plenary, once a month. I, II, IV. 483 Leo XIII, December 13, 1898.

These Indulgences are gained by reading the Gospel for at least a quarter of an hour.

484. Prayer to the Sacred Heart for Pope Pius X.

i. 300 Days. T.Q. ii. Seven Years and Seven Quarantines, if said before the Blessed Sacrament exposed. iii. Plenary, if said every day in June, on the last day of the month. I, II, III, IV. (See Instructions.) 484 Pius X, May 27, 1908.

MOST Sacred Heart of JESUS, with humble confidence we earnestly pray to Thee for thy Vicar, our Holy Father Pius X, to whom on earth Thou hast been pleased to confide thy joys and thy sorrows. O good JESUS, Thou didst make a special promise to all priests who are devout to thy Heart, that they should enjoy the gift of moving the most hardened hearts, and should gather marvellous fruits from their apostolic labours. Oh, may that promise be realized to the full in the Pontiff of thy Eucharist and of thy adorable Heart. And since he is the universal High Priest, give him power to stir the hardened hearts of the entire human family; may his words, inspired by thy Divine Heart, fill with light, humility and love all who are hardened by ignorance, rebellious pride, or earthly lusts; and with strenuous zeal all who are feeble, slothful, or lukewarm in thy service. O sweetest Heart, renew in him the joys of the sacerdotal unction; lighten the burdens of the Pontifical Office; and do Thou hasten on the fulfilment of his apostolic desire to " restore all things in Thee." Grant that the Holy Father, who has so well understood the love of thy Heart in its desire for sacramental union with men, may see the accomplishment of that other desire of thine, the prayer of the Cœnaculum, " that they may be one." O Heart infinitely powerful and merciful, unite round him all those committed to Thee by the FATHER, and to thy Vicar by Thee; so that we may be all one among ourselves by the love which alone makes us brethren, and one with the Pontiff by the obedience which alone makes us free, and one with Thee, as Thou art one with the FATHER. Amen.

485. Prayer to the Queen of Angels by the Ven. Louis Edward Gestac.

300 Days, once a day. (See Instructions.) 485 Pius X, July 8. 1908.

AUGUST Queen of Heaven and Mistress of Angels, who hast been commissioned by GOD with power to crush the head of Satan, we humbly beseech thee to send forth the legions of Heaven, that under thy command they may seek out all evil spirits, everywhere put them to flight, curb their insolence, and hurl them back into the abyss.

Who is like unto GOD?

Holy Angels and Archangels, defend and keep us. O good and tender Mother, thou shalt ever be our love and our hope. O Mother of GOD, send the holy Angels to defend me, and drive far away from me the cruel enemy.

486. Ejaculation to the Sacred Heart.
300 Days. T.Q. (See Instructions.) 486 Pius X, Off. Nov. 26, 1908.
ALL for Thee, most Sacred Heart of JESUS.

487. The Twelve Saturdays immediately preceding the Immaculate Conception.
Plenary on each Saturday, I, II, IV. (See Instructions). 487 Pius X. Off. November 26, 1908.
Some time must be spent in prayer or pious meditation in honour of the Immaculate Conception.

488. Prayer to St Paul.
300 Days once a day. (See Instructions) 488 Pius X, Off. December 10, 1908.
O MOST glorious Apostle, who didst labour with so much zeal at Ephesus to destroy the writings which thou knewest full well would pervert the minds of the faithful; deign in these times to turn upon us thy loving regard. Thou seest how an unbelieving and unbridled press endeavours to steal from mans heart its precious treasures of faith and moral purity. We beseech thee, O great Apostle, to enlighten the minds of all these perverse writers, that at length they may cease from injuring souls by their wicked doctrines and perfidious suggestions; move their hearts to renounce the evil which they do to the chosen sheep of CHRIST'S fold ; obtain for us the grace that, being always obedient to the voice of the supreme Pastor, we may never give ourselves up to the reading of evil books, but may, on the contrary, seek to read, and, as far as possible, diffuse, such works as may by their wholesome influence help all to promote the greater glory of GOD, the exaltation of the Church, and the salvation of souls. Amen.

489. Litany of St Joseph.
300 Days, once a day. (See Instructions). 489 Pius X, Rit. March 18, 1909.
N.B. The public recitation of this Litany is now authorized.

KYRIE, eleison.	LORD, have mercy.
CHRISTE, eleison	CHRIST, have mercy.
KYRIE, eleison.	LORD, have mercy.
CHRISTE, audi nos.	CHRIST, hear us.
CHRISTE, exaudi nos.	CHRIST, graciously hear us
PATER de cælis, DEUS, FILI REDEMPTOR mundi, DEUS, SPIRITUS SANCTE, DEUS, Sancta Trinitas, unus DEUS, *Miserere nobis*	GOD, the Father of Heaven, GOD the SON, Redeemer of the world GOD, the HOLY GHOST, Holy Trinity one GOD, *Have mercy on us*

Sancta Maria,	*Ora pro nobis*	Holy Mary,	*pray for us.*
Sancte Joseph,		St. Joseph	
Proles David inclyta,		Renowned offspring of David,	
Lumen Patriarcharum,		Light of Patriarchs,	
DEI Genitricis sponse,		Spouse of the Mother of GOD,	
Custos pudice Virginis,		Chaste guardian of the Virgin,	
FILII DEI nutritie,		Foster father of the SON of GOD,	
CHRISTI defensor sedule,		Diligent protector of CHRIST,	
Almæ Familiæ præses,		Head of the Holy Family,	
Joseph justissime,		Joseph most just,	
Joseph castissime,		Joseph most chaste,	
Joseph prudentissime,		Joseph most prudent,	
Joseph fortissime,		Joseph most strong,	
Joseph obedientissime,		Joseph most obedient,	
Joseph fidelissime,		Joseph most faithful,	
Speculum patientissime,		Mirror of patience,	
Amator paupertatis,		Lover of poverty,	
Exemplar opificum,		Model of artisans,	
Domesticæ vitæ decus,		Glory of home life,	
Custos virginum,		Guardian of virgins,	
Familiarum columen,		Pillar of families,	
Solatium miserorum,		Solace of the wretched,	
Spes ægrotantium,		Hope of the sick,	
Patrone morientium,		Patron of the dying,	
Terror dæmonum,		Terror of demons,	
Protector sanctæ Ecclesiæ,		Protector of Holy Church,	

Agnus DEI, qui tollis peccata mundi, parce nobis DOMINE.
Agnus DEI, qui tollis peccata mundi, exaudi nos DOMINE.
Agnus DEI, qui tollis peccata mundi, miserere nobis.
V/. Constituit eum dominum domus suæ
R/. Et principem omnis possessionis suæ.

Oremus
DEUS, qui ineffabili providentia beatum Joseph sanctissimae Genitricis tuæ sponsum eligere dignatus es: præsta quæsumus ut quem protectorem veneramur in terris, intercessorem habere mereamur in cœlis: qui vivis et regnas in sæcula sæculorum. Amen.

Lamb of GOD, who takest away the sins of the world, spare us, O LORD.
Lamb of GOD, who takest away the sins of the world, graciously hear us, O LORD.
Lamb of GOD, who takest away the sins of the world, have mercy on us
V/. He made him the lord of his household,
R/. And prince over all his possessions.

Let us pray.
O GOD, who in thy ineffable providence didst vouchsafe to choose blessed Joseph to be the spouse of thy most holy Mother; grant, we beseech thee, that we may have him for our intercessor in Heaven, whom we venerate as our protector on earth: who livest and reignest world without end. Amen.

490. Medals of the Child JESUS.
i. 50 Days. T.Q. ii. Plenary, in articulo mortis. (See Instructions.) 490 Plus X, Off. March 18, 1909.
The medals must be blessed by one having faculties for bestowing the apostolic benediction on rosaries, crosses, etc. For the partial indulgence, the medal must be reverently kissed with the invocation below. The conditions for the plenary indulgence are Confession and Communion if possible, the invocation of the Holy Name, and the patient acceptance, at the hand of GOD, of death as the wages of sin.
HOLY Child JESUS, bless us.

491. Kissing the Ring of a Cardinal or Bishop.
50 Days. (See Instructions) 491 Pius X, Off. March 18, 1909.
Addendum. Invocation "JESUS, Mary, Joseph." Seven Years and Seven Quarantines T.Q. Plenary once a month. Pius X, June 8, 1906.

Letchworth: At the Arden Press